Faith After Foundationalism

Also by D. Z. Phillips

Faith After Foundationalism

Plantinga-Rorty-Lindbeck-Berger—
Critiques and Alternatives

D. Z. Phillips

Westview Press
BOULDER • SAN FRANCISCO • OXFORD

Copyright © 1995, 1988 by Westview Press, Inc.

First published in 1988 by Routledge

Published in 1995 in the United States of America by Westview Press, Inc., 5500 Central Avenue, Boulder, Colorado 80301-2877, and in the United Kingdom by Westview Press, 12 Hid's Copse Road, Cumnor Hill, Oxford OX2 9JJ

Library of Congress Cataloging-in-Publication Data
Phillips, D. Z. (Dewi Zephaniah)
Faith after foundationalism : Plantinga-Rorty-Lindbeck-Berger : critiques and alternatives / by D. Z. Phillips.
    p. cm.
Originally published: London ; New York : Routledge, 1988.
Includes bibliographical references and index.
ISBN 0-8133-2645-1
    1. Knowledge, Theory of (Religion) 2. Hermeneutics. 3. Language and languages—Religious aspects—Christianity. I. Title.
[BL51.P517 1995]
200'.1—dc20   95-2371
                                                               CIP

Printed and bound in the United States of America

The paper used in this publication meets the requirements of the American National Standard for Permanence of Paper for Printed Library Materials Z39.48-1984.

10   9   8   7   6   5   4   3   2   1

To
Roy Holland and Peter Winch

Contents

Contents

Part Four: Religion and Concept-Formation

Acknowledgements

This book was written during the academic year 1985/6. I am grateful to the University College of Swansea for granting me the sabbatical leave which allowed me to concentrate on it. During the Fall Semester, I was a Visiting Professor and Research Fellow at Yale, and during the Spring Semester, a Visiting Professor and Fellow at Claremont Graduate School, California. During these visits I received many kindnesses from students and staff, academic and administrative, for which I am deeply grateful.

Concern with Wittgenstein's *On Certainty* and with Reformed epistemology is central in Part One of the book. I am indebted to discussions with Rush Rhees concerning *On Certainty*, and to fruitful disagreements with H.O. Mounce over how that work is to be read. In this context, I have also learned from discussions with Peter Winch, Donald Evans and David Sims, and from papers on related topics by Samuel Fleischacker which he was good enough to show me at Yale. Stephen Davis of Claremont McKenna College kindly read this section of the book, providing helpful comments on my exposition of Reformed Epistemology. For purposes of discussion, I presented my main contentions in a paper called 'Foundationalism, Reformed epistemology and Wittgenstein's *On Certainty*', which I read at the University of Illinois at Urbana, Illinois State University, the University of Arizona at Phoenix and the University of California at Santa Barbara. I benefited from the discussions on these occasions. The main issues, with a slightly different emphasis, were presented as the 1987 Aquinas Lecture, 'Shaking Foundationalism', delivered at Blackfriars, Oxford, in January 1987.

In Part One, and elsewhere in the book, I have made use of selected material from 'Primitive Reactions and the Reactions of Primitives', the 1983 Marett Lecture delivered at Exeter College, Oxford, on 17 May 1983. In 1984, the lecture was also presented at the State University of New York at Albany and Buffalo, and at the California State University at Hayward. I am grateful to those who contributed to the discussions on those occasions. The Marett Lecture was printed for private circulation initially, but was later published in *Religious Studies*, vol. 22. I have also made use in Part One and elsewhere in the book of selected material from 'The Friends of Cleanthes', *Modern Theology*, Jan. 1985. I am grateful for permission to use this material here.

In Part Two, Chapters 13 and 14 on Peter Berger's work are a revision of my contribution to the symposium 'The Sociologizing of Meaning' with A.R. Manser, *Proceedings of the Aristotelian Society*, Supp. Vol. LIII, 1979. My revision has benefited from A.R. Manser's criticisms on that occasion, although he would probably still be unhappy with some of my conclusions. I am grateful for permission to use some of the original material here.

Part Three of the book consists of material which I wrote in the form of two papers while at Yale Divinity School, designed to invite discussion, namely, 'Lindbeck's Audience' and 'Holmer's Audience'. It was not until the following semester that this material fell into place as the third part of the book. By that time, the papers had aroused a certain amount of interest as independent pieces. 'Lindbeck's Audience' was a reaction to George Lindbeck's *The Nature of Doctrine*. Because of the interest in that book, I was persuaded that there was good reason to publish my paper in *Modern Theology*, Oct. 1987. I wish to acknowledge the gracious way in which George Lindbeck accepted and discussed my criticisms, and to thank the Editor of *Modern Theology* for permission to use the material here. 'Holmer's Audience' is a reaction to Paul Holmer's *The Grammar of Faith* which I already knew and had found philosophically congenial. I benefited from the discussions I had with Paul Holmer at Yale. David Gibson was extremely helpful, in informal discussions, in pointing out similarities and differences between Paul Holmer's work and my own. 'Holmer's Audience' is to appear as 'Grammarians and Guardians' in a *festschrift* for Paul Holmer edited by Richard Bell.

In Part Four of the book, Chapters 19 and 20 grew out of an unpublished paper, 'God and Mystery'. The paper was one of the lectures I gave as Agnes Cuming Visitor at University College, Dublin in 1982. I am indebted to the discussion on that occasion and to the discussions when the paper was read at Louisiana State University, Baton Rouge, and University College, Cardiff in 1982, at the College of Wooster, Ohio in 1983, and at the University of Leeds in 1984.

Chapter 21 grew out of a paper on 'Grace and Works' given at the Centre for Philosophic Exchange at the State University of New York at Brockport. The lecture, in its original form, was published in *Philosophic Exchange*, 1984/5, nos. 15 and 16. I benefited from the discussion of the paper at the Centre where a video of the discussion is available. I am also grateful for a discussion of the paper at Tulane University in 1982. In arriving at the version of the material used in the book, I have benefited from the perceptive comments of Donald Evans. 'God and Mystery' and 'Grace and Works', in their original form, were responses to the work of John Whittaker. Discussions with him at Louisiana State University were extremely rewarding.

In the remainder of Part Four of the book, I have selected and revised material from two published papers. I am grateful for permission to make this use of the material here. 'Mystery and Mediation' was read at one of the plenary sessions of the first National Conference on Religion and Literature at the University of Durham in September 1982. The paper was published in *Images of Belief in Literature* edited by David Jasper (Macmillan and St Martin's Press 1984). The paper was read as a Convocation Lecture at the College of Wooster, Ohio and to a meeting under the auspices of the Alumni Association at Georgia College, Milledge-ville in 1982, and as a public lecture at Nazareth College, Rochester in 1984. I am grateful for the discussions on these occasions.

'The Devil's Disguises' was a lecture in the Royal Institute of Philosophy Series, *Objectivity and Cultural Divergence*, edited by Stuart Brown, Cambridge University Press 1984. The paper was also read at the University of Virginia at Charlottesville, the University of Georgia and Louisiana State University in 1982, and at Vassar College and California State University at San Bernardino in 1984. This material was also used in my seminars at Yale and Claremont. I benefited from all the discussions on these various occasions.

It is obvious that my intellectual debts are numerous. No one to whom I am indebted would agree with all the conclusions I have reached. Indeed, many would disagree with most of them. Nevertheless, without their help, I could not have written the book. I am also grateful to Mrs Sonia Hughes for the preparation of the typescript for publication and Donald Evans for being ready, as usual, to help me with the proof-reading.

D.Z.P.
Swansea

Preface

Contemporary philosophy of religion is dominated by foundationalism, and by a post-Enlightenment conception of rationality. Foundationalism is the view that propositions are of two kinds, those which stand in need of evidence, and those which provide the required evidence. The latter are said to be foundational, since they do not stand in need of further evidence. Most philosophers assume that belief in God cannot be given foundational status. That belief, it is said, stands in need of supporting evidence. Even when the evidence is considered to be favourable, the most that can be said is that it is highly probable that there is a God.

The embarrassment for foundationalism has always been that it does not do justice to the primary language of faith. Strong belief is not tentative or hypothetical. Believers do not pray to a God who probably exists. But if foundationalism is inadequate, to what philosophical alternative can one turn?

In Part One of the book, I discuss the powerful attack on foundationalism by Reformed epistemologists in recent years. The Reformed epistemologist argues that the religious believer has every right to place belief in God among his foundational propositions. The foundationalist denies this right. He appeals to the post-Enlightenment conception of rationality and its notion of sovereign reason, by reference to which epistemic practices are to be judged. The Reformed epistemologist points out that the possibility of such judgement depends on producing a criterion of basicality. Such a criterion would determine which propositions are and are not properly foundational. But no such criterion has been produced. The classical foundationalist claims that only self-evident propositions and the incorrigible propositions of sense experience are properly foundational. But how does he know this? It is certainly not self-evident that this is so.

The theist cannot demonstrate his right to place belief in God among his foundational propositions, but the foundationalist is in precisely the same position with respect to the foundational propositions he recognises. The foundationalist does not arrive at his commitment to his foundational propositions as a result of intellectual investigation. On the contrary, he takes this commitment for granted in his investigations. He trusts in his epistemic practices. The Reformed epistemologist, unlike the foundational-

Preface

ist, does not claim to know that his foundational propositions reflect reality, but he believes that they do. The Reformers were right: justification is by faith, not by reason.

Reformed epistemology, despite its attacks on classical foundationalism, remains within a foundationalist tradition. Both make a final appeal to foundational propositions. For Wittgenstein, basic propositions are not foundational. They enjoy their status within practices where they are held fast by all that surrounds them. Further, foundationalists and Reformed epistemologists regard epistemic practices as though they were descriptions of a reality which lies beyond them. Wittgenstein, far more radically, insists that distinctions between the real and the unreal get their sense within epistemic practices.

On Wittgenstein's view, philosophers must wait on epistemic practices and the complex relations in which they stand to each other. His task is to give perspicuous representations of this situation when faced with conceptual confusions concerning it. These representations will include accounts of co-operation and conflict between practices. Sometimes, the conflict between belief and unbelief is itself a conflict between different grammars, rather than a difference of opinion within an agreed grammatical framework. Such conflicts are distorted by the post-Enlightenment conception of rationality and by Reformed epistemology. According to the former, religious beliefs are not regarded as false beliefs, but as ideologies, instances of bad faith. According to the latter, those who deny the existence of God are in the grip of various forms of self-deception. Both points of view espouse totalitarian epistemic claims.

For Wittgenstein, philosophy is not the arbiter of rationality, the bar to which epistemic practices have to come for a verdict. In this respect, it may be thought that his conception of philosophy resembles the hermeneutic and sociological turns some have thought enquiry must take after foundationalism. I discuss these turns in Part Two of the book.

In hermeneutics, too, philosophy has ceased to adjudicate the rationality of epistemic practices. It relocates philosophy as simply one participant in the cultural conversation that is hermeneutics. To realise this, it is said, is to free oneself from philosophy's metaphysical pretensions; from a world well lost. But are we brought back to our ordinary world as a result? It seems that, in hermeneutics, much of that world is distorted too.

This conclusion may be difficult to accept, since the hermeneutic conversation presents itself as if it were simply ordinary conversation. But the hermeneutic conversation has hidden values. Those who enter it, it is said, must be ready and eager to talk. The conversation has agreement as its aim; an agreement not given prior to the conversation, but one which is supposed to emerge from it. Any agreement reached must not be static. It must be prepared for further changes and modifications as novelties appear on the horizon. As a result, we are told that no values are absolute.

The hidden values of hermeneutics are not the necessary consequences of exposing the defects of foundationalism. The postulation of the hermeneutic conversation is prescriptive, and there is no reason why religious believers should follow the prescription. In certain circumstances, religious believers will want to stress the differences between their practices and those of other people. Common agreement will not be their aim and they will not be prepared to talk to all and sundry. The hermeneutic conversation turns out to be no more than one set of responses some may wish to engage in faced by a plurality of epistemic practices.

After foundationalism, some have suggested that enquiry should take a sociological rather than a hermeneutic turn. Instead of a hermeneutic conversation, we are offered a sociological story. Like the conversation the story, if adopted, promises to bring us back from metaphysical to ordinary conceptions of reality. According to the story, men became victims of meanings and values they themselves have created. They allow this to happen because they want to be protected from anomy; from meaninglessness. But there are many different clusters of meanings, some strong, some weak. When religious meanings find themselves in an unsympathetic cultural milieu, they have to accommodate existing fashions in order to survive.

The sociological story is descriptive rather than prescriptive. But what does it describe? The concepts it employs are appropriate to describe the behaviour of those who simply conform to whatever is the done thing, engage in activities from ulterior motives, and are ready to compromise with anything in order to survive. In short, the concepts employed describe behaviour which deviates from a norm, deviates from the genuine. But the sociological story offers itself as a description of the norm and the genuine! As such, it obscures the possibilities of the genuine from us.

Theology, like philosophy, has wanted to learn from a critique of foundationalism. In Part Three of the book, I discuss some theological forms of foundationalism, and attempts within theology to take a Wittgensteinian turn after foundationalism. One form of theological foundationalism is found in cognitivist theories of religious belief. Such theories see theologies as descriptions of a divine object to which they refer. Competing theologies are competing descriptions, on this view. Another form of theological foundationalism is found in experiential-expressive theories of religious belief, whereby different theologies are seen as different interpretations of an underlying religious experience to which they refer. But these references to 'a common object' or 'a common experience' are idle, since it is only within theological and religious contexts that we have criteria to determine what is meant by speaking of 'the same God' or 'the same religious experience'. Wittgenstein expressed these insights by calling theology a grammar.

Yet Wittgenstein's conclusion is often turned into a foundationalist theory, a so-called 'cultural linguistic' approach to religious belief. On such a view, different theologies are seen as different interpretations of the grammar of a common doctrine. In this way, Wittgenstein's view is made to lend support to a perspective in which religious differences are seen as superficial phenomena hiding an underlying unity. Nothing in Wittgenstein supports such a view. Philosophy's task is to give a perspicuous representation of religious differences when we are tempted to mischaracterise them. No single account can be given of the various contexts in which differences occur. Sometimes, however, theological differences are themselves grammatical clashes, rather than a clash of interpretations within an agreed common grammar. Sometimes, one man's God is another man's devil.

Theological foundationalism can take many forms. For example, it is said that theism is the implicit foundation of religious belief. Others say that religious belief depends on the outcome of historical evidence. Alternatively, it is said that religious belief is grounded in 'religious facts' or 'religious history'. Again it has been said that religious belief is based on religious experience; an experience given prior to all religious beliefs and theologies. When these forms of foundationalism are subjected to Wittgensteinian criticisms, the criticisms are often seen as if they were an additional metaphysical theory called Wittgensteinian fideism. In this way, the metaphysical game perpetuates itself.

There is an important difference, however, between the philosopher and the theologian. The philosopher is the guardian of grammar. His concern is to free us from the conceptual confusions which bewitch us. The theologian, however, is the guardian of the Faith. He is not content with giving perspicuous representations of religious agreements and differences. He has the task of proclaiming, from among these agreements and differences, his own religious and theological pespective. The philosopher informs, but the theologian incites.

In Part Four of the book, I explore what happens, in the case of some central religious concepts, when we turn from foundationalism to examine concept-formation in religious belief. Where the notion of mystery is concerned, we see how foundationalists turn religious mysteries into epistemological mysteries. In philosophical theism, our task is said to be how to move from the world to God. A gap is opened up between a language, said to be necessarily inadequate, and the reality of God. When we pay attention to concept-formation, we see that, far from hiding God from us, the conception of God in the language is of a hidden God. Thus, to say 'God is beyond mortal telling' is not to report an epistemological failure to praise God. On the contrary, the expression is one form such praise takes.

Our philosophical task is to let the concept of mystery come in at the right place; to show how the concept is mediated in human life. I try to show the internal relations which exist between a belief in mystery and the notion of grace, the way we react to the contingencies of life, and the ways in which we judge and think of other people. This recognition of the religious place for mystery is very different from the recognition and the place which philosophy often gives to mystery.

What conception can philosophy have of itself after foundationalism? First, the enormous confidence philosophy has in itself as the demonstrator of religion's necessary confusions is overthrown. Second, wholesale condemnation of religion is not replaced by wholesale endorsement of it. Religion is a ragged phenomenon. Given the diverse influences we have mentioned, it would be astonishing if no form of religious belief had ever been infiltrated by, or even born of, various kinds of confusion.

In endeavouring to give perspicuous representations of the grammar of religious belief, the philosopher cannot take his audience for granted. I have already mentioned the anti-religious sense of intellectual superiority by which he will be confronted. This sense is destroyed at considerable cost to the philosophers concerned. They would have to recognise that they are often in the grip of the very superstitions they condemn in others. It is difficult to clarify the grammar of religious belief in a pervasively secular age.

Even where a philosopher provides grammatical clarifications, it cannot be assumed that they will be appreciated by those whom he addresses. Some will not merely misunderstand them; they will fail to understand them. The elucidations offered fail to get off the ground for them; the language means nothing to them. Some may be blind to what the philosopher of religion wants to show, as he may be blind to some perspectives other than his own. We do not share all the concepts in our language. We do not learn to talk by being able to talk to anyone about everything. These considerations should lead philosophy to revise its assumption that it possesses the resources to understand, and to convey to others, the character of any practice presented to it. That conception of itself may well be another illusion, which, after foundationalism, philosophy is called on to surrender.

Part One

Can There Be A Religious Epistemology?

It is difficult to find the *beginning*. Or, better: it is difficult to begin at the beginning. And not try to go further back.

Wittgenstein, *On Certainty*

1
Foundationalism and Religion: a Philosophical Scandal

It has been one of the scandals of the philosophy of religion that foundationalism in epistemology has been thought, and still is thought, to be the only philosophical perspective capable of doing justice to the nature of religious belief. Foundationalism is the view that a belief is a rational belief only if it is related, in appropriate ways, to a set of propositions which constitute the foundations of what we believe. It assumes, from the outset, that belief in God is not among these foundational propositions. Belief in the existence of God, it is said, stands in need of justifications, grounds, reasons, foundations. We have to ask whether it is rational to believe in God. We are acquainted with countless cases where it is appropriate to be asked why we believe what we say we believe, and it is simply assumed that belief in God is another belief of this kind. Once this assimilation of belief in God to other kinds of belief takes place, asking whether belief in God is rational quickly becomes a matter of seeking evidence for the existence of God. Such evidence, if it can be found, will constitute the foundation of the belief. If it cannot be found, it will have been shown that there is no good reason for believing in God. To continue to believe, without good reason, was held by W.K. Clifford, in the nineteenth century, to be itself a sin; to indulge in the pleasure of believing in such a way, he claimed, is to indulge in a 'stolen' pleasure:

> Not only does it deceive ourselves by giving us a sense of power which we do not really possess, but it is sinful, because it is stolen in defiance of our duty to mankind. That duty is to guard ourselves from such beliefs as from a pestilence, which may shortly master our body and spread to the rest of the town.[1]

3

Clifford's view culminated in the following remark: 'To sum up: it is wrong always, everywhere, and for anyone to believe anything upon insufficient evidence.'[2]

While, for the most part, continuing to believe without sufficient evidence is not condemned in religious terms by philosophers today, nevertheless, it is considered sufficient to place the believer beyond the pale as far as reasoned intellectual discussion is concerned. And so, within the philosophy of religion, the weighing of evidence, for and against the existence of God, proceeds. This is the mode of argument which is still dominant *within* the practice of the philosophy of religion. Philosophers who argue in this way are the friends of Cleanthes. For example, some philosophers, such as Richard Swinburne, argue that the preponderance of evidence is in favour of belief in God, while others, such as J.L. Mackie, have argued that the preponderance of evidence points against belief in God. But, as Alvin Plantinga has said, such philosophers 'concur in holding that belief in God is rational, only if there is, on balance, a preponderance of evidence for it — or less radically, only if there is not, on balance, a preponderance of evidence against it.'[3] Little wonder that Swinburne has been called our twentieth-century Cleanthes. Yet, if Swinburne is the Cleanthes of believers, Mackie may well be called the Cleanthes of unbelievers.

This evidentialism, where God's reality is in question, shows that, for the most part, philosophy of religion is still at an animistic stage. According to E.B. Tylor's 'animism', primitives react to the unknown in the world which confronts them by postulating the existence of beings higher than themselves to explain otherwise inexplicable events. It is extremely important to note that, for Tylor, religious belief is not irrational. Religious beliefs are *mistakes*, but they might have been true. Tylor would agree with Frazer when he said of the primitives:

> their errors were not wilful extravagances or the ravings of insanity, but simply hypotheses, justifiable as such at the time they were propounded, but which a full experience has proved to be inadequate. It is only by the successive testing of hypotheses and the rejection of the false that truth is at last elicited.[4]

Notice, 'the rejection of the false', not the rejection of the unintelligible. Swinburne's reaction has been to reaffirm that the hypothesis of God's existence *is* the best explanation of the world as we know it.[5] But, as Mackie shows, he has failed to come to terms with Hume's criticisms in his *Dialogues Concerning Natural Religion* which haunt all forms of argument from or to design or cosmological arguments. We cannot avoid these criticisms either by suggesting that the reasonableness of religious beliefs depends on the cumulative effect of considerations in themselves inconclusive.[6] In *Religion Without Explanation*,[7] I tried to show how Hume argues on three levels. At the first level, Hume emphasises that we do not have direct knowledge of God. His nature must be determined from the character of his works. From every reasonable point of view, the character of the works seems mixed, including good and bad features. At the very best, therefore, God seems to have a mixed or capricious character. At the second level, however, Hume asks why it is necessary to regard nature as an artifact in the first place. By so regarding it, we already assume that we have to look outside nature for an explanation of it. But is there not a perfectly natural way of explaining natural facts without reference to God? But what of the existence of the world as such? Is that not something which still stands in need of explanation? At the third level, however, Hume argues against the intelligibility of postulating God as the explanation of the world. First, we do not know what it means to ask for the cause of everything. The world is not some kind of object of which it makes sense to seek the cause. Second, we have no grounds for speaking of a maker of the world. We have experience of building houses. Therefore, when we see a house, we know that someone, somewhere, built the house. But when we look at the world about us, we have no idea of what it is to speak of worlds being made. We have no basis in our experience to speak of the world as God's artifact. Hume's arguments, at each level, are logical arguments. If, then, Hume's arguments are successful, their conclusion is not that it is highly unlikely that the world is a product of a divine plan. Hume's conclusion is that such talk is unintelligible.

There are times when Mackie seems to recognise the *logical* force of Hume's arguments. Consider, for example, his reaction to Swinburne's attempts to resuscitate the argument from design. In summing up the effect of Hume's and Kant's arguments on Swinburne's arguments, Mackie says, 'The advance of science has destroyed the starting-points which made it initially plausible and attractive to the eighteenth century, while the general philosophical objections which were brought against it by Kant and,

above all, by Hume, remain in force against Swinburne's restate-
ment of it, and, I surmise, *against all possible reconstructions*.[8] In the
first part of the quotation, Mackie speaks of the traditional proof
as something which has been undermined by science. But, if this
were accepted, the believer could reply by saying, 'Perhaps the
evidence will turn in my direction once again. It is true that the
existence of a divine plan seems highly unlikely at the moment,
but perhaps new facts will emerge in the future which will show
that the existence of a divine plan is highly likely, as likely as it
appeared to be in the eighteenth century.' But this response would
not be open to the believer in response to what Mackie says of
the criticisms of Hume and Kant. He says that these criticisms
show that the conception of an argument from design is a product
of conceptual confusion. Speaking of the traditional proofs of the
existence of God, Mackie says, 'Since the early nineteenth century,
and particularly through Kant's influence the traditional "proofs"
of theistic doctrines have been widely rejected or abandoned.'[9]
Were the proofs abandoned because their conclusions were
unlikely to be true? If so, perhaps there is always the likelihood
that, were appropriate facts to come to light, the proofs'
conclusions could be held to be likely to be true after all. But
Mackie recognises that this is not the way in which the proofs
have been rejected or abandoned. They have been rejected as the
products of conceptual confusion. Mackie recognises that I see
Hume's achievements as the exposure of such confusion:

> D.Z. Phillips ... refers, indeed, to the 'enormous influence'
> of Hume on contemporary philosophy of religion, and says
> that 'given its assumptions, Hume's attack on certain theistic
> arguments is entirely successful'; ... Phillips concedes to
> Hume ... that we cannot infer a god from the world either
> by a design argument or a cosmological argument; in fact
> 'The whole notion of a God and another world which we
> can infer from the world we know is discredited'.[10]

Ironically, I am prepared to give more credit to Hume's argument
against metaphysical tendencies in the philosophy of religion than
Mackie is prepared to give.

Why, given all his objections, does Mackie spend ten of the
fourteen chapters of his book coming to the wholly expected
conclusion that design arguments or cosmological arguments do
not work? The answer lies in the fact that Mackie, like so many

philosophers of religion, can see no alternative way of discussing religious beliefs. He equates philosophical theism with religious belief. He refuses to call anything else an example of real religion. Further, despite his occasional insights into its *conceptual* defects, for most of the time he discusses that theism in terms of probabilities. For example, according to Mackie, God is a person without a body. In his opinion, there could be such a person; there is nothing unintelligible in such an assumption. Of course, Mackie's conclusion is that it is highly unlikely that there are persons without bodies. The majority of philosophers today would not argue in this way. They would say that the notion of a person without a body is meaningless. We may speak of the soul and the body, but in doing so we are not talking of two separate elements in a human being. Rather, we are talking of a human being under different aspects. Of course, the Bible does say that God is a spirit, and that they who worship him should worship him in spirit and in truth. Let's make the philosophical substitution: 'God is a person without a body and they who ...' On the other hand, let's forget it! For Mackie, however, and for the majority of philosophical theists who argue with him, all these matters are matters of probability.

My main aim, at the moment, however, is not to enter into these disputes, but to bring their *character* to your attention. They are disputes between opposing hypotheses, so that believer and non-believer may be said to hold opposite beliefs from each other. But if this is still the dominant way of philosophising about religion, then it fits in perfectly well with the methodological procedures proposed by Tylor and Frazer: 'It is only by the successive testing of hypotheses and rejection of the false that truth is at last elicited.' Speaking of such theories, Evans-Pritchard says: 'For the most part the theories ... are, for anthropologists at least, as dead as mutton, and today are chiefly of interest as specimens of the thought of their time.'[11] Whatever we may say of anthropologists, animism is alive and well among contemporary philosophers of religion.

Most philosophers would say that philosophers of religion and believers today have less excuse than the primitives for their animistic practices. As we have seen, of the primitives, at least, it could be said that their hypotheses were justifiable at the time, although, now, a full experience has shown them to be inadequate. But now, it seems, not everyone can have had a full experience, or, at least, not everyone could have appreciated its significance,

7

since there are still people who believe in God. This stubborn remnant, however, can hardly expect the same consideration from today's intellectuals as Frazer thought he was giving to the primitives: 'We shall do well to look with leniency upon their errors as inevitable slips made in the search for truth.'[12] Now, as Norman Malcolm points out, the tone is very different:

> In our Western academic philosophy, religious belief is commonly regarded as unreasonable and is viewed with condescension or even contempt. It is said that religion is a refuge for those who, because of weakness of intellect or character, are unable to confront the stern realities of the world. The objective, mature, *strong* attitude is to hold beliefs solely on the basis of *evidence*.[13]

When religious beliefs are discussed within the parameters of these assumptions the results are predictable enough:

> In American universities there must be hundreds of courses in which [proofs for the existence of God] are the main topic. We can be sure that nearly always the critical verdict is that the proofs are invalid and consequently that, up to the present time at least, religious belief has received no rational justification.[14]

The stubborn remnant, it seems, is also a stupid remnant.

Notice, all that can be said on this view, is that *up to the present time* no rational justification has been given of religious belief. Echoing Mackie's sentiments in *The Miracle of Theism*, T.A. Roberts says,

> For better or for worse we cannot escape the fact that we live in an age where the fate of Christianity as a system of beliefs which can be afforded to the intelligent man is in the balance. And, for the most part, what accounts for this anti-religious conceptual turn today is the growth and development of our detailed knowledge of the workings of nature which came in the wake of the scientific revolution since the seventeenth century. One consequence of this scientific knowledge is to make many things which it was reasonable to believe in the Middle Ages or in the time of Calvin unreasonable to believe in our age. If this is so, is

there any reasonable ground now for holding any religious belief? The strong message of Mackie's book is that there is not.[15]

But what of the stubborn remnant? Need Mackie's arguments deter them? Not necessarily. As we have already seen, they might well take on the arguments on their own terms. They might be prepared to admit that, at the moment, the preponderance of evidence is against belief in God, but remain convinced that this is a temporary setback and that sufficient evidence will turn up sooner or later. Believing this, they continue, in the face of conflicting evidence, to believe in God. More radically, they may be prepared to admit that they have never had, and neither has anyone else had, sufficient evidence for belief in God. Such evidence, it may be said, is never available in this life. They believe, however, that this evidence will be made available after death. If asked for their reasons for believing this, they may give none apart from their trust in the promises of Jesus, so understood, that all will be made known one day. They might argue that the presence of sufficient evidence would destroy and negate the character of faith and the very need for faith. Faith, it might be said, is living in the trust and hope that there is evidence for the existence of God in the absence of such evidence here and now.

But, now, is any of this satisfactory? Let us recall that the whole point of the philosophical enterprise was to establish the rationality of belief in God. In order to do this, however, there must surely be a correspondence between the subject of philosophical investigation and the subject of religious worship. Otherwise, of what use would the philosophical reflections be if they concerned a philosophical fiction and not the God of Scripture? But when we turn to Scripture it is patently obvious that belief in God is not a matter of believers entertaining a hypothesis. It is not a matter of embracing the best available explanation given the evidence at hand. Faith does not seem to be readiness to postpone a desire for evidence in the belief that it will turn up at a later date or after death. All this is obvious from countless passages from the Bible, but let us simply quote a well-known passage from Psalm 139 to illustrate the point:

Whither shall I go from thy Spirit? or whither shall I flee from thy presence? If I ascend into heaven, thou art there: if I make my bed in hell, behold thou art there. If I take

9

the wings of the morning, and dwell in the uttermost parts
of the sea; Even there shall thy hand lead me, and thy right
hand shall hold me. If I say, surely the darkness shall cover
me; even the night shall be light about me. Yea, the darkness
hideth not from thee; but the night shineth as the day; the
darkness and the light are both alike to thee.

What would be a foundationalist reading of the psalm? 'Whither
shall I go from thy Spirit? or whither shall I flee from thy presence?
If I ascend up into heaven, it is highly probable that thou art
there: if I make my bed in hell, behold it is highly probable that
thou art there also?' The following reading fares no better: 'If I
ascend up into heaven, it is cumulatively apparent that thou are
there; if I make my bed in hell, behold it is cumulatively apparent
that thou art there also.' Surely, in the original[16] the Psalmist
testifies to the inescapable reality of God. Inescapable? This seems
a far cry from the competing probabilities of the arguments of
animistic philosophical foundationalism. As A.B. Davidson says,
'It never occurred to any prophet or writer of the Old Testament
to prove the existence of God.'[17] This is quite a jolt to anyone
who believes that people cannot believe in something without
proof or evidence. It seems as if all these writers were shirking
their essential task: failing to attempt to prove God's existence or
to seek evidence for his existence. The question of God's existence,
as something for which evidence must be sought, simply does not
find a place in the traffic of their discourse. They agree or disagree
over whether someone or something is of God, or from God, but
not over whether there is a God at all.

It is no good suggesting that they presupposed the existence of
God, or took for granted what an outcome of an enquiry into it
would be, since presupposing something, or taking the outcome
of an enquiry for granted, is something we do, something which
does enter the traffic of our language, and, in their case, there is
no sign of their doing either. It may be said that, for them, God
was manifest in all things; that his reality underlies their commerce
with each other. This is true, but, as we shall see, the fundamental
issue concerns the sense in which God's reality underlies their
lives; is basic to them. Whatever of this, however, the God in
question is certainly not thought of as a god who may not exist.

But, it might be said, we no longer live in the world of the
Psalmist. In that world, it may have been possible to speak of
the inescapable reality of God. In a certain sense, God's reality

was taken for granted; all things spoke of him. But that world is not our world. We have already spoken of believers as a stubborn remnant. Since they are a remnant, is it not obvious that they have to give reasons to the unbelievers who surround them for the Faith they still have to proclaim? We do not live in a world in which God's reality is inescapable. Our problem, it seems, is not how to escape God, but how to find him. There are even theologians who say that God cannot be found on high. They insist that we should speak of him as deep inside us, but secular psychiatric and psychoanalytic explanations threaten to monopolise explanations of what can be found there. Height and depth: both domains seem to be already appropriated. Astronauts and analysts — between them they seem to have covered the terrain. Given all this, how can we possibly say that the Faith can be proclaimed without proof, evidence, a foundation or a justification?

This argument, which seems so powerful, is, in fact, misleadingly seductive. Suppose that we grant that believers make up what we have called a stubborn remnant. We have already seen that the God in whom they believe is one of whom it makes no sense to say that he may or may not exist. As Cornelius Van Til says,

> To ask *whether* the triune God of Scripture exists and *whether* the space–time world is what it is because of this God, is to presuppose that abstract possibility is back of God. A God of whom it is possible to ask intelligently *whether* he exists is not the God of Scripture. The God of Scripture is back of all possible eventuation in the space–time world. It is an insult to this God to argue for his *possible* existence. An argument for his possible existence *presupposes* the idea that he may possibly not exist. But *the God of Scripture tells us that he cannot possibly not exist. He presents himself as the selfreferential source of all that exists in the universe.*[18]

Further, for the believer, God is the sovereign measure of all things. For him, how can such a measure be subject to measurement? Making God subject to the assessment of probabilities makes him subject to criteria of assessment which seem to be endowed with greater authority than the divine object of the assessment. But, as Camus has said, he who submits God to judgement kills him in his own heart. For the believer, it is the sovereign God who judges man, not man who judges God.

What if the apologist wants to convey the character of a God who is not to be judged, and whose reality cannot be merely possible or probable, to a person who can make little of such a notion? Could he do it by employing the methods advocated by philosophical foundationalism? If, *per impossibile*, the sceptical enquirer is convinced by these methods, the most he would be able to say is that it is highly probable that there is a God. But, then, it would make sense to say that such a god might not exist. If this is so, then, whatever the apologist has conveyed, it cannot be the notion of an inescapable God, since according to *that* notion, it does not make sense to say that God might not exist. The philosophical scandal mentioned at the outset consists precisely in this: we are asked to accept as the only appropriate philosophical method for establishing the rationality of religious belief, a method which actually distorts the character of religious belief. The age in which we live may be extremely tentative about recognising the sense of belief in an inescapable God. But that tentativeness is in people's relation to the belief. Tentativeness must not be admitted to the grammar of the belief itself. When that is done, the logic of belief in an inescapable God is turned into a belief in a god who may or may not exist. But, is it not clear, as Plantinga has said, that 'The mature believer, the mature theist, does not typically accept belief in God tentatively, or hypothetically, or until something better comes along. Nor ... does he accept it as a conclusion from other things he believes.'[19] Yet, typically, epistemological foundationalism, which dominates contemporary philosophy of religion, depicts the religious believer in precisely this way. Something has gone wrong, something which cannot be rectified until we examine some of the assumptions which underlie foundationalism.

Notes

1. W.K. Clifford, 'The Ethics of Belief' in *Lectures and Essays*, (Macmillan, London, 1879), p. 184.
2. Ibid., p. 186. Both passages from Clifford are quoted by Alvin Plantinga in 'Reason and Belief in God' in Alvin Plantinga and Nicholas Wolterstorff (eds) *Faith and Rationality* (University of Notre Dame Press, Indiana, 1983), pp. 24–5.
3. Alvin Plantinga, 'Is Belief in God Rational?' in C.F. Delaney (ed.) *Rationality and Religious Belief* (University of Notre Dame Press, 1979), p. 9.
4. James Frazer, *The Golden Bough* (abridged edn) (Macmillan, London, 1924), p. 264.
5. Richard Swinburne, *The Coherence of Theism* (Oxford University Press, 1977), *The Existence of God* (Oxford University Press, 1979), *Faith and Reason* (Oxford University Press, 1981).
6. Basil Mitchell, *The Justification of Religious Belief* (Macmillan, London, 1973).
7. D.Z. Phillips, *Religion Without Explanation* (Basil Blackwell, Oxford, 1976).
8. J.L. Mackie, *The Miracle of Theism* (Oxford University Press, 1982), p. 149. My italics.
9. Ibid., p. 177.
10. Ibid., p. 222; quoting from Phillips, *Religion Without Explanation*, p. 21.
11. E.E. Evans-Pritchard, *Theories of Primitive Religion* (Clarendon Press, Oxford, 1965), p. 100.
12. Frazer, *Golden Bough*, p. 264.
13. Norman Malcolm, 'The Groundlessness of Belief' in *Thought and Knowledge* (Cornell University Press, 1977), p. 204.
14. Ibid.
15. T.A. Roberts, 'Crefydd a Rheswm' (Religion and Reason), *Y Traethodydd*, April 1984. My translation.
16. The two readings would represent Scripture if the philosophical views of Richard Swinburne and Basil Mitchell, respectively, were applied to it.
17. A.B. Davidson, *Theology of the Old Testament* (Edinburgh, 1904), p. 30.
18. Cornelius Van Til, *A Christian Theory of Knowledge* (Presbyterian and Reformed Publishing Co., New Jersey, 1969), p. 263.
19. Plantinga, 'Is Belief in God Rational?', p. 27.

2
The Reformed Challenge to Foundationalism

In recent years, there has been a philosophical challenge to foundationalism by a group of philosophers who conform to, or, at least, are influenced by, one version or other of Calvinist Reformed theology. I am not suggesting that these philosophers agree entirely with each other; they do not. Some of the differences between them may be regarded by them as extremely important. For present purposes, however, it is their unity in their common criticism and rejection of foundationalism which is of interest. In this section I want to give an outline of what their philosophical challenge amounts to.

Their challenge to foundationalism begins from a clear recognition of the scandal in the philosophy of religion we discussed in the previous section. They see that no philosophical system in which it makes sense to speculate about God's existence as though it were a matter of probability can do justice to the notion of God's inescapable reality. To embrace such a system, a system which has dominated philosophical reflection about religion since the Enlightenment, is already to presuppose the necessary answerability of religious belief to criteria of intelligibility wider than itself. Cornelius Van Til voices his misgivings about this presupposition as follows:

The essence of the non-Christian position is that man is assumed to be ultimate or autonomous. Man is thought of as the final reference point in predication. The facts of his environment are 'just there'; they are assumed to have come into being by chance. Possibility is placed above both God and man alike. The laws of logic are assumed as somehow operative in the universe, or at least as legislative for what man can or cannot accept as possible or probable. If a god exists, he must at least be subject to conditions that are similar to, if not the same as, those to which humanity is subject.[1]

The Reformed epistemologists (as I shall call them) point out that it is simply assumed in foundationalism that belief in the existence of God is a belief which stands in need of evidence. As we have seen, the evidence is to be provided by the relation in which the belief stands to propositions which constitute the foundations of our beliefs, propositions for the truth of which no evidence is needed. Again, it is simply assumed that belief in God cannot appear in these foundational propositions. The essence of the Reformed challenge is to ask the foundationalist how he knows this. The foundationalist claims to walk by reason alone. Therefore, if reason tells him which propositions are properly foundational, and which are not, he seems to have in his possession a rational criterion for foundational propositions, a criterion of basicality. By reference to this criterion it could be seen whether belief in God can function as a foundational proposition. The Reformed philosophers challenge the foundationalist to make this criterion explicit. They argue that he cannot, because he does not possess any such criterion. But in the absence of such a criterion to adjudicate between propositions which claim to be basic propositions, how can the foundationalist say that belief in God cannot appear among basic propositions? Having stated the Reformed challenge in broad outline, let us look at it in more detail, initially, in the version of it we find in the arguments of Alvin Plantinga.

Plantinga puts the case as follows:

Suppose we say that the assemblage of beliefs a person holds, together with the various logical and epistemic relations that hold among them, constitutes that person's *noetic structure*. Now ... for each person S there is a set F of beliefs such that a proposition p is rational or rationally acceptable for S only if p is evident with respect to F — only if, that is, the propositions in evidence constitute, on balance, evidence for p. Let us say that this set F of propositions is the *foundation of S's noetic structure*. On this view every noetic structure has a foundation; and a proposition is rational for

S, or known by *S*, or certain for *S*, only if it stands in the appropriate relation to the foundation of *S*'s noetic structure. Suppose we call this view *foundationalism* ... Might it not be that my belief in God is itself in the foundations of my noetic structure? Perhaps it is a member of *F*, in which case, of course, it will automatically be evident with respect to *F*.[2]

Plantinga reminds us of the force which foundational propositions are meant to play:

> The propositions in *F*, of course, are not inferred from other propositions and are not accepted on the basis of other propositions. I know the propositions of my noetic structure, but not by virtue of knowing *other* propositions; for these are the ones I start with. And so the question the foundationalist asks about belief in God, namely, what is the evidence for it — is not properly asked about the members of *F*; these items don't require to be evident with respect to other propositions in order to be rationally believed. Accordingly, says the foundationalist, not just any proposition is capable of functioning foundationally; to be so capable with respect to a person *S*, a proposition must not need the evidential support of other propositions; it must be such that it is possible that *S* knew *p* but have no evidence for *p*.[3]

What kinds of propositions are capable of functioning foundationally? Philosophers have differed in the answers they give to this question, but these differences will not be important as far as the Reformed challenge to foundationalism is concerned. The challenge remains essentially the same no matter what candidates are advanced as foundational propositions. The most favoured candidates advanced are, undoubtedly, self-evident propositions and incorrigible propositions relating to the senses. These propositions, such as $2+1=3$ and 'I seem to see a red patch', have embarrassed those who want to claim that their belief in God functions foundationally. The proposition that God exists is neither self-evident nor incorrigible, so it seems that it cannot function foundationally in any noetic structure. But what if the theist, true to his understanding of his noetic structure, insists that belief in God is the foundation of it? What if he insists that God's reality is evident to him, but is not based on the evidential support of other propositions? Clearly, the foundationalist will want to know by what right the theist places his belief in God in the foundations of his noetic structure. He wants the theist to produce a reason for doing so. Plantinga admits that the theist will be hard pressed to answer. But, Plantinga insists, the foundationalist is equally hard pressed if the same question is asked of him. He, too, is embarrassed if asked to give a justifying reason why he places his propositions in the foundations of his noetic structure. Let us consider the two favoured classes of foundational propositions.

First, self-evident propositions. These are said to have epistemic and phenomenological properties. The epistemic property is that of simply being seen to be true once understood. The phenomenological property is the luminous aura which accompanies them and leads us to accept them, or which may be our impulsion to accept them. But, Plantinga argues, it is conceivable that we could be sure of these characteristics and yet it be the case that the propositions we think are self-evident are not self-evident. We need a criterion, therefore, by which to show that the propositions we take to be self-evident, really are self-evident. But if the criterion produced is said to be self-evident, the same question of how we can be sure can be asked of it, and so on *ad infinitum*. It seems that our justifications can have no end. Plantinga asks, 'How does the foundationalist know — how does anyone know — that, indeed, a given proposition *is* self-evident? How do we tell? Isn't it possible that a proposition should seem to be self-evident when in fact it is not?'[4] The foundationalist is revealed as someone who takes on *trust* the proposition that what seems to be self-evident is very likely to be true, and the proposition that most propositions which appear to be self-evident really are self-evident. But neither of these propositions, which he takes on trust, is self-evident. The foundationalist has no reason for accepting them. He simply commits himself to them. Yet it is this very commitment that he objects to in the religious believer. Plantinga says of the foundationalist: 'We might say that he commits himself to the trustworthiness of his noetic equipment. More elegantly, he commits himself to the reliability of his epistemic endowment.'[5] It is important to recognise that when the foundationalist expresses his conviction that most propositions which seem self-evident are self-evident and that what appears to be self-evident is very likely to be true, he has not arrived at this conviction as the result of any kind of investigation. On the contrary, the commitment is in advance of any investigation and plays a foundational role in the subsequent investigations. So the foundationalist who says that only what is self-evident should play a foundational role in a noetic structure, and that this is dictated by reason, in fact commits himself to the reliability of these epistemic procedures without reason.

As we saw, the foundationalist objects to the religious believer ascribing a foundational role to his belief in God in his noetic structure. He accuses him of having no reason for doing so. But, as we have just shown, the foundationalist has no criterion by which he can demonstrate the reliability of the propositions he places in the foundations of his noetic structure. He simply trusts in his practice of doing so. But in that case, why should not the religious believer trust in his practice too? Plantinga gives the following verdict on the foundationalist:

> He means to commit himself to reason and to nothing more; he therefore declares irrational any noetic structure that contains more — belief in God, for example — in its foundations. But here there is no reason for the theist to follow his example; the believer is not obliged to take his word for it. So far we have found no reason at all for excluding belief in God from the foundations; so far we have found no reason at all for believing that belief in God cannot be basic in a rational noetic structure. To accept belief in God as basic is clearly not irrational in the sense of being proscribed by reason or in conflict with the deliverances of reason. The dictum that belief in God is not basic in a rational noetic structure is neither apparently self-evident nor apparently incorrigible. Nor does it seem to be a deductive consequence of what is self-evident or incorrigible. Is there, then, any reason at all for holding that a noetic structure including belief in God as basic is irrational? If there is, it remains to be specified.[6]

To many, this conclusion may appear unsatisfactory and inconclusive, for while it is the case that the foundationalist can offer no criterion by which belief in God can be excluded from the foundations of a noetic structure, it is also the case that the theist can offer no criterion by which the belief should be included. Foundationalist and theist seem to share a common failure: neither can produce a criterion for proper basicality. In the absence of such a criterion it may be asked why *any* proposition could not be placed in the foundations of a noetic structure. Plantinga attempts to meet this objection by saying that we do not need a criterion of basicality before we can accept certain propositions as basic in our noetic structures. He argues that we recognise, in *certain circumstances*, the proper basicality of certain propositions without actually forming any formal criteria. Of course, it may turn out that we should not have accepted as basic certain propositions which we thought were basic. That fact in itself, however, should not lead us to leap to the irrational conclusion that all propositions which seem to us self-evident or incorrigible are not, in fact, self-evident or incorrigible. Our procedures, in these matters, Plantinga says, will be inductive: 'We must assemble examples of beliefs and conditions such that the former are obviously properly basic in the latter, and examples of beliefs and conditions such that the former are obviously *not* properly basic in the latter.'[7] This reference to the obviousness of the propriety or impropriety of the candidates for basic propositions should not lead us to think that we can produce a neat set of necessary and sufficient conditions for basicality on which every one will agree. It is no part of Plantinga's case to claim that such conditions can be produced. The situation we find ourselves in is messier than that. The circumstances will vary enormously. In some it may be possible to produce no more than *some* necessary conditions and *some* sufficient conditions. In any case, we must always be ready, he claims, to revise these conditions in the light of new theories.

Plantinga's procedure, then, relies on a consideration of the particular examples in question. There is no reason to believe, however, that everyone will agree about the examples. Obviously, the non-believer will not assent to the example of the religious noetic structure in which belief in God functions foundationally, although he may admit that the believer has behaved appropriately with respect to his epistemic claims. But, of course, he believes that the believer has an erroneous point of departure. In the same way, however, the believer holds that the non-believer's exclusion of belief in God from the foundations of his noetic structure is erroneous. It does not follow, for Plantinga, that no question of truth is involved. The question of truth is now raised at the level of the clashing noetic structures. Plantinga says:

Of course it does not follow that there is no truth of the matter; if our criteria conflict, then at least one of them is mistaken, even if we cannot by further discussion agree as to which it is. Similarly, either I am mistaken in holding that *B* (belief in God) is properly basic in *C* (certain conditions), or you are mistaken in holding that it is not. Still further, if I *am* mistaken in this matter, then if I take *B* to be basic in *C* — that is, if I am in *C* and believe *B* without the evidential support of other beliefs — then I am irrational in so doing. Particularism does not imply subjectivism.[8]

So although neither believer nor unbeliever can give the other a reason why belief in God is or is not a foundational belief, it remains a fact that one or the other is mistaken in his claim. What being mistaken amounts to, it seems, is unanalysed in this context.

It may be thought that because Plantinga conceives of his views as an attack on foundationalism, he thinks belief in the existence of God is groundless. This is not so. Although the relations between the conditions in which we believe in God and the belief itself are not evidential, this does not mean that there are no relations between them. What Plantinga has to say about these is illustrated best by the second class of propositions which foundationalists have placed in the foundations of our noetic structures, namely, incorrigible propositions of sense experience. If I say I see a tree, my belief in its existence is not based on the *evidence* of my seeing the tree or on my being appeared treely to, to use Chisholm's language. Nevertheless, Plantinga argues, these experiences play a vital part in the formation of my belief. Plantinga says,

> my being appeared to in this characteristic way (together with other circumstances) is what confers on me the right to hold the belief in question; this is what justifies me in accepting it. We could say, if we wish, that this experience is what justifies me in holding it; this is the *ground* of my justification, and, by extension, the ground of the belief itself.[9]

In a similar way, Plantinga wants to argue that belief in God, although not dependent on evidence for being known, is also grounded in and justified by the conditions in which it is held. These conditions are experiences in which the believer is aware of God in his creation, aware of God's anger at his sins, aware of God's presence and of the need to thank and praise him, and so on. If we were to speak strictly, Plantinga says, belief in God is not properly basic. What is properly basic are such beliefs as 'God is speaking to me', 'God has created all this', 'God is to be thanked and praised'. Plantinga concludes: 'It is not the relatively high-level and general proposition *God exists* that is properly basic, but instead propositions detailing some of his attributes and actions.'[10] In this way, it can be seen that religious beliefs are not groundless or gratuitous.

It may be thought in the light of Plantinga's emphasis on the basicality of propositions that he has left little room for argument with respect to them. This is an impression he is anxious to correct. He raises the worry someone may have about the believer who accepts belief in God as basic:

> Does it not follow that he will hold this belief in such a way that no argument could move him or cause him to give it up? Will he not hold it come what may, in the teeth of any evidence or argument with which he could be presented? Does he not thereby adopt a posture in which argument and other rational methods of settling disagreements are implicitly declared irrelevant?[11]

In Plantinga's view, real though the worry is, it is not one which need be caused by anything he has said. Let us suppose that belief in God clashes with some other basic propositions in the noetic structure. The propositions cannot rationally co-exist with each other, so a choice has to be made between them. In this way, a believer may become an atheist and an atheist may become a believer. Therefore a person who holds that belief in God is properly basic does not hold the belief dogmatically. The mere possibility that he may be wrong means that, strictly speaking, what we have called the justifying conditions of basic propositions are, in fact, only prima-facie, rather than ultima-facie all-things-considered, justifications. A proposition may be put to me which seems self-evident to me. Accepting it may entail that I can no longer hold on to my belief in God. Plantinga says:

> we may say that a condition that overrides my *prima-facie* justification for *p* is *defeating condition* or *defeater* for *p* (for me). Defeaters, of course, are themselves *prima-facie* defeaters, for the defeater can be defeated. Perhaps I spot

a fallacy in the initially convincing argument; perhaps I discover a convincing argument for the denial of one of its premises; perhaps I learn on reliable authority that someone else has done one of these things. Then the defeater is defeated, and I am once again within my rights in accepting *p*. Of course a similar remark must be made about defeater-defeaters: they are subject to defeat by defeater-defeater-defeaters and so on.[12]

It must be borne in mind, however, that if a potential defeater is defeated, where belief in God is concerned, it does not follow that belief in the defeater-defeater is the foundation of my original belief.

Plantinga recognises that more needs to be said on all these issues. He says that he has been talking about weak justifications, the justifications which enable us to say we *believe* something. But what if there are strong justifications, justifications which enable us to say we *know* something? In the case of 'I see a tree', whether the justification is strong or weak, no question about the character of the justifying experience need arise when I say 'I see a tree'. Are there strong justifications where religious belief is concerned? What if the justifying experiences he has mentioned, experience of God in his creation, of God's anger, of the need to thank and praise God, constitute strong justifications, the justifications which enable us to say not simply that we believe God exists, but that we know God exists? But whether the justification is strong or weak no question or belief regarding its character need arise in the condition which enables the believer to say he believes in God. They may and do arise in the course of philosophical discussion, but they need not arise in the life of a believer when he comes to believe or holds on to his belief. The implications of this admission, which Plantinga does not discuss have, as we shall see, far-reaching implications for his arguments against foundationalism.

In the light of Plantinga's attack on foundationalism, what kind of rationality, what kind of coherence, can be ascribed to belief in God? The answer is the kind guaranteed by 'negative coherence theories'. We have not been provided with a criterion which can determine whether belief in God should be placed in the foundations of a noetic structure. What we have seen, however, is that no good reason has been given to show why this should not be done. William P. Alston puts the matter by saying that while foundationalism holds our epistemic practices guilty until proved innocent, in Reformed epistemology, our epistemic practices are held to be innocent until proved guilty. The difficulty is that no justification of an epistemic practice can be given without invoking the very practice one is pretending to justify. Alston says:

> Our only reason for supposing that memory is generally reliable is that its past track record is a good one, and we have no way of ascertaining that without relying on memory. Again, it is obviously impossible to *argue* for the reliability of reasoning without relying on reason to do so. And so on.[13]

So when the foundationalist asks religious believers to provide external justifications for their epistemic practices, and they fail to provide them, what we need to remember is that no epistemic practice is better off than religious epistemic practices in this respect.

Notes

1. Van Til, *A Christian Theory of Knowledge*, pp. 12-13.
2. Plantinga, 'Is Belief in God Rational?', pp. 12-13.
3. Ibid., p. 13.
4. Ibid., p. 21.
5. Ibid., p. 24.
6. Ibid., p. 26.
7. Plantinga, 'Reason and Belief in God', p. 76.
8. Ibid., p. 78.
9. Ibid., p. 79.
10. Ibid., p. 81.
11. Ibid., p. 82.
12. Ibid., p. 84.
13. William P. Alston, 'Christian Experience and Christian Belief' in Alvin Plantinga and Nicholas Wolterstorff (eds), *Faith and Rationality*, (University of Notre Dame Press, Indiana,1983) p. 119.

3
Preliminary Criticism of the Reformed Challenge

The essence of the Reformed challenge is to accuse the foundationalist of claiming to have a criterion of rationality which, in fact, he does not possess. By means of this alleged criterion the foundationalist claims to discern which epistemic practices are rational and which are not. Among those practices which are not rational, he claims, are those of religion. In criticising the Reformed challenge to foundationalism, it is no part of my intention to deny the conclusion that foundationalism fails to provide a coherent account of the reason, by reference to which, the rationality of epistemic practices is to be judged. The difficulties are in the route by which Reformed philosophers reach these conclusions. Here is the same conclusion arrived at by arguments from a rather different philosophical perspective. J.D. Kenyon says:

> there is an attitude which is perhaps characteristic of scientific dogmatism, namely that since God is something we can never really know about, agnosticism is intellectually more proper than either theism or atheism. If 'know' implies only internal justification, the premiss is false; if it implies external justification, it is true, but so is the parallel premiss for the physical world, and the dogmatism consists in not drawing the same conclusion for belief on that topic as well. The mistake is to let the word 'know' go on holiday abroad from its religious home and engage in the entirely spurious activity of undermining the function it has at home. Holidays are for rest. The scientism consists in acknowledging this for the word 'know' as it occurs internally to science, but not otherwise.[1]

But there is one big difference between Kenyon's remarks and Plantinga's arguments. When Kenyon refers to the attempt to give external justifications to epistemic practices he says that in the attempt language goes on holiday. In other words, the attempt is *confused* and misconceived. Plantinga, on the other hand, says that the attempt fails. He does not say it is confused or unintelligible. Failure is not an instance of language on holiday, or of language idling. Further, in what he asks us to imagine as he illustrates the failure of the foundationalist, Plantinga shows how far removed he is, philosophically, from those who accuse foundationalism not of failure, but of confusion. This distance is revealed most clearly in Plantinga's discussion of basic propositions.

As we have seen, the fundamental issue for Reformed epistemology is whether the believer is justified in placing belief in God in the foundations of his noetic structure. To show that he is not justified in doing so, it is argued, we need a criterion of basicality by reference to which it could be shown that the self-evident and incorrigible propositions, favoured by the foundationalist, should be among the foundational propositions, and that belief in God should not. But no such criterion can be found. In its absence, how do we know, Plantinga asks, whether the propositions we say are self-evident and incorrigible really are self-evident or incorrigible. He replies that what we have is not knowledge, but trust. Yet it is a trust in face of the possibility that all our epistemic practices could be wrong. But what if the whole notion of an external justification of epistemic practices, of the kind Plantinga is seeking, is confused? In that event, the possibility of their being wrong is also confused. If showing that the practices are correct is confused, so is showing that they are incorrect. Alston, we recall, marked the difference between the foundationalists and Reformed epistemologists by saying that for the former, our epistemic practices are guilty until proved innocent, whereas, for the latter, they are innocent until proved guilty. But if the notion of external justification is a confused one in this context, it makes no sense to call our epistemic practices innocent or guilty. We might say, with Wittgenstein, that they are simply there, like our life. Plantinga is able to contemplate all our epistemic practices being wrong because of his introduction of a relativism and psychologism into epistemology which confuse the fundamental philosophical issues involved.

25

Consider, first, his discussion of simple self-evident propositions in arithmetic, such as 2 + 1 = 3. Plantinga says

> Understanding a self-evident proposition is sufficient for apprehending its truth. Of course this notion must be relativized to *persons*; what is self-evident to you might not be to me. Very simple arithmetical truths will be self-evident to nearly all of us; but a truth like 17 + 18 = 35 may be self-evident only to some. And of course a proposition is self-evident to a person only if he does in fact grasp it; so a proposition will not be self-evident to those who do not apprehend the concepts involved in the proposition.[2]

Here is a good example of Plantinga conflating logical and psychological considerations. The self-evidence of the arithmetical proposition is made a function of an individual's reaction. Plantinga says that simple arithmetical propositions are self-evident to nearly all of us. But if self-evidence is a function of an individual's grasp, what is it that the minority can be said to *fail* to grasp? His relativism makes the self-evidence of 2 + 1 = 3 a strangely intermittent affair: self-evident when one of the majority happens to react to it, but not self-evident when one of the minority reacts to it. It is as if the minority lack a certain experience, an intuition, perhaps, which the majority possess when they react to 2 + 1 = 3. Some have an intuition of self-evidence, but others do not.

Does teaching someone 2 + 1 = 3 make any reference to these individual experiences or intuitions? Normally we would not refer to any experiences we had in writing or thinking about 2 + 1 = 3, and in trying to teach a child we wouldn't want to know what experiences, if any, he was having either. What we want to try to do is to get the child to go on in a certain way, the way we call the correct way in arithmetic. Of course, what we mean by 'correct' is not independent of how people respond, but the responses in question are within the activity we call arithmetic. If a child does not respond in a certain way, it may be because he has made a mistake, a mistake we correct by making use of arithmetical procedures. What if the child were to say that he had had certain experiences, certain intuitions, in arriving at the right answer? What if he said he had arrived at the right answer without any of these experiences? In either case, would not the presence or absence of these experiences be quite irrelevant to what is meant by the correct answer?

Sometimes, the conviction that learning must involve having an experience is confused with the correct observation that the child must be brought to calculate for himself. The child must not be simply memorising the next number in the series. Correcting his mistakes is not a matter of getting him to conform to what the majority are doing. The teacher tries to get the child to see his mistakes for himself. He will point out his mistake by getting the child to see how he has calculated elsewhere and so on. What if the child said that his having had a certain experience was sufficient to show that he had seen his mistake? Would that convince the teacher? Hardly. If there were a teacher who accepted the assurance, then it would soon reveal its worthlessness if the child continued to make the same mistake. So when the teacher endeavours to get the child to see for himself the mistake he has made, his endeavours do not depend on the presence of certain experiences in the child.[3] By relativising and psychologising the notion of self-evidence Plantinga makes the reaction of the individual all-important and self-evidence a mere function of it. He puts the emphasis on the individual's psychology instead of on the practice.

But what of the more radical case where we may fail to teach the child? I refer to situations in which we cannot get the child to go on in the same way at all, cannot get the child to count. What if the child remains tentative about $2 + 1 = 3$, accepting it some days, but unable to grasp it on others? Do we say that the matter is *simply* not self-evident to the child? Of course not. What this particular child needs is not correction, but training. As yet, the child is not in a position to make arithmetical mistakes. If training in arithmetic is *unsuccessful*, the point of saying that cannot be brought out by saying that one psychological reaction happens to be different from the psychological reactions of the majority. The child is cut off from a practice, the practice of arithmetic. What is at stake is not the absence of self-evidence, understood as a function of a reaction lacking in the child, but a child's lack of ability to engage in a certain practice. Exclusion from the practice means exclusion from the myriad ways in which counting and calculating enter our lives.

The question of whether something appears to be self-evident to a person is different from the question of whether a person can see what is self-evident. Plantinga's relativism and psychologism lead him to conflate these questions. The self-evidence of $2+1=3$

does not emanate from the epistemic and phenomenological properties of the proposition considered in relation to the reactions of an isolated individual. The proposition enjoys its self-evident status *in* arithmetic. It is within the practice that the proposition has its application and its sense.

This emphasis on the *practice* is something on which, as we have seen, Plantinga himself relies in order to meet the objection that, in the absence of a criterion of basicality, *anything*, for example, belief in the Great Pumpkin, could be a basic proposition. He emphasises, quite rightly, that in certain *circumstances*, it is obvious that something is properly basic. He says, as we saw, 'We must assemble examples of beliefs and conditions such that the former are obviously properly basic in the latter, and examples of beliefs and conditions such that the former are obviously *not* properly basic in the latter.'[4] Notice, beliefs and *conditions*. These conditions are our practices. We do not have any choice about where to look. Without appeal to these conditions, Plantinga could not appeal either to what is 'obviously properly basic', for it is within practices that the notions of 'obviousness' and 'what is proper' have their purchase. But in relativising these notions to the reactions of individuals, Plantinga is cutting away the ground of the argument he needs to deny that *anything* could be properly basic.

It may be thought, in the later developments of Plantinga's argument, that nothing prevents him from acknowledging that basic religious propositions have their status within religious practices. Yet, this is not so, for once Plantinga makes foundation-less practices his final appeal, rather than foundationless propositions, much of his strategy against foundationalism is undermined, a strategy which depended on considering foundational propositions *in isolation* and asking for a criterion for their basicality.

This is seen in Plantinga's more radical proposal that all our epistemic practices could be mistaken. Speaking of the foundationalist, he asks:

> How does he know that a given proposition — 7 + 5 = 12, for example, — *is* self-evident? Might we not be mistaken in our judgements of self-evidence? It seems obviously possible that there should be a race of persons — on some other planet, let's say — who think they find *other* propositions self-evident, some of those others being denials

of propositions *we* find self-evident. Perhaps this race invariably makes mistakes about what is self-evident. But might not the same thing be true of us? A proposition is self-evident, after all, only if it is *true*; and it certainly seems possible that we should believe a proposition self-evident when in fact it is not.[5]

What are we to make of this supposition? One of its features is its lack of content. We are not told what activities the people on the other planet are supposed to be engaged in. What if the activity has no resemblance to arithmetic? Suppose that the marks $7 + 5 = 12$ only appear on wallpaper patterns. Could we find out whether $7 + 5 = 12$ in that context was a self-evident proposition by concentrating, however, intensely, on the marks and waiting on our individual reactions? Of course not. In that context the question would not make sense.

More importantly, what if the activity on the other planet which Plantinga has in mind is some kind of alternative arithmetic? Plantinga is quite right in insisting that no external justification of our arithmetic can be given to show it is the right arithmetic, but quite wrong to conclude that, consequently, the whole of our arithmetic could be mistaken. Because he allows this to be a possibility, we shall see, that in denying that there can be an external justification of arithmetic, Plantinga is engaged on a very different enterprise from that of Wittgenstein when the latter said that justification must come to an end somewhere. Plantinga is still in the grip of the foundationalism he set out to criticise.

Like Plantinga, Rush Rhees, in his discussion of Wittgenstein's ideas in 1938 on continuity, asks us to imagine a society where, in certain circumstances, the elementary conclusions in arithmetic are not drawn:

> But what I am suggesting is that we can imagine a community in which circumstances — special conditions in which arithmetic was applied, perhaps, or combinations of ancient customs — inclined people to say that if you add in that way, then the result of adding 3 to 3 is 5. They might say that if you said anything else you would not be following the elementary rules of addition.[6]

We are tempted, when faced with an example of this kind, to say that, if these people are doing arithmetic, they *cannot* calculate in this way. We may say that the meaning of '3' determines that we calculate as we do. But does it? Rhees says that to speak in this way is to speak 'as though arithmetic sprang out of the meaning of "3" like shoots from a bulb. It is less misleading to say that the meaning of 3 is contained or is given in the whole arithmetic of it.'[7] But this does not rule out the possibility of alternative arithmetics, different ways of calculating. Of course, if we begin by taking our arithmetical operations for granted, then, within those parameters, our arithmetic is the only possible one. But to say this is no more than to emphasise the ways in which we calculate. It does not lead to the confused conclusion that the ways in which we calculate rule out the possibility of other ways of calculating. This is why we cannot say, as Plantinga does, that the alternative way of calculating on the other planet *contradicts* what we do. As Rush Rhees say, 'No technique for using an expression can contradict the meaning of that expression because the meaning is in the technique.'[8]

At this point a familiar worry may make itself heard. Rhees expresses it as follows:

'But is there no *justification* for our teaching people to do mathematics in this way — beyond the fact that that's the way that everybody does it? Is it a matter of sheer accident that people *do* happen to do mathematics in this way? Are you really saying that there is nothing about the nature of mathematics which gives any reason why it should have developed in this form rather than another?'[9]

Rhees say that we can give various reasons why we do mathematics in the way we do, but that none of these reasons would establish the necessity of doing mathematics in the way we do. The reasons Rhees lists are various: some have to do with the kinds of objects we need to measure in our practical affairs (we need to know in our practical affairs whether objects will fit into available spaces); reasons why we need to measure with instruments such as rulers which do not expand or contract; the behaviour of the objects we count, the fact that they are fairly static and do not vanish suddenly; that objects are not constantly changing their shape; our interests in calculating, that the symbolism in which we calculate can be written down and recorded; our desire to be as systematic as possible and to eliminate what is cumbersome, etc,

etc. All these reasons and more may lead us to conclude that it is *natural* that we calculate in the way we do, and so it is, but none of these reasons show that an alternative mathematics can be ruled out as self-contradictory. If, for some reason, a people preferred what seems to us the unnatural and cumbersome method of proceeding, that would be that. Rhees gives the following example:

> Eddie Cantor, in his film *Strike me Pink*, measures cloth with an elastic yardstick, using the extended yardstick when he is taking the cloth off the roll and when he is asking the customer: 'Is that enough?' and using the shrunken yardstick when he cuts the cloth. It might be a universal practice to have elastic yardsticks, and further each person might pride himself on having his own special degree of elasticity in the yardstick he used. Business in such a community would be rather different from business in ours. But it might go on, and people might, if you asked them, give reasons for preferring it that way.[10]

The way they would do arithmetic would not contradict the way we do it. Plantinga argues as if the possibility of an alternative way of calculating makes it intelligible to say that the way in which we calculate could have been wrong all along. It makes sense to say that it could turn out that we had been making mistakes all along without knowing it. These suppositions are an instance of language idling. They do not link up with anything or have any implications. In what sense can these doubts be entertained? The whole point about the elementary propositions of mathematics is that we do not entertain doubts about them. Notice, we say *do not*, not *could not*. We do not have a metaphysical proof to show that we must proceed arithmetically in the way we do. As we have seen, we can conceive of an alternative arithmetic. But the philosophical point of postulating such alternatives is to rid us of the conviction that there must be some queer kind of necessity underpinning our procedures. *On the other hand, the philosophical postulation of other possibilities is not meant to cast doubt on our own procedures.* Philosophers have changed the philosophical postulation into an actual postulation, so making it look as if we had an *option* to calculate in one way or another. This confusion has led to a vulgarisation of Wittgenstein's thought in recent philosophical literature.[11] The result has been to make it look as if the ways we think are options which we choose from some vantage point outside them. That perspective removes us from anything Wittgenstein was trying to do. *It cannot be over-emphasised that his postulation of other possibilities is not meant to deny the naturalness of the way we calculate, but to emphasise it.* If someone in our midst actually began 'doubting' the elementary propositions of mathematics we would not know what to make of him. Put differently, we would know what to make of him all too well: he would be one of the unfortunate in our midst who does not know how to count, who cannot be taught to count. What Wittgenstein emphasises is that we would not say this individual has made a mistake. Rather, he is cut off from the language-game in which talk of being correct and being mistaken have their application. He is cut off from our agreed procedures in counting, not procedures we agreed on prior to counting. but agreements which show themselves *in* the ways we count. Wittgenstein says:

> In certain circumstances, for example, we regard a calculation as sufficiently checked. What gives us the right to do so? Experience? May that not have deceived us? Somewhere we must be finished with justification and there remains the proposition that *this* is how we calculate...

> If someone supposed that *all* our calculations were uncertain and that we could rely on none of them (justifying himself by saying that mistakes are always possible) perhaps we would say he was crazy. But can we say he is in error? Does he not just react differently? We rely on calculations, he doesn't; we are sure, he isn't.[12]

Plantinga attacks the foundationalist for thinking that all propositions depend for their rationality on standing in appropriate relations to other propositions which cannot be doubted, foundational propositions such as self-evident or incorrigible propositions. But the essence of his attack consists in berating the foundationalist for claiming to have a criterion, which in fact he does not possess, by which he can show why what is basic within the various noetic structures are worthy members and the only members of the class of foundational propositions. The foundationalist's failure then enables Plantinga to play the same foundationalist game and place belief in God in the foundations of his noetic structure in the absence of any epistemological criterion which would forbid him from doing so. It seems to me that Jesse de Boer is correct in saying: 'While Plantinga protests that foundationalism ought to be abandoned, what he in fact does himself is add to the foundations our belief in God. He calls this belief "properly basic" and so, by the sense of his idiom, he stays inside the foundationalist camp.'[13] But, if, as we have seen, the kind of justification of practices Plantinga requires does not make sense, the failure of which the foundationalist stands accused must be understood in the light of the fact. Plantinga admits that Reformed epistemology lacks a criterion of basicality, meaning by this a justification of why, within our practices, what is basic is called basic.[14] But he does not see this lack as freedom from confusion. He admits the criterion is lacking, but thinks there ought to be one. He does not see that the reason such a criterion is lacking has nothing to do with lack of diligence or ingenuity on his part. What he seeks is a philosophical will-o'-the-wisp; it is not there to be found because what is sought does not make sense. The real illusion in foundationalism is its claim that reason will give a foundation and a justification for the ways in which we distinguish between what is reasonable and unreasonable in various epistemic practices. According to the foundationalist, religious practices can then be judged by the law of reason, so conceived, to see whether they are a rational or irrational practice. Plantinga is one with the foundationalists in thinking that our practices need such a justification. Since the criterion has not been arrived at yet, our practices can be deemed innocent until proved guilty. What we have seen is that the intelligibility of our practices await no such verdict, neither do they need it. They are simply there as part of our lives.

Similar difficulties occur for Plantinga when we turn from the elementary self-evident propositions of arithmetic to what he says about incorrigible propositions concerning the senses. These, along with the self-evident propositions, are the favoured propositions of the foundationalist when he considers which propositions are properly basic. The attractiveness of the propositions in question is that they cannot be denied without talking nonsense. Plantinga says that Aquinas was prepared to put propositions such as 'There's a tree over there' among the incorrigible propositions. Descartes, however, was more cautious and presented propositions such as 'I seem to see a red book' or 'I seem to see something red' as incorrigible propositions. It is obvious that Plantinga thinks this greater caution is commendable. He thinks that Roderick Chisholm is even more commendable in proposing propositions such as 'I am appeared redly to' to fill this role. Why does Plantinga commend this ever-growing philosophical caution, a caution which, of course, does not reflect how the word 'know' is used outside philosophy? Although he probably would not admit this, it is because he is impressed, as many philosophers have been, with the grammar of 'know' and the grammar of first-person psychological statements. What I mean is this: if we claim to know something our claim must have some justification. We are expected to be able to say how we know what we say we know. Further, if it turns out that what I said I knew was not the case, I have to say, 'I thought I knew it, but I didn't'. This is not so with beliefs. If I say I believe something and it turns out not to be the case, then, although I have to say that I am wrong, I am not called on to say that I did not believe it. So it is tempting for the philosopher to restrict the use of 'know' to those cases where the knowledge is always justified, where the claim to know *could not* be mistaken. Hence the appeal of self-evident propositions, such as the elementary propositions of mathematics we have already considered. In the same context, first-person psychological statements such as 'I am in pain' do not fall foul of the challenge 'How do you know?' The person cannot be wrong. He may not know how to use the word 'pain' or he may be lying or joking, but such considerations apart, what would it mean to think that someone who said 'I am in pain' or 'I seem to see a red patch' could be wrong? But why should the grammatical features of self-evident propositions in logic and mathematics and first-person psychological statements legislate for all uses of the word 'know'? After all, we do say 'I thought I knew, but I didn't', which shows that there is a proper use for 'I thought I knew and I did'. No reason has been given for saying that 'know' should be restricted to uses where we could not be mistaken. If you ask me whether I know there is a chair available in the store room, I have good reason to say that I know a chair is available if I put one there five minutes ago. Of course, someone could have gone there in the meantime and taken the chair away, but that *possibility* doesn't make my use of 'know' illegitimate, despite the fact that if the possibility became an actuality, I'll have to say I did not know when I thought I did. If we think of the ways in which we come to learn to use the word 'know', it is hard to imagine our use of it without giving considerable prominence to circumstances such as these.

Ironically, although Plantinga wants to discuss knowledge in connection with incorrigible statements relating to the senses, what he does not see is that where the statements really *are* incorrigible it is odd to speak of knowledge. There are a host of such propositions and they were Wittgenstein's main concern in *On Certainty*. They are the very propositions about which Plantinga is doubtful with respect to their inclusion as basic propositions: propositions such as 'This is a tree' and 'There is an ink-well on my desk'. The doubts Plantinga entertains are those quarterly familiars with which philosophers have become acquainted. I may be looking at the tree in a fog and I may be having an hallucination when I see the ink-well. These possibilities cannot be denied. But the conversations between G.E. Moore and Norman Malcolm which Wittgenstein was interested in took place in Moore's garden, the garden of the house he had lived in for many years and in which there was a tree. There is no question of fog or unfavourable circumstances of any kind. What would it mean *in these circumstances* to doubt the existence of the tree? Plantinga invokes hallucinations and colour-blindness to illustrate how we can be misled by familiar things. But his very invoking of them shows that these are occurrences we find out about. In fact, we cannot say what they are without explaining the difference between what seems to be the case and what is the case. No one denies that there are circumstances where it makes sense to doubt empirical propositions, but does it follow that it makes sense to doubt these propositions in all circumstances? When we make mistakes the conception of a mistake fits in with our beliefs. We correct our mistakes. But the corrections I make take place within a context where there is a great deal we take for granted. What we take for granted covers a wide range of propositions. They do not form a class of which all the members have something in common. We would not know what to say to anyone who suggested that they could be doubted. What could we say to someone who doubted the existence of a tree we were both sitting under? What would we say if, on opening the door of his familiar room, the door which leads to the equally familiar corridor which leads to the equally familiar staircase, instead of seeing this familiar scene, he said he saw the sea lapping at his feet? What if we could convince him that although he thought he saw his class before him and thought he was giving a lecture, the room was in fact empty and he was in a hospital room? Would we in any of these instances say he had made a mistake? Of course not. He would be terrified. He would think he was going insane. Unlike mistakes, his experiences cannot be fitted into the loose network of our other beliefs. On the contrary, they disorientate him. He no longer knows his way about. Matters are disrupted which previously he took for granted. But it is important to realise that these experiences do not make us doubt where we had not doubted before. No, they have the effect of plunging us into confusion in such a way that we do not know what to believe or doubt any more. We have been taken out of the traffic of normal discourse. Alternatively, if there is one in our midst who cannot participate in some fundamental aspects of this discourse; if, for example, he denies that the earth has existed for a long time, that people are ever in pain, that $3 + 3 = 6$, we do not know what to make of him. His presence does not throw our practices into confusion. On the contrary, our practices mark him off as the strange one, the outsider. But this does not mean that such a man contradicts what we do, or that what we do renders what he does self-contradictory. He is too strange to be self-contradictory. To be sure in our dealings, then, we do not have to produce, as Plantinga thinks we must, a criterion which shows why we should take for granted what we take for granted. Nor do we have to suspend judgement, as Alston suggests, treating the strange ones, or the unteachable ones, as 'innocent' in the meantime. No, they *are* the strange ones. What we do is to show how fundamental in our thinking and in our practices what we take for granted is. To show this, what we need is not a foundation for our practices but attention to the roles played by what is basic in them. Basicality is not a matter of what *cannot* be otherwise, but a matter of what cannot be otherwise in the ways we think.

Notes

1. J.D. Kenyon, 'Doubts About the Concept of Reason', *Proceedings of the Aristotelian Society*, supp. vol. LIX, 1985, p. 264.

2. Plantinga, 'Is belief in God rational?', p. 17.

3. Here, I have simply been repeating the arguments in Rush Rhees's 'On Continuity: Wittgenstein's ideas 1938' in his *Discussions of Wittgenstein* (Routledge and Kegan Paul, London, and Shocken Books, New York, 1970).

4. Plantinga, 'Reason and Belief in God', p. 76.

5. Alvin Plantinga.

6. Rhees, 'On Continuity', p. 113.

7. Ibid., p. 114.

8. Ibid.

9. Ibid., p. 120.

10. Ibid.

11. See Part Two, Chs. 10, 11 and 12.

12. Ludwig Wittgenstein, *On Certainty*, trans. Denis Paul and G.E.M. Anscombe (Basil Blackwell, Oxford, 1979), paras. 212 and 217.

13. Jesse de Boer, 'Reformed Epistemology', *The Reformed Journal*, vol. 32, issue 4 (April 1982), p. 25.

14. Plantinga, 'Reason and Belief in God', see pp. 90-91.

4
Basic Propositions: Reformed Epistemology and Wittgenstein's *On Certainty*

To the philosophically unwary, it may seem as if there is a great similarity between what Reformed philosophers want to say about basic propositions and Wittgenstein's treatment of the problem in *On Certainty*. Two major considerations may tempt us to think in this way. First, it is true that Reformed philosophers and philosophers influenced by Wittgenstein in the philosophy of religion are one in their rejection of foundationalism. Second, they say that God is believed in without God's existence being seen as a presupposition for which prior evidence must be sought. Jesse de Boer, despite saying, with good reason, that Plantinga is still in the grip of foundationalism also says this: 'I get from Plantinga's sketch of Reformed epistemology and his rejection of "foundationalism" a sense of *déjà vu*, Wittgenstein had done the job more thoroughly years ago; Plantinga generalizes his work so as to include religious belief.'[1] True, the ignoring of the critiques of foundationalism by Wittgenstein and J.L. Austin, different though they are, is one of the more curious features of the Reformed philosophers' reading of the history of recent philosophy. That apart, however, it cannot be said that Plantinga's philosophical enterprise bears any positive relation to what Wittgenstein was concerned with. Certainly, Plantinga cannot be understood as someone who applies Wittgenstein's insight to the philosophy of religion. The deep-going differences between them can be explored in terms of their respective discussions of basic propositions.

First, it is clear that, for the Reformed epistemologists, basic propositions in noetic structures are thought of as the *foundations* of those structures. That this is so is evident from the function which such propositions are said to perform. As Plantinga says, a foundational proposition 'must be capable of bearing its share

38

of the weight of the entire noetic structure'.[2] It is also clear that the foundational propositions are thought of as logically prior to all others. Plantinga says, 'I know the propositions in the foundations of my noetic structure, but not by virtue of knowing *other* propositions; for these are the ones I start with.'[3]

With Wittgenstein, in *On Certainty*, matters are different. He was interested in basic propositions because, while they were certainly not propositions of logic and had the form of empirical propositions, there were important differences between them and many of the ways in which we normally talk of empirical propositions. Wittgenstein had in mind propositions such as 'I was born', 'The earth has existed for many years', 'There are material objects', 'There are human beings', etc., etc. We do not investigate the truth or falsity of these propositions. Neither do we believe them because we have found out that they are correct, for when did we do that? Propositions such as these seem to underlie other propositions. Without taking them for granted we wouldn't know how to speak of truth or falsity at all in the various contexts they enter into. But the crucial question for Wittgenstein is *the sense* in which these basic propositions do underlie other propositions. He did not think there was simply one answer to this question. Different examples have to be treated differently. For example, in some cases, something which begins by being discovered experimentally hardens into a norm for description. A physiologist on dissecting the human skull finds the brain. He makes relatively few dissections and yet he says that it is obvious that every skull contains a brain. How does he know that? How does what he has found justify his confident expectation for all other cases? But would not any physiologist be amazed if these questions were asked of him? He would be at a loss to know what the questioner wanted. He would say that the way he proceeds is obvious. He has no reason for proceeding in that way, which is not to say that he proceeds unreasonably. What makes sense is shown *in* the way he proceeds and for that he has no reason. One is reminded of the famous 'Candid Camera' series in which a car was secretly pushed down an incline into a garage. The owners complained that the car had given them trouble throughout their journey south from the north. When the mechanic opened the bonnet, he found the car had no engine. He was, of course, utterly at a loss. Once we know what the function of an engine is in a car, how can a car travel without an engine? In fact, that question does not arise. Similar conclusions follow in the case of 'There is a heart in every body'. In other cases, such as the proposition 'I was born' or 'Mountains have existed for a long time', it is odd to say that the conclusions were arrived at experimentally. Questions about such matters do not arise.

> I am told, for example, that someone climbed this mountain many years ago. Do I always enquire into the reliability of the teller of this story, and whether the mountains did exist years ago? A child learns there are reliable and unreliable informants much later than it learns facts which are told it. It doesn't learn *at all* that that mountain has existed for a long time: that is, the question whether it is so doesn't arise at all. It swallows this consequence down, so to speak, together with *what* it learns.[4]

Wittgenstein would also say that it is involved *in* what it learns. Experience cannot be appealed to as a foundation, in the way Alston suggested, for we are talking about what is involved in that very experience.[5]

> The child learns to believe a host of things. I.e. it learns to act according to these beliefs. Bit by bit there forms a system of what is believed, and in that system some things stand unshakeably fast and some are more or less liable to shift. What stands fast does so, not because it is intrinsically obvious or convincing; it is rather held fast by what lies around it.[6]

It is clear from these remarks that in saying that basic propositions *underlie* other propositions, Wittgenstein does not mean to imply that these propositions are the foundations or the first principles on which the other propositions are based. Unlike the Reformed philosophers, Wittgenstein would not say that one could *start* with these propositions, because the propositions have their sense, are held fast, by all that surrounds them. So before we can be sure of the ways in which we think and behave, we do not have to start from these propositions. How could we since the propositions have their life *in* the ways we think and behave. The propositions are not hypothetical in any way. On the contrary, they are taken for granted, rarely formulated, and taken out of the traffic of discourse as far as any doubt, conjecture or proof in relation to them is concerned.

The child is introduced to basic propositions in being taught *other* things. For example, the child does not believe in the existence of chairs and tables because it has been taught that material objects exist. It is taught to sit on a chair or at a table, and that, one might say, is what shows one's belief in the existence of material objects. A child comes to know people in its dealings with them – its mother, father, brothers, sisters, friends, the butcher, the milkman, the grocer, etc., etc. In this is shown its belief in human beings. The belief is not the presupposition of its actions, but shows itself, has its sense, in those actions. In being taught these, however, the child is also learning what can be taken for granted. These propositions hang together, but if we say they form a system, we must not think of this as a formal system. The way the propositions hang together make up what Wittgenstein calls our world-picture. The child is introduced to this world-picture as it grows up, but not by being given a course of instruction in it. Once again, our world-picture cannot be thought of as the foundation of our thinking. It is what shows itself by being taken for granted *in* our thinking. Similarly, we cannot think of our world-picture as the presupposition of the ways in which we think, as though those ways of thinking could be derived from it. We cannot first identify our world-picture and then go on to describe the ways in which we think, because it is only in terms of how we think that we can speak of our world-picture. We are not talking of any priority over the ways we think, logical or temporal, when we speak of our world-picture.

By contrast with the way in which Wittgenstein speaks of basic propositions being held fast in all that surrounds them, the basic propositions of Reformed epistemology seem isolated and even arbitrary. To say this does not imply a desire to reopen the search for a criterion which will determine by what right we place our basic proposition in the foundations of our noetic structures, to use Plantinga's language. To say this does imply, to use Wittgenstein's language, that we are not shown the way in which belief in God underlies other things in the noetic structure. We are not shown how belief in God is held fast in all that surrounds it. In short, the belief in God seems to be unmediated, casting illumination on nothing. Peter Losin is worried by the fact that this is how belief in God will appear to the unbeliever, given Plantinga's analysis. Obviously, the unbeliever will not accept the basic propositions of religion. Plantinga considers that, given

41

his own criteria, the unbeliever acts reasonably in refusing to believe. But Plantinga accuses the unbeliever of being in the grip of false reasoning, reasoning which is bereft of belief in God in its foundations. But, Losin asks, how does Plantinga know this? It looks as if he is claiming to know, independently of his own mode of reasoning, and that of the unbeliever, that the unbeliever's mode of reasoning is false. But in order to know this he would have to possess the very neutral epistemological criterion which he denied that the foundationalist, or anyone else, possessed. Plantinga says that the believer has a right to place belief in God in the foundations of the noetic structure, but what the right consists in is a rather thin affair, namely, that no one has been able to show him why he should not. But, of course, as Losin says, the unbeliever does not see this. Plantinga may say that the existence of God is as evident to the believer as $2 + 2 = 4$, but the unbeliever may say that the existence of God is as self-contradictory to him as the claim that there is an Euclidean triangle whose interior angles do not add up to 180°. Who is to say who is right? Losin sees no way in which either believer or unbeliever can appeal to anything other than their right to place different beliefs in the foundations of their respective noetic structures. As a result, Losin sees no alternative, if this logical isolation of the foundational propositions is to be avoided, to going back to weighing up evidence for and against belief in the existence of God.[7] This conclusion need not be embraced, but Losin's point is independent of his apologetic concerns. His main point is to insist on the necessity of mediating the concept of God's reality. Without such mediation, the concept seems 'basic' in some magical way. In his reply to Losin, Plantinga says: 'One task laid on Christian philosophers, I think, is that of working out a Christian epistemology – a theory of knowledge, justification, rationality and allied topics which takes for granted the central contours of the Christian scheme of things'.[8] His purpose in doing so, however, he insists, is not to convince the sceptics, but to endeavour to become clear about how Christians should think about these things. George Mavrodes says of the Reformed philosophers: 'Like Calvin they have no intention of providing unbelievers with reasons to believe or, for that matter, of providing believers with reasons to continue in their faith.'[9] If the belief is meant to stand in evidential dependence on the reasons, the point is well taken. But not all reasons take the form of evidence. There is the provision of *elucidation* as well as the provision of evidence.

Why do we assume that a request for elucidation must be a request for evidence? Without elucidation of the central contours of the Christian faith, without any attempt to show how its central concepts are mediated in human life, the assertion that belief in God is foundational in one's noetic structure will seem a pretty empty assertion to make. The proposition that God exists will seem isolated from the rest of the noetic structure it is said to support, or at least its foundational function will be, to say the least, obscure.

By contrast, no such metaphysical isolation surrounds Wittgenstein's basic propositions since, so far from being said to be the *foundation* of our thinking, they are said to be involved *in* our thinking. In Reformed epistemology the foundations seem to be an arbitrary point of departure. But this cannot be said of Wittgenstein's informal system of basic propositions:

> All testing, all confirmation and disconfirmation of a hypothesis takes place already within a system. And this system is not a more or less arbitrary and doubtful point of departure for all our arguments: no, it belongs to the essence of what we call an argument. The system is not so much the point of departure, as the element in which arguments have their life.[10]

This will apply as much to religious systems (practices) loosely conceived, as to any other. These too will be no arbitrary points of departure, but will constitute the context within which belief in God has its life and meaning. The meaning of belief in God is shown in the light it casts on all that surrounds it. Not: 'God be the foundation of my thinking' but 'God be *in* my thinking'. The basicality of the belief is shown in this involvement.

The second major difference between Reformed epistemology's and Wittgenstein's treatment of basic propositions is seen in the way they discuss the sense in which basic propositions are held fast in all that surrounds them. At first, this comparison may seem puzzling. Have we not just accused Reformed epistemology of isolating its basic propositions from all else in the noetic structure? How, then, is it possible now to speak of the basic proposition's relation to all that holds it fast? The answer lies in the fact that although Reformed epistemologists assert that foundational propositions are not conclusions based on evidence, they deny that foundational propositions are *groundless*. This is

43

said to be true, therefore, when we are considering propositions which have been held to be foundational, such as 'I see a tree' and the religious foundational belief that God exists. As we shall see, however, the claim that these propositions are well grounded does not lead us to retract what has been said about the metaphysical isolation of basic propositions in Reformed epistemology, since, when we consider the relations said to pertain between the basic proposition and its alleged grounds in the noetic structure, the metaphysical isolation of the basic propositions becomes even more pronounced. Let us examine how this comes about in the two cases.

As we have seen, strictly speaking, Plantinga tells us, 'I see a tree' is not properly basic. Partly he says this because of the possibility of circumstances where we can be mistaken about the existence of a tree. But even when we see the tree without impediment, Plantinga would still say that 'I see a tree' is not properly basic. This is because he claims that the proposition is grounded in experience, the experience he describes as 'I am being appeared treely to'. Yet as we saw in the exposition of the Reformed challenge, Plantinga does not want to say that the experience is evidence for the belief, but that it plays a vital part in its formation. Not a great deal is said about what this 'vital part in its formation' consists in, but, as a result of it, he says that the assertion 'I see a tree' can be said to be grounded in and justified by the experience.

The attraction of 'I am appeared treely to' (perverse though the construction is) is that it does not invite the question, 'How do you know?' Unless the person is lying, joking, or does not know the meaning of the words he is using, the possibility of a mistake is ruled out. And, after all, that is what Plantinga is searching for, an incorrigible proposition of sense experience. 'I see a tree' hardly seems to qualify. This is because we can think of plenty of circumstances in which the person making the utterance is mistaken, does not know what he thinks he knows. But when a tree is seen in what we would call ideal circumstances, what then? What happens if we analyse 'I see a tree' in terms of the more ultimate experiences in terms of which it is supposed to be analysed? What happens if we suggest that 'I see a tree' is a logical construct of 'I am appeared treely to'? J.L. Austin has shown that the consequence is that a logically unbridgeable gap is opened up between the appearances, the sense data, and the object said to be experienced, such that we are robbed of our normal conceptions of certainty concerning the latter.

Plantinga seems to be looking for an absolute distinction between propositions which are properly basic and those which are not. He is searching for conceptions of minimal experiences, experiences which are immediate and cannot be mistaken. The assumption that you could be mistaken would be meaningless. Unfortunately the statement of immediate perception does not tell us very much, as Plantinga's example 'I am appeared treely to', bears out. But if, of necessity, we have to begin with such experiences, how do we ever speak with any confidence of the things about us? For example, how do we know how to distinguish, among our many experiences of 'being appeared treely to', which among them are imaginations, hallucinations, or perceptions? For after all, Plantinga is claiming to show us the sense in which 'I see a tree' is a well-grounded claim. We have reason to suppose that what is emerging in these views is something like the very foundationalism Plantinga wants to oppose. True, he does not speak of propositions which stand in need of evidence and propositions which provide evidence, but he does speak of corrigible experiences and their grounds in incorrigible experiences.

For Plantinga, 'I see a tree' cannot be an incorrigible proposition of sense experience, since it is not a minimal claim. The reason for saying this is that we can imagine circumstances where to say 'I see a tree' is to claim too much. I claim to see a tree in a fog and it turns out that I am mistaken. It is assumed that the circumstances are unfavourable. But what if I am standing in front of the tree on a clear day; what if I am touching it, climbing, sitting in its branches, trimming it, chopping it down, etc, etc. What could I be unsure of? The distinction between being sure or unsure breaks down. There is nothing to occasion it. It does not enter into the traffic of our discourse.

But suppose that one *does* say that the claim 'I see a tree' is well-grounded in incorrigible propositions of sense experience, what then? The consequences are that it is hard to see how 'I see a tree' can ever be a well-grounded claim. Plantinga's difficulties can be illustrated by reference to the difficulties surrounding the speculations of Locke and Berkeley on similar questions. For Locke, in order for my experiences to be experiences of seeing a tree, there had to be a correspondence between my experiences and that which caused me to have them, namely, the tree. If my experiences were caused by some other object, they could not be called experiences of seeing a tree. The difficulty is that since Locke holds that our knowledge is knowledge of our ideas, there is no way in which this correspondence can be established. As Warnock points out,[11] if I say an object is causing a bulge in my stocking, I can take the object out to verify this. But the objects which cause our ideas are, on this reading of Locke, necessarily inaccessible. Berkeley is not faced with these difficulties because he claims that what we mean when we say 'I see a tree' is that our experiences have a certain consistent pattern. But, as Warnock points out, this analysis won't do. If 'I see a tree' as a well-grounded statement is to be understood as 'It seems to me, God and everyone else as if there were a tree', one should not be able to deny the first statement and assert the second. Similarly, if what we mean by saying 'I see a tree' is a well-grounded statement is 'I, God and everyone else are appeared treely to', the same condition should hold. Yet, in both cases, it clearly does not hold. We could have all the 'seeming as ifs' or 'appearings to' in creation and it still be the case that we were not seeing a tree. 'I am appeared treely to' will not guarantee, or yield in analysis, statements concerning what is the case. In fact, as Austin points out, the 'experiences' which are supposed to make the assertion 'I see a tree' a well-grounded one in fact take us further and further away from the assurance that we are seeing a tree. The sequence of beliefs in search of incorrigibility may read as follows: 'I see a tree'; 'I seem to see a tree'; 'It seems to me that I see a tree'; 'It seems to me now that I see a tree'; 'It seems to me now as if I were seeing a tree'. The philosophical problem is posed as one of determining when we can stop hedging and have the right to say, 'I see a tree', whereas, as Austin says, what ought to be asked is why we should *start* hedging in the first place.[12] Warnock's own suggestion is that 'I see a tree' could be understood as a verdict on the relevant experiences. But the same objections can be made to this suggestion as were made earlier against the assumption that 'I see a tree' can be said, *in vacuo, always* to be related to supporting evidence (foundationalism), or to formative grounds (Plantinga). J.L. Austin points out that verdicts are normally needed in unfavourable circumstances; they are given by people who are not in a position to see things. But verdicts are not needed when something is under one's nose. When I see the tree, climb it, chop it down, etc., I do not need a verdict relating to the tree's existence. An umpire in cricket may give his verdict in difficult circumstances, circumstances in which it was hard to see whether the ball touched the ground before the fieldsman caught it. True, he may give a verdict when all is clear, but this is because it is a formality demanded by the game. Imagine our reaction to someone who, just as we were about to commence climbing a tree, demanded a prior verdict on its existence!

Although Plantinga denies that the incorrigible sensory statements constitute evidence for saying 'I see a tree', he does, as we have seen, claim that these statements are the grounds and justifications for saying 'I see a tree'; they play a vital part in the formation of the claim 'I see a tree'. That being so, the incorrigible statements serve the purpose of advancing us in the direction of the statement 'I see a tree'. For the foundationalist, the advance is via evidence; for Plantinga, the advance is, more obscurely, via formation of the belief. But in both cases, the requirement is to *advance*. Yet, as I have said, as we extend the search for the incorrigible statement of sense experience, so far from advancing towards the desired factual claim, we are going further and further away from it.

It seems that the incorrigible statements of sense experience, so far from being formative of 'I see a tree', take one further and further away from the assertion. But why should we accept the problem in these terms? Austin's insight that we must have something on our plates before we start messing with it can be applied in this case too.

In appealing to Austin's insights, I do not mean to suggest that Plantinga is unaware of the difficulty of moving from what is properly basic in sense experience to the assertion 'I see a tree'. But he does not draw any of the philosophical conclusions from this insight which Austin draws. On the contrary, instead of asking himself what reasons he would have, in ideal circumstances, for doubting that he saw a tree, Plantinga continues to hedge. Not only does he deny that 'I see a tree' is properly basic but goes on to deny that the condition for the assertion of the tree's existence, namely, 'I am appeared treely to', is properly basic. He now says that that condition itself is only a prima-facie condition for saying that the tree exists. These conditions, as we saw in the exposition of the Reformed critique of foundationalism, are capable of being overthrown by considerations which he calls defeaters. But the defeaters are only prima-facie defeaters, and may be defeated by defeater-defeaters, which may in turn be defeated by defeater-defeater-defeaters, and so on. We may well wonder what has happened to our certainty when we claim to see a tree in ideal circumstances. To introduce a tentativeness into this assertion is meaningless. It is a philosophical tentativeness which plays no part in our actual discourse. Of course, Plantinga would say that he, too, in practice, is certain of the tree's existence. He denies, however, that there is something called reason, external to our practice, which can show that the practice *could not* be mistaken. Therefore, he must allow the possibility that he could be wrong, while acting with certainty in practice. We shall have more to say about this notion of 'possibility' in the next chapter. For the moment, let us note that we do not counter Plantinga's argument by saying that we *do* possess a conception of rationality external to perception which shows it to be 'real'. In that sense, it is not a matter of saying that we *'could not'* be mistaken or that we *'could'* be mistaken. Within what we call perception, within the context of what we actually do, the question does not arise. Furthermore, if a person could be convinced that he was in a hospital bed all the time when he thought he was seeing, climbing and resting in a tree, he would not conclude that he had made a mistake. He would be terrified, thinking, with good reason, that he was going insane. But, note, that is something he *finds out*. We cannot extrapolate, from that case, the suggestion that perhaps we can never find out whether we are really seeing the tree.

What needs to be emphasised at the moment is Plantinga's admission that, in fact, he is as certain as anyone else that he is seeing a tree when he sees one in normal circumstances. Yet he also wants to say that he could be mistaken. I have suggested that he entertains this possibility of being mistaken as a philosopher, although it does not enter into his practical judgements. Even so, it ought to give us reason to ponder on the status of a philosophical analysis which robs us of the certainty which plays such a crucial role in our everyday lives. That apart, my reason for dwelling on Plantinga's analysis of 'I see a tree' is to draw a parallel between it and his discussion of the proposition 'God exists'. Many steps in the argument will be similar with one important difference. When we reach the conclusion of the argument we find it difficult to make the same distinction, in the context of Reformed epistemology, between acting with certainty on the one hand, and entertaining philosophical doubts on the other hand, doubts which do not enter into the practice being discussed. As we shall see, the philosophical doubt seems to lead to a modification of the certitude of faith. Were this not the case, it would be difficult to account for the debate within Reformed epistemology concerning what constitutes a proper response on the part of the Christian in face of this possibility of error. If the possibility did not affect the practice of faith, no response would be called for, and no discussion made necessary.

Just as he does not believe that 'The tree exists' or 'I see a tree' are, strictly speaking, basic propositions, so Plantinga does not believe that 'God exists' is, strictly speaking, properly basic. Once again, we find what is properly basic in certain conditions in which it is appropriate to say 'God exists'. These conditions are further experiences such as the awareness of the world as God's creation, conviction of sin, and the need to thank and praise God. At first, this suggestion looks promising. Belief in God seems to be placed in the context of a living faith in which it has its sense. Without taking such a placement into account, we cannot even begin to appreciate the character of concept-formation in religious belief.[13] In this religious context, the conditions invoked, unlike the appeal to incorrigible experiences in the previous context, *are* the conditions relevant to concept-formation where the notion of God's reality is concerned. Unfortunately, the philosophical promise is short-lived, since Plantinga treats these conditions, too, as no more than prima-facie justifications for belief in God. They, too, are said to be subject to defeater-defeaters, and so on. Just as in his analysis of 'I see a tree', the possibility of being mistaken is maintained, so also in the analysis of 'God exists', the possibility of error is allowed. But in this case, the possibility of error does not operate solely in the realm of philosophical speculation while practice goes on unheeded and unimpeded. The possibility seems to invade the very practice of belief. In that case, it is difficult to make the overall development of Plantinga's arguments consistent.

In his criticisms of foundationalism, Plantinga reminded us that the mature believer does not, typically, accept belief in God tentatively or hypothetically. Of course, the tentativeness in question then had to do with evidentialism, the worry that belief in God is based on insufficient evidence. Because the evidence is never as good as we would like, religious beliefs, the foundationalist tells us, are matters of probability. It then seems that we should reformulate religious beliefs so that the natural expressions of them become less misleading. On this view, should we not say from now on, 'I believe that it is highly probable that there is an almighty God, maker of heaven and earth', 'I believe it is highly probable that God forgives sins', and so on? Do these reformulations do justice to the nature of religious belief? Hardly. It is even less plausible to regard them, not as reformulations, but as expressions of what confessions of faith already are. Plantinga would agree, and he rejects the evidentialism which leads us to think such reformulations or analyses are necessary.

Having noted Plantinga's criticisms of foundationalism, do we not have to say, when we come to consider his own discussion, that he, too, introduces a tentativeness, a necessary tentativeness, into the nature of religious belief? To be sure, on Plantinga's view, the believer is not waiting, tentatively, in case contrary evidence should turn up, but he *is* waiting tentatively in case defeaters turn up, logical objections he cannot answer. But, to quote Plantinga's own words back at him: 'The mature believer, the mature theist, does not typically accept belief in God tentatively or hypothetically, or until something better [a superior logical argument] comes along.' What is more, the constant logical possibility of error is made to affect the very *character* of belief, on Plantinga's view: it is the condition for avoiding dogmatism. Dogmatism will not take the form of believing despite *insufficient evidence*, but it can take the form of believing *insufficient arguments*. Yet, as I have said, it is difficult to make Plantinga consistent on this question. For example, in expounding the Reformed objection to natural theology, Plantinga summarises what he takes to be a confused account of the believer's reliance on argument:

> If my belief in God is based on argument, then if I am to be properly rational, epistemically responsible, I shall have to keep checking the philosophical journals to see whether, say, Anthony Flew has finally come up with a good objection to my favourite argument. This could be bothersome and time-consuming; and what do I do if someone does find a flaw in my argument? Stop going to church? From Calvin's point of view believing in the existence of God on the basis of rational argument is like believing in the existence of your spouse on the basis of the analogical argument for other minds — whimsical at best and unlikely to delight the person concerned.[14]

As we know, Plantinga's apologetics are negative apologetics. He does not want to base religious beliefs on arguments, but he does claim to have shown that no good arguments have been advanced to show why belief in God should not be properly basic for the believer. But now we have seen that, for Plantinga, such belief is, strictly speaking, *not* properly basic. It is itself formed by and grounded in certain experiences. Are these beliefs that these experiences are what they claim to be properly basic? We have seen that these experiences in which the belief in God is grounded are themselves said to be prima-facie grounds, subject to defeaters. Of course, Plantinga says that the defeater is a prima-facie defeater, itself subject to defeat by a defeater-defeater, which is, in turn, subject to defeat by a defeater-defeater-defeater, and so on. The picture of the believer, who would be properly rational, awaiting the quarterly onslaught of the philosophical journals does not, on this view, seem so ludicrous after all.

Furthermore, the possibility of recurring defeaters of one kind or another is made, by Plantinga, into a real threat to faith. True, Plantinga emphasises that if a believer finds a defeater-defeater when faced with a potential defeater for the belief that God exists, it does not follow that his belief in God was based on the argument which defeats the potential defeater. Nevertheless, the crucial question concerns the believer's *failure* to find an argument to defeat the potential defeater in these circumstances. What then? Plantinga says that if the potential defeater cannot be defeated, the believer should not continue to hold the belief dogmatically. Here, then, the defeaters which Plantinga has in mind clearly do affect the very substance and possibility of believing in God. Were that not the case, the whole issue of the desirability or otherwise of a dogmatic faith would not arise. There would be no need, for example, for Nicholas Wolterstorff to disagree with Plantinga's view on dogmatism. Wolterstorff argues that it may be part of a believer's noetic structure that belief in the existence of God is more important than any other belief. In that event, no matter how successful the defeating argument against that belief may be, and despite his inability to answer it, a believer will continue to believe in God. Wolterstorff says:

> Of course, for a believer who is a member of modern Western intelligentsia to have his theistic conclusions proved nonrational is to be put into a deeply troubling situation. There is a biblical category which applies to such a situation. It is a *trial*, which the believer is called on to endure. Sometimes suffering is a trial. May it not be that sometimes the nonrationality of one's conviction that God exists is a

trial, to be endured?[15]

These remarks may find echoes in the obvious truth that faith is tried again and again, but that truth is placed here in a curious context. Enduring in the faith despite suffering is often a deepening of the faith. Indeed, the suffering has often been a formative factor in the development of faith. But what would it mean to say, in terms of Reformed epistemology, that enduring in a faith which you cannot show has not been defeated rationally is a deepening of that faith? What would it mean to say that the very argument which seems to show that it is irrational to believe in God is an aspect of the formation of that belief? Thus, Wolterstorff's comparison between the enduring of suffering by the believer and the endurance of accusations of irrationality in one's believing is not a felicitous one.

It seems, then, that if we accept Plantinga's account of belief in God as being grounded in conditions which turn out to be prima-facie conditions or justifications of the belief, subject to defeaters which are, in turn, subject to defeater-defeaters, and so on, the possibility of the radical irrationality of religion is a trial which never ends. It may be thought this conclusion is of little consequence, since Reformed epistemologists do not indulge in positive apologetics. This is not so, for in terms of negative apologetics the consequences of a successful defeater are enormous. Plantinga's whole case is that *no* good reason can be given to prevent the believer placing belief in God in the foundations of his noetic structure. But if a good reason is provided, if a defeater emerges which cannot itself be defeated, then the believer has no right to place belief in God in the foundations of his noetic structure. The very foundations of his beliefs have been denied him. In that event, the foundations have been destroyed. Yet the *possibility* of defeating arguments is supposed to be forever present. On this view, even if the foundations are not destroyed or shaking, there is always the threat of earthquakes. In Plantinga's epistemology, the trial of faith's rationality never ends for one simple reason: justifications never come to an end either.

Notes

1. De Boer, 'Reformed epistemology', p. 24.
2. Plantinga, 'Is Belief in God Rational?', p. 13.
3. Ibid.
4. Wittgenstein, *On Certainty*, para. 143.
5. Alston recognises the circularity of the appeal but draws the wrong conclusions from it.
6. Wittgenstein, *On Certainty*, para. 144.
7. See Peter Losin, 'Reformed Epistemology', *The Reformed Journal*, vol. 32, issue 4 (April 1982), pp. 21-3.
8. Alvin Plantinga, 'Reformed Epistemology Again', *The Reformed Journal*, vol. 32, issue 7 (July 1982), p. 7.
9. George I. Mavrodes, 'Jerusalem and Athens Revisited' in Alvin Plantinga and Nicholas Wolterstorff (eds), *Faith and Rationality* (University of Notre Dame Press, Indiana, 1983), p. 195.
10. Wittgenstein, *On Certainty*, para. 105.
11. G.J. Warnock, *Berkeley* (Peregrine Books, London, 1969).
12. See J.L. Austin, *Sense and Sensibilia*, ed. G.J. Warnock (Clarendon Press, Oxford, 1962).
13. This issue will be our central concern in Part Four.
14. Plantinga, 'Reason and Belief in God', pp. 67-8.
15. Nicholas Wolterstorff, 'Can Belief in God Be Rational?' in Alvin Plantinga and Nicholas Wolterstorff (eds), *Faith and Rationality* (University of Notre Dame Press, Indiana, 1983), p. 177.

5
Epistemology and Justification by Faith

We have seen two important differences between the treatment of basic propositions in Reformed epistemology and Wittgenstein's treatment of basic propositions in *On Certainty*. First we saw that these propositions are foundational for the Reformed epistemologist whereas they are not for Wittgenstein. Second, there is a big difference in both cases between these propositions and their relation to the noetic structures, to use Plantinga's phrase, in which they appear. The foundational propositions of Reformed epistemology seem isolated. Though the believer trusts that they are true, they remain always open to the possibility of error. In Wittgenstein, on the other hand, the emphasis is on the way basic propositions underlie our ways of thinking without themselves being subject to doubt and speculation. Wittgenstein says, 'It may be for example that *all enquiry on our part* is set so as to exempt certain propositions from doubt, if they are ever formulated. They lie apart from the route travelled by enquiry.'[1]

This marks an important difference between the nature of the enterprises that Reformed epistemology and Wittgenstein are engaged in. Plantinga's purpose is the discovery of what in fact is true. He wants to give a correct picture of the world. This is very different from Wittgenstein's conception of philosophy. For Plantinga, people have different noetic structures. Some have belief in God among their foundational beliefs and some have not. For him, the vital question concerns which noetic structure truly shows things as they really are. In Wittgenstein, on the other hand, his discussion of what he calls a world-picture has nothing to do with endeavouring to draw up a list of approved propositions which can be known or believed to be true. He is not raising the question of what *can* be known. Rather, he is investigating what goes deep in our ways of thinking, what constitutes bedrock in them. He is not helping us to make a discovery of things which we did not know before, but he is concerned to investigate what is involved in the ways we think. There will be no one answer to this question. The language-games we play vary enormously. No one account of what 'agreement with reality' amounts to can be given, since the meaning of what agreement with reality comes to is itself determined by the language-games we play and the forms of life they enter into. The ways in which basic propositions hang together in these contexts, Wittgenstein calls our world-picture. As we have already noted, he says

> The child learns to believe a host of things. I.e. it learns to act according to these beliefs. Bit by bit there forms a system of what is believed, and in that system some things stand unshakeably fast and some are more or less liable to shift. What stands fast does so, not because it is intrinsically obvious or convincing; it is rather held fast by what lies around it.[2]

It might be said that whereas Wittgenstein discusses our world-picture, Plantinga discusses pictures of the world. For Wittgenstein, it would make no sense to speak of establishing a world-picture or of asking whether our world-picture is the right one. For Plantinga, however, these questions concerning our pictures of the world, our noetic structures, are fundamental. Of course, he does not say that we can *know* that the picture of the world which has belief in God in its foundations really pictures the world, pictures reality. But we believe, have faith, that it does. The mistake of the foundationalist is to claim more than this. He claims to be able to show, by means of reason, which among our pictures of the world really picture reality. He is a child of the Enlightenment. The Reformed epistemologist not only denies this, but claims to show that the foundationalist too, though he does not realise it, lives by faith. He does not have a criterion of basicality, a reason, which will show him why the propositions he takes to be basic are properly basic or why the propositions he takes to be basic are the only properly basic propositions. That is something he believes. He does not find it out by any kind of investigation, for it plays an essential part in any investigation he conducts. He commits himself to his epistemic endowment.

He has faith in it. But, now, that is precisely the position of the Reformed epistemologist. The big difference, of course, is that the latter has belief in God among his foundational beliefs, whereas the unbelieving foundationalist does not. What the Reformed epistemologist believes by faith, however, is that his noetic structure, as opposed to the others, shows things as they really are, where there is some possibility that it might not. The Reformed epistemologist, in expressing his faith in this way, is raising the question of whether his noetic structure does show him how things are. This is not to raise a question about whether we can be sure of some claim to knowledge within an epistemic practice, but to ask how we know that the epistemic practice as such tells us how things are. It is not like asking how I know that I am seeing a tree, but like asking how we know, when we see things, that we are seeing things as they are.

As we have seen, the Reformed epistemologist's apologetics are negative rather than positive. The same applies in this epistemological context. We have already noted Alston's point that we trust our practices until we have reason to do otherwise. Such reasons could exist. All our epistemic practices *could* be mistaken. Of course, we do not believe they are. That, however, is a matter of faith, not of knowledge. Our belief that God exists could be mistaken too. We have no conclusive reason not to believe that God exists. We may believe that no such reasons exist. But that, again, is a matter of faith, not of knowledge. Yet, in this respect, belief in God is no different from our trust in our other foundational beliefs. They are taken on trust too. All justification, in this context, is justification by faith. But what is it that we are justified in believing? — That our epistemic practices do, in fact, show us how things are.

I have contrasted Wittgenstein's whole enterprise in philosophy with this way of thinking. Wittgenstein's conception of a world-picture must be distinguished from Reformed epistemology's conception of pictures of the world. At the heart of the disagreement is the conception of epistemic practices as descriptions or hypotheses concerning reality. To put the matter in Wittgenstein's terms, the issue is whether the different grammars of the ways in which we speak are to be understood as a set of beliefs or descriptions of how reality or the world really is.

It may be argued, however, that the contrast I have drawn between Reformed epistemology and Wittgenstein's philosophy is a premature one which depends on ignoring certain features of

56

Wittgenstein's work in *On Certainty*. Further, it may be said, when these features are taken into account, there is *no* contrast between the two enterprises. On the contrary, properly understood, it may be argued, Wittgenstein's *On Certainty* is itself a brilliant vindication of the doctrine of justification by faith in epistemology. How does it come about that Wittgenstein, too, may be taken as endorsing the Reformed conception of justification by faith? I believe through a seductive, but mistaken, reading of certain important features of *On Certainty*.

It is well known that in his *Philosophical Investigations* Wittgenstein insists over and over again that our justifications come to an end at some point if someone, looking at our practices, asks why we go on in *this* way rather than another. What is to justify our calling *this* way of going on, going on in the *same* way? How does someone whom we teach grasp this? How does he get to know what is to count as going on in the same way?

> How can he *know* how he is to continue a pattern by himself — whatever instruction you give him? — Well, how do I know? — If that means 'Have I reasons?' the answer is: my reasons will soon give out. And then I shall act, without reasons.[3]

We do not continue heaping justification on justification in teaching how a rule or a procedure is to be followed. As we have already seen, if a child fails to grasp what it means to go on in the same way, it will be cut off from the practice in which the particular rule has its life. The practice, what we do, is not based on prior rules. It is only in the context of what we do that the rules have their life. Wittgenstein says, 'If I have exhausted the justifications I have reached bedrock, and my spade is turned. Then I am inclined to say: "This is simply what I do".'[4]

Notice that Wittgenstein says that this is what we *do*, not what we *must* do. There is no necessity, external to our practices, which determines that they are as they are. The foundationalist seeks such a necessity in reason, a reason which dictates that all our practices are based on certain foundational propositions. In Wittgenstein, as we have just noted, matters are very different: 'But the end is not an ungrounded presupposition: it is an ungrounded way of acting.'[5]

So far, so good. But, now, Wittgenstein notes in *On Certainty* not only that there is a plurality of practices, but that practices undergo change. Some of the practices clash with one another. Is there no question of right and wrong when this occurs? Does it not make sense to say that our previous practices were mistaken? Further, when our practices undergo change, cannot it come about that we discover that what we took for granted is in fact a misplaced trust and has to be corrected? In contexts such as these, the practices are themselves being questioned. The practices themselves seem to be concepts of reality which can be subjected to further scrutiny. Experience may show that our concepts of reality do not, in fact, reflect reality.

In *On Certainty* Wittgenstein is constantly emphasising other *possibilities*, other ways of doing things. On the reading of *On Certainty* we are considering, this notion of possibility is taken to mean something like 'possible description of reality' or 'possible hypothesis about reality'. So at the level where practices are compared, there may be other possible descriptions of reality besides those we are acquainted with. Our practices are simply hypotheses among many possible alternatives concerning how things really are. Of course, we cannot *know* whether our practices do reflect the way things are. We trust that they do. That trust can be shown to be misplaced, but until that happens we are justified in exercising it. As we shall see, there is an incoherence in this notion, but, at the moment, I am simply expounding this proposed reading of Wittgenstein.

It is not hard to see why this reading should appeal to a Reformed epistemologist. First, it shows that the religious believer's trust in his practices does not stand in need of a further foundation or justification. But it does more than this, since, secondly, the believer, it is said, is asked to believe much that is not only not the case at the moment, but which he has no reason to believe could happen apart from the fact that it has been promised to him. He is asked to believe that he is going to survive his death; that somehow he is going to shed his present body and inherit a new one; is asked to believe that, if he is faithful in certain respects, he will go to a kind of place called heaven, and that if he is unfaithful, he will go to another kind of place called hell. What it would be for these promises to be fulfilled does not fall within the range of his present experience. Yet, now, on this reading of Wittgenstein, this need not trouble him unduly. Does not Wittgenstein himself insist that there is no necessity about our ways of going about things, or about the ways we see things? Things *could* be seen in very different ways. The religious believer, on this view, is told of a different state of affairs which will come to pass. Because things *can* always be different, he has reason to exercise his trust in the promises he has been given which say that these different states of affairs will come about.

Religion, it is argued, teaches us that a radical change is going to take place at the end of our lives; that at the end of time we enter into a reality very different from the one we have known. All through our lives we have looked through a glass darkly, but, then, face to face. For all we know, we have lived our whole lives in a distorted medium. Think of ourselves as though we were fish who never left the ocean's depths. The fish believe, falsely, that there is nothing above the ocean, whereas, all the time, apart from the world they know, there is a greater reality above them. Or again, think of ourselves as domestic dogs who share and understand a minimal part of the life of the household, while, all the time, the wider and greater life in the house goes on. May not God's world be greater than our world and his ways higher than our ways? When all distortions pass away, the believer will see God and himself as they really are. Of course, the believer thinks God is no deceiver. He does not expect his trust in all human practices to be thwarted. On the other hand, he does not say that all he sees is all there is to see. The believer does not say that how he sees things *must* be the way things are. There is always the possibility that his practices are mistaken or incomplete. As a believer, he holds this to be the case, since human practices are subject to correction and completion, not in this life, but in the world to come. Until that day, the believer travels in trust and faith.

This is a reading of Wittgenstein's *On Certainty* which a Reformed epistemologist might well be happy with, but is it a reading of Wittgenstein which can be sustained? I suggest not, for a number of reasons. Central to the worry being expressed in the reading concerning human epistemic practices is the fear that the practice as *such* does not reflect how things are. In order for that worry to be expressed we need a conception of 'how things are' which is independent of *all* human practices. Remember, we are not dealing with the question of errors and misjudgements *within* epistemic practices, but with the issue of the reliability of the epistemic practices as such. The worry here is of a familiar sceptical kind. As Peter Winch says, these are 'worries about whether the world can be known to be such as our forms of thought seem to presuppose'.[6] But the worry cannot be expressed in the way our reading presupposes. As we saw, not only was it suggested that we can only trust that epistemic practices reflect how things are, but also that we have found, on occasion, this trust to be misplaced. We have discovered that an epistemic practice is mistaken or incomplete. But what can 'mistaken' or 'incomplete' mean in this context? After all, what is discovered is also, of necessity, in the context of an epistemic practice. But in that case, how do we know that this context or discovery corrects or completes the previous one? How would we know whether the new discovery takes us closer or further away from how things are? To know that we would need to *know* that the epistemic practice which we call correct or complete is nearer to reality than the one we are correcting. But it is just that knowledge which, according to this reading of Wittgenstein, we do not possess. It is no good either saying that we simply *trust* that the new or modified epistemic practice is correct or more complete, since our problem is the prior one of giving any sense to the terms 'correct' and 'complete', whether we speak of knowledge or faith in connection with them. We need a relation to reality of the epistemic practices outside any context where we could speak of checking whether something is real or not. Wittgenstein says, 'Forget this transcendent certainty.'[7]

Another factor which leads us to think of epistemic practices as referring to a reality which transcends them all, is a view of these practices as hypotheses or descriptions about the world. Throughout the reading we are considering there is talk of whether our epistemic practices in fact show us how things are. What needs to be remembered is Wittgenstein's remark, 'It is what human beings *say* that is true or false; and they agree in the *language* they use. That is not agreement in opinions but in form of life.'[8] In the reading of *On Certainty* we are considering, the language in which we distinguish between the real and the unreal is itself discussed as though it were an opinion, a hypothesis or description of the real in which we trust. Peter Winch refers to this as 'the seductive idea that the grammar of our language is itself the expression of a set of beliefs or theories about how the world is, which might in principle be justified or refuted by an examination of how the world *actually* is'.[9] Peter Winch shows how this idea leads to incoherence. He does so in discussing Roger Trigg's view that 'An essential function of language... is to concern itself with what is actually the case. Its business is to communicate *truth*.'[10] Winch responds by saying, 'It is *speakers* of a language who attempt to say what is true, to describe how things are. They do so *in* the language they speak; and this language attempts no such thing, either successfully or unsuccessfully.'[11] Winch illustrates the incoherence involved in Trigg's views by means of a telling example worthy of complete quotation:

> If Tom believes that Harry is in pain and Dick that he is not, then, in the ordinary sense of the word 'belief', Tom and Dick have different beliefs. But according to Trigg's way of speaking, Tom and Dick, because they both speak the same language and mean the same thing by the word 'pain', share a common belief: even though their descriptions of Harry are mutually contradictory — indeed precisely because they are — they in a sense share a common belief about reality: perhaps that it contains such a thing as pain. But if it is possible to affirm that there is such a thing as pain, it might be possible to deny it too. The language in which the denial is couched must be meaningful; and it must mean the same as the language in which what is denied might be affirmed, else the denial would not contradict the affirmation. So to deny that there is such a thing as pain, I must mean by 'pain' just what someone who affirms that there is such a thing means by 'pain'. Hence we are still both speaking the same language and still, according to Trigg's way of thinking, offering the 'same description of reality'.[12]

Winch claims, quite rightly, that the example illustrates how important it is to recognise that the grammar of a language, the concept of reality in terms of which denials and affirmations may be made, is not itself a belief or a theory about the nature of reality. That is why, for example, although we can investigate whether there are physical objects of such-and-such a kind, we would not know what would be meant by saying that we must investigate to find out whether there are physical objects. Wittgenstein says,

> 'A is a physical object' is a piece of instruction which we give to someone who doesn't yet understand either what 'A' means or what 'physical object' means. Thus it is instruction about the use of words; and 'physical object' is a logical concept. (Like colour, quantity ...) And that is why no such

proposition as 'There are physical objects' can be formulated.[13]

Yet, as Winch admits, it is not always easy to distinguish between what belongs to grammar and what belongs to theories or beliefs. This is because the distinction is not itself a stable one, as Wittgenstein shows in *On Certainty*. There is two-way traffic between the grammar of our practices on the other hand, and our facts and theories on the other. Changes in the latter can affect the grammar of our epistemic practices. Nevertheless, as I hope to show, none of this constitutes an endorsement of the reading of *On Certainty* which would make it akin to Reformed epistemology.

How does it come about that Wittgenstein's talk of changes in our epistemic practices leads to the view that we *trust* that the practices show us how things are? I believe that much of the answer has to do with the way in which Wittgenstein's references to *alternative possibilities* is taken in *On Certainty*. What kind of possibility is he talking about here? On the reading of *On Certainty* that we are considering, clearly, the talk of possibilities is taken to mean 'the possibility that how things are may turn out to be other than we had supposed'. Since this possibility is forever before us, it seems that we can never be certain about how things are. Perhaps to say we are *uncertain* is to exaggerate, for we do have faith in our epistemic practices. But that is all we do have, *faith, trust*, in what we take for granted.

This is a bad misunderstanding of the kind of possibility Wittgenstein is discussing. In asking us to imagine practices other than our own, other ways in which things might be done, Wittgenstein's purpose is not to make us uncertain about our own practices. The possibilities he ask us to imagine are *logical* possibilities, not predictions about what he thinks might happen. The purpose of directing our attention to such possibilities is to disabuse us of certain misunderstandings about our own practices. For example, to disabuse us of the assumption that our practices are underpinned by some kind of necessity which makes them what they are, the only practices they could be. The grammar of the language we speak is not grounded in such a necessity. So far, it might be thought, there is a similarity between these conclusions and the insistence of Reformed epistemologists that the foundations of our noetic structures are not guaranteed by reason. Yet, the similarity is misleading, for when the Reformed epistemologist says that he trusts in the foundations of his noetic structure, it is trust in the fact that the noetic structure *has* the underpinning in reality which we lack knowledge of. Wittgenstein's point, on the other hand, is that the whole conception of such an underpinning is confused. The difference is seen in the fact that, for Wittgenstein, our epistemic practices are groundless. Plantinga distances himself from that view, saying that they are well grounded, although our conviction to that effect is itself a matter of faith rather than knowledge. But as I said in Chapter 3, it cannot be emphasised too strongly that Wittgenstein's postulation of alternative possibilities is not meant to cast doubt on our own procedures. The same holds for those cases where he considers actual changes which have affected the grammar of the language we use in various contexts. But, once again, the consideration of other possibilities in either context has, above all, a logical aim: not to undermine or deny the naturalness of our practices, but to emphasise it. On the other hand, in stressing the naturalness of our world-picture Wittgenstein is not establishing it as the *right* one. No world-picture is the *right* one. But in saying this Wittgenstein is not embracing a form of relativity. He is not saying that every person has a right or that every group has a right to his or their world-picture as the right one. If he were saying this, Wittgenstein would be taking the task of philosophy to be the establishing of what can be known, the establishing of which world-picture is the right one. But that is not how Wittgenstein conceives of his task. In noting changes in ways of thinking which may occur or have occurred, Wittgenstein is not testing hypotheses about the structure of the world. Rather, he is bringing out what is involved in these ways of thinking. He is not testing their foundations for they have no foundations. He says they are groundless. To avoid *that* misunderstanding in foundationalism, he calls our ways of thinking arbitrary.

The fact that the distinction between grammar, theories and beliefs is not a stable one may tempt us back to some form of foundationalism or, in avoiding it, tempt us to embrace an alternative akin to Reformed epistemology. Wittgenstein says, 'The mythology may change back into a state of flux, the river-bed of thoughts may shift. But I distinguish between the movement of the waters on the river-bed and the shift of the bed itself; though there is not a sharp division of the one from the other.'[14] In considering what is involved in these shifts, it is important to remember that Wittgenstein does not believe that all the cases can be given the same treatment. It will not do, therefore, to jump from one context to another as if what can be said in one context can be applied in some general way to another. As always, everything depends on the grammar of the cases in question.

Sometimes, what is fixed, what cannot be doubted, was once arrived at experimentally: 'It might be imagined that some propositions of the form of empirical propositions were hardened and functioned as channels for such empirical propositions as were not hardened but fluid; and that this relation altered with time, in that fluid propositions hardened, and hard ones become fluid.'[15] Take, for example, the way in which some experimental findings are so central that they become a norm within which further experiments are discussed, without themselves being questioned. For example:

> Think of chemical investigations. Lavoisier makes experiments with substances in his laboratory and now he concludes that this and that takes place when there is burning. He does not say that it might happen otherwise another time. He has got hold of a definite world-picture — not of course one that he invented: he learned it as a child. I say world-picture and not hypothesis, because it is the matter-of-course foundation for his research and as such also goes unmentioned.[16]

Other scientists would not have been surprised at the way in which Lavoisier drew his conclusions. They would take his procedures as obvious. But, of course, some experimental findings may have major repercussions within a science. They may shift our whole way of looking at things scientifically, so that, in this instance, the experimental findings shift the framework within which we investigate. Think of the shift from a Ptolemaic system to a heliocentric system in physics. Obviously, this had major implications for investigation. A system which once seemed fixed was overthrown, but the overthrow was not like the overthrow of a hypothesis within a scientific system, but was the overthrow of the system itself. It must be remembered, however, that the Ptolemaic system can still be used. In the heliocentric system things are viewed by taking the sun as central. It has proved far less cumbersome and more fruitful in terms of empirical results to use this system. This is why science finally went in that direction. It is important to remember that: it is a direction in which physics went. True, the new direction meant that what was not doubted before, namely, that the sun rotates around the earth, was no longer accepted. Physicists can give reasons for the greater fruitfulness of the new theory. But what would it mean to ask them why they relied on physics? That would be a different question for which no answer could be given.

The difference can be brought out if we think of what is wrong in describing Wittgenstein as discussing the *categories* in which we think. To talk of categories will encourage us to think of *employing* categories. This talk is most at home in science where a physicist may switch from one frame of reference to another, in one context, for example, using a corpuscular theory of light, in another, wave theory. A physicist will be able to tell us why he made the switch. In the example of the switch to the heliocentric system, the change is more fundamental, as we have seen, but it is still a category which the physicist employs. But Wittgenstein wants to move from these examples to others where talk of employing categories would be forced and strained. Wittgenstein, in these other contexts, wants to emphasise that we do not employ our ways of thinking; we are employed *in* them.

Think of a different but related example. One of the propositions which Wittgenstein says we do not question is that the earth has existed for many years. We do not formulate this proposition, but it is involved in what we do in a myriad ways, and it is these ways of acting which hold the proposition fast. Wittgenstein says:

> The existence of the earth is rather part of the whole *picture* which forms the starting-point of belief for me. Does my telephone to New York strengthen my conviction that the earth exists? Much seems to be fixed and it is removed from the traffic. It is so to speak shunted onto an unused siding.[17]

Again, note, Wittgenstein says that we *do* not doubt, not that we *cannot*. But that does not mean that we can doubt it if we want to. Wittgenstein asks, 'Can I doubt at *will?*' It is because Wittgenstein has been taken to answer that question in the affirmative that some have argued that we *cannot* be other-minded.[18] They look for some kind of necessity in the ways we think on which our thinking in these ways can be based. Wittgenstein's point is that we do not need such a notion of transcendental necessity to capture the fact that we have no choice about these fundamental ways in which we think.

But, now, what happens when this way of thinking is confronted by another which seems to conflict with it? How are we to think of this? Wittgenstein says:

> Men have believed that they could make rain, why should not a king be brought up in the belief that the world began with him? And if Moore and this king were to meet and discuss, could Moore really prove his belief to be the right one? I do not say that Moore could not convert the king to his view, but it would be a conversion of a special kind; the king would be brought to look at the world in a different way. Remember that one is sometimes convinced of the *correctness* of a view by its *simplicity* or *symmetry*, i.e. these are what induce one to go over to this point of view. One then simply says something like '*That's* how it must be'.[19]

The important difference between this example and the fundamental changes within physics, is that here we have no reference to a subject within which the different ways of looking at the world compete. No, Moore would be trying to awaken the king to all that is involved in his way of looking at the world. The way the king looks at it may seem awkward and cumbersome. We are not told that it appears so to the king, for that would presuppose that he had the kind of interests we have in looking at the world. Wittgenstein cannot be read as meaning that in the case of this clash, 'the world' is what the two views have as their common topic, standing as competing hypotheses or descriptions of it. If that were the case, then Moore would be saying that he had already checked *his* way of looking at the world and found it *more* satisfying than the king's. Wittgenstein says, 'But I did not get my picture of the world by satisfying myself of its correctness; nor do I have it because I am satisfied of its correctness. No: it is the inherited background against which I distinguish between true and false.'[20] If Moore fails to persuade the king what he has failed to give him is any interest in or sense of history. Moore can distinguish between true and false statements about alleged events which have taken place on earth, but he doesn't check on whether the earth itself exists. As Wittgenstein says, 'If the true is what is grounded, then the ground is not *true*, nor yet false.'[21] But what of the questioning king? Wittgenstein replies, 'If someone asked us "but is that *true*?" he might say "yes" to him; and if he demanded grounds we might say "I can't give you any grounds, but if you learn more you too will think the same." If this didn't come about, that would mean that he couldn't for example learn history.'[22] What Moore tries to do in relation to the king is not so much correct him, but initiate him into an interest in history. The absence of such interests and the inability to answer such questions may lead us to say that our way of looking at things is far richer than the king's. But the use of the comparative should not mislead us. What this comes to is that *given* an interest in certain questions, we can answer them and the king can't. But, then, those interests are precisely *our* interests, part of the interest we have in things. The king may not have these interests. Of course, we may persuade him to have them, but that would be to awaken him to a sense of history. The temptation is to think that we *must* have an interest in history or questions about the duration of the earth. This example is unlike the one in which Wittgenstein speaks of a game becoming pointless once it is discovered that its outcome can be determined by the second move in it. There, the game *is* rendered pointless because of more general features it shares with other competitive games. Moore and the king are not competitors in this sense.

Let us consider a further example which will bring us nearer to the religious examples we want to come to in the end. Wittgenstein wrote *On Certainty* before anyone had landed on the moon. At that time, it made no sense to doubt whether one had been on the moon. The doubt could not connect up with anything, nothing would hang on it. Wittgenstein says, 'Everything that I have seen or heard gives me the conviction that no man has ever been far from the earth. Nothing in my picture of the world speaks in favour of the opposite.'[23] As we all know, things have changed and man has landed on the moon. The fact that this has happened obviously changes the parameters of what it is and is not reasonable to believe. On the other hand, the present position is an interesting one. Because very few people have been on the moon, it still makes no sense to me to doubt whether I have been there any more than it makes sense for me to doubt whether I was in India last year. The change is that the content of the doubt is no longer ruled out as unimaginable. But, on the other hand, it is not like doubting whether it was Ystalyfera or Ystradgynlais I went to in the Swansea Valley, where one could easily be mistaken for the other. Yet, if space travel became commonplace, then doubting whether one has been on the moon could itself be a commonplace doubt, as would assurances that one knew one had been there:' "I *know* that I have never been on the moon." That sounds quite different in the circumstances which actually hold, to the way it would if a good many men had been on the moon, and some perhaps without knowing it. In *this* case one could give grounds for this knowledge.'[24]

But, at the time of writing, when no one had been on the moon, Wittgenstein imagines what it might be like to be confronted by a counter-claim. First, he imagines this in a child who has been told this by an adult:

> Suppose some adult has told a child that he had been on the moon. The child tells me the story, and I say it was only a joke, the man hadn't been on the moon; no one has ever been on the moon; the moon is a long way off and it is impossible to climb up there — If now the child insists, saying perhaps that there is a way of getting there which I don't know etc. what reply could I make to him?... — But a child will not ordinarily stick to such a belief and will soon be convinced by what we tell him seriously.[25]

That the child should react in this way is extremely important; it is a condition of the child's entry into the world we know about. And it is part of our expectation that a child will react in this way. The child shares our world and teaching children in the expectation of certain responses is part of that world. They soon put away childish things.

But in the middle of the paragraph in which he cites the example of the child, Wittgenstein also says this: 'What reply could I make to the adults of a tribe who believe that people sometimes go to the moon (perhaps that is how they interpret their dreams), and who indeed grant that there are no ordinary means of climbing up to it or flying there?[26] This is different from the example of the child, for now we are talking about the adults of a tribe. In the case of the child, its surroundings were such that the surroundings it wanted to give to the story of going to the moon would not be sustainable. Wittgenstein has in mind considerations such as the following in face of someone asking,

> 'But is there no objective truth? Isn't it true, or false, that someone has been on the moon? If we are thinking within

our system, then it is certain that no one has ever been on the moon. Not merely is nothing of the sort ever seriously reported to us by reasonable people, but our whole system of physics forbids us to believe it. For this demands answers to the question. 'How did he overcome the force of gravity?' 'How could he live without an atmosphere?' and a thousand others which could not be answered.[27]

Now, in one sense, the tribe understand the force of these questions, for as we have already noted, they 'grant that there are no ordinary means of climbing up to it or flying there'. But instead of this admission leading in the direction we expect in the child's replies, when instructed, we get this: 'Instead of all these answers we met the reply, "We don't know *how* one gets to the moon, but those who get there know at once that they are there; and even you can't explain everything." ' Wittgenstein says 'We should feel ourselves intellectually very distant from someone who said this.'[28] Immediately after this discussion comes the following remark: 'Isn't this altogether like the way one can instruct a child to believe in a God, or that none exists, and it will accordingly be able to produce apparently telling grounds for the one or the other?'[29]

Wittgenstein's remark about a feeling of intellectual distance is an interesting one. It suggests that there is something there, a way of looking at things, which one may be intellectually distant from. It is not like the sense of distance experienced between us and the mentally unbalanced or the deranged who may wander among us muttering about their frequent visits to the moon. Their words lack connection with what lies around them; in fact, it is their disconnectedness, their obsessiveness, which marks them off. But it is not like that with the tribe Wittgenstein refers to. Presumably, their remark *does* link up with the surroundings of their lives, but it is the *character* of that link which eludes us. Of course, many among us will simply say 'What a load of superstitious rubbish!' In saying that, presumably, they mean that such a remark made in the context of the network of beliefs in which we were teaching the child would not merely fail to fit in, but would not qualify as something which *could* fit in. But the same reasonable appeal to surroundings should be applied to the tribe; that is, we should surely endeavour to see and appreciate the character of the network of beliefs in which the remark *is* made. We may fail in the attempt. Consider a similar example

Wittgenstein considers elsewhere. He asks:

> How am I to find out whether this proposition is to be
> regarded as an empirical proposition — 'You'll see your
> dead friend again?' Would I say: 'He is a bit superstitious?'
> Not a bit. He might have been apologetic (The man who
> stated it categorically was more intelligent than the man
> who was apologetic about it). 'Seeing a dead friend', again
> means nothing much to me at all. I don't think in these
> terms. I don't say to myself, 'I shall see so and so again'
> ever. He always says it, but he doesn't make any search.
> He puts on a queer smile. 'His story had that dreamlike
> quality'. My answer would be in this case 'Yes', and a
> particular explanation.[30]

The explanation, presumably, would be in terms of the grammar
of the language being used. There is an obvious connection with
ordinary uses of 'see', but also 'the grammar is modified in the
new circumstances and it thereby comes to bear a different
sense'.[31] What determines whether such modification has taken
place is the surroundings of the language, the connections it has
with other aspects — hopes, fears, aspirations, etc. — of the lives
of the people who speak in this way.

Peter Winch has emphasised the special difficulties which may
occur when the surroundings in which expressions we may find
strange have their use, belong to a culture other than our own.[32]
Yet, similar difficulties may arise within our own culture where
familiarity with religion can so easily breed contempt. We
assimilate the religious utterances to surroundings to which they
do not belong, saying 'We do not believe...' as if we were presenting
an *opposite* point of view. We say we do not believe in the
resurrection of the dead, that we do not believe in a last judgement,
etc., etc., as though we were debating alternatives within a
common framework. Yet if we start telling a believer what we
mean, we often find he does not take it in that way at all. Further,
when we say we do not believe it we, too, often mean that we
can make nothing of it. Taken in the way we are tempted to take
it, the believer's claims do not even *begin* to be credible.
Wittgenstein illustrates these points well as follows:

> I have a moderate education, as all of you have, and therefore
> know what is meant by insufficient evidence for a forecast.

Suppose someone dreamt of the Last Judgement, and said he now knew what it would be like. Suppose someone said: 'This is poor evidence.' I would say: 'If you want to compare it with the evidence for it's raining tomorrow it is no evidence at all.' He may make it sound as if by stretching the point you may call it evidence. But it may be more than ridiculous as evidence. But now, would I be prepared to say: 'You are basing your belief on extremely slender evidence, to put it mildly.' Why should I regard this dream as evidence — measuring its validity as though I were measuring the validity of the evidence for meteorological events?

If you compare it with anything in Science which we call evidence, you can't credit that anyone could soberly argue: 'Well, I had this dream... therefore... Last Judgement'. You might say: 'For a blunder, that's too big.'...

I mean, if a man said to me after a dream that he believed in the Last Judgement, I'd try to find out what sort of impression it gave him. One attitude: 'It will be in about 2,000 years. It will be bad for so and so and so, etc.' Or it may be one of terror. In the case where there is hope, terror, etc., would I say there is insufficient evidence if he says, 'I believe...? I can't treat these words as I normally treat 'I believe so and so'. It would be entirely beside the point...[33]

The person who fails to understand what the believer is saying finds himself at an intellectual distance from what is being said. He is not confronted by competing hypotheses within a common system:

> Suppose someone were a believer and said: 'I believe in a Last Judgement', and I said: 'Well, I'm not so sure. Possibly.' You would say that there is an enormous gulf between us. If he said 'There is a German aeroplane overhead', and I said 'Possibly, I'm not so sure', you'd say we were fairly near.[34]

The enormous gulf which separates them is not the enormous gulf between two vastly different hypotheses, but the gap between someone for whom belief in the Last Judgement guides his whole life and someone who misunderstands the character of the belief and treats it as one which is akin to a hypothesis. It is clear that Wittgenstein does not treat religious belief in that way:

Also, there is this extraordinary use of the word 'believe'. One talks of believing and at the same time one doesn't use belief as one does ordinarily. You might say (in the normal use): 'You only believe — oh well...'[35]

In *On Certainty*, Wittgenstein gives the following examples of religious beliefs where he speaks in terms of what is said contradicting what is normally said:

I believe that every human being has two parents; but Catholics believe that Jesus only had a human mother. And other people might believe that there are human beings with no parents, and give no credence to all the contrary evidence. Catholics believe as well that in certain circumstances a wafer completely changes its nature, and at the same time that all evidence proves the contrary. And so Moore said 'I know that this is wine and not blood', Catholics would contradict him.[36]

I do not think this is a particularly good example because it is not accurate. What Catholics in fact say is that the wafer has become the body of Christ while *not* denying that any physical analysis would show that the consecrated host had not changed its physical characteristics. They do not say that all evidence *proves* that the wafer has not become the body of Christ. Of course, it may be extremely difficult for someone to understand what is meant by saying that the wafer *has become* something else in this context. Perhaps in the sense in which the enquiry is carried on, there is nothing to understand. Calling the sacrament a mystery might be one way of indicating that one must die to a certain kind of understanding in order to be able to accept it. Wittgenstein would accept that if we were to call this clash between Moore and the Catholic over the Eucharist a contradiction, it is not contradiction within a common system of beliefs. The case of the Virgin Birth is a much harder one to understand, since it might be argued that, there, we do have a clash within a common way of speaking.

In the preceding paragraph Wittgenstein says:

I might therefore interrogate someone who said that the earth did not exist before his birth, in order to find out which of my convictions he was at odds with. And then it *might* be that he was contradicting my fundamental attitudes, and if that were how it was, I should have to put up with it.[37]

But if the contradictions were within a common system there would be no question of putting up with it. Of course, someone may be rejected as unteachable. But this is not the kind of context, as we have seen, that Wittgenstein has in mind, and in the *Lectures and Conversations* he says that it is odd to say that the unbeliever has the *opposite* belief from the believer. He says that while he may *call* it believing the opposite, what it amounts to saying is that the believer and the unbeliever think in different ways. Wittgenstein says that it is tempting to ask of one's way of thinking, 'Isn't this an hypothesis, which, as I *believe*, is again and again completely confirmed?'[38] but he corrects this immediately by saying 'Mustn't we say at every turn: "I *believe* this with certainty"?'[39] which does not mean, as we have seen, that one is trusting an unconfirmed hypothesis. But on the reading of *On Certainty* which would make it akin to Reformed epistemology, that is what all epistemic practices become — unconfirmed hypotheses about the nature of reality. Reality never changes, only concepts of reality change and we trust, have faith, that our concept of reality is correct.

Notes

1. Wittgenstein, *On Certainty*, para.88.
2. Ibid., para.21.
3. Ludwig Wittgenstein, *Philisophical Investigations*, trans. G.E.M. Anscombe (Basil Blackwell, Oxford, 1953), vol.1, p.211.
4. Ibid., vol.1, p.217.
5. Wittgenstein, *On Certainty*, para.110.
6. Peter Winch, 'Language, Belief and Relativism' in H.D. Lewis (ed.), *Contemporary British Philosophy*, 4th series, p.328.
7. Wittgenstein, *On Certainty*, para.47.
8. Wittgenstein, *Investigations*, vol.1, p.241.
9. Winch, 'Language, Belief and Relativism', p.336.
10. Ibid., pp.324-5.
11. Ibid., p.324.
12. Ibid., p.325.
13. Wittgenstein, *On Certainty*, para.36.
14. Ibid., para.97.
15. Ibid., para.76.
16. Ibid., para.167.
17. Ibid., paras. 209 and 210.
18. See Jonathan Lear, 'Leaving the World Alone', *Journal of Philosophy* (1982).
19. Wittgenstein, *On Certainty*, para.92.
20. Ibid., para.94.
21. Ibid., para.205.
22. Ibid., para.206.
23. Ibid., para.102.
24. Ibid., para.111.
25. Ibid., para.106.
26. Ibid.
27. Ibid., para.108.
28. Ibid., para.106.
29. Ibid., para.107.
30. Ludwig Wittgenstein, 'Lectures on Religious Belief' in Cyril Barrett (ed.), *Lectures and Conversations on Aesthetics, Psychology and Religious Belief* (Basil Blackwell, Oxford, 1966) pp.62-3.
31. Winch, 'Language, Belief and Relativism'.
32. See Peter Winch, 'Understanding a Primitive Society' in his *Ethics and Action* (Routledge and Kegan Paul, London, 1972) and 'Language, Belief and Relativism'.
33. Wittgenstein, *Lectures and Conversations*, pp.61-2.
34. Ibid., p.53.
35. Ibid., pp.59-60.
36. Wittgenstein, *On Certainty*, para.239.
37. Ibid., para.238.
38. Ibid., para.241.
39. Ibid., para.242.

6
Religion and Epistemology

In considering various examples of basic propositions in *On Certainty*, we have been asked, by Wittgenstein, to appreciate what goes deep in our ways of thinking. These ways of thinking are misunderstood if they are thought of as hypotheses concerning descriptions of an unchanging reality which transcends them all. This remains the case even though ways of thinking undergo changes and may be eroded. Above all, we have seen the necessity of looking at each example of basic propositions from the standpoint of the mode of discourse in which they are found.

There are special difficulties, however, relating to the religious examples. As we have seen, Wittgenstein, in postulating certain 'alternatives' to our ways of thinking, is concerned to emphasise and underline what is fundamental to us in our attitudes. It is in order to bring this out, to disabuse us of a notion of necessity underpinning these attitudes, that talk of alternatives is introduced. It must be remembered, however, that not all his examples admit of this treatment. In imagining certain other ways of going on, Wittgenstein has to fill out, as best he can, rudimentary sketches of what these alternative possibilities amount to — other ways of buying and selling, other ways of ascribing blame, other ways of talking about distant planets, etc., etc. The changes, if they were to come about, would make enormous differences. Nevertheless, that's what they would be — differences, and things would go on in these very different ways. But in other cases, Wittgenstein says, if someone came to doubt his surroundings we would say he had gone insane. What if someone I had known for a long time suddenly started claiming that for a long time he had been living elsewhere? Wittgenstein says, 'I should not call this a *mistake*, but rather a mental disturbance, perhaps a transient one.'[1] But, of course, religious beliefs are not of this sort. If they are denied we do not regard those who deny them as mentally disturbed. On the contrary, it may be more likely that, for the majority of people, it is the religious believers who are regarded as in some way confused. What are the special difficulties relating to the religious cases?

First, as we have seen, most of the 'alternatives' Wittgenstein talks of are logical alternatives. He does speak at times of beliefs and ways of looking at things which people have actually held, but, for the most part, his references to other ways of doing things are to imaginary states of affairs. I have argued that his main purpose in doing so is to show that there is no queer kind of necessity underpinning our practices; but that does not mean that we are in any doubt about them. In the case of religious beliefs, however, it may be thought, this is simply not true. After all, we are not thinking here of logical alternatives, other ways of doing things. On the contrary, this way of doing things is in our midst and we are called on to make a decision with respect to it. Some believe in it, others do not believe it, and some, believers and unbelievers alike, have doubts about it. So the presence of religious practices in our midst may tempt us to revert to some kind of foundationalism or to something akin to Reformed epistemology with respect to it.

Second, within religion itself a central place is given to religious mystery. God is a mystery which human understanding cannot exhaust. If this religious mystery is turned into an epistemological mystery, if instead of seeing that the God who is worshipped *is* a hidden God, we start thinking of all our ways of thinking as screens which hide God from us, then it is easy to see how we can regard all our ways of seeing things as based on trust, a trust that they point to an unchanging reality. In fact, I am tempted to think that in the reading of *On Certainty* we have been considering, a religious influence has been at work. A certain understanding of the *religious* distinction between the unreality of this world and the reality of God's world has become a general epistemological view. Calvin writes:

> For as long as our views are bounded by the earth, perfectly content with our own righteousness, wisdom and strength, we fondly flatter ourselves, and fancy we are little less than demigods. But, if we once elevate our thoughts to God, and consider his nature, and the consummate perfection of his

76

righteousness, wisdom, and strength, to which we ought to be conformed — what before charmed us in ourselves under the false pretext of righteousness, will soon be loathed as the greatest iniquity; what strangely deceived us under the title of wisdom, will be despised as extreme folly; and what wore the appearance of strength, will be proved to be most wretched impotence. So very remote from the divine purity is what seems in us the highest perfection.[2]

Understood in a certain way, these religious distinctions may be taken to imply, epistemologically, that even our best knowledge and certainties are but incomplete expressions of something awaiting completion in a world to come. In this way all our ways of thinking are regarded as mere opinions and the possibilities to which Wittgenstein draws our attention become, not ways of illuminating what is fundamental in our ways of thinking, but indications that reality may be very different from the ways in which we think of it. In religious contexts, calling life on earth incomplete has its points, but in epistemological contexts calling our ways of thinking opinions has no practical import. Wittgenstein says:

But imagine people who were never quite certain of these things, but said that they were *very* probably so, and that it did not pay to doubt them. Such a person, then, would say in my situation 'It is extremely unlikely that I have ever been on the moon', etc., etc. *How* would the life of these people differ from ours? For there *are* people who say that it is merely extremely probable that water over a fire will boil and not freeze, and that therefore strictly speaking what we consider impossible is only improbable. What difference does this make in their lives? Isn't it just that they talk rather more about certain things than the rest of us?[3]

What of these two arguments from religious to general epistemological conclusions? They fail because they do violence to the grammar of religious belief. With respect to the appeal to mystery in religion, I do not pretend to have given an alternative account of its religious significance. That will be one of our chief concerns when we come to consider concept-formation in religion.[4] All I am pointing out at the moment is that if such talk is imported into epistemology in the way suggested, it becomes idle talk, having no practical import — rather an odd effect for an allegedly momentous religious truth to have.

But with respect to the first argument relating to the presence of religious belief among us as an alternative among others, enough has already been said to show that its presence need not entail either foundationalism or Reformed epistemology as the appropriate analyses of the fact. The reason why can be brought out by a brief consideration of an interesting attempt to reconcile these two standpoints. Stephen J. Wykstra has pointed out that many basic beliefs Plantinga appeals to would turn out not to be basic at all, in the eyes of foundationalists, if 'basic' were understood to mean that the beliefs are *in fact* not checked by an individual for evidence in favour of them. To say that all beliefs must have evidence in *this* sense is a form of what Wykstra calls *extravagant evidentialism* which no foundationalist need hold. Yet this is the form of foundationalism which Plantinga often attacks. According to this view, a belief could be properly basic if an individual himself had not carried out the appropriate inferences to its conclusion for himself. But plenty of our beliefs are acceptable without question by us — the conclusions of scientists, a newspaper report of an air disaster, etc., etc., without our checking the reports for ourselves. But this does not show that the beliefs do not stand in need of evidence. Wykstra's suggestion is that extravagant evidentialism should be replaced by *sensible evidentialism*, which suggests that to say a belief is evidence-essential, is to say it stands in need of evidence, *only* in the sense that the belief *would* be in trouble if it were discovered in the community that no evidential case for it is available. For Wykstra, the issue is whether belief in God is evidence-essential for the community of theists. It would not be a matter of indifference, he claims, if no evidence were thought to be available. On the other hand, he recognises that many think there is something amiss with the suggestion that belief in God is evidence-essential. He says:

> For one thing, this seems to presuppose that it is epistemically better to believe in God on the basis of an inferential case than to believe in a basic way — even though our exemplars of religious faith (Moses, or Isaiah, or Jesus, for example) seem to believe in and know God in a basic rather than inferential way. Further, sensible evidentialism

seems here to put the uneducated believer in an inferior and epistemically dependent position, relative to some Christian intellectual elite that has the competence to assess the inferential case for God's existence.[5]

Wykstra does not want to dismiss these considerations lightly, but it seems to me that this is what he does, nevertheless, in his attempt to reconcile the religious perspective with sensible evidentialism. He tries to distinguish between propositional knowledge of God and existential knowledge of God, the latter being the only one that matters in the end. He says that this does not give Christian intellectuals the edge over believers any more than the evidence sought by Biblical scholars gives them an edge over simple readers of the Bible. Yet this begs the question. Whether Moses saw God in the burning bush or whether Jesus was the Son of God are not matters based on historical evidence. But sensible evidentialism must regard these matters of faith as something which could, in principle, be disproved by showing that there is no evidence available for them. That there is no evidence available outside religious categories, it seems to me, is one of the important defining characteristics of the grammar of these religious truths. Also, it seems that Wykstra ducks the main issue. What if the intellectuals *did* conclude that no evidence for belief in God is available; would that overthrow the exemplars of faith, which provide, on Wykstra's own admission, the most important sense of belief? Surely, what is needed, instead of conjuring up a philosophical use of 'reasoning to religious conclusions', is to pay attention to the sense of the exemplars, something which would itself be a proper pursuit for philosophical enquiry. It may be that the tensions in the analogy to which I am referring have some force for Wykstra, for when we come to his suggestions concerning what it might mean for intellectuals to find sufficient evidence for God's existence, we find him saying this:

> And if there is a case for theism of the sort that evidentialists see as essential, one might not be able to show to another that this is so as one can for a scientific theory; for another's capacity to apprehend it may well depend in part upon knowing God existentially, upon living one's life in that project of redemptive love that only His grace makes possible. This dependence of the cognitive upon something

79

deeper than the cognitive is, it seems to me, entirely compatible with sensible evidentialism.[6]

This last sentence needs considerable further argument, since, from what has been said, the analogy with other enquiries has made any application of sensible evidentialism to the existence of God strained in the extreme.

If, indeed, the cognitive (philosophical) interests *did* pay attention to the non-cognitive (religious) beliefs, then we would see that the tension between belief and unbelief cannot be satisfactorily accounted for in evidentialist terms. On that matter, it seems to me, Plantinga is right. The dispute between belief and unbelief is not one in which probabilities and evidence are weighed within a common system. The gap between what the believer wants to say and what the unbeliever denies is itself a *grammatical* gap. To reject religion, or to come to God, is not to reject or embrace a hypothesis within a common way of looking at things, but, rather, to reject or embrace a whole way of looking at things. That is why we have a word like conversion to characterise coming to believe. The convert turns around, comes to things from a new direction.

Speaking of that direction, worship of God, Wykstra says that we all enter it as children or not at all. The religious import of that remark, the sense in which we are all as little children before God, has its home within religious worship. It encapsulates the spirit in which we are asked to worship God. It is *not* a remark about the epistemological status of worship. There is nothing uncertain about how we are to come to God; we must come as little children. There is a deep misunderstanding, therefore, if such remarks are taken as signs of the relative uncertainty of religious views of the world when compared, let us say, with physics or ordinary perception. Yet, curiously enough, this is what has happened from both some Calvinist and some Catholic perspectives in relation to the epistemic status of religious practices.

First, let us see how this has happened from a Calvinist perspective. William P. Alston characterises perception and religious belief as ways of objectifying our experience. The crucial question for him, therefore, is whether these epistemic practices *do*, in fact, give us information about the reality they claim to convey to us. He says, 'The tough problem is to determine whether we are justified in conceptualizing our experience in these terms.'[7] As we have seen, there are difficulties from the outset in this way of stating the problem. To what are we supposed to refer to decide whether one practice objectifies reality more or less than another, or, indeed, to determine whether it objectifies reality at all? Whatever we appeal to will itself be some epistemic practice which, in being such, is logically on a par with the practices being assessed and so can be of no help in the metaphysical assessment. Alston cannot tell us what he means by the 'experience' we are supposed to objectify in our conceptualisations. So in asking whether the latter are successful, there is no question of comparison between 'experience' and our conceptualisations. Alston, in fact, accepts these difficulties, and says that all judgements about the success of our conceptualisations are internal to them. Our epistemic practices are to be judged from the fruits of experience. To this, Wittgenstein replies

> But isn't it experience that teaches us to judge like *this*, that is to say, that it is correct to judge like this? But how does experience *teach* us, then? *We* may derive it from experience, but experience does not direct us to derive anything from experience. If it is the *ground* of our judging like this, and not just the cause, still we do not have a ground for seeing this in turn as a ground. No, experience is not the ground for our game of judging. Nor is its outstanding success.[8]

Since Alston thinks there *is* something which we do not possess, namely, the comparison of the epistemic practices with reality, at best, the practices can tell us what *seems* to be the case, but never what *is* the case. As we have seen, the expression of this qualification before our certainties is idle and has no practical import. Of course, the needless distinction is vital to the whole enterprise of Reformed epistemology. We do not have knowledge of reality. Rather, it is said we have faith in the fruits of our epistemic practices. But, as we have already seen, if these fruits can only express what *seems* to be the case, no amount of compounding of what seems to be the case can yield what *is* the case. We live by faith, not by knowledge. The only justification we have of our epistemic practices is faith in their fruits.

But Alston is concerned with a comparison of the fruits of various epistemic practices. Of course, for Alston, relying on perception is just as much a matter of faith as relying on God. On the other hand, there seems to be far more agreement about the fruits of perception than there is about the fruits of religious faith. Most people are convinced by the former, but this cannot be said of the latter. This disparity may be thought to cast doubt on the fruits of the life of the spirit, but Alston says that the comparison is hardly a fair one:

> It is really inappropriate to compare the situation of the ordinary believer, vis-à-vis [Christian practice] with the situation of the normal adult human being vis-à-vis [the practice of perception]. For we are all masters of the latter practice. We emerged from our apprenticeship in early childhood long before we reached the age of philosophical reflection on these matters. But in Christian practice we are, almost all of us, at the stage of early infancy, just beginning to learn to recognize the other reality from ourselves, just beginning to recognize the major outlines of the landscape, and one should add, just beginning to respond to them appropriately. Hence we must look outside our own experience to the tiny minority that qualify as masters of the spiritual life, both for some intimation of what mastery of this practice is like and for an answer to the question whether this enterprise proves itself by its fruits. We cannot hope to arrive at a definitive answer to that question from the outside. Of course there is a remedy for that — to get inside. But that is an arduous and time-consuming task, not one to be attempted in the course of an essay. Meanwhile we must glean such hints as we can from the lives, works and thoughts of the likes of Mother Teresa of Calcutta as to what it is to be more than babes in the experience of God, and as to what it is to respond to this experience in the way it indicates.[9]

Alston's argument oscillates disastrously between conceptual and religious reflection. It conflates the grammar of a practice with the relation in which an individual stands to the practice. We must bear in mind, throughout, that Alston's aim is meant to throw light on the issue whether, in comparison with perception, we are justified in conceptualising our experience in terms of Christian practice. Compared with the agreement evidenced in perception, as when, on a clear day, we all agree that we are seeing a tree, Alston points out that the weak in the Faith vastly outnumber the strong. But this observation does nothing to aid

82

the comparison of the practices as *practices*, since the distinction between weakness and strength in believers is one which is drawn *within* religious practice; they are weak or strong *in the Faith*. Alston conflates the issue of how strong religious belief is among the adherents to a practice with the issue of the epistemic status of the practice itself. If the majority of believers are weak in their adherence to a practice, of course, the practice is weakened. But this weakness is not a sign of doubt about the character of spirituality, for if the weaknesses are confessed or recognised, it is only in the light of knowledge of the exemplars of faith that such confession or recognition can, logically, occur. Alston conflates the issues in such a way that the weaknesses of the majority of believers casts doubt on the *conceptual* parameters of the practice, even when within the practice itself is found the view that only a minority will be strong in it. What would make the logic and grammar of Faith *really* obscure would be an inability among people to be sure of what is meant by tentativeness or strength in the Faith, or a confusion of seriousness with mediocrity and banality. There is a further complication concerning being like children before God. True, Paul does distinguish between those who are babes in the Faith and those who are ready for the strong meat of the Word. On the other hand, coming before God as helpless as a child is hardly an expression of a beginner's stage in Christianity, since that is the paradigm of the disposition towards God which believers are told to strive for. Saints often say they are the greatest sinners. But if someone did confess to being a babe in the Faith in the Pauline sense, that would not be, as Alston seems to think, a remark of someone outside a practice who would like to get inside it, but, rather, an expression of one of the most familiar confessions heard *within* Christianity. Of course, if other rival ways of thinking begin to exercise a hold on the believer, doubts of another kind may beset him: not doubts about his growth in grace, but doubts about whether the concern really means anything at all. Alston's mistake is to think that doubts of the latter kind can be answered in terms of doubts of the first kind.

A similar move, it seems to me, is made by Jamie Ferreira in comparing Wittgenstein with John Henry Newman. This comparison, as we shall see, can be an extremely fruitful one, but Ferreira is prevented from seeing this by the epistemological presuppositions she brings to the discussion. This need not have been the case, for much of the groundwork for a comparison between Newman and Wittgenstein had been already accomplished in two remarkable essays by James Cameron published as early as 1957 and 1960. Little attention has been paid to them, but they merit our attention in the present climate of philosophical opinion more than ever. Cameron points out that, throughout his life, Newman wrestled with the issue of the relations between faith and reason and their bearing on religious belief. Naturally, his views altered during the course of their development. What I present here is what Cameron takes to be his most mature thoughts.

Newman came to the conclusion that trying to meet arguments against religious belief by appeal to evidence which was supposed, somehow, to tip the balance in its favour, was an intellectually unfruitful exercise. He regarded those who relied on evidentialism, in the manner of Paley, as the old 'high and dry' party. In his *University Sermons* he speaks of 'the age of evidences as "a time when love was cold"'.[10] Instead of such approaches, he endeavoured to meet scepticism head-on in a manner reminiscent of Hume. Hume insisted that, at a certain level, although it might be maintained in the study, philosophical scepticism could not be maintained in practice. Hume's final appeal is to nature, to what we in fact do. But if someone were to require a further justification of our practices, there is none at hand. Hume says, 'Where reason is lively, and mixes itself with some propensity, it ought to be assented to.'[11] Writing of the sceptic Hume says that 'he must assent to the principle concerning the existence of body, tho' he cannot pretend by any arguments of philosophy to maintain its veracity. Nature has not left this to his choice, and has doubtless esteem'd it an affair of too great importance to be trusted to our uncertain reasonings and speculations.'[12] Newman writes 'Nature certainly does give sentence against scepticism.'[13] We think too of Wittgenstein's remark that while we may just about sustain the thought in our philosophical imaginings that human beings may be automata, we cannot sustain it out on the streets when, for example, we may be confronted by a group of playing children.[14] To mistake the policeman in Madame Tussaud's for a human being is one thing, to try to extend *that* mistake to all our dealing with human beings is ludicrous. Our trust in nature and in human beings is shown in the various ways we act with respect to them. So far, the Reformed epistemologist might be happy to say that we are justified in what we do by faith and not by reason. Our reasons, good and bad, operate within the sphere of our trust. All concerned, Hume, Newman, Wittgenstein and Reformed epistemologists, are as one, against foundationalists who claim that, underlying our practices, we possess a concept of reason on which those practices depend and which justifies their rationality. In this emphasis, as Cameron says, Newman was not using scepticism to press men into faith, but raising, in a fresh way, a fundamental issue in epistemology.

Yet Newman, as Cameron also points out, regarded Hume as an intellectual enemy of religion, despite the obvious respect he had for him. Newman pointed out that Hume's deficiencies with respect to religious belief were due to the fact that he did not extend his epistemological insights to that sphere. Here, Hume did not believe that Nature had left us with no choice. Cameron expresses Hume's position well.

It is frivolous to raise doubts about the validity of the methods of the natural sciences; here the 'experimental philosophy'[15] shows its worth by its power to unify within a consistent scheme the world of our perceptions and to make the natural world serve our purposes. It is equally frivolous to raise doubts as to the claims of the *consensus humani* in questions of morals.[16] But there are, for Hume, no such good reasons, there is no happy coincidence of natural propensity and rational hypothesis, when questions connected with philosophical theology come to be considered. In these cases the destructive process of philosophical analysis is not inhibited: here we can face without too much anxiety, and with a certain satisfaction that no rational human interests are put in peril, the results of such an analysis. 'The whole is a riddle, an enigma, an inexplicable mystery. Doubt, uncertainty, suspense of judgement, appear the only result of our most accurate scrutiny concerning this subject.'[17]

What Hume did not see, because he did not feel it in his own case, nor was it perceived thus in the philosophical culture which surrounded him, was that religion too could be based on an antecedent presumption, what we have called a whole way of looking at the world. What Newman came to see was that, properly extended, Hume's originality would show that belief *and* unbelief go beyond reason. Put in the Wittgensteinian terms we have already used, the gap between belief and unbelief is itself a *grammatical* one. Here is Newman extending Hume's insights to examples of religious belief:

> we trust our senses, and that in spite of their often deceiving us. They even contradict each other at times, yet we trust them. But even were they ever consistent, never unfaithful, yet their fidelity would not be thereby proved. We consider that there is so strong an antecedent presumption that they are faithful that we dispense with proof. We take the point for granted; or, if we have grounds for it, these either lie in our secret belief in the stability of nature, or in the preserving presence and uniformity of Divine Providence — which, again, are points assumed. As, then, the senses may and do deceive us, and yet we trust them from a secret instinct, so it need not be weakness or rashness, if upon a certain presentiment of mind we trust to the fidelity of testimony offered for a revelation.[18]

In Wittgenstein's terms, trust in the uniformity of nature or trust in divine providence is held fast by all that surrounds them for their adherents. The lack of consensus concerning religious belief tempts us to think of that belief as a hypothesis to be judged within a common system of assessment. But, as Newman points out, the certainties involved in religion are not the same certainties in which the natural sciences are interested. Nevertheless in not seeing that these very differences allowed him to extend his epistemological insights to religion, Hume was guilty of the philosophical dogmatism which I noted in Chapter 2 where I quoted J.D. Kenyon's observation that

> there is an attitude ... which is perhaps characteristic of scientific dogmatism, namely that since God is something we can never really know about, agnosticism is intellectually more proper than either theism or atheism. If 'know' implies only internal justification, the premiss is false; if it implies external justification, it is true, but so is the parallel premiss for the physical world, and the dogmatism consists in not drawing the same conclusion for belief in that topic as well.[19]

But what if we *do* draw the same conclusion, what, then? As Cameron points out, the issue then becomes one of why one should embrace the one outlook rather than the other. Why belief rather

than unbelief? Although at times tempted to embrace a version
of Pascal's wager, Cameron shows that Newman is again highly
original in the way he tackles this question. He suggests that
reflection on our common experience of conscience may lead us
to a sense of a transcendent God. Perhaps Newman is relying too
much on the *common* character of an appeal to conscience, not
taking into account how varied a phenomenon conscience can be.
That apart, however, Cameron is correct in addressing himself
to the issue of the *sense* in which such reflection may *lead* someone
to belief in God or some understanding of it. He points out that
Newman cannot mean that as a *matter of fact* such reflection leads
to belief, or that in the event of it not leading to it, a person would
be guilty of self-contradiction in continuing to talk of conscience
without coming to these conclusions. The reflection only works
for someone who has a rudimentary belief already or who, maybe,
is making rudimentary moves in that direction. Now, it will be
said, if the reflective move from conscience to God is itself part
of some kind of predisposition to make the move, the whole
sequence, as an argument, is viciously circular. So it is, but
Newman had already come to the conclusion that you could not
argue your way to religious belief in the way evidentialism
assumed. What he is talking about here, is something different.
Cameron says,

> The solution to the difficulty is, I believe, this. In neither
> case are we faced with an *argument* in the usual sense. In
> neither case is there a movement from premises to
> conclusion. We are faced rather with an insight or an
> intuition — these are unfortunate and much-abused words
> but I can think of no better ones — which can indeed be
> *analysed,* and this is what we do if we say that a scrutiny of
> conscience leads us to a belief in God or that an act of
> cruelty being what it is is evidence for its being morally bad.
> Such an analysis has meaning and carries conviction only
> to those who share the insight or intuition and *recognise* the
> analysis as a true explication of what they already possess.
> This is why in the field of ethics and religion, the field of
> what Newman calls 'moral truth', we tend to use the
> ambiguous language of feeling and to suppose that in this
> field a different mode of reasoning is appropriate, a different
> logic; perhaps, to echo Pascal yet again, a 'logic of the
> heart'.[20]

Cameron does not think philosophers should have to excuse themselves for making observations of this kind. He says

> To suppose that in the fields of morality and religion we can use the same criteria as those we use in history, natural science and mathematics is as absurd as to suppose that we can employ moral and religious criteria to determine questions of science or formal logic. Such a mistake springs from our failure to recognise that religious utterances have (to use the terminology of some philosophers of today) their own logical grammar.[21]

Yet having said that, it must be admitted that Cameron's use of terms like 'insight' and 'intuition' are unfortunate. Although this is not his intention, they are associated with images of sudden graspings of meaning or flashes of inspiration, associations which play down the reflective context in which, after all, Newman and Cameron are insisting these 'insights' or 'intuitions' occur. More seriously, Cameron's 'solution' does not address itself to the important problem he claims Newman poses for us. Having seen that belief and unbelief are not competing hypotheses to be assessed by a sovereign reason to which they are both subject, the question posed concerned *the choice* between belief or unbelief; why one *rather than* the other? It is no solution to this question to be given examples of reflections which work for those who *already* believe. Surely, Cameron needs to take his own closing remarks more seriously where he recognises the grammatical differences involved. In 'Newman and Empiricism' he stresses how Newman emphasises the fundamental role which action plays in religious belief, the role of a commitment in which religious belief has its life, but he still does not get to grips with the important question he posed for us. How would one man pass from not understanding the grammar of religious belief to understanding it? How would a person pass from unbelief to belief?

We have seen a more promising answer in our exposition of Wittgenstein's *On Certainty*: when reasons come to an end, there is *persuasion*. Of course, this term is as dangerous in its way as those which Cameron used. This is especially the case if we think of persuasion as an *alternative* means of convincing someone, as when we say, 'When reason fails, try persuasion' or as when we refer to persuasive as distinct from rational methods. That is not what

Wittgenstein has in mind. The kind of persuasion he has in mind is a form of imaginative elucidation, something which will bring about the dawning of an aspect not previously appreciated. We must not forget, once again, that, for Wittgenstein, the basic propositions he discusses in *On Certainty* are not foundations, not prior assumptions. On the contrary, they are held fast by all that surrounds them. The persuasion, if it occurs, will be persuasion in the context of trying to make all that surrounds what is basic come alive. When the surroundings come alive, what is basic also comes alive; it is, Wittgenstein says, swallowed down with it. This is not a matter of grounding from without. Our beliefs, in this context, are groundless. But it is a matter of elucidating from within. In such elucidation the belief may or may not come alive for the listener. Think of the way we speak of *instruction* in the Faith. But what we hear may come alive in different ways. One way is where we say, 'Now I see the kind of thing it is', where we understand something we did not understand before. Another way is where we say 'I believe it' where we actively embrace that to which we were passive before. The difference in these modes of acceptance are shown in the way they enter our lives. The possibility of this elucidation, which may have no effect, of course, or which may lead in the directions I have indicated, seems to me to contrast with the relative isolation of foundational religious beliefs to which we have already called attention in Reformed epistemology. It also contrasts sharply with the negative character of apologetics in that epistemology. What Wittgenstein has to say with regard to persuasion shows the possibility of giving a perspicuous representation of religious beliefs, but not for apologetic purposes, without any implication of methods of proof which claim to be neutral as between belief and unbelief.

It does not seem to me that the scope of these exciting possibilities in epistemology have been appreciated by Jamie Ferreira. She finds ambiguity in Cameron's claim, on the one hand, that Newman deepened Hume's empiricism by showing that the logical issues were deeper than he had supposed, and his claim, on the other hand, that religious certainties are grammatically different from other kinds of certainties. She says that this latter claim implies 'that Newman did not think we could get speculative certainty in religion'.[22] Ferreira then gives quotations to show how Newman distinguished between practical and speculative certainty where the former would be a case of taking something as true 'for practical purposes'. My aim is not to get embroiled in problems of interpretation, where Newman is concerned, but, if *that* is the kind of practical certainty Ferreira has in mind, it is not what Cameron has been talking about or what Wittgenstein meant in his emphasis on the primacy of *action.* Wittgenstein is not saying that in learning to sit on chairs, set tables, climb stairs, etc., we are learning to act *as if* there are chairs, tables and stairs for practical purposes. His point is that it is in these responses that the concepts of chairs, tables, stairs have their grammar and their life. According to Cameron, Newman is not contrasting the practical and the speculative in such contexts, but, rather, through the originality of his epistemological insights, endeavouring to shift our conception of that very contrast. He is suggesting that the very possibility of speculating about truth or falsity is rooted in contexts where active responses are taken for granted in relation to the subject being discussed. Speculation itself depends, in the end, on ungrounded practice. It is in doing so that he opens up the new possibilities for philosophical discussion we have been noting.

There are indications, however, that it is precisely the character of these epistemological insights which eludes Ferreira. This can be shown in considering the way she endeavours to show that doubt is compatible with religious commitment. This doubt she wants to discuss, however, does not lead to any practical uncertainty. A doubt which did lead to such uncertainty would be incompatible with the absolute commitment Newman says the Faith calls for. It bids us to feel ashamed of such doubts. What kind of doubt, then, does Ferreira have in mind? Is Newman referring to logical dubitability? If he were, Newman would be pointing out that our ability to frame the contradictory of a true proposition need not constitute reasonable grounds for practical doubt. For example, if I am sitting in a room full of friends, I can construct the proposition, 'I am not sitting in a room full of friends,' but this does not give me the slightest reason to doubt the facts of my situation. Ferreira argues that Newman has in mind the possibility of a more-than-logical doubt. 'Not p is "really" possible — possible without changing the constitution of the world as we know it — yet it cannot "come to pass in matter of fact" in a given case. Thus, more-than-logical dubitability does not necessarily provide reasonable grounds for doubt.'[23] For Newman, actual assent is not withdrawn while the truth of the proposition is being investigated. Of course, this suggestion, so far, would be consistent with the negative apologetics of Reformed epistemology. One's religious practice is innocent until proved guilty. One may believe that every objection will in fact be overcome although there is always the possibility that an objection will occur which one will not be able to meet. Until then, one lives in trust.

Ferreira reaches similar conclusions by attempting to assimilate Newman's more-than-logical doubt with Wittgenstein's discussion in *On Certainty* of the possibility of other ways of thinking and doing things. As we have seen, Wittgenstein's primary purpose in these examples is a logical one, namely, to rid us of the idea that our ways of doing things are underpinned by some kind of necessity. Such an underpinning it seems, would be given in Ferreira's unexplained reference to 'the unchanging constitution of the world'. Wittgenstein's view is not, as Ferreira seems to think, that since we cannot have knowledge of this constitution, we must act on trust. On this view, we justify our epistemic practices by faith without knowing whether they correspond to reality. If Newman were saying this, he would be close to the Reformed epistemologist. But, of course, he would also inherit all the difficulties we have seen to be associated with that view.

Whatever of that, what can be said is that this is not Wittgenstein's view. For Wittgenstein, a fundamental shift in our epistemic practices would constitute a fundamental change in our world-view. Such shifts would not be shifts in hypotheses, where the world remains unchanged as something existing independently of them all. We are back to the view that the grammar of our language is a description of the world as it actually is. Ferreira quotes a paragraph in *On Certainty* in support of her reading of Wittgenstein where in fact her reading is exactly what he is opposing. Wittgenstein has been emphasising that when we claim to know something we can often be asked for our grounds. He says that, within our language-games, these grounds can be provided. For example, I say I know there is a chair in the next room because I've just checked that this is so. But, then, what if we are asked why such grounds are good grounds? We are tempted to say that we *know* they are good grounds, which suggests that we have further grounds for saying so. Here, Wittgenstein says, we are trying to use 'know' outside the restricted contexts in which it makes sense to do so. For that reason, Wittgenstein says, 'But as soon as I say this sentence outside its context, it appears in a false light. For then it is as if I wanted to insist that there are things that I *know*. God himself can't say anything to me about them.'[24] Ferreira reads this as meaning that beyond all our epistemic practices there is the unchanging knowledge of how things are which God possesses. We trust that our practices correspond to it, but we can never know. But that is exactly what Wittgenstein is denying! He is saying that not even God himself could tell us anything about such a speculation because it does not make sense. To think of God otherwise, as Ferreira seems to do, is to have a conception of God which is as metaphysical as the suppositions which lead one to embrace it.

In discussing Reformed epistemology, we have had reason in this chapter, and on other occasions, to comment on the relatively isolated character of belief in God as a foundational proposition in the noetic structure. God is an object of trust, his reality lying behind all there is. In Ferreira's analysis which we have just invoked, God seems to be a limited conception, a regulative idea beyond our epistemic practices. Of course, we trust he is there, but we can never know this. This transcendental foundationalism is foreign to the whole tenor of Wittgenstein's *On Certainty*. The basic propositions which he discusses are not grounded in a something we know not what beyond our epistemic practices. On the contrary, they are said to be held fast by all that surrounds them. Just like 'Physical objects exist' or 'Human beings exist' so 'God exists' should be explored in this way.[25] It is in this context that we should look to see what is meant by the inescapable reality of God. Yet, when we turn to look at the ways in which Reformed epistemologists have sought to discuss God's inescapability, further difficulties await us.

Notes

1. Wittgenstein, *On Certainty*, para. 71.
2. John Calvin, *Institutes of the Christian Religion*, trans. John Allen (Presbyterian Board of Publication, Philadelphia, 1813), vol. I, bk. 1, ch. 1, pp. 47-8.
3. Wittgenstein, *On Certainty*, para. 338.
4. See Part Four.
5. Stephen J. Wykstra, 'Plantinga versus evidentialism: relocating the issue', unpublished paper.
6. Ibid.
7. Alston, 'Christian Experience and Christian Belief', p. 106.
8. Wittgenstein, *On Certainty*, paras. 130 and 131.
9. Alston, 'Christian Experience and Christian Belief', p. 132.
10. John Henry Newman, *Sermons Chiefly on the Theory of Religious Belief, preached before the University of Oxford* (1843), p. 189. Quoted by James Cameron in 'Newman and Empiricism' in his *The Night Battle* (Helicon Press, Baltimore, 1962), p. 232.
11. David Hume, *A Treatise of Human Nature*, ed. L.A. Selby-Bigge, (Clarendon Press, Oxford, 1896), p. 270.
12. Ibid., p. 187.
13. John Henry Newman, 'Lectures on the Scripture Proof of the Doctrines of the Church', *Tracts for the Times*, no. 85, 2nd edn, 1840, p. 72.
14. Wittgenstein, *Investigations*, vol. 1, p. 420.
15. Hume, *Treatise*, p. xx.
16. I think this conclusion is premature, the case of morals being close to that of religious belief.
17. Cameron, *The Night Battle*, p. 229. Quotation from David Hume, 'The Natural History of Religion' in his *Essays and Treatises on Several Subjects*, a new edition, 1822, vol. 11, p. 449. This apparent open-mindedness is quite consistent with my stronger view that when *actual* philosophical arguments for religion are considered, they can be shown to harbour *logical* confusions and, therefore, could not *possibly* be valid.
18. Newman, *Sermons*, p. 206. Quoted by Cameron in 'The Logic of the Heart' in *The Night Battle*, pp. 210-11.
19. Kenyon, 'Doubts about the Concept of Reason', p. 264.
20. Cameron, 'The Logic of the Heart', *The Night Battle*, p. 216.
21. Ibid., pp. 217-18.
22. M. Jamie Ferreira, *Doubt and Religious Commitment* (Clarendon Press, Oxford, 1980), p. 47, fn. 49.
23. Ibid., p. 93.
24. Wittgenstein, *On Certainty*, para. 554.
25. For a discussion of this point see Phillips, *Religion Without Explanation*, ch. 10.

7
A Reformed Epistemology?

We saw, at the outset, that the notion of God's inescapable reality is hardly captured by the war of competing probabilities to which foundationalism reduces disputes between belief and unbelief. At best, the prize for winning the dispute is the right to say, 'It is highly probable that God exists'. Reformed epistemology endeavours to do justice to the foundational character of religious belief, and to the notion of God's inescapable reality. Therefore, as we have seen, they resist the notion of a sovereign reason to which religious belief is answerable. For them, anyone who admits to such a conception of reason as a measure by which belief in God is to be assessed becomes 'an unwitting tool of the Enlightenment, of rational humanism'.[1] At the same time, however, *within* the Reformed epistemologists' view of religious belief there is the conception of a God who is sovereign over all things, reason included. There is a tension, therefore, between Plantinga's emphasis on negative apologetics and the temptation to think that belief in an all-embracing God should yield, in the Christian philosopher, an all-embracing metaphysical system. For the believing philosopher who can see things clearly, it may be thought, the sovereignty of God, which he acknowledges as a believer, should be reflected in his philosophy in the working out of an epistemology which is itself sovereign over all alternatives. No doubt a believer does not have to give himself to philosophy, but *if* he did, then a proper use of reasoning, it is said, should lead to this result.

Garry Gutting's concern is with the fact that this result has not been forthcoming in contemporary philosophy of religion. Though highly complimentary about the work Plantinga and I have done, he expresses considerable misgivings about what he regards as our self-imposed philosophical limitations: 'They've both done excellent work in showing the confusions and *non sequiturs* of intellectual attacks on belief, but they give us little idea of why we should believe or why they themselves believe.'[2] Further, he suggests that we should at the very least be concerned to find that, in this respect, we are at odds with a long tradition of Christian apologetics:

> You keep saying that positive apologetics is wrong-headed. But what of the long tradition it has within the Christian church? Augustine's *City of God* was written to argue for the superiority of Christianity to its pagan rivals, to, as he said, 'persuade the proud how great is the virtue of humility'. Thomas Aquinas wrote his *Summa contra Gentiles* to argue for the truth of the Catholic faith against Jewish and Moslem nonbelievers ... But even after the Reformation and among Christians who put a very strong emphasis on the limits of reason and the need for grace, we find the tradition of positive apologetics strong. Think of Pascal, with the elaborate scheme for his *Apology* or Schleiermacher's *Speeches on Religion to its Cultured Despisers,* specifically designed to convince romantic pagans of the intellectual credibility of Christianity. From the days of the Fathers on, there has been a series of major Christian thinkers who have been strikingly successful in making a case for Christianity to nonbelieving intellectuals. Pascal even made Voltaire feel uncomfortable at his 'shadow across the path' to a rejection of Christianity. But contemporary nonbelievers can read the very best current Christian philosophers (and theologians too, but that's another matter) and feel entirely unchallenged in their nonbelief. At most, they'll be more cautious in condemning Christians for believing.[3]

The first thing to be said about my own work in response to these charges is that I do not conceive of it as the work of a Christian philosopher or a Christian scholar. Hopefully, it is the work of a philosopher endeavouring to become clear about a cluster of beliefs which have been and are extremely important in the lives of men and women. The aim is not to persuade people to believe, but to understand the character of their beliefs. The aim is not to persuade them that there is a God, but to see what it may mean to be so persuaded. As we have seen, Plantinga's concerns are the concerns of a Christian philosopher asking whether Christians have a right to believe what they say they believe. He thinks it can be shown, by means of negative apologetics, that no known philosophical argument can deprive them of this right. Of course, in so far as I have been concerned to understand the character of religious belief, I too have concluded that the philosophical attacks on the intelligibility of religious belief have, for the most part, been due to confused understandings of its character. Yet, these differences apart, Gutting's concerns do raise important philosophical issues which bring them within the orbit of the work I take myself to be engaged in. What I mean is this: if I can get a philosopher to see that his objections to religious belief are confused, he may or may not become a believer as a result. Nevertheless, he must appreciate something about the character of religious belief which he did not appreciate before. As we saw in the previous chapter, this in itself takes us, in certain respects, beyond the limits of negative apologetics. This is more important than we may realise, and we shall return to this issue later in the chapter.

For the moment, however, let us stay with the responses of Reformed epistemologists to the tensions I have mentioned. The lack of emphasis on positive apologetics may have led Gutting to underestimate the extent of their metaphysical ambitions. It might be assumed that epistemology's task is limited to noting the various noetic structures and taking account of what is basic in each of them. After all, we have been told that practices are innocent until proved to be guilty and that the epistemological resources for such a proof are, in a large number of cases, unavailable. From this it might be assumed that, for the time being at least, the noetic structures which exclude belief in God from their foundational beliefs should be deemed innocent too. But, here, matters become complicated. Once it can be shown that there is no reason why a believer should not have belief in God in the foundations of his noetic structure, the content and character of that belief has implications for what can be said of other noetic structures. The judgement on other noetic structures from within the religious noetic structure is necessitated, it seems, by belief in a sovereign God. But, as we shall see, in the elucidation of what is involved in such judgement, there is a constant danger of turning religious beliefs into epistemological theories.

In order to do justice to the character of religious belief, Reformed epistemologists also insist that the whole religious noetic structure with its foundational beliefs is, in fact, true. This can only be believed. It cannot be proved. Nevertheless, that *is* what is believed, trusted in. It follows, then, that when Reformed epistemologists ask whether there can be a religious epistemology, they are asking for far more than an epistemology of religion. The latter would be familiar enough. It would consist in asking epistemological questions concerning religion that are asked of other human activities as well. In this way, important grammatical differences may come to light; for example, surrounding the use of 'existence' where God's existence is concerned:

If the question arises as to the existence of God, it plays an entirely different role to that of the existence of any person or object I ever heard of. One said, had to say, that one *believed* in the existence, and if one did not believe, this was regarded as something bad. Normally if I did not believe in the existence of something no one would think there was anything wrong in this.[4]

Making observations such as these is not what is proposed by the possibility of a Reformed epistemology. What is being proposed is an epistemology, a mode of enquiry, which is itself religious in character. Since epistemologies are regarded as theories or hypotheses about the nature of reality, which are either true or false, Reformed philosophers cannot tolerate a plurality of noetic structures. There is an issue of correctness or incorrectness involved. There can only be one true theory of knowledge. It seems that, according to the Reformed philosophers we are considering, they trust that the only true theory of knowledge is not only religious, but Christian; not only Christian, but Protestant; not only Protestant, but Calvinistic. Of course, even within the Reformed tradition there are further differences. What is essential to note is that a true theory of knowledge is one which gives a true account of reality. This brings us back full circle to problems we have already discussed. My aim, at this point, is not to reopen them, but to show how they set the scene for the problem of the relation of the religious noetic structure to non-religious or irreligious noetic structures. In some sense or other it is clear that, for Reformed epistemology, the non-religious structures have to be deficient. But the difficulties facing the very *possibility* of a Reformed epistemology become apparent when we try to explicate this sense.

Can Reformed epistemologists say that the adherents to non-religious noetic structures are mistaken? When we ordinarily speak of someone having made a mistake, we think of him as someone engaged in the same activity as the person who is correct with respect to the matter in hand. A simple example would be the case of an arithmetical mistake. The person who makes a mistake in calculating is governed by the same criteria of correctness as the person who calculates correctly. The criteria are found in the activity in which they both participate, and it is by reference to them that the mistake is pointed out and corrected. Here the criteria are formal, but essentially the same point can be made where the criteria are informal. For example, a person may say, 'You were mistaken when you said that he married her for her money.' When this person corrects the mistake, he does not change his conception or that of his friend of what it is to marry a woman for her money. It is in terms of this conception that the discovery of the mistake is made. He finds out, that his friend was factually wrong in this particular case, that is all. Both share a common standard of behaviour, but one finds out that he had made a mistake in applying it. In the arithmetical example and in the case of the personal judgement, both participants, it may be said, take part in a procedure which is independent of them individually. The meanings involved are neutral in relation to the two participants. Judgements of correctness or incorrectness are made within these agreed criteria.

Let us now go back to the question of whether Reformed philosophers can say that those who exclude God from their noetic structures are mistaken. Do we find, in this case, too, that those who say persons are mistaken share common criteria which would be accepted by the persons said to be mistaken? Put differently, do we have, in this case, too, meanings which are neutral with respect to the participants? Notoriously, the answer must be that we do not. This is a fact which Reformed philosophers are not only happy to assent to, but which they go out of their way to emphasise. Cornelius Van Til is happy to accept the following description of his presuppositionalist viewpoint which he quotes: 'They have held that it is impossible to prove the existence of God to an unbeliever; that one must *assume* his existence as a basis for argument with an unbeliever, because the unbeliever and the believer have no common ground on which they can meet in argument.'[5] But, in that case, how is the believer to convince the unbeliever; does not the very possibility of it depend on a neutral common ground? After all, the Christian wants the non-Christian to forsake his position.

It is extremely important to note that, in one respect, Reformed philosophers share a common assumption with foundationalists: they take for granted that unless there is *common* ground between believers and unbelievers, believers would have no justification for saying that the unbeliever is in the wrong. Where they differ is in the foundationalists' claim that this common ground is common *neutral* ground, namely, the weighing of probabilities in terms of evidence available to believer and unbeliever alike. This is what Reformed philosophers deny. But a denial of neutral common ground is not a denial of common ground. The reasons why common ground is denied is obvious enough: time and time again, as the history of theology and philosophy shows, when religious belief is submitted to allegedly neutral criteria of assessment, its character is distorted. It is subjected to criteria which are quite alien to it. The absurd result is that religious belief is asked to answer to tests of intelligibility which are inapplicable and inappropriate in the first place.

But what common ground can be appealed to if neutral common ground is unavailable? The answer of Reformed philosophers is: that common ground which actually represents the situation accurately, namely, Christianity itself. An appeal is made to Calvin's view that God implanted an innate tendency in all men to know him:

We lay it down as a position, not to be contraverted, that the human mind, even by natural instinct, possesses some sense of a Deity. For that no man might shelter himself under the pretext of ignorance, God hath given to all some apprehension of his existence, the memory of which he frequently and insensibly renews; so that men universally know that there is a God, and that he is their Maker, they must be condemned by their own testimony, for not having worshipped him and consecrated their lives to his service. If we seek for ignorance of a Deity, it is nowhere more likely to be found, than among tribes the most stupid and furthest from civilization. But, as the celebrated Cicero observes, there is no nation so barbarous, no race so savage, as not to be firmly persuaded of the being of a God. Even those who in other respects appear to differ but little from brutes, always retain some sense of religion; so fully are the minds of men possessed with this common principle, which is closely interwoven with their original composition. Now, since there has never been a country or family, from the beginning of the world, totally destitute of religion, it is a tacit confession, that some sense of the Divinity is inscribed on every heart.[6]

As we shall see, Calvin's view cannot be constructed from this passage alone. It is difficult to extract a consistent reading from the different emphases in what he has to say. For the moment, let us confine our attention to what Reformed philosophers have made of his remarks, to return later to other possible readings of what he has to say. From the passage we have quoted, it does not look as if Calvin intends his remarks to be an *a priori* pronouncement. Man's natural tendency to have some sense of a Deity is not evidence on which belief in God is based, but Calvin *is* offering evidence for the existence of this natural tendency. In fact, it is odd to call it a tendency, since, on this reading, all men have a sense of the divine. Nature never permits them to forget it. These matters are said by Calvin to be beyond controversy. In fact, their sense is hard to determine.

If it is said that everyone has some sense of the Divine, what is to be said of the many people who say that they do not? The Reformed philosophers say that, in these cases, the knowledge is still present, but has been overlaid and obscured by sin. Sin is introduced into the account as a fundamental explanatory concept. But what kind of explanation is it? Compare the following: 'I cannot play football because of my cartilage trouble' and 'I cannot resist temptation because of my weak will.' In the first case, the cause of the trouble is identifiable quite independently of its consequence. The cartilage trouble is one thing, the inability to play football another. But in the case of weakness of will this is not so. The weakness of will is not identifiable independently of the failure to resist temptation. That failure *is* the weakness. What makes the weakness of the will seem to be an independent explanation is that others can be told of a person's weak-willed disposition. We may say, 'He won't stand by you because he's too weak.' Here, a prediction is made on the basis of what is known of the person involved. But if we were asked why we said he was weak-willed, we would have to appeal to acts such as not standing by someone when the occasion demanded it.

When we speak of someone being in the grip of sin, our remark is grammatically akin to the reference to weakness of the will. So in what sense does the reference to sin *explain* man's separation from God? Why are men separated from God? Reply: sin. What is sin? Reply: separation from God. If, in describing the separation, we are describing the sin, in what sense does the latter explain the former? Again, the reference to a sinful disposition in a person may mislead us in this context. We may say, 'He won't resist the temptation because he is in the grip of sin.' Here, we are making a prediction based on what we know of the person. Where that temptation is concerned, he won't resist it, because he is in the grip of sin. But 'being in the grip of sin' is not contingently related to the falling to temptation, since if asked to expound what is meant by 'being in the grip of sin', we would have to refer to the innumerable times on which he had fallen to temptation. An added consideration in this context may explain the confusion of treating sin as causally related to being separated from God, or as the explanation of the separation. If we want to explain the attractiveness of temptations, money, position, etc, we should have to refer to the prestige and status of much that tempts people. That prestige and status cannot be explained by reference to the individual alone. That prestige and status exist in the community whether he likes it or not and it may tempt him. Sin walks abroad. Nevertheless, when he *is* tempted, this does not have the *consequence* of separating him from God. It is part of what we mean by such separation.

Let us now return to our main problem. Reformed philosophers say that all men have some sense of the Divine. Obviously, some men say that they do not. This is explained by reference to sin. But the sin, in this case, would be the denial of knowledge of God. Therefore, so far, nothing has been explained. The problem seems to remain: on the one hand, the Reformed philosophers want to say that God has inscribed knowledge of himself on the hearts of all men in such a way that nature never allows them to forget it; and on the other hand they have to admit that there are many who deny all knowledge of God. Given this understanding of the problem, there is only one solution to it, a solution which Reformed philosophers embrace. All the emphasis has to be put on saying that knowledge of God is *overlaid* by sin. In other words, although the sin does not explain the separation from God, the correct description of the sin is as *overlaid knowledge*. In other words, there must be something about the denial of those who say they have no knowledge of God, some features of their separation from God, such that even when they deny all knowledge of God, there is something about their denial which shows that they still have knowledge of him. This answer, if plausible, would indeed meet the problem facing the Reformed philosophers. They would now be able to say that all men have knowledge of God because those who deny knowledge of him are in the grip of self-deception. If this could be established, it would also show the nature of the common ground which exists between believer and unbeliever and which enables the former to assess the latter. The unbeliever is in the grip of self-deception when he denies knowledge of God. Therefore, on his own terms, if he understood his situation, he would see that he knew God. But knowledge of God is precisely what the believer possesses. This knowledge, explicit in the believer, overlaid in the unbeliever, is the common ground which makes it possible for the former to judge the latter. Van Til puts the matter bluntly: 'The Christian knows the truth about the non-Christian.'[7] Such a claim is an extremely ambitious one. If it could be established, it would achieve everything Reformed philosophers seek in their claim that the believer can only judge the non-believer if there is common ground between them. But, as we shall see, the ambition of the claim is its undoing, inheriting new difficulties for it which cannot be answered.

Understood in a modified form, the thesis presents no difficulty. The claim would simply be that many who deny all knowledge of God are deceiving themselves. Such a claim has to be proved in the particular case. There may be features of a person's behaviour, various tensions and strategies, which lead us to say that he is deceiving himself. We may say that he protests too much. My aim, at this point, is not to explore in detail the logic of this kind of self-deception,[8] but simply to point out that the presence of self-deception, in this sense, is something which has to be established. Sometimes Calvin seems to be responding to just such a challenge. The denials of the unbeliever are shown in their true colours when certain crises engulf him: 'But if any despair oppress them, it stimulates them to seek him, and dictate concise prayers, which prove that they are not altogether ignorant of God, but that what ought to have appeared before had been suppressed by obstinacy.'[9] That being so, it makes sense to say that self-deception may or may not be present in the case under examination, and, of course, this may be said of the believer as well as the unbeliever. When a man says he has knowledge of

God, or when a man denies all knowledge of him, *he may or may not* be in the grip of self-deception. But this modified and modest claim is insufficient to meet the ambitions of the Reformed philosophers. They are not content to say that unbelievers *may* be deceiving themselves; they say they *must* be deceiving themselves. Van Til says, 'How then we ask is the Christian to challenge this non-Christian approach to the interpretation of human experience? He can do so only if he shows that man *must* presuppose God as the final reference point in predication... He can do so only if he shows the non-Christian that he cannot deny God unless he must first affirm him.'[10] This thesis about the *necessary* presence of self-deception, in the sense discussed, in the unbeliever, cannot be maintained. Reformed philosophers give a number of examples to illustrate their thesis, but, as we shall see, none of them achieve the desired result.

The first of these is Van Til's suggestion that 'The unbeliever is the man with yellow glasses on his face. He sees himself and his world through these glasses.'[11] For a moment, let us consider the case of a colour-blind person. In his case, it can be said that his very description of his condition invokes the standard from which he deviates. After all, he is blind to something. This is something he finds out, and while this does not mean he is cured of his colour-blindness, he learns to cope with it. The same may be said of other deficiencies of sight. Our common reactions in what come to be regarded as standard conditions set the parameters of the normal. In this sense, the standards set are neutral as between individuals. But, for Reformed philosophers, there is no neutral common ground between the believer and the unbeliever. In saying that he does not know God, so far from invoking a norm he recognises, the unbeliever is denying that there is such a norm. It is a travesty of what he is saying, and a mere begging of the question, to compare him with a colour-blind person. The same distinctions apply to a man who wears coloured spectacles. By calling the spectacles coloured, he is already admitting that what he sees through them deviates from the colours things have in reality. He learns the distinction by putting on the glasses, taking them off, and noting the changes in how things look through the glasses. Of course, the unbeliever need make no such admission. His standards need not be distortions of anything. They are simply different standards. One cannot escape from the logical deficiencies of the analogy by saying that the person cannot remove his glasses,[12] or that 'these coloured

103

glasses are cemented to his face'.[13] The logical distinctions do not depend on the contingency of whether a person can, in fact, remove his coloured glasses, but in what it means to call the glasses coloured. If the glasses can be removed, the person can be taught, like everyone else, the distinction between appearance and reality where colours are concerned. If the glasses cannot be removed, he finds himself in the same position as the colour-blind person, and will acknowledge this as the colour-blind man does. Such acknowledgements can be understood because to talk of colour-blindness and coloured glasses is already to invoke the norm on which such talk is logically parasitic. What the Reformed philosophers have not even begun to show is how viewpoints which deny all knowledge of God are, *in the same way*, logically parasitic on a standard, in this case, knowledge of God, which such viewpoints are supposed to invoke.

The second example which attempts to show that a man who denies knowledge of God really has knowledge of him relies on the presence of a troubled conscience in the unbeliever. Van Til argues:

> Even man's negative ethical reaction to God's revelation within his own psychological constitution is revelational of God. His conscience troubles him when he disobeys; he knows deep down in his heart that he is disobeying his creator. There is no escape from God for any human being. Every human being is by virtue of his being made in the image of God accessible to God. As such he is accessible to one who without compromise presses upon him the claims of God. Every man has capacity to reason logically. He can intellectually understand what the Christian position claims to be. Conjoined with this is the moral sense that he knows he is doing wrong when he interprets human experience without reference to his Creator.[14]

Van Til may well have in mind men whose denials or protests against God reveal a longing for him. One can locate signs of a troubled conscience even in their acts of denial or rebellion. No one would want to deny such cases. Calvin seems to have such cases in mind when he says,

> They try every refuge to hide themselves from the Lord's presence, and to efface it from their minds; but their attempts

to elude it are all in vain. Though it may seem to disappear for a moment, it presumably returns with increased violence; so that, if they have any remission of the anguish of conscience, it resembles the sleep of persons intoxicated, or subject to frenzy, who enjoy no placid rest while sleeping, being continually harassed with horrible and tremendous dreams. The iniquitous themselves, therefore, exemplify the observation, that the idea of God is never lost in the human mind.[15]

But this is hardly enough to establish Van Til's claims. He has to say that these features are a *necessary* feature of all ethical protests against religion. But those who utter ethical protests against religion need have no troubled consciences. On the contrary, they may believe that it is those who believe in God who should have troubled consciences. They do not know deep down in their hearts that they are wrong, or that they are disobeying their Creator. On the contrary, they may know deep down in their hearts that they are in the right, and that there is no Creator. I am talking here about what such people would say and their psychological state. There is no reason to accept Van Til's claims regarding what these *must* constitute. At the heart of his confusion is his assumption that the religious assertion that no man escapes God's demands and depends on metaphysical theses about ethical protests against religion such as those he is propounding.

The third example is similar to the one we have just considered. It must not be thought, it is said, that the denial of God is always self-conscious. On the contrary, God, by his general grace, allows a man to be better than the principles he adopts. As Van Til says, 'He will live a "good" normal life. He will be anxious to promote the welfare of his fellow men. In all this he is not a hypocrite. He is not sufficiently self-conscious to be a hypocrite.'[16] Therefore, since in denying God, his conduct, 'his principle', as Van Til puts it, 'drives him on to the swine trough', some account must be given of his good deeds. God, by his general grace, allows him to perform such deeds. The explanation is that in saying he is free of God he is deceiving himself. 'Like the prodigal of the scriptural parable he cannot forget the father's voice and the father's house.'[17] This view may or may not be acceptable as a religious perspective on the morality of the unbeliever, but it claims to be more than that. It locates some residue of knowledge of God in the unbeliever. Again, the point is not to deny that this may be the case, but to deny that it *must* be the case. Van Til tends to talk of morality as if it were one thing. He is then able to talk of it as the conduct required of the Christian, but which has become detached from its divine source. Even in these cases, there need be no self-deception in the sense being discussed. The morality may have become an end in itself for the unbeliever. But there are other cases where a person's perception of what is required morally of him does *not* accord with a Christian morality. It would be ludicrous to attribute *that* conduct to God's general grace, but it is conduct in accord with a morality nevertheless. To say that within these moralities there *must* be a lingering knowledge of the father does not even begin to be plausible. Van Til tends to assume that any moral viewpoint must have grown from Christianity. He speaks of the adherents as failing to forget their father's voice and house. But what if the moral view concerned owed nothing to religion, that its beginnings and developments were quite independent of religious concepts? To say that these *must* be understood as deviations from religion is simply to be guilty of a condescending misunderstanding in relation to them. Once again, the fundamental assumption is being made that to have a religious *perspective* on other moralities entails having a religious *explanation* of them. It is clear that Van Til is making this assumption from the following:

> A son that has gone away from home and has been away for a long time might suddenly be put face to face with his father. Would it be possible for him not to recognize his father for what he actually is? So impossible is it for a sinner to deny that Christianity is true. The sense of deity within him constantly gives the lie to all his theories short of the recognition of God as Creator and Judge. So also when confronted with Scripture as the Word of God the natural man can apply his reductionistic theories only at the cost of an evil conscience. He may be intellectually honest in his research. But at bottom he maintains his theories against better knowledge.[18]

If the person *is* intellectually honest, where is the realm in which he has the better knowledge? Whatever of difficulties such as these, however, the fundamental assumption which needs to be questioned is that religious belief in the inescapable reality of God entails giving an explanation of other moralities, etc., in the way the Reformed philosophers attempt to do. The question which needs to be faced is whether religion stands, or needs to stand, in an *explanatory* relation to these other possibilies.

The fourth example is more bizarre than the other three we have examined. According to Alvin Plantinga, 'The fact is, Calvin thinks, one who does not believe in God is in an epistemically substandard position — rather like a man who does not believe that his wife exists, or thinks she is a cleverly constructed robot and has no thoughts, feelings or consciousness.'[19] Plantinga does not give us any context in which we are to understand a man who behaves in this way. If he is asking us to imagine a man's actual behaviour, we are not talking about someone who is epistemically substandard, but about someone who is insane. I am taking it for granted that we are talking of a wife who is alive and who goes about her daily work in and out of the home in the normal way. I do not suppose that Plantinga would want to say that people who do not believe in God are insane. On the other hand, it may be that he is speaking of people who hold certain philosophical theories in terms of which they say (perhaps to their wives) that they cannot know that their wives exist or that they are not made of clockwork. In that case, our task would be to trace the route by which a philosopher came to these confused conclusions and attempt to rescue him from them. Here, however, there is no difference in the behaviour of the disputants in relation to the wife. They differ philosophically. But the difference between religious and non-religious perspectives is not a philosophical difference. What separates them in their beliefs and convictions is constitutive of their different ways of life. These different ways of living are not interpretations of anything more ultimate than themselves. It is one of the deepest temptations in philosophy to so regard them. Rush Rhees expresses the temptation as follows:

In considering a different system of ethics there may be a strong temptation to think that what seems to *us* to express the justification of an action must be what really justifies it there, whereas the real reasons are the reasons that are given. These *are* the reasons for *or* against the action. 'Reason' doesn't always mean the same thing; and in ethics we have to keep from assuming that reasons must really be of a different sort from what they are seen to be.[20]

In the fifth and final example, we see how Reformed philosophers are guilty of falling to the temptation of which Rhees speaks. In saying that the unbeliever does not believe because of sin, Nicholas Wolterstorff believes that 'sin' may usefully be construed as a form of ideology or rationalisation. In this respect, he thinks that believers, in their treatment of unbelievers, have much to learn from the methods of Freud and Marx:

> Given its sources, the way to relieve someone of an ideology or rationalization is not to lay in front of him or her evidence for its falsehood. Usually that won't work. One must get at those hidden dynamics and bring them to light. Critique or therapy, rather than presenting evidence, is what is required.[21]

It may be thought that although no one example we have considered need be true in the case of all unbelievers, *some* example of that kind *must* be true in all cases. To insist that unbelief always stems from a particular rationalisation may be too ambitious, but some form of rationalisation *must* be present. That is about the best that can be done for the Reformed philosophers' case. Ironically, Eugene Kamenka came to exactly the same conclusion about Feuerbach's, Freud's and Marx's attempts to show that religious belief is the product of rationalisation. Kamenka argues that while their analyses may not be true for every religious belief one considers, *some* analysis of this kind is, as a matter of fact, always true of every religious belief.[22]

It can be seen that claims relating to rationalisation are totalitarian on either side of the fence. Belief accuses unbelief and unbelief accuses belief of being the product of rationalisation. I have argued, in relation to the various attempts to explain religion away as some form of rationalisation, that the attempts violate their own procedural principles.[23] We can only accuse something of being a rationalisation if the 'real' explanation we want to substitute for it is not only intelligible to the people accused of being the victims of rationalisation, but is shown to be present in the details of the life and behaviour of the people concerned. In attempting to show how religion is a product of rationalisation, these fundamental requirements were violated by Feuerbach, Freud and Marx. But, within the contexts of the examples we have considered so far, it appears that Reformed epistemologists, too, are guilty of violating the same fundamental requirements for the legitimate use of the term 'rationalisation'. If we say that all unbelievers are in the grip of some form of rationalisation, then, as when philosophers make similar claims about all believers, we do violence to the notion of rationalisation by divorcing it from the conditions and contexts in which it has its sense.

Why have theologians felt it so important to make judgements which encompass unbelievers? The answer is, surely, that if we say man is created in God's image and that God is sovereign, man, even in his unbelief, is not placed outside God's judgement. He remains a child of God. The difficulty arises when talk of the *imago Dei* is taken to imply some kind of remnant of knowledge of God which survives man's separation from God. If we say that all knowledge of God can never be eradicated or must always be present in every man's heart, we are led into the kinds of difficulties we have been discussing. There can be no doubt that there are times when Calvin speaks in a way which inherits these difficulties. Emil Brunner says that Calvin, like Luther, employs the notion of a *remnant* of the imago. 'Therefore', Brunner concludes, 'it is not permissible to deprecate or abuse man. Even in his sin man is yet honourable, since he still bears the image of God within him, even though it be obscured and "painted over".'[24] This remark, as we shall see, contains an important religious truth, but one which is distorted if we speak of the unbeliever as distorting or painting over something he already knows. In short, we need not have recourse to accusations of self-deception, in the senses discussed, in order to say that men have no excuse for not believing in God. At times, Calvin does use such arguments, arguments which seem to allow him to reach a bold conclusion:

> Whence we infer, that this is a doctrine, not first to be learned in the schools, but which every man from his birth is self-taught, and which, though many strain every nerve to banish it from them, yet nature itself permits none to forget.[25]

There are times when Calvin argues differently. He appeals to actual distortions, as in idolatry or false worship, to show how a warped conception of God can be found in men. First idolatry: 'while experience testifies that the seeds of religion are sown by God in every heart, we scarcely find one man in a hundred who cherishes what he has received, and not one in whom they grow to maturity, much less bear fruit in due season... Their conceptions of him are formed, not according to the representations he gives of himself, but by the inventions of their own presumptuous imaginations.'[26] Second, a false worship in which men think that their sins can be eradicated by expiations which are magically efficacious without requiring any true repentance in the believer: 'That seed, which it is impossible to eradicate, a sense of the existence of a Deity, yet remains; but so corrupted as to produce only the worse of fruits.'[27] The difficulty, once again, is that if idol worship and corrupted worship are taken as *evidence* of the fact that the seeds of religion are never eradicated in the human heart, then, as in the case of self-deception, it is clear that idol worship and distortion may, but need not, necessarily, be present. In the case of the fool, in the psalm, who says in his heart, 'There is no God', Calvin takes this to be a denial of the glory due to God, but not a denial of his existence.

All these difficulties come into being if the notion of the *imago Dei* is taken to imply some kind of remnant of belief in God which is to be seen as evidence of the seeds of belief in God in all men. But need the notion be understood in this way? Instead of looking at it as providing *evidence* for religious claims, the situation is very different if we remind ourselves that the notion of the *imago Dei* is already a religious notion, one having its sense within a religious perspective. Here, what would be being said is that the unbeliever, in his unbelief, does not cease to be a child of God. This being so, the possibility of any man coming to God cannot be ruled out. That must mean, however, that that person must be capable of being addressed by God. This comes to saying that *if* he came to God, it would not be by by-passing what he already possesses. Brunner makes the point by distinguishing between a formal sense and a material sense of the *imago Dei*. The receptivity to God's word expressed in this formal sense is minimal, but important: 'This receptivity says nothing as to his acceptance or rejection of the Word of God. It is the purely formal possibility of his being addressed.'[28] To give the *imago Dei* a material sense would be to say that there is always a remnant of belief in all men. It is important to note that I am not entering the dispute as to whether there is always a remnant or never a remnant of God's image after the Fall, where that dispute has to do with how the natural world is regarded religiously. My point has to do with what it is for a person to be addressed by the Word of God. In some cases, the people addressed may be in a state of self-deception. In others the people may be idolatrous or superstitious. In other cases, the Word of God comes to a man as something entirely new in his life. It seems pointless to try to turn any of these possibilities into a universal thesis, and even more strained to attempt to make all the available counter-evidence fit such a claim. Karl Barth is correct to point out that Brunner is not consistent either in his discussion of the *imago Dei*. Although he denies that he is using the notion in any material sense, he does say such things as, 'Only a being that can be addressed is responsible, for it alone can make decisions. Only a being that can be addressed is capable of sin. But in sinning, while being responsible, it somehow or other knows of its sin. This knowledge of sin is a necessary presupposition of the understanding of the divine message of grace;'[29] and again: 'The Word of God could not reach a man who had lost his consciousness of God entirely. A man without conscience cannot be struck by the call "Repent ye and believe the Gospel." What the natural man knows of God, of the law and of his own dependence upon God, may be very confused and distorted. But even so it is the necessary, indispensable point of contact for divine grace.'[30] These claims inherit all the difficulties we have already discussed. Barth objected strongly to these suggestions because he wanted to insist that when a person truly comes to God he comes to something new, not to something he possesses imperfectly already. He pointed out that, even in the case of knowledge of God in nature,

> According to the Roman Catholic, reason, if left entirely without grace, is incurably sick and incapable of any serious theological activity. Only when it has been illumined, or at least provisionally shone upon by faith, does reason serve to produce those statements concerning God, man and the world, which, according to Roman Catholic doctrine, are not only articles of revelation but have to be considered as truths of reason. Neither the doctrine of grace which has come from the Augustinian–Thomist school, nor the Roman Catholic doctrine of knowledge which has been brought into accord with it, is as crudely Pelagian as some Protestant controversialists would make it out to be.[31]

But, now, even if Barth wants to insist on God's revelation as something new, that revelation must still illuminate what was in the person's life prior to the revelation. That is what makes it a revelation. Barth says that the revelation calls on a person to *reject* what he has prior to it. Even allowing that, it must cast light on those aspects of life which are rejected. In other words, the warring factions within the theological disputes would *all* have to recognise the necessity of mediating the sense of religious concepts. Without such mediation, we cannot show the sense the concepts have in human life; *the way in which they illuminate* must be brought out. As far as theology is concerned, the way the connections are made can be regarded as God's work, as the work of a God-given grace. In fact, *one* of the ways in which Brunner considers the problem expresses this point perfectly:

> The Word of God does not have to create man's capacity for words. He has never lost it, it is the presupposition of his ability to hear the Word of God. But the Word of God itself creates man's ability to believe the Word of God, *i.e.* the ability to hear it in *such a way* as is only possible in faith. It is evident that the doctrine of *sola gratia* is not in the least endangered by such a doctrine of the point of contact.[32]

The points of contact are not arbitrary: conscience, nature, birth, death, relations between men and women. It is in these contexts that we would look for hints in exploring the meaning of the beliefs of any religion. It is in the contexts of these points of contact that the grammar of the belief is to be explored.

Like Gutting, Brunner too is concerned about the kind of contact which must be made between religious belief and the surroundings of human life. At times, both Reformed epistemology and Barthianism can give the impression of isolating religious belief from the life that surrounds it. Of course, in stressing contacts, the relations revealed may be treated as though they were justifications. They are not, they are elucidations. Brunner is alive to the dangers:

> At this point there is a danger of the true principles being betrayed. As early as the second century the Apologists did this, and since then it has happened again and again. But the task remains. The fact that there is a false apologetic way of making contact does not mean that there is not a right way.[33]

Brunner says,

What I should say to a man on his death-bed is a holy matter;
but it is a matter no less holy how I am to say it to him in
such a way that he shall understand and appreciate it... To
despise the question of the How is a sign, not of theological
seriousness but of theological intellectualism.[34]

Brunner says that the proofs for the existence of God have been
one of the wrong ways of trying to make the connections. Gutting
is still looking for efficacious arguments such that to follow them
would be to become a believer. Plantinga rightly resists the
invitation to supply such arguments. On the other hand, his
negative apologetics are in danger of suffering from what Brunner
calls 'theological intellectualism'.

Yet, these matters are all cast in an apologetic context and
show how difficult the appropriation, and how easy the
misappropriation, of Wittgenstein's philosophy is for theology
and Reformed epistemology. The difficulty Wittgenstein's work
presents is that it stands outside the apologetic context. It is
difficult to appreciate this if philosophy is itself conceived to be
a way of assessing religious belief *pro* and *contra*. The sense in
which conceptual analysis goes beyond Plantinga's negative
apologetics is not that it provides a positive apologetics, but that
it endeavours to elucidate the kind of beliefs religious beliefs are.
In doing this the issue of concept-formation in religion becomes
central. Here is a conception of philosophy and epistemology
which is neither for nor against religion. To understand it is to
see why attempting to establish a Reformed epistemology to free
us from the confusions of foundationalism is still to remain captive
to an apologetic conception of epistemology.

Notes

1. Gary Gutting, 'The Catholic and the Calvinist: a Dialogue on Faith and Reason', *Faith and Philosophy*, vol. 2, no. 3 (July 1985), p. 254.
2. Ibid., p. 237.
3. Ibid., p. 238.
4. Wittgenstein, *Lectures and Conversations*, p. 59.
5. Van Til, *A Christian Theory of Knowledge*, pp. 255–6.
6. Calvin, *Institutes*, vol. 1, pp. 51–2.
7. Van Til, *A Christian Theory of Knowledge*, p. 18.
8. For a discussion of this kind see I. Dilman and D.Z. Phillips, *Sense and Delusion* (Routledge and Kegan Paul, London, 1971).
9. Calvin, *Institutes*, vol. 1, p. 57.
10. Van Til, *A Christian Theory of Knowledge*, p. 13.
11. Ibid., p. 259.
12. Ibid.
13. Ibid., p. 295.
14. Ibid., p. 292.
15. Calvin, *Institutes*, vol. 1, pp. 52–3.
16. Van Til, *A Christian Theory of Knowledge*, p. 225.
17. Ibid.
18. Ibid., p. 244.
19. Plantinga, 'Reason and Belief in God', p. 66.
20. Rush Rhees, 'Wittgenstein's View of Ethics' in his *Discussions of Wittgenstein* (Routledge and Kegan Paul, London, 1970), p. 103.
21. Nicholas Wolterstorff, 'Is Reason Enough?' *The Reformed Journal*, vol. 34, no. 4 (April 1981), p. 23.
22. Eugene Kamenka, *The Philosophy of Ludwig Feuerbach* (Routledge and Kegan Paul, London, 1970), p. 47.
23. Phillips, *Religion Without Explanation*, chs. 5 and 6.
24. Emil Brunner, 'Nature and Grace' in John Baillie (ed.), *Natural Theology* (Geoffrey Bles, The Centenary Press, London, 1946), p. 42.
25. Calvin, *Institutes*, vol. 1, p. 53.
26. Ibid., p. 54.
27. Ibid., p. 57.
28. Brunner, 'Nature and Grace', p. 31.
29. Ibid., p. 31.
30. Ibid., p. 32–3.
31. Karl Barth 'No!' in John Baillie (ed.), *Natural Theology* (Geoffrey Bles, The Centenary Press, London, 1946), p. 96.
32. Brunner, 'Nature and Grace', p. 32.
33. Ibid., p. 58.
34. Ibid.

8
Religious and Non-Religious Perspectives

We have seen the difficulties which are created for the conception of a Reformed epistemology by its basic assumption that to do justice to the sovereignty of God and his inescapable reality, it is necessary to devise an all-embracing metaphysical system which stands in an explanatory relation to all other possible perspectives. Since Reformed philosophers hold that no common neutral ground exists between the believer and the unbeliever, but that no judgement of the unbeliever is possible unless common ground exists, they conclude that that common ground is Christianity itself. The unbeliever can legitimately be seen as a religious phenomenon since he is essentially a prodigal son incapable of really denying or forgetting his true home. As we have seen, however, this attempt to show that all non-believers are in the grip of self-deception runs into insuperable difficulties. And so it may seem that we are caught in a hopeless philosophical tangle. On the one hand, Reformed philosophers want to say that belief in God is foundational, but on the other hand, noetic structures which exclude God do not seem to be within the orbit of religious judgement. For Reformed philosophers, this admission would severely damage their claim that belief in God is foundational.

Of course, exactly the same dilemma faces the secular rationalist or foundationalist. He has placed a certain concept of reason at the basis of his judgements. As we have seen, however, his conception of reason does not do justice to the character of religious belief. He wants to move from certain ways of thinking to the assertion that there can be no other ways of thinking. In this he is at one with the Reformed epistemologist who seeks to do exactly the same thing. Both claim that if only we thought as we ought to think, we would think as they do. He tries to underpin the way of thinking he is advocating with a metaphysical necessity. As we saw in the discussion of basic propositions in Wittgenstein's *On Certainty*, this cannot be done. To show how deep our ways of thinking go with us Wittgenstein presents us with a dramatic case which emphasises the fact:

> Is it wrong for me to be guided in my actions by the propositions of physics? Am I to say I have no good ground for doing so? Isn't precisely this what we call a 'good ground'?

> Supposing we met people who did not regard that as a telling reason. Now, how do we imagine this? Instead of the physicist, they consult an oracle. (And for that we consider them primitive.) Is it wrong for them to consult an oracle and be guided by it — If we call this 'wrong' aren't we using our language-game as a base from which to *combat* theirs?[1]

As we have already noted, Wittgenstein's point here is certainly not to suggest that we need not rely on physics in the way we do, or that we have a choice between relying on physics and consulting oracles. As always, his emphasis on other *possibilities* has as its aim the exposure of bogus notions of necessity where our ways of thinking are concerned. The postulating of the other possibilities is not meant to characterise our present ways of thinking as options, but, on the contrary, to show how deep they go with us. The logical issues remain the same when the possibilities envisaged are actually present in our world or in our society. It is interesting to observe how the actual proximity of other ways of living tempt us all too easily to fall back into the traps of essentialism. Perhaps Wittgenstein's postulation of people who consulted oracles seemed remote enough not to be worrying, but when Peter Winch began discussing witchcraft and oracles among the Azande the philosophical mood soon changed, although the philosophical issues involved were exactly the same.[2] Once again, assumptions became entrenched about the ways in which the Azande *must* be thinking, namely, our ways, and confidence was expressed in the irrationality of witchcraft. The main issue escaped most commentators. The question was not whether Winch was correct in describing the ways of the Azande, but whether he *could* have been correct or whether there is something, the ways in which we *must* think, which rules out the *possibility* of his being correct.

How much more urgent, it may be thought, is the issue concerning the relation between religious and non-religious perspectives. These are not possibilities invoked to make a logical observation, but different ways of living and of looking at life *which are actually present in our society*. It may be thought that the presence of alternatives makes Wittgenstein's treatment of basic propositions in *On Certainty* of limited value in relation to them. I want to argue that this is not so, and that a comparison of Wittgenstein's treatment of basic propositions with the basic beliefs of religion is highly instructive and relevant to our present concerns.[3]

In discussing Wittgenstein's treatment of basic propositions we saw how, with regard to many of them, they could not be denied without our being cut off from reason. This is one difference, and an important one, between basic propositions such as 'This is a tree', 'I was born', 'There is a corridor outside my door', etc., etc., and religious beliefs. The latter *are* denied. This fact may tempt one back into the foundationalist camp, to treat religious beliefs, unlike Wittgenstein's basic propositions, as alternatives within a class of propositions whose truth or falsity can be assessed by common neutral criteria. But Wittgenstein shows that religious beliefs are not of this kind. He gives the following example:

> Suppose someone is ill and he says: 'This is a punishment', and I say: 'If I'm ill, I don't think of punishment at all.' If you say: 'Do you believe the opposite?' — you can call it believing the opposite, but it is entirely different from what we would normally call believing the opposite.
>
> I think differently, in a different way. I say different things to myself. I have different pictures.
>
> It is this way: if someone said: 'Wittgenstein, you don't take illness as punishment, so what do you believe?' — I'd say: 'I don't have any thoughts of punishment.'
>
> There are, for instance, these entirely different ways of thinking first of all — which needn't be expressed by one person saying one thing, another person another thing.[4]

On the one hand, then, thinking of illness as a punishment from God is not to be construed, as evidentialists construe it, as one explanation competing within the same system with others of the same kind. On the other hand, it would be bizarre to claim, with Reformed philosophers, that every time an unbeliever is ill, deep down in his heart he knows that God is punishing him. Yet it is something basic for the believer. He does not believe it on evidence and it determines how he looks on his illness or misfortune. Yet, it can be denied. Indeed, this way of thinking may and does make some people very angry and they want to put a stop to it. There are people who do not believe it. How is the relationship between one who believes and one who does not believe to be understood in this context?

Here, we must remember that although Wittgenstein said the role of the basic propositions he was discussing was similar in different contexts, he was careful to point out that they do not constitute a distinct class of propositions. The same things cannot be said about them all. In some cases, if the familiar things you took for granted were doubted, it would be hard to see how you could go on. If, for example, I found that I could never be sure of where I was, I'd say I was going insane. In other cases, changes may enable you to go on, but not in the same way as you went on before. For example, if the behaviour of seeds were not seen to be connected with their structure, this would revolutionise our conception of botany, but it wouldn't mean that everything would have to be given up. You would go on with different emphases, emphases on what the seeds grew into, rather than on the structure of the seeds.

What light do these considerations throw on the relation of religious beliefs to other beliefs? Is it not illuminating here, too, to point out that when a person comes to see a religious sense in things, he is certainly not proving a hypothesis or relying on probabilities? Neither need he be coming to recognise something he was already deceiving himself about. No, he comes to something new, something which does not stop him going on, .but which nevertheless *demands that he does not go on in the same way*. Coming to God is not a change of opinion, but a change of direction; a reorientation of one's whole life. Using Plantinga's language, it would be to come to embrace a whole noetic structure for the first time. Of course, a person may have been deceiving himself or, in his sin, fearing God. In Benjamin Britten's opera *Billy Budd*, Claggart, in one of his arias, says, on seeing Billy's purity, that the light has shone in the darkness and that the darkness comprehends it and suffers.[5] That possibility cannot be denied, and in my criticisms of the notion of Reformed epistemology it was not denied. But Reformed philosophers tried to turn this possibility into a necessary scheme of things, so robbing it of its point and obscuring other cases. After all, it must be remembered that Britten's aria is a departure from the Biblical original where we are told that when light shone in darkness, the *darkness comprehended it not*. No question here of the darkness not comprehending against its better knowledge. No, it simply did not comprehend. This is why religion has a special word to describe the way people come to God: conversion. Coming to believe in God, then, is not to win the war of probabilities, or to be free of self-deception in the sense discussed. It is to come to something new, to be shaken at the foundations, and to make a spiritual reality basic in one's life.

It may be thought that this emphasis on conversion, on coming to God as something new, still leaves us with the issue of what right the believer has to judge the perspectives of unbelievers. Indeed, it may be thought that, in these terms, the problem becomes insuperable. But, if we think this, is it not because we are still hanging on to the assumption shared by foundationalists and Reformed philosophers, namely, that in order for one person to judge another there must be common ground between them? Without this common ground, it is thought, moral and religious judgements are impossible. But why should we accept this assumption? We are, after all, acquainted with plenty of ordinary examples to show that it is untenable. We condemn a mean action from the standpoint of generosity. We condemn pride from the standpoint of humility. We condemn unfaithfulness from the standpoint of faithfulness. No one, presumably, would deny that such judgements are made and everyone can think of scores of additional examples. But what does generosity have in common with meanness, humility have in common with pride, faithfulness have in common with unfaithfulness? Nothing, but moral judgements are made nevertheless. It would be ludicrous to suggest that there is some good better achieved by the virtues than the vices, according to some common criteria, or to suggest that inside every vicious man there is a virtuous man struggling to get out. The moral judgements that are made, despite the lack of common ground, are in terms of the virtues, not in terms of something more ultimate than them.

The same is true of religious judgements. What is appealed to, namely, what God requires of man, is not assessed by anything more ultimate than itself. Reformed philosophers should be happy to agree with this because they want to give belief in God a foundational role and to deny that God's sovereignty is answerable to anything more ultimate than itself. It is odd, therefore, that they cannot see that as long as what is done is contrary to God's will, that is sufficient *in itself* to make it the object of Christian judgement. In so far as Christianity stands in a relation of judgement to other perspectives, it need not think of them, as Marx or Freud might, as ideologies or rationalisations. When Marxism or Freudianism treats perspectives in this way, they have to say, sooner or later, that the participants in these perspectives cannot be saying or doing what they think they are doing. Christian judgement carries no such implications. *This is because its primary aim is not explanation, but judgement.* Marxism and Freudianism reject the explanations offered, because they claim to be the possessors of the real explanations. Christians, on the other hand, can accept as accurate what the perspectives they judge say they want and live by. *That* is why they are judging them. Their plans and aims need not be re-explained. If they are contrary to the will of God they are judged as sinful. Where is the logical difficulty supposed to be which prevents this judgement being made?

But, it may be asked, what about the inescapable reality of God and the claim that no man can escape his judgement? Of course, a man may escape formal punishment by some institution for the wrong he has done. Neither need he see any natural disaster under the aspect of punishment, or feel any remorse for his wrongdoing. Yet, as Plato says, the evil man is necessarily punished. What this comes to is that he is an object of pity.[6] Students often find it difficult to grasp this point. They are tempted to say that Archelaus has got away with his wrongdoing. But is not this a vulgar notion of 'getting away with it'? One way in which students come to see this is in being asked which man is in the worse state: a man who feels remorse for his despicable deeds or one who actually delights in his depravity? They have no hesitation in saying that the latter is in the worse state. Is *that* not his punishment? Surely, the same applies to the inescapable judgement of God. Sometimes, believers seem to talk as if the man who does not repent of his sins, and who does not suffer a punishment externally related to them, can be said to have escaped God's judgement. But is not this, too, a vulgar conception of what it is to escape from God's judgement? What is divine judgement other than separation from God? What more should any Christian want it to be? To pray not to be the object of divine wrath is not to pray, 'God, do not do that to me', but, rather, 'God, do not let me become that.'[7] This being so, the unrepentant sinner, the man who actually revels and rejoices in evil, has not escaped God's judgement. On the contrary, he is separated from God, an object of pity. If someone is not content with this, thinking that the person has got away with it, is he not discontented with divine punishment, wishing it were accompanied by punishments of other kinds? What we have seen is that the possibility of judgement of unbelievers, a possibility informed by a conception of the inescapable reality of God, does not entail or imply that the unbelievers are sinning against a latent better knowledge they possess, or that Christian judgement stands in an explanatory relation to them.

It may be thought that, as a result of the criticisms we have noted, religious believers have to withdraw all talk of unbelievers deceiving themselves, except in those contexts in which evidence of internal tensions in the behaviour of the person judged gives warrant for such talk. But this is not so. This is because there is a different context in which we talk about self-deception which is untouched by the criticisms we have noted. To appreciate what self-deception comes to in this context, let us think again of the example of the man who says that a person is deceiving himself in thinking that he loves a woman. He is really marrying her for her money. Here, as we saw, the judgement cannot be made without corroborating evidence in the person's behaviour. It was the absence of this corroborating evidence which led to difficulties in the Reformed philosophers' claim that the unbeliever is *always* sinning against the better knowledge of God which he knows deep down in his heart. But now consider the case in which someone says, 'All those years I thought I knew what love was, but I was deceiving myself. Now I see what love really is.' The possibility of this judgement does not depend on the person showing that throughout the years he had not really wanted what he said he had wanted, and that he had really wanted, but suppressed, what he now recognises to be really love. The realisation he comes to is a realisation of something new, something in the light of which his former life is reassessed.

It may be asked why we want to speak of self-deception in this context. Why is it not enough to say that the person was mistaken in what he thought love was? The reference to a mistake is misleading because it may give the impression of a mistake made

121

within an already existing set of values. We may think a person married someone else for her money and find out we were wrong. But, here, we find out we were wrong within an already existing set of beliefs. We do not have to change our conceptions to make such a judgement, because it is in terms of these conceptions that our judgements are made. But when a person says he has been deceiving himself about what true love is, he is not simply changing an opinion. He is changing as a person. He is not changing his mind within a set of values. His values are changing. But why talk of *self*-deception? Why not say he was deceived in what he thought previously? But by whom? The conception of love he had previously was part of him. He sustained it in his own life. When he comes to a new understanding of love, therefore, he can say with good reason, that he has been deceiving himself.[8]

The same point can be applied to the unbeliever who comes to God. Here, too, it is misleading to talk of him correcting a mistake within an already existing system of values. To come to God is to change as a person and to look back on one's previous life as a deception sustained by oneself — a self-deception. Speaking of the unbeliever from within a religious perspective, the believer may say that he is deceiving himself. What we have seen is that this judgement is possible without claiming to explain the other's condition by reference to a suppression of better latent knowledge. Giving up this claim does not rob believers of their traditional claims that when the unbeliever is deceiving himself, he is still encompassed by the inescapable reality of God.

Notes

1. Wittgenstein, *On Certainty*, paras. 608 and 609.
2. See Winch, 'Understanding a Primitive Society'.
3. I undertook such a comparison in *Religion Without Explanation*, ch.10.
4. Wittgenstein, 'Lectures on Religious Belief' in *Lectures and Conversations*, p. 55.
5. *Billy Budd*, opera by Benjamin Britten, libretto by E.M. Forster and Eric Crozier, Boosey and Hawkes, London, 1951.
6. See Peter Winch, 'Ethical Reward and Punishment' in his *Ethics and Action*, p. 226.
7. See D.Z. Phillips, *The Concept of Prayer* (paperback edition, Basil Blackwell, Oxford, 1981), p. 51.
8. For a more detailed discussion of the difference between these two kinds of self-deception, see Dilman and Phillips, *Sense and Delusion*.

9

Philosophy, Description and Religion

In all the observations made from the outset of this essay, the *descriptive* task of philosophy has been emphasised. Philosophical description can often be confused with sociological or anthropological description, especially when examples common to all these disciplines are discussed. The point of the *philosophical* descriptive task, however, cannot be appreciated if its interest is thought to be in simply pointing out that there are different ways of living, and in emphasising that attempting to force them all into a unitary account is to be guilty of a condescending misunderstanding. As we have seen, these matters are not unimportant, but they do not get us to the heart of the philosophical problems in which Wittgenstein was engaged in *On Certainty*.

These fundamental problems, as we have seen, are *logical* in character. They have had to do with Wittgenstein's treatment of basic propositions, a treatment which does justice to their fundamental character without falling into the pitfalls of foundationalism. For Wittgenstein, the basic propositions he discusses are not the foundations or presuppositions of the ways we think, and neither can the ways in which we think be derived or inferred from them. Rather, the basic propositions are held fast by all that surrounds them. They are not the bases *on* which our ways of thinking depend (foundationalism), but are basic *in* our ways of thinking.

This logical point is as true of religious ways of thinking as of any other. Here, too, the notion of God's reality is held fast in all that surrounds it; it is involved *in* the ways we think.[1] As we have seen, the fact that not everyone thinks in this way is an added factor which may tempt us back to thinking that assenting to religious truths is a matter of assessing the evidence for them, by some method which is given logically prior to the consideration of the context in which the religious truths are expressed. The role of basic propositions, these matters which we take for granted in the ways we think, determine how it is possible to say anything at all, to draw a distinction between truth and falsity, in the respective spheres. To be unable to go along with them, in many cases, would be to go insane. In all cases, it would be to cut oneself off from the possibility of the discourse in question. To be unable to see God involved in our ways of thinking is to be cut off from the possibility of talking to God; to be cut off from God in one's life. To be unable to acknowledge basic propositions is not, as we have seen, to be guilty of a mistake, but it is to be cut off from the possibility of truth or mistake. To cut oneself off from talking to God is not to make a mistake within a system of beliefs one continues to possess after such a severance. Rather it is to cut oneself off from this cluster of beliefs altogether.

The ways of thinking in which the basic propositions are held fast are not themselves founded on anything more ultimate than themselves. They are groundless. We saw how Reformed epistemology, while striving to free itself from foundationalism, could not bring itself to embrace this conclusion. It claimed that although not dependent on foundations, belief in God is not groundless. In saying it is grounded in worship and religious experience, Reformed epistemology comes, on one view, extremely close to the emphasis found in *On Certainty* whereby we would say that the existence of God is held fast, shows itself, in worship and religious experience. But the metaphysical surroundings of Reformed epistemology revealed this similarity to be more apparent than real. As we saw, a fatal tentativeness was reintroduced into Reformed epistemology, where the primary language of religion is concerned, in an appeal to prima-facie justifications which, finally, brought it nearer to foundationalism than to what Wittgenstein was trying to show.

Once philosophy has shown the fundamental roles played by basic propositions in our ways of thinking, its task is over. In showing how talk of the possibility of being mistaken in these contexts cannot get a foothold, Wittgenstein is not suggesting that our ways of thinking are optional for us. In emphasising that there is no necessity underpinning our ways of thinking, that other possibilities can be conceived, we have seen that Wittgenstein was not undermining our ways of thinking or suggesting that they are uncertain in any way. On the contrary, he was stressing how natural these ways of thinking are for us and how deep they go in our lives. The same conclusion is drawn concerning our religious ways of thinking. For some people, these go deep too. That this should be so is something which, in philosophy's descriptive task, is noted. Philosophical misunderstandings of basic propositions in religion, as elsewhere, are combated. That has been my aim in this essay. Whether one is glad or dismayed that there are religious ways of thinking which go deep with human beings is a matter which takes us beyond philosophy's descriptive task.

Yet, without withdrawing anything I have said, I want to raise the question of how there might be a natural religious response to the descriptive task of philosophy which I have attempted to outline and participate in.

The natural religious response I have in mind may be brought out if we begin by considering some remarks Norman Malcolm made in his discussion of 'the groundlessness of belief'. What I have been calling basic propositions in this essay, in order to emphasise the difference between Wittgenstein's treatment of them, and their treatment in Reformed epistemology, Malcolm calls 'framework propositions':

We do not decide to accept framework propositions. We do not decide that we live on the earth, any more than we decide to learn our native tongue. We do come to adhere to a framework proposition, in the sense that it forms the way we think. The framework propositions that we accept, grow into, are not idiosyncrasies but common ways of speaking and thinking that are pressed on us by our human community. For our acceptances to have been withheld would have meant that we had not learned how to count, to measure, to use names, to play games, or even *to talk*. Wittgenstein remarks that 'a language-game is only possible if one trusts something.' Not *can*, but *does* trust something. (*O.C.*, 509). I think he means by this trust or acceptance what he calls belief 'in the sense of religious belief' (*O.C.*, 459). What does he mean by belief 'in the sense of religious belief'? He explicitly distinguishes it from *conjecture* (*Vermutung*: ibid). I think this means that there is nothing tentative about it; it is not adopted as a hypothesis that might later be withdrawn in the light of new evidence. This also makes explicit an important feature of Wittgenstein's understanding of belief, in the sense of 'religious belief', namely, that it does not rise or fall on the basis of evidence or grounds: it is 'groundless'.[2]

In his reply to the paper, Colin Lyas criticises Malcolm for suggesting that all groundless belief is religious belief. He does not think this suggestion need detain us long. Together with the remarks we have just quoted, he refers to Malcolm's following comment:

> Wittgenstein observes that it would strike him as nonsense to say, 'I know that the Law of Induction is true'... It would be more correct to say, 'I believe in the Law of Induction.' This way of putting it is better because it shows that the attitude towards induction is belief in the sense of 'religious' belief — that is to say, an acceptance which is not conjecture or surmise and for which there is no reason — it is a groundless acceptance.[3]

Lyas comments, 'Now if we decide to christen 'groundless acceptance' as 'religious belief' then it will, of course, be true that, in this sense of the term, religious belief is groundless.'[4] He also comments, that 'even if theistic religious belief and belief in the Law of Induction do have a feature, groundlessness, in common it seems to me to be stretching things to make this a reason for calling a belief in the Law of Induction a *religious* belief.'[5] It would indeed, but Malcolm is doing no such thing. Lyas misreads Malcolm. Malcolm is wanting to show no more than Lyas says he could show, legitimately, namely, 'Religious belief and belief in the Law of Induction have a feature in common, namely, they are groundless.'[6] When Malcolm speaks of the 'religious' sense of belief he is referring only to the groundless aspect of the believing in this context, not to its religious content. The point of doing so being, of course, as we have seen in this essay, that those who appeal to inductive procedures to criticise the groundlessness of religious belief do so without realising that, in the context in which they do so, their inductive procedures are equally groundless. *That* is Malcolm's point.

Having made that point, however, is it not easy to see how the various groundless ways of thinking may themselves evoke a religious response? As we have seen, Wittgenstein evokes other 'possibilities', not in order to suggest that our ways of thinking are optional or uncertain. His work, after all, is called *On Certainty*. He does show, however, that our ways of acting and thinking are not dependent on any metaphysical underpinning in the form of some notion of necessity. The agreement that we show in our ways of acting, is a brute fact. *That* we do agree in the way we do is given. That it is so may well be an object of wonder: wonder at the agreement which makes possible our talk of colours; wonder at the agreement in our reactions to sounds without which what we call music would be impossible; and so on and so on. I do not say that any of this need be the cause of wonder, only that it *may* be. It may well be said that Wittgenstein is a philosopher who makes us see the wonderfulness of the ordinary, the wonderfulness of what is given. If this wonder takes a religious form, it is not difficult to see how these gifts of nature can be seen as gifts of grace — a grace of nature, one might say. But, someone might object, aren't religious possibilities *given* too; doesn't it follow from what has been said that the existence of religious modes of thought too are not guaranteed by any kind of necessity? That is correct. But, then, why should we assume that there is any necessity in our coming to God? Is not that possibility, too, a gift of grace?

Notes

1. For a comparison and contrast of the ways in which 'There are material objects' and 'There is a God' are held fast in all that surrounds them see Phillips, *Religion Without Explanation*, ch.10.

2. Norman Malcolm, 'The Groundlessness of Belief' in S. Brown (ed.) *Reason and Religion* (Cornell University Press, Ithaca, New York, 1977), pp. 147-8. This passage is unchanged in Malcolm's revised paper, of the same title, in his *Thought and Knowledge* (Cornell University Press, Ithaca, New York, 1977), see pp. 203-4.

3. Ibid., pp. 152-3.

4. Colin Lyas, 'The Groundlessness of Religious Belief' in Brown, *Reason and Religion*, p. 164.

5. Ibid., p. 165.

6. Ibid.

Part Two

Manners Without Grammar

Anything your reader can do for himself leave to him.

Wittgenstein, Culture and Value

10
The Hermeneutic Option

We concluded the first part of the book by coming to see what is involved in saying that our epistemic practices are not underpinned by any kind of metaphysical necessity. We saw that this does not entail that the practitioners of these practices are in a state of doubt as to whether the practice corresponds to reality. That notion of doubt is as metaphysical as the foundations the practices were thought to need. To be delivered from these metaphysical preconceptions is to be free of stumbling blocks which obscure from us the way things really are. Our task has been the one described by Wittgenstein as endeavouring to bring words back from their metaphysical to their ordinary use. But the task is not an easy one, because the recovery of the ordinary can only be achieved by retracing all the steps which tempted us to forsake it in the first place.

We have seen how foundationalism in epistemology distorts our ordinary everyday understanding of our surroundings. It claims to have in its possession a concept of reason which can assess the rationality or irrationality of our epistemic practices. According to reason, so conceived, we can determine, it is said, which propositions can be properly foundational in any practice. Belief in God cannot be among foundational propositions in any practice; it is based on evidence, which may or may not be sufficient to sustain the belief. What has been argued against such a view, however, is that basic propositions in an epistemic practice are not the foundations or presuppositions of the practice. On the contrary, the basic propositions are held fast by all that surrounds them in the practice; they are involved *in* the ways in which we think. This applies to belief in God which is basic within a religious practice. That practice does not stand in need of the kind of justification foundationalism insists must be provided.

Where do we turn to after foundationalism? This is a dangerous moment for philosophers, dangerous because, in overthrowing one theory, they assume it must be because they have a better one to put in its place. Once again, as one metaphysical system succeeds the other, we lose sight of our surroundings. This is what happens in Reformed epistemology where justification by reason is replaced by justification by faith. The Reformed epistemologist argues that the foundationalist can produce no satisfactory criterion for the proper basicality of propositions. That being so, he is no position to say that only self-evident propositions and the incorrigible propositions of sense experience are properly basic, and that belief in God is not. Of course, the Reformed epistemologist can produce no satisfactory criterion either, but, at least, he has as much right to make belief in God foundational as others have in the case of their foundational propositions. We believe that our foundational propositions, including belief in God, are properly basic, but we cannot know this. We justify our epistemic practices by faith. We believe that they correspond to reality, but it is possible that they could all be mistaken. It cannot be denied that people have doubts about their faith or that people lose their faith, but these doubts are not the metaphysical doubts of Reformed epistemology. In substituting faith for reason, the Reformed epistemologist hankers after the same metaphysical justification as the foundationalist. He simply says it is unavailable for us, and that we must have faith in its availability in God. Once again, however, ordinary trust in God has been transformed into a metaphysical trust. Trust in God, what that comes to, is shown by all that surrounds it in the lives of human beings. The reality of God is not far off for the believer. On the contrary, if his belief is strong, it is that in which he lives and moves and has his being.

Once again, therefore, after foundationalism, we should not be tempted by the metaphysical theories of Reformed epistemology. We need to put all such theories aside. At this point, further, and, perhaps, more subtle, dangers await us. The call to put aside metaphysical theories has been the motto of another contemporary challenge to foundationalism. I refer to hermeneutics. After foundationalism, according to Richard Rorty in his book *Philosophy and the Mirror of Nature*, there is only one direction in which we can go: hermeneutics.

We may be tempted by the hermeneutical turn because it shares, with our argument, the attack on foundationalism. It was because of the claims for reason as the adjudicator of epistemic practices that epistemology, in the eighteenth century, enjoyed the status of a foundational discipline. By the nineteenth century, philosophy had become a substitute for religion for man: 'It was the area of culture where one touched bottom, where one found the vocabulary and the convictions which permitted one to explain and justify one's activity *as* an intellectual, and thus to discover the significance of one's life.'[1] With the growth of science, however, philosophy ceased to be regarded as the custodian of rationality or as the major guardian against superstition. By the early twentieth century, the scientist, with the increasing specialisation in the various branches of his discipline, had become as culturally remote as the philosopher. As for philosophy, Rorty tells us, it was simply shrugged off by those seeking an ideology or a self-image.

Rorty does not regret the decline of epistemology as a foundational discipline. Its status as such depended on metaphysical pretension. To be rid of it, Rorty says, is to be rid of a world well lost. But what world does Rorty leave us with? As we shall see, in ridding us of a metaphysical world, he robs us of much of our ordinary world at the same time. When Wittgenstein said, 'What *we* do is to bring words back from their metaphysical use to their ordinary use',[2] the ordinary use obviously remains untampered with. It does not change as a result of the attack on metaphysics. On the contrary, it plays a vital role in that attack. But with Rorty's strategies things are different. When he criticises metaphysics, he offers something else in its place. He is not content with clarity about the ordinary; instead, he preaches a new gospel, the gospel of hermeneutics.

To illustrate this fact, let us remind ourselves of some ordinary, but central, religious convictions. A religious believer may claim, with certainty, to be in communion with a divine reality. He does not regard that reality as an optional set of descriptions; as one option among many. On the contrary, for him, the divine reality in which he believes constitutes an eternal standard. The believer may not think he is under any obligation to reach agreement with religious or non-religious perspectives which are other than his own. With some he may be ready to converse, but he may want to have nothing to do with others. He believes that God has made him into a new being and that his task is to deepen his acknowledgement of this.

It has to be admitted that in talking about these matters, a philosopher may misleadingly transform them into metaphysical theories or systems. But if these transformations are avoided, the religious concepts are once again allowed to be themselves. Rorty's invitation to hermeneutics also invites us to eschew metaphysics, but, as we shall see, it does not allow religious concepts to be themselves. On the contrary, according to Rorty, hermeneutical insights enable us to see that we are never in contact with anything other than human realities. Further, our certainty with respect to them is always a matter of consensus opinion. The realities we meet are sets of descriptions which are optional for us. None of them merit being called an eternal standard. On the contrary, new descriptions, deviant discourses, are always being presented to us in the culture. Our endeavours, it is said, should be directed towards bringing about an agreement between normal discourse and abnormal discourse, but an agreement which is always open-ended in the consideration of further possibilities. In these endeavours, the virtue of understanding is born, and therein is the possibility of our becoming new beings.

We can see, even from this summary, that hermeneutics has pretensions of its own. It is interesting to note that when Rorty referred to the status epistemology enjoyed in the eighteenth century as a foundational discipline, he also thought that this status enabled it to make the lives of its intellectual adherents significant. Thus philosophy provided a meaning for their lives, and became, he claims, in the nineteenth century, a substitute for religion. When philosophy in the twentieth century became peripheral, according to Rorty, those looking for an ideology or self-image simply shrugged it off as an irrelevance. Now, of course, Rorty does not regret epistemology's loss of status. Neither does he think it can have *the* dominant voice in the hermeneutic conversation with different aspects of the culture. Nevertheless, at no time does he sever the link between philosophical enquiry and searches for the meaning of life, an ideology or a self-image. On the contrary, as we have seen, engaging in hermeneutics is meant to be the path to virtue. There is the possibility of the enquirer becoming a new being. It appears, then, that as with philosophy in the nineteenth century, hermeneutics in the twentieth century is offered as a substitute for religion. Rorty is not prepared to settle for philosophy's modest, but important task: the striving for clarity.

Why is it so difficult to disentangle the hidden programme in

Rorty's hermeneutics from his often acute criticisms of epistemological foundationalism? Much of the answer lies in the fact that he *does* recognise the moves by which epistemology overreaches itself. Concentrating on these, the hidden agenda may slip by us unnoticed. Yet, not to notice it, as we shall see, is to allow hermeneutics, in its turn, to overreach itself. In the first part of the book, we saw that one of the ways in which epistemology overreaches itself is in thinking that the *grammars* of the various forms of discourse we engage in are themselves descriptions of, or hypotheses about, a reality which is independent of them all. Sceptical worries then take the form of worries about whether the language within which claims of truth and falsity are made *itself* makes any contact with reality. As we saw, the epistemological foundationalist claims to make that contact secure in certain indubitable propositions, on the basis of which he thinks we can build our epistemic practices with confidence. But, as we have argued, our practices are not based on these propositions, since it is only within our practices that the propositions enjoy their status. The Reformed epistemologist has faith that our practices refer to reality, and, by so doing, misses the references to reality made within them. In both cases, justifications are sought for the epistemic practices themselves. As Peter Winch has said, the

> sceptical difficulties do not concern doubts about whether someone is right on a particular occasion in the claim about how much time has passed, what caused such and such an event, what kind of object he is perceiving. They concern rather the possibility of making *any* such claims; they tend to undermine confidence in there being any genuine distinction between truth and falsity in such judgements; they attack, that is, the possibility of making any sense of them at all.[3]

Winch points out,

> Much of the difficulty in all these cases springs from the fact that the forms in which we think seem, on a certain sort of examination, to suggest a kind of application to the world which is not the application they in fact have. When we do, in the course of our lives, apply them in the appropriate way, the sceptical worries strike us, in Hume's

phrase, as 'strain'd and ridiculous', but the worries are not laid to rest until we have succeeded in the surprisingly difficult tasks of attaining a clear view of the *actual* application of our ways of thinking and of the nature of the obstacles which stood in the way of our taking proper stock of these.[4]

Rorty, in his reactions to foundationalist attempts to answer scepticism, seems to share Winch's views. He, too, wants to expose the attempt to provide epistemic justifications beyond the point where it makes sense to do so. 'For epistemology is the attempt to see the patterns of justification within normal discourse as *more* than just such patterns. It is the attempt to see them as hooked on to something which demands moral commitment – Reality, Truth, Objectivity, Reason.'[5] In opposition to requests to provide the justificatory links between the language-games we play and the elements of a reality of which they are taken to be descriptions, Rorty insists 'if we understand the rules of a language-game, we understand all there is to understand about why moves in the language-game are made.'[6] We have no conception of reality in abstraction, to which our epistemic practices must conform. 'Our choice of elements will be dictated by our understanding of the practice, rather than the practice's being "legitimated" by a common ground.'[7] Winch, too, wants to undermine the seductive idea we have encountered, namely, 'that the grammar of our language is itself the expression of a set of beliefs or theories about how the world is, which might in principle be justified or refuted by an examination of how the world actually is.'[8] So far so good, but does Rorty leave our language-games as they are?

In case it be thought that one's objections to Rorty's analysis apply only to its consequences for religious belief, it is as well to look at what seems to be an extremely straightforward example: our descriptions of a physical object. This example is not an arbitrary one, since it concerns a thinker to whom Rorty pays considerable attention, namely, John Locke. Locke's worries about our descriptions of physical objects reflect the sceptical worries to which Winch called our attention. In dispelling these worries, Rorty concludes that we see that we are never confronted by a non-human reality. In this conclusion, Rorty takes from us, not only the pretensions of metaphysics, a world well lost, but also features of our ordinary world at the same time. Let us see how this comes about, since if this happens even in *this* case, how much more likely is it to happen in the case of religious language, where there are additional temptations to speak of a world which our language can never reach.

We may play a game in which we are asked to guess what object is being referred to by a set of descriptions we are given. Sometimes we answer correctly and sometimes we answer incorrectly. But this worry about whether we have given the correct answer is not Locke's worry. His worry is not over whether, on a specific occasion, our descriptions are correct. Locke's worry is about how we can *ever* know whether our descriptions are correct. In order to know whether they are correct, we need to know what they are descriptions of, and how can we ever know *that?* One way of putting the matter, which we find in Rorty, is to ask how we *can* know whether our ideas mirror nature. What if there is no connection between our *ideas* of how things are, and the *things themselves?*

If we are given sets of descriptions, and are asked to say what they are descriptions of, we might say that they are descriptions of tables, chairs, etc. There seems to be no difficulty about distinguishing between the offered descriptions, and those things, tables and chairs, which they may or may not be descriptions of. But this answer would not satisfy Locke at all. He points out that we do have ideas in our experience that are correctly identified as ideas of things like tables and chairs:

> I appeal to everyone's experience. It is the ordinary qualities observable in iron, or a diamond, put together, that make the true complex idea of those substances, which a smith or a jeweller commonly knows better than a philosopher; who, whatever *substantial forms* he may talk of, has no other idea of those substances than what is framed by a collection of those simple ideas which we found in them.[9]

So far, then, we do not need philosophers to supplement the knowledge which smiths possess about iron, jewellers possess about diamonds, and we possess about table and chairs. But this knowledge does not silence our sceptical worries, for whether we have ideas of secondary qualities such as colour, hardness, etc., or whether we have ideas of primary qualities, such as extension, figure or solidity, the question remains of what *any* of these ideas, these qualities, are ideas or qualities *of. What* they are ideas or qualities of, is *not* itself given in experience, but it seems to Locke

137

to be necessarily suggested or *implied by* our experience. Having noted that we do meet ideas of tables and chairs in our experience and ideas of the qualities they are composed of, Locke goes on to say that all these ideas imply a

> Something to which they belong, and in which they subsist; and therefore when we speak of any sort of substance, we say it is a thing having such or such qualities: a body is a thing that is extended, figured, and capable of motion; a spirit is a thing capable of thinking; and so hardness, friability, and power to draw iron, we say, are qualities in a loadstone. These, and the like fashions of speaking, intimate that the substance is supposed always *something besides* the extension, figure, solidity, motion, thinking, or other observable ideas, though we know not what it is.[10]

It is not hard to detect the scepticism implicit in Locke's position, for if all we ever experience are ideas, or sets of descriptions, how are we ever going to know what they are ideas or descriptions of?

How are we to deal with the problem? There are times when Locke's own language encourages us to think that the problem we are discussing is an empirical one. This is never more so than when Locke distinguishes between nominal essences and the real essence of things. He says,

> This, though it be all the essence of natural substances that we know, or by which we distinguish them into sorts, yet I call it by a peculiar name, the *nominal essence*, to distinguish it from that real constitution of substances, upon which depends this nominal essence, and all the properties of that sort; which, therefore, as has been said, may be called the *real essence.*[11]

But although we have knowledge of nominal essences, we do not have knowledge of their real essence:

> Our faculties carry us no further towards the knowledge and distinction of substances than a collection of those sensible ideas which we observe in them; which, however made with the greatest diligence and exactness we are capable of, yet is more remote from the true intenal constitution from which those qualities flow, than, as I said,

a countryman's idea is from the inward contrivance of that famous clock at Strasbourg, whereof he only sees the outward figure and motions.[12]

On the basis of this analogy, Locke would appear to be advocating no more than commendable caution. In the case of the clock, we have a distinction between how the clock appears to be and how the clock really is. The countryman could come to knowledge of the inner constitution of the clock. It would appear, on this analogy, that the enquirer could come to a knowledge of the real essence of things. Enquiry progresses from our acquaintance with nominal essences to an investigation of greater empirical analysis. This impression is reinforced when Locke makes remarks such as the following:

Blood, to the naked eye, appears all red, but by a good microscope, wherein its lesser parts appear, shows only some globules of red, swimming in a pellucid liquor, and how these red globules would appear, if glasses could be found that yet could magnify them a thousand or ten thousand times more, is uncertain.[13]

For reasons such as these, Jonathan Bennett suggests that we ought to distinguish between Locke's general conception of substance and his notion of real essence. He suggests that the latter notion is a regulative idea, representing a commendable caution about our knowledge of the natural world at any particular time. Caution about the real essence indicates no more than the 'open' character of our conclusions, our readiness to revise our conclusions in the light of further investigations. Thus, Bennett concludes, 'With characteristic intelligence, insight and humility, Locke took every possible chance...to stress the gap between the intellectual control which we do impose on the world and the science-plus-conceptual-scheme which we might find appropriate if we "cured our ignorance".'[14] Thus, Bennett concludes that in *this* context, in his discussion of real essences, Locke is not arguing that knowledge is, in principle, impossible. 'What he says is not that real essences are in principle unknowable, but only that there are reasons for suspecting that full knowledge of them would require scientific inquiries of a depth and scope that lie beyond our capacities.'[15]

There are reasons, however, for resisting Bennett's distinction between Locke's conception of real essence and the general idea of substance. Bennett argues that knowledge of real essence should be understood in the context of our readiness to revise our scientific findings. This being so, there would have to be a logical continuity between the use of the concept of real essence and what we mean by the use of our faculties in scientific enquiry. To say that knowledge of the real essence is beyond our present capacities must mean, in this context, 'beyond our present capacities'. We can be cured of our ignorance in successive instances. But is this how we find Locke talking? Having said what he means by the nominal essence of 'man', he goes on to contrast it with what might be meant by the real essence of man.

> The foundation of all those qualities which are the ingredients of our complex idea is something quite different, and had we such a knowledge of that constitution of man, from which his faculties of moving, sensation, and reasoning, and other powers flow, and on which his so regular shape depends, as it is possible angels have, and it *is* certain his Maker has, we should have quite other ideas of his essence than what now is contained in our definition of that species, be it what it will.[16]

It is clear that what Locke has in mind is a distinction between human knowledge at any particular time and a knowledge which lies beyond human attainment. There is no continuity between *these* kinds of knowledge, as there would be if all Locke were talking about were the developments within a scientific discipline and the essential readiness to be open to further developments.

To see what is involved in Locke's concept of substance, we have to appreciate that he is concerned, as many philosophers have been, with the question of the limits of human knowledge, the question of what *can* be known. These limits are misunderstood if they are taken to refer to the limitations of what we know at any particular time. Philosophers, including Locke, have not always been careful to distinguish between the different contexts in which they have spoken of what can be known. It is that fact which gives Bennett's reading its plausibility. When we look inside the clock at Strasbourg, we come to the inner workings of the clock. When we look through the microscope, we are getting closer to an appreciation of what blood really is. Yet, even in these contexts, we must be careful not to assume that knowledge sought in one context is more fundamental and a necessary corrective to what is said in other contexts. For example, from what the microscope shows us about blood, it does not follow that we are incorrect when we say that blood is red. Our interests in the different contexts determine what we mean by more or less fundamental knowledge. In the same way, if our interest is in the aesthetic appearance of a clock, knowledge of its inner workings may be held to be relatively unimportant.

But when Locke speaks of the limits of what *can* be known, no discovery, whether it be arrived at by looking through a microscope or by opening a clock, could constitute, for Locke, knowledge of the real nature of things. We find, as Bennett agrees, that Locke's general notion of substance does not allow that substance to have a nature. If we begin with an object such as a coloured table, it is noted that the table may lose its colour. It is concluded that, therefore, the colour is not an essential part of the table — an odd conclusion in itself. The colour only belongs to the appearance of the table, it is said, and not to its inner nature. Colour only belongs to the surface of things. What we want is to penetrate below the surface to the thing itself. But what is this *thing*? Is the smoothness or solidity of the table part of its real nature? As we use more scientific instruments, we may begin to doubt this. For whatever we mention can be said to be a property of something, the something which, no matter how many properties we name, we never seem to arrive at.

In this way of speaking, the fascination with the subject–predicate proposition and form of speech plays a dominant role. If anything we mention with respect to an object is thought of as a property of the object, it looks as if we should have a conception of the object apart from all its properties. When we say of something that *it* has a certain colour, *it* has a certain shape, *it* is solid, *it* has a certain smell, *it* has a certain weight, etc., etc., we may become puzzled about what this *it* we keep referring to really is. It seems that it ought to be an extra item alongside all the properties we have mentioned, one which underlies them in some way or other. Yet, although this *it* must be there, it seems we can have no knowledge of it. No amount of revision of our empirical conclusions brings us any nearer to this knowledge. As Locke puts it, 'I am apt to doubt that, how far soever human industry may advance useful and experimental philosophy in *physical* things, scientifical will still be out of reach, because we want perfect and adequate ideas of those very bodies which are nearest to us, and most under our command.'[17] So it is not a matter of wondering whether we will ever solve some scientific problem which is proving particularly resistant to our enquiries. Even in relation to the table we sit at, the chair we sit on, Locke is saying that we only have knowledge of nominal essences. We can never know what the thing in itself is, the *it* which is a table or a chair. Yet, he is convinced of the reality of this *it*, the *it* to which the properties belong and to which our descriptions refer. 'The idea that we have, to which we give the general name "substance", being nothing but the supposed, but unknown, support of those qualities we find existing, which we imagine cannot subsist *sine re substante*, without something to support them, we call that support *substantia*; which, according to the true import of the word, is, in plain English, standing under or upholding.'[18] Here we can see the influence of the subject–predicate form at work; the way it can lead us to conclude, as it did Locke, 'that the substance is supposed always *something besides* the extension, figure, solidity, motion, thinking, or other observable ideas, though we know not what it is.'[19] If we are under the influence of this way of thinking we are likely to think of the problem facing philosophy in the way Wittgenstein describes: 'For they see in the essence, not something that already lies open to view and that becomes surveyable by a rearrangement, but something that lies *beneath* the surface. Something that lies within, which we see when we look *into* the thing, and which an analysis digs out.'[20] The 'rearrangement' necessary in Locke's talk of substance is the way in which we need to be brought to see that what we mean by a 'thing' is not an element which stands apart from everything we can say about it. We talk as if all we ever have are descriptions which approximate to, but never exhaust, the nature of the thing they are supposed to be descriptions of. We forget that we are already acquainted with the distinction between adequate and inadequate descriptions of, say, a table. The table, in this context, is not a *further* set of descriptions, descriptions of something we can never know.

Looking back at our discussion we can, using Rorty's language, say that in it there is a world well lost, namely, the world of the metaphysical conception of a thing which can never really be known. In losing this world, Wittgenstein's point is that we are freed from confusions about our ordinary world. In losing the metaphysical thing, of which 'table' was supposed to be predicated, we gain in clarity with respect to the ordinary table of our everyday surroundings. But when we turn to Rorty's own conclusion, do we find that he leaves us with our ordinary conception of a table? On the contrary, Rorty concludes, 'Our certainty will be a matter of conversation between persons, rather than a matter of interaction with nonhuman reality.'[21] What does this conclusion amount to? Is Rorty simply saying that the non-human reality is Locke's metaphysical conception of substance? It would appear not, since Rorty presents us with the following choice when it comes to talking of our knowledge of ordinary things: 'we can think of knowledge as a relation to propositions, and thus of justification as a relation between the propositions in question and other propositions from which the former may be inferred. Or we may think of both knowledge and justification as privileged relations to the objects those propositions are about.'[22] It is clear that Rorty favours the first way of talking about our knowledge of things. But what if we do? Rorty replies,

> If we think in the first way, we will see no need to end the potentially infinite regress of propositions-brought-forward-in-defence-of-other propositions. It would be foolish to keep conversation on the subject going once everyone, or the majority, or the wise, are satisfied, but of course we *can*. If we think of knowledge in the second way, we will want to get behind reason to causes, beyond argument to compulsion from the object known, to a situation in which argument would be not just silly but impossible, for anyone gripped by the object in the required way will be *unable* to doubt or to see an alternative. To reach that point is to reach the foundations of knowledge.[23]

What if we try to apply Rorty's analysis to our ordinary talk of tables and chairs? This talk should not be considered in terms of propositions or objects considered in abstraction or in isolation. Wittgenstein emphasises, 'Children do not learn that books exist, that armchairs exist, etc., etc., — they learn to fetch books, sit in armchairs etc. etc.'[24] Of course, in certain circumstances, doubts may be expressed about the existence of such objects. But in the circumstances Wittgenstein describes, are we faced with a potentially infinite series of justifications? Obviously not, since the question of the existence of the books and armchairs does not even arise. Contrary to Rorty's suggestion, requests for justifications would not simply be silly, they *would* be unintelligible. Also, contrary to Rorty, the impossibility of doubt, in these circumstances, does not commit one to any kind of foundationalism. Wittgenstein asks, 'Can I doubt at *will?*'[25] But what makes doubt impossible, is not that we are somehow gripped by the object in isolation, but the circumstances in which we fetch books and sit in armchairs. We can see no alternative. The objects are not the determinants or foundations of our certainty. Our certainty gets its sense from the circumstances which pertain within the epistemic practice. Rorty seems close to such a view when he says 'We will say with Quine that knowledge is not like an architectonic structure but like a field of force', but he adds, 'and that there are no assertions which are immune from revision'.[26] But is this addition intelligible? In certain circumstances there would be no question of revising the fact that we were fetching books or sitting on armchairs. If we saw someone constantly checking that he was holding a book or sitting in an armchair, we would not say that he was making sure of these facts, but that he was unbalanced. What he would need would not be correction, but cure.

What does Rorty mean when he says 'Our certainty will be a matter of conversation between persons, rather than a matter of interaction with non-human reality'?[27] Perhaps all Rorty means is that to understand what we mean by certainty we must see what it amounts to in the context of human epistemic practices. If so, it is highly misleading to say that when we are certain we do not come into contact with non-human realities. In a perfectly obvious sense, books and armchairs are non-human realities as are trees, mountains and countless other things.

The conclusions we have arrived at have important implications for the philosophy of religion. Of course, there are important grammatical differences between talk of physical objects and talk of God. We have already seen in the first part of the book how easy it is to turn our talk of God into metaphysical speculation. Our task where the concept of God is concerned, as with the concept of a physical object, is not the metaphysical one of wondering how we can ever arrive at such concepts. On the contrary, these concepts are already given in the discourses in which they have their natural home. Within religious practices, distinctions are made between those who say they know God but do not, and those who truly know him. To appreciate what religious certainties amount to, we must explore the role such talk has within these practices. These matters will be explored later.[28] My point now is a far more limited one, namely, to point out that religious certainties, like any other certainties, have their sense within human epistemic practices. Yet, why should *that* fact lead us to say, with Rorty, that we do not interact with non-human realities? It would be incredible if, as a result of emphasising that religious concepts have their sense in human epistemic practices, we were told that we *had* to conclude, for no other reason than this, that when someone says he knows God, the reality he comes into contact with *cannot* be a non-human reality! I am not prejudging the issue of whether alleged divine realities are, in fact, human realities.[29] What I am protesting against is the *a priori* thesis that from the epistemological considerations we have been given by Rorty, it follows that no realities in our experience can be called non-human realities.

It can be seen that, in fact, Rorty is in the grip of the very metaphysical tendencies he opposes. He assumes that if we *do* speak of non-human realities, such talk *must* involve us in metaphysical pretensions. We have seen already that this is not the case. It no more follows where talk of God is concerned than it does from our talk of tables, chairs, mountains and trees. Rorty ignores the natural contexts of such talk. To insist that our normal talk should be reformed simply because there are metaphysical misrepresentations of it is to remain in the grip of those misrepresentations. A final example will illustrate this fact.

As we have seen, Rorty accuses foundational epistemology of wanting 'to see the patterns of justification within normal discourse as more than just such patterns'.[30] For example, we saw that in relation to our talk of physical objects, we may be tempted to think that we can never know whether our descriptions are accurate, because 'the thing', the substance, which they are supposed to be descriptions of, lies necessarily beyond our acquaintance. The *x* which is a table and brown can never be known. Rorty, rightly, wants to rid us of this *x*, the metaphysical subject. In doing so, however, he robs us of ordinary subjects at the same time. Rorty says it is absurd to think 'that the vocabulary used by present science, morality or whatever has some privileged attachment to reality, which makes it *more* than just a further set of descriptions'.[31] We have already seen, in discussing Winch's refutation of Roger Trigg,[32] that the vocabulary, the language, in which we make our judgements, is not *itself* a description of anything. It neither succeeds nor fails to attach itself to reality, since neither assumption makes sense. Retaining the view of language as being in itself, a set of descriptions, is to retain at least half of the metaphysical picture Rorty takes himself to be opposing. On the other hand, if we turn to the judgements we do make within our various ways of speaking, it is ludicrous to suppose that all we ever encounter is a further set of descriptions. In unfavourable circumstances, I may offer a set of descriptions when I fail to identify precisely what I am looking at. But when, in good light, I sit on a chair or at a table, my reference to the chair and the table is not a reference to a further set of descriptions. I could describe these objects if asked, but, in the circumstances described, the objects themselves are not a further description of anything. To think they are is still to be in the grip of Locke's notion of an *x*, which, by definition, can have no nature.

The same lessons hold in our talk of God. Here, as we have seen, the matter is complicated by the fact that the gap or tension between belief and non-belief is itself a grammatical one. Nevertheless, that complication notwithstanding, it still remains that in speaking of God we are not confined to sets of descriptions which approximate to, but never capture, his reality. On the contrary, our talk of God, for example, saying that 'God is love', is constitutive of what we mean by divine reality. 'God is love' is not a description of God which may be true or false, but a grammatical rule for one use, albeit a primary one, of the word 'God'. In the mouth of a believer it takes the form of a confession of faith.

What we have seen is that in elucidating the metaphysical world which he wants to lose, Rorty places much in jeopardy which belongs to our ordinary world. Despite the fact that, for the most part, in this chapter, religion has not been our central preoccupation, it has been important to observe that the metaphysical tendencies which stand in the way of giving religious epistemic practices the attention they merit, are the same tendencies which stand in the way of giving proper attention to our ordinary talk of physical objects. Of course, much else may stand in the way of our failure to understand religious beliefs; matters which have more to do with the content of those beliefs. Yet, if the epistemological misapprehensions we have discussed are not overcome, the enquirer is hardly likely to get that far. On the contrary, his reflections can barely get started in a profitable direction. The further difficulties discussed in the next two chapters illustrate this truth all too well.

Notes

1. Richard Rorty, *Philosophy and the Mirror of Nature* (Princeton University Press, Princeton, New Jersey, and Basil Blackwell, Oxford, 1980), p. 4.
2. Wittgenstein, *Investigations*, vol. 1, p. 116.
3. Winch, 'Language, Belief and Relativism', p. 329.
4. Ibid.
5. Rorty, *Philosophy and the Mirror of Nature*, p. 385.
6. Ibid., p. 174.
7. Ibid., p. 318.
8. Winch, 'Language, Belief and Relativism', p. 329.
9. John Locke, *An Essay Concerning Human Understanding*, ed. and abridged by A.D. Woozley (Fontana Library, London, 1969), bk 2 xxiii 3, p. 186.
10. Ibid., bk 2 xxiii 3 pp. 186-7.
11. Ibid., bk 3 vi 2 pp. 283-4.
12. Ibid., bk 3 vi 9 p. 287.
13. Ibid., bk 2 xxiii 11 p. 191.
14. Jonathan Bennett, *Locke, Berkeley, Hume: Central Themes* (Clarendon Press, Oxford, 1971), p. 121.
15. Ibid., p. 122.
16. Locke, *Essay*, bk 3 vi 3 p. 284.
17. Ibid., bk 4 iii 26 p. 343.
18. Ibid., bk 2 xxiii 2 p. 186.
19. Ibid., p. 187.
20. Wittgenstein, *Investigations*, vol. 1 p. 92.
21. Rorty, *Philosophy and the Mirror of Nature*, p. 157.
22. Ibid., p. 159.
23. Ibid.
24. Wittgenstein, *On Certainty*, para. 476.
25. Ibid., para. 221.
26. Rorty, *Philosophy and the Mirror of Nature*, p. 181.
27. Ibid., p. 157.
28. In Part Four.
29. I have discussed reductionist explanations of religious belief in *Religion Without Explanation*.
30. Rorty, *Philosophy and the Mirror of Nature*, p. 385.
31. Ibid., p. 361.
32. See Part One, Ch. 5.

11
Optional Descriptions?

In attacking the pretensions of epistemological foundationalism, Rorty also attacks a conception of philosophy as the assessor or adjudicator of human practices. As we have seen, we cannot reduce what 'corresponding to reality' comes to to a single definition. As we have also seen, epistemology cannot pretend to be the possessor or provider of such a definition. Yet, as Rorty says, 'Philosophy as a discipline capable of giving us a "right method of seeking truth" depends upon finding some permanent neutral framework of all possible enquiry.'[1] To abandon the search for such a framework is 'to abandon the notion of philosophy as a discipline which adjudicates the claims of science and religion, mathematics and poetry, reason and sentiment, allocating an appropriate place to each'.[1]

We have seen how religious belief has been misunderstood by philosophers because they have mischaracterised it, subjecting it to criteria of meaning which were irrelevant. Once philosophers give up their pretensions regarding this general test of intelligibility, we should expect them to recognise, respect, and wait on the various activities and modes of discourse we engage in. When they do so, they discover that these various activities do not presuppose a common ground or a common goal to which they all conform. It is presumptuous of the philosopher to insist that, although all the participants deny any knowledge of a common foundation or goal of their activities, such a foundation or goal *must* be present in some way or other. A philosopher who argues in this way sees himself as 'the cultural overseer who knows everyone's common ground — the Platonic philosopher-king who knows what everybody else is really doing whether *they* know it or not, because he knows about the ultimate context (the Forms, the Mind, Language) within which they are doing it'.[3] Once these presuppositions are given up, the philosopher, instead of imposing *his* conception of 'correspondence to reality', 'truth', 'goodness', etc., etc., on to the various practices, can wait on the practices themselves to explore what *they* mean by these various concepts.

But this is not what we find Rorty doing. Rather, as a result of the fall of foundational epistemology, he concludes that it has the beneficial consequence of 'preventing man from deluding himself with the notion that he knows himself, or anything else, except under optional descriptions'.[4] This is a deeply misleading conclusion and one, once again, which shows that Rorty is still in the grip of the metaphysical views he thinks he has freed himself from.

Rorty takes himself to be sharing Wittgenstein's aim to bring words back from their metaphysical to their ordinary use. For example, if we rescue the word 'know' from its metaphysical use, we rescue it from the philosophical restrictiveness of a single paradigmatic use. We show that the word can be used in a variety of contexts. These contexts will represent the ordinary uses of the word. According to Rorty, however, in these contexts, anything we say we know can only be known under an optional description. But that, clearly, is *not* our ordinary use of the word 'know'. What constitutes knowledge and knowing something varies significantly in different contexts. That does not mean, however, that what is known within these contexts is known under an optional description.

Consider some examples. I am working in a bakery and I am asked how many loaves of bread we have left. I count them and reply, 'Ten.' In what sense is what I know an optional description? If I want to give a correct answer to the question I have been asked, I have no option at all. Nor will it be any different if I am told of a tribe who do not count. They conduct their business transactions with only two categories: 'enough' and 'not enough'. This may stop me thinking, if I ever had such a thought, that our way of counting is the only possible way in which business could be conducted. But this does not mean that I have an option about the way I conduct my business or that I have any choice when asked to say how many loaves are left in the bakery.

I am asked whether a certain book is on an armchair. I go into the room, see a book on the armchair, pick it up, check its title, and call out to the person who wants to know, 'Yes, it's here.' In what sense, given that I do not want to lie or play a joke, is my reply optional for me? Even if I do want to lie or play a joke, what I want to lie or joke about is not a state of affairs which falls under optional descriptions. If the descriptions seemed optional, the book appearing to be on the armchair one moment, but not the other, in my hand and then seeming to vanish, I would not say I had a choice of descriptions. I'd say I was going crazy.

I witness a car crash. People are flung out of the two cars which have collided. They writhe and scream in agony before me. Some are badly cut, while others hold themselves doubled-up though the cause of it is not visible to my untrained eye. When I bear witness later to what I saw, I have no option when I say that these people were in pain. Once again, I may have been told of a tribe who only react as we do to pain when wounds are visible. Otherwise neither they, nor the person we would describe as doubled up in pain, react as we would do in such situations. But this information does not leave me in any doubt or confronted by any option when it comes to describing the pain I witnessed in the car crash.

Now it is true that our talk of mathematics, physical objects and pain differs in important respects and what knowing something in these different contexts comes to varies accordingly. We have no paradigm of knowledge which transcends all these contexts. But that does not mean that all we ever know within them are sets of optional descriptions. If Rorty says that the absence of a transcendent paradigm leads to this conclusion, then he is still in the grip of the metaphysical assumption that the possibility of knowledge *is* dependent on such a paradigm. The only difference between Rorty and the metaphysician would be that the latter believes that a transcendent paradigm of knowledge is available, while Rorty does not. What we have seen, however, is that our ordinary uses of 'know' are not dependent on this metaphysical requirement.

As we have seen, Rorty holds that a person deludes himself if he thinks he knows himself, or anything else, except under optional descriptions. We have given examples to show that this is not the case. Still, it might be said that these are not the examples Rorty has in mind. Rorty, it could be argued, is thinking in the main of the plurality of moral, political and religious perspectives in a culture. He is protesting, quite rightly, against philosophers who attempt to reduce the genuine plurality of such perspectives to a spurious unity. Such philosophers regard the perspectives as surface phenomena, hiding from us all the common good which underlies them all, or the common goal they are all really pursuing. If that were all Rorty was doing, I should have no complaints against him.

Yet, philosophers who begin by noting a plurality of perspectives often go on to suggest, misleadingly, that the recognition of such a plurality *must* be reflected in a certain attitude on the part of the adherents to the particular perspectives. That does not follow at all. A person may have thought that one could not call one's own viewpoint moral if one recognised the existence of other moral viewpoints. He may have thought that their existence robbed his own moral viewpoint of its imperative. This is a logical confusion which reflection on the plurality of perspectives may help to clear up. But this is quite different from the suggestion that once this plurality has been recognised, one's own moral perspective can only be seen as an option for one. The recognition that there are many viewpoints is quite consistent with a wide range of moral attitudes to those viewpoints.

Consider an example from matters of taste. A drinker recognises that people's choices, where drinks are concerned, vary widely. A choice of drinks is open to him in the sense that they are available at the bar and he is free to make his choice. Yet, even here, having made his choice, he may regard the drinks he seldom chooses as pleasant, unpleasant, interesting, uninteresting, disgusting, and so on. But the reason why talk of options is at home here is because we are discussing drinks, a matter of taste. Although some make quite a fuss about such matters, saying that to follow a drink of one kind with a certain other kind of drink is quite impossible, these matters remain questions of taste.

Moral questions are not matters of taste, but matters of decency. Here, too, there will be a whole range of attitudes to moral viewpoints other than one's own. Some will say that some of them contain important insights. Others will disagree. In the case of a specific viewpoint there may be no agreement on whether it should be called a *moral* viewpoint. But, even if it is, this fact need not lead a person to regard his own viewpoint as optional. On the contrary, he may regard the other viewpoint as terrible, and as being all the worse for being a moral viewpoint. So far from viewing his own standpoint as optional, he may think that any decent person should adhere to it and it is essential that he should do so. My aim is not to tidy up these differences. The differences are important grammatical features of the use of the word 'moral'.

I find the suggestion that someone could regard *all* moral viewpoints as options bizarre, but we do not have to establish that point. All we need to show, and have shown, is that the absence of a transcendent paradigm of the 'moral' does not reduce all moral perspectives to the status of 'optional descriptions'. As with our earlier examples, to think that *this* fact rules out the possibility of absolute commitments, is to remain in the grip of the very foundationalism in ethics one is supposed to be opposing.

Rorty also believes that once foundationalism has been overthrown, criticism of the culture can only proceed piecemeal. There can be no reference to 'eternal standards'.[5] But what does Rorty mean by eternal standards? He may be attacking certain metaphysical conceptions. The idea of eternal standards he attacks may be linked with the suggestion that a 'permanent neutral matrix' could be established by reference to which any cultural activity is to be assessed. If so, his criticisms have a point. But, one suspects, Rorty would like to go further and put a stop to talk of eternal standards *per se*. Talk of 'eternity' has its natural home in religious contexts. Its sense depends on distinctions between time and eternity, the temporal and the eternal in matters of the spirit. But these religious uses do not depend on the metaphysics Rorty wants to reject. Kierkegaard, in his *Purity of Heart*,[6] discusses 'commitment to the Eternal', but would be as opposed as Rorty to epistemological foundationalism. He is, of course, one of the great opponents of such foundationalism in the history of philosophy. In short, in ridding ourselves of metaphysical conceptions of transcendence we do not rid ourselves of religious conceptions of transcendence.[7] On the contrary, ridding ourselves of the metaphysical conception should help us to see the ordinary conception, in this case a religious one, more clearly. Needless to say, if a believer is committed to obeying the eternal will of God, he is hardly likely to view this as an optional description which is open to him. Once again, in getting rid of a metaphysical world, Rorty gets rid of much of our ordinary world at the same time.

Rorty sees himself as having to make a choice between two options: on the one hand, systematic philosophy, and on the other hand, edifying philosophy. By systematic philosophy he means, more or less, foundational epistemology. Edifying philosophy, of which we shall have more to say in the next chapter, comes about when philosophy engages in conversations with participants in other aspects of our culture. What these participants produce, according to Rorty, are different optional descriptions under which the world can be perceived and understood. The conversation they engage in, philosophers included, is what Rorty means by hermeneutics.

Because he takes himself to be faced with a choice between systematic and edifying philosophy, Rorty does not give enough attention to the possibility of non-systematic philosophy, by which I mean a philosophy which, while sharing Rorty's attack on foundationalism, leaves the variety of moral, political and religious perspective undisturbed. The non-systematic philosopher is interested in clarity and is therefore anxious to recognise the diversity of perspectives within our culture. Within some of these there is talk of absolute standards and even of eternity. Rather than endeavour to get rid of such talk in the wake of an attack on foundational epistemology, he will try to see what it amounts to. The danger in Rorty's mode of enquiry is, that in freeing us from the pretensions of metaphysics, he makes us captive to the pretensions of hermeneutics. The extent of this captivity is yet to be explored.

Notes

1. Rorty, *Philosophy and the Mirror of Nature*, p. 211.
2. Ibid., p. 212.
3. Ibid., p. 317-18.
4. Ibid., p. 379.
5. Ibid., p. 179.
6. Søren Kierkegaard, *Purity of Heart*, trans. Douglas Steere (Harper Torch Books, New York, 1956).
7. See D.Z. Phillips, *Death and Immortality* (Macmillan, London, 1970).

12
The Hidden Values of Hermeneutics

What is the nature of the hermeneutic conversation to which Rorty invites us? I shall endeavour to show that it is a conversation which has hidden values. When these values are made explicit we can see why Rorty will not settle for philosophy's modest task: the search for clarity. According to him, philosophy cannot fulfil the aspirations of foundational epistemology. These were pretentious and led philosophy to overreach itself. Yet, as we shall see, the role of philosophy in the hermeneutic conversation is just as pretentious, perhaps more so, for being hidden.

Exposition of the nature of the hermeneutic conversation is difficult, because Rorty himself is not consistent nor always clear in what he has to say about it. He tells us,

> Hermeneutics sees the relation between various discourses as those of strands in a possible conversation, a conversation which presupposes no disciplinary matrix which unites the speakers, but where the hope of agreement is never lost as long as the conversation lasts. This hope is not a hope for the discovery of antecedently existing common ground, but *simply* hope for agreement, or, at least, exciting and fruitful disagreement. Epistemology sees the hope of agreement as a token of the existence of common ground, which, perhaps unknown to the speakers, unites them in a common rationality.[1]

From this quotation it is at least clear what Rorty is denying. He is denying that philosophy can fulfil the role of foundational epistemology. He does this in two ways: first, he denies that epistemology can provide a neutral yardstick by which to measure

154

the different claims of our epistemic practices; second, he denies that epistemology's task is to make explicit a supposed implicit rational foundation or rational goal which all human epistemic practices are said to possess. While the second task being denied avoids imposing external criteria of rationality on human practices, it imposes on them a unity they do not possess.

But what positive hopes does Rorty have for philosophy once it has taken a hermeneutical turn? The hope is that the hermeneutic conversation will end in agreement, or, at least, fruitful disagreement. What fruitful disagreement amounts to is not at all clear. In any case disagreement, not to mention radical and irrevocable disagreement, does not feature large in Rorty's discussion. It is hope of agreement through the hermeneutic conversation which predominates. But what does this hoped for agreement amount to? Surely, it is not to be interpreted so widely so as to include 'agreeing to differ'. Agreement entails common ground, but neither the agreement nor the common ground need exist before the conversation. In this, Rorty differs from foundational epistemologists and Reformed epistemologists. For him, agreement is hoped for subsequent to the hermeneutic conversation. If we note what actually happens, such agreement may, in fact, occur in a number of ways. First, one of the parties may realise his views are confused. Second, agreement may be reached by some kind of compromise. Third, agreement may be reached where one party sees it is going to lose and simply withdraws to fight another day. Agreements in industrial disputes often take this form. One side may accept an offer, the perceived inadequacy of which caused the dispute in the first place. Yet, even in these circumstances, it is said that an agreement in the dispute has been reached. These cases, and others one could mention, require separate treatment and cannot be run together. We never find out from Rorty the details of the situations he has in mind. Worse, at times he seems to espouse a purely pragmatic conception of agreement, where 'agreement' simply means that, as a matter of fact, someone has come out top in the conversation. Here, the best argument is simply the one that works.

Even at this early stage in the hermeneutic turn, a hidden value has come to light: agreement is good, and disagreement is bad. Despite the earlier reference to fruitful disagreement, it is highly unlikely to be accorded more than a stage in the hermeneutic conversation, a conversation which has agreement as its aim. Rorty has not put aside the grand designs in philosophy he seemed to be attacking. On the contrary, the only difference between foundational epistemology and hermeneutics is that the former assumed agreement to be already present, while the latter has it as a goal to aspire to. As Rorty says, 'the hope of agreement is never lost as long as the conversation lasts'.[2] In fact, there may be more to be said for the certainty foundationalism claimed to appeal to. At least it was something definite; a paradigm taken from a particular mode of discourse and illegitimately elevated to be a paradigm for all modes of discourse. The certainty hoped for in the hermeneutic conversation may turn out to be far more elusive to grasp.

Once we see the hope for such agreement to be a hidden value in hermeneutics, a second hidden value follows quickly in its wake. Since agreement is to come via conversation, readiness to engage in the hermeneutic conversation is assumed, without argument, to be a good thing. But has Rorty the right to make that assumption? He says, 'Epistemology views the participants as united in what Oakeshott calls an *universitas* — a group united by mutual interests in achieving a common end. Hermeneutics views them as united in what he calls a *societas* — persons whose paths through life have fallen together, united by civility rather than by a common goal, much less by a common ground.'[3] But if we look at contexts such as this, a society in which, as Rorty says, people have been thrown together, because their paths have happened to cross, it is clear that conversations will not be conversations with everyone. Further, invitations to converse may be accepted or refused. After all, it is often a criticism to say of someone that he'll talk to anyone. People will take the view that there are conversations they should engage in and others which they should have nothing to do with. And, of course, people will differ widely over which conversations these are. So if religious believers refuse to engage in certain conversations, this will not be peculiar to them. On the contrary, it is a characteristic which almost everyone shares. Rorty cannot escape from these observations by arguing that by civility he means the readiness to converse with those with whom we disagree. No doubt such readiness is apparent in innumerable cases. It must also be noted that, in other cases, such civility would be frowned on. Where certain viewpoints are concerned, uncivil relations with them may be praised and conversation positively discouraged or even forbidden.

The role of the philosopher is to note that there are these

agreements and disagreements when, for some reason or another, a philosopher is tempted to distort or ignore them. The question of whether those who disagree with each other *should* engage in conversation, in the hope of agreement, is not one that philosophy can answer, even when it calls itself hermeneutics. If some invitations to converse are greeted with enthusiasm, while others are told, 'Get thee behind me, Satan!', philosophy possesses no *a priori* method by which it can be shown that the latter response is necessarily misplaced or that the former response is always to be welcomed. Philosophy has to leave logical space for these different reactions. In identifying civility with readiness to converse, Rorty is doing no more than expressing his own opinions about the matter. What he is *not* doing is delineating the role philosophy must have after foundationalism.

What does a philosopher look like after he has taken a hermeneutic turn? As we have seen, he can no longer be regarded as 'the cultural overseer who knows everyone's common ground'. Rorty describes his new role as that of 'the informed dilettante, the polypragmatic, Socratic intermediary between various discourses. In his salon, so to speak, hermetic thinkers are charmed out of their self-enclosed practices. Disagreements between disciplines and discourses are compromised or transcended in the course of the conversation.'[4] Once again, however, we have to ask why it is thought that people ought to be charmed out of or compromise their practices. As we have seen, it may be necessary to clear up the confusion of someone who thinks that, in order to defend the 'truths' of his practices, he must deny the descriptive terms 'moral' or 'religious' to any practices other than his own. Yet, this has nothing to do with persuading someone to change his practices. If a person were asked to enter a conversation with adherents of a view he found extremely distasteful, and if he were told that civility demanded that his differences with them should be transcended, he might reply, with good reason, 'So much the worse for civility!'.

We see a third hidden value emerge in the hermeneutical assumptions of the kind of philosopher Rorty has in mind: he assumes that there is such a thing as normal discourse and abnormal discourse. Normal discourse is that discourse within which, for the most part, the participants agree with each other. Within normal discourse there are settled, well-established procedures by reference to which any disputes, should they arise, can be settled. Abnormal discourse occurs when someone joins the conversation who does not share or conform to the standards of normal discourse. Rorty gives, as an analogy, Kuhn's distinction between normal science and revolutionary science. The analogy is misleading, in this context, since however revolutionary the change, we are still talking about a change in the course of science. Rorty's use of 'abnormal discourse' is so wide, by contrast, that it is meant to span from utter nonsense to revolutions!

What exactly is abnormal discourse? It must have some context in which it has its sense. Even Rorty admits that to attempt abnormal discourse *de novo* is madness. One kind of situation Rorty has in mind is this: a scientist, with scientistic pretensions of being able to reduce everything to a common denominator, is resisted by adherents to moral, political and religious perspectives. They argue against scientism. If such a confrontation is called abnormal discourse, the term simply refers to the clash, the disagreement, between the perspectives involved. But Rorty wants to call the perspectives themselves instances of abnormal discourse. If so, this cannot be because there are no procedures for reaching agreement *within* these perspectives. For example, within a religious perspective there may be procedures for determining when a spirit is or is not of God. If, then, this religious perspective is called abnormal discourse, it is not because the participants cannot reach agreement within it, but *because non-participants cannot reach agreement about it*. But why should the fact that those who do not participate in a practice cannot agree about it, entitle us to call the discourse of that practice abnormal? Another hidden value begins to emerge in the form of an appeal to some kind of observers' view of human practices. Who are these observers? What status do they have? The answers to these questions have yet to emerge.

At this point we are confronted, not by a hidden value in hermeneutics, but by an explicit one. Once we put aside foundational epistemologies, we are left with edifying philosophy. Edification occurs when abnormal discourse is viewed from the perspective of normal discourse. What does this edification amount to? Rorty replies,

> The attempt to edify (ourselves or others) may consist in the hermeneutic activity of making connections between our culture and some exotic culture or historical period, or between our own discipline and another discipline which seems to pursue incommensurable aims in an

incommensurable vocabulary. But it may instead consist in the 'poetic' activity of thinking up such new aims, new words or new disciplines, followed by, so to speak, the inverse of hermeneutics: the attempt to reinterpret our familiar surroundings in the unfamiliar terms of our new inventions. In either case, the activity is (despite the etymological relation between the two words) edifying without being constructive — at least if 'constructive' means the sort of co-operation in the accomplishment of research programmes which takes place in normal discourse. For edifying discourse is *supposed* to be abnormal, to take us out of our old selves by the power of strangeness, to aid us in becoming new beings.[5]

This long passage illustrates how vague a notion Rorty's conception of edification is. He thinks in the hermeneutic conversation 'that the preservation of the values of the Enlightenment is our best hope.'[6] But these values must be stripped of their foundationalist pretensions. The parties in the hermeneutic conversation are not subject to a sovereign concept of reason. On the contrary, edifying philosophy overthrows all attempts to discover 'the final commensurating vocabulary for all *possible* rational discourse'.[7] Rorty would not only be opposed to the foundationalism which seeks an external foundation for all human practices. He would also be opposed to those Reformed epistemologists who argued as though all the practices already have a common foundation in God even when the participants fail to recognise this.[8] Rorty sees any attempt to reduce all vocabularies to one as a denial of our humanity.

Another hidden value emerges at this stage of the argument. When Rorty resists any attempt to reduce the variety of human perspectives and practices to a commensurable measure, he is speaking as an enquirer who wants to respect the differences he sees in the account he gives of them. So far, so good. But Rorty wants to go further. He claims that no individual can identify himself completely with any of the styles of discourse involved in the hermeneutic conversation. This is a much bolder claim. It is a recommendation that the individual should have a determinate attitude towards the modes of discourse he encounters. But this recommendation does not follow from any kind of philosophical analysis. What if the discourse with which a person identifies himself is religious? What if he says that, in God, he lives and moves and has his being? What kind of confusion is he supposed to be guilty of? Rorty says that the edifying philosopher's aim is to keep the conversation going rather than aim for objective truth. He says that no one can be acquainted or provided with 'all of Truth'. But the believer may insist that Jesus is the Way, the Life and the Truth.

What has happened here is that, once again, Rorty has conflated the metaphysical concepts he wants to attack with some important concepts in the practices he says he wants to respect. Thus, when he attacks the notions of 'objective truth' or 'all of Truth', he is referring to the kind of foundational knowledge systematic philosophies claimed they could provide. He is attacking the possibility of a science of values. But when Christians say that Jesus is the Truth, they are not putting forward any such science. They are confessing their Faith. Rorty objects to an individual finding his identity in such a confession, as though that contravened his insights when attacking foundational epistemology. Of course, it does no such thing. A believer may be quite aware of the values and truths proclaimed in other practices. Their existence and difference need not be denied by his confession.

The hidden values of hermeneutics emerge all the more clearly if we ask whether Rorty objects to an absolute religious allegiance on the part of the believer. It may seem, at first, that he does not want to interfere with the allegiances of individuals. After all, he does say that the burden of choice cannot pass from an individual. He must reach his conclusions for himself. But these appearances are deceptive. It is hard to see how Rorty could condone refusal to engage in the hermeneutic conversation, since he says that 'getting into a conversation with strangers is like acquiring a new virtue'.[9]

If Rorty were simply recommending the hermeneutic conversation to those, like himself, who are attracted by it, they could be left to their business, confused though it might be. But he is doing more than that: he is giving philosophy a new prescriptive role after the demise of foundationalism. He is not prepared to settle for clarity. The prescriptive character of his enterprise is shown in his advocacy of talking to strangers and coming to feel at ease with what was strange previously. But how can such advocacy be made *in vacuo*? Of course, it is easy enough to think of situations in which closer contact has led to greater understanding and the clearing up of fear, prejudice and baseless suspicion. On the other hand, it is equally easy to think of situations where distance should be maintained, since contact would be contact with what is evil and base. In that event, it is better that such things should remain strange to us. 'Don't speak to strangers' is often good advice. I have refrained from giving examples because another feature of such situations to be noted, is that there will be differences and disagreements in many cases over what we should draw near to and what we should keep away from. *That* is the kind of complexity philosophy must respect and refrain from tidying up. Rorty, like the epistemologists he criticises, cannot settle for differences. They insisted on providing foundations. He insists on edifying us.

Let us see further what this involves. Consider a religious believer who sees certain non-religious perspectives as greatly distanced from his own perspective. They seem strange to him. This may be due to misunderstandings on his part. If all Rorty were saying were that when these misunderstandings are cleared up, the perspectives no longer seem strange, there would be no objections to his rather obvious claim. But that is *not* what Rorty is saying. He is claiming that the aim of a hermeneutic conversation is that we should feel at ease with what was strange to us before. But why should it not be otherwise? Why should what was strange to us before the hermeneutic conversation not be even stranger after it? Faced with a readiness to accommodate on the part of the believers, the prophet remonstrated, 'Woe to them that are at ease in Zion!'

Rorty goes further: he suggests that another aim of the hermeneutic conversation is 'to reinterpret our familiar surroundings in the unfamiliar terms of our new inventions',[10] the new inventions being new aims, words, or disciplines which may emerge from our conversations. He gives the examples of Freudianism and Marxism being incorporated into people's vocabularies. If Rorty is referring to the values associated with these movements they have, undoubtedly, eroded old values, including religious ones, in the lives of many people. But if by Freudianism and Marxism we mean their pretensions to be systematic philosophies, then Rorty should attack the same essentialism in them as he did in foundational epistemology. There is little evidence of Rorty allowing that there could be a religious critique of these movements. His emphasis is always on the incorporation of the new and the innovative.

The reason for this emphasis is to be found in Rorty's conviction that one of the purposes of hermeneutic philosophy is to break the hold of convention. Once again, however, it is essential to distinguish between philosophical conventions and ordinary conventions. Rorty's attack on the foundationalist conventions of epistemology must not be confused with an attack on established moral and religious conventions. In this latter context, as we have seen, there will be different and conflicting judgements. 'Sticking to one's ways' will be an accusation in the mouths of some and a congratulation in the mouths of others. That this is so is a datum for philosophy to observe, not a problem for philosophy to clear up.

Despite his emphasis on historical considerations, Rorty, curiously enough, shows little real interest in the *content* of any moral, political or religious perspective. Instead, he emphasises the confusions about *any* perspective from which hermeneutics is supposed to deliver us. The story, applied here to religious belief, goes something like this: we may be confused about the logical character of our religious belief. Because we say we are in contact with an ultimate reality, we may think this entails that we have a conception of reality as the external foundation of all those practices in which we distinguish, in various ways, between the real and the unreal. Once we are delivered from this misconception we see that our religious perspective enjoys no absolute metaphysical status. In the culture, it is simply one option among others. But what happens when, as Rorty recommends, we begin sampling the options? There are times when the sampling is simply a matter of noting who wins that particular conversation. But once some voice or other has become the dominant one, we are not to be satisfied with *that* either. We are called on again to pastures new. And so another conversation is won and another contentment guarded against. It seems that when Rorty called his philosopher 'an informed dilettante' he said more than he realised, for the character who emerges from the hermeneutic story is the dabbler who cannot give himself to anything for very long. The interest of the dabbler seems to be captured by the following description:

> To say we become different people, that we 'remake' ourselves as we read more, talk more and write more, is simply a dramatic way of saying that the sentences which become true of us by virtue of such activities are often more important to us than the sentences which become true of

us when we drink more, earn more, and so on. The events which make us able to say new and interesting things about ourselves are, in this nonmetaphysical sense, more 'essential' to us (at least to us relatively leisured intellectuals inhabiting a stable and prosperous part of the world) than the events which change our shapes or our standards of living.[11]

Put a little more flatteringly, it could be argued that Rorty's notion of a hermeneutic conversation is simply a philosophical reconstruction of his own interests as an historian of the intellect for whom philosophy becomes a ' "voice in the conversation of mankind"... which centres on one topic rather than another at some given time not by dialectical necessity but as a result of various things happening elsewhere in the conversations'.[12] Rorty insists that edifying philosophy must leave room for wonder at the new. What we have seen is that an over-emphasis in this direction leaves no room for wonder at the ordinary.

The values of the dilettante *cannot* be reflected in the attitudes of the participants in the practices the dilettante is reflecting on. This is because, in seeking his own edification, he does not give them the attention they deserve from a philosopher; he does not wait on them. To analyse the attitudes of the participants in terms of the dabbler's attitudes would lead to radical incoherence. The dilettante does not commit himself to any perspective. He claims to be absorbed in their history, in their comings and goings, their formations and declines. But to be truly absorbed in the history of various practices is to wait on the conceptions found in them. Among these, as in religious perspectives, there are conceptions of truth and eternal standards. People have died for the truth. Could Rorty's informed dilettante give an account of that fact? Was it that martyrs did not realise there were other options open to them? If Rorty had waited on the religious perspective he would have seen that the knowledge of God believers possess, after foundationalism, does not have to be identified by the outcome of the hermeneutic conversation. It might survive such a conversation or get lost in it. But its primary meaning is to be found in the ordinary context of praise and worship.

How is a believer to respond if the hermeneutic conversation seems to be going against him? Can he say, with Rorty, 'It would be foolish to keep conversation on the subject going once everyone, or the majority, or the wise, are satisfied, but of course we *can*.'[13] Rorty says that by knowledge we mean what our peers will let us get away with. Religious believers will not be impressed by this view. After all, they have been told that God has made foolish the wisdom of this world, and they have been warned to beware of those who are wise in the ways of the world. Why, then, should they seek a consensus opinion? No reason at all, unless they become entrapped by Rorty's relativistic conception of knowledge as consensus opinion.

Objections to Rorty's view of knowledge as that which our peers will let us get away with do not depend, however, on taking the allegiances of minority groups as our examples. On the contrary, the objections hold in the case of the most ordinary examples of normal discourse. Consider, for example, our talk of colours. It is a fact, of course, that when I see a red object I expect any other normally sighted person to see that it is red too. But I do not consult the majority in calling the object red. I do not agree with them to react in the way I do. I simply react and find that they agree. It is an agreement *in* our reactions. On Rorty's analysis what *the* colour of the object is, is a matter of what the consensus is among opinions first reached on an individual basis. On such a view, each individual could have his own conception of red, green, blue, etc. The logical point, however, is that there is no conception of colours prior to the agreement in reactions, and *in* those reactions, no reference is made to the majority at all. On a given occasion, the individual could be right, and the majority wrong.

When we turn to moral, political and religious perspectives it is even more important to resist Rorty's analysis. Although we do not learn what to value in the way we learn colour, here, too, agreement in reactions is important. I may be introduced to a moral, political or religious perspective. The likelihood, in the vast majority of cases, is that this perspective has been established long before I was born. Yet, making it my own is not a matter of conforming to what the majority say. I could adhere to it for that reason, but, then, my adherence is conventional and not real. This distinction lies at the root of Plato's separation of philosophical virtues from popular virtues. A soldier who has popular virtue may act in conformity to what courage demands, but only because he fears public condemnation more. He is not courageous. He barters fear for fear. If a person simply conforms to a majority consensus, he will do *whatever* the majority say he ought to do. A man who believes in something morally will not abandon it simply because the majority who once supported it now abandon it. For him, knowing what is right is not a matter of what his peers let him get away with. Indeed, the trouble with the peers may be precisely their readiness to let us get away with such things.

Looking back at the hidden values of hermeneutics, it is hard to see any good reason why philosophy should take this turn after foundationalism. We have seen what these hidden values come to: we must be ready to enter into a conversation with those with whom we disagree in the culture in the hope of transcending our disagreements. Yet, should agreement be reached, we are not to rest content in it, but are to be called on to further innovative conversations. All this is said to be the consequence of seeing through the foundational pretensions of epistemology. The world of these pretensions is a world well lost. Yet in the course of his criticisms we have seen Rorty demolish much of our ordinary world at the same time. He also thinks that no such thing as a distinctively philosophical method survives his criticisms. If by 'method' he means the establishing of epistemological foundations, this may be true. But philosophical method, as we have seen in Wittgenstein, need not amount to this. Its characteristic method will be to get us to see things as they are by recalling our ways of speaking from what our metaphysical tendencies have made of them, to the natural place they have in people's lives. This task, as we have seen, may be far more arduous than we might suppose. Our conceptual confusions may have a strong hold on us. My contention has been that Rorty does not give us back our natural ways of talking. They are distorted by his conception of hermeneutics. Rorty says, 'For hermeneutics, inquiry is routine conversation'.[14] Unfortunately, as conceptual clarification shows, this is not the case: in hermeneutics, routine conversation is vulgarised. Rorty complains about the lack of agreement over what constitutes a successful conceptual analysis. That lack of agreement no doubt exists. But impatience with a philosophical conversation is not a good reason for forsaking it for the conversation called hermeneutics.

Notes

1. Rorty, *Philosophy and the Mirror of Nature*, p. 318.
2. Ibid., p. 318.
3. Ibid.
4. Ibid., p. 317.
5. Ibid., p. 360.
6. Ibid., pp. 335-6.
7. Ibid., p. 387.
8. See Chapter 6.
9. Rorty, *Philosophy and the Mirror of Nature*, p. 319.
10. Ibid., p. 360.
11. Ibid., p. 359.
12. Ibid., p. 264.
13. Ibid., p. 159.
14. Ibid., p. 318.

13

The Sociologising of Values

We have seen that, in wanting to be the philosophical successors to foundational epistemology, Reformed epistemology and hermeneutics take us away from the world we already know. Opposing the metaphysical pretensions of foundationalism, these philosophies fall foul of pretensions of their own. Despite the fact that these were exposed by means of philosophical arguments, arguments influenced by Wittgenstein, many have come to the conclusion that the kind of conceptual attention our surroundings deserve cannot be supplied from within philosophy itself. After foundationalism, they argue, we must turn elsewhere. The direction in which we should turn, it is suggested, is that which leads us to the sociology of knowledge. At first, it may seem, that in the criticisms we are about to consider, sociologists of knowledge are close to Wittgenstein's strictures on philosophical theorising.

> The theoretical formulations of reality, whether they be scientific or philosophical or even mythological, do not exhaust what is 'real' for the members of a society. Since this is so, the sociology of knowledge must first of all concern itself with what people 'know' as 'reality' in their everyday non- or pre-theoretical lives. In other words, common-sense 'knowledge' rather than 'ideas' must be the central focus for the sociology of knowledge. It is precisely this 'knowledge' that constitutes the fabric of meanings without which no society could exist.[1]

It is true that Peter Berger and Thomas Luckmann say that philosophy's task is 'to obtain maximal clarity as to the ultimate status of what the man in the street believes to be "reality" and "knowledge" ',[2] but they also think that philosophy has failed in this task:

The sociology of knowledge understands human reality as socially constructed reality. Since the constitution of reality has traditionally been a central problem of philosophy, this understanding has certain philosophical implications. In so far as there has been a strong tendency for this problem, with all the questions it involves, to become trivialized in contemporary philosophy, the sociologist may find himself, to his surprise perhaps, the inheritor of philosophical questions that the professional philosophers are no longer interested in considering.[3]

This is a bold claim. If my answer to it is not to be misunderstood, the context in which it is offered must be clear from the outset. Berger has accused philosophers of failing in the task of clearing up confusions about our ordinary uses of 'knowledge', 'belief', 'truth', etc. He offers to give us that clear view. My concern is with the language he offers us in his attempt to do so. The object of my criticisms, therefore, is not sociology as a subject, but the language offered by a particular sociologist as the means of clarity. That this should be thought necessary is due to the fact that, although confused, this language has been influential. The language is, in fact, conceptually confused, an instance of language idling. But, as we shall see, this does not mean that it has no effect. It invites us to think in a way which obscures from us the very possibilities it claims to be clarifying. What Berger presents is a persuasive story. Our only hope of seeing through it is by a criticism of each stage in its development. We shall find that there are many echoes of Rorty's notion of hermeneutics in Berger's sociological story.

At the first stage of the story, we find man presented as the radical inventor of the world in which he lives. Berger tells us, 'Man manufactures a tool and by that action enriches the totality of physical objects present in the world. Once produced, the tool has a being of its own that cannot readily be changed by those who employ it.'[4] Unaware of any change of grammatical context Berger proceeds to say, 'Man invents a language and then finds that both his speaking and thinking are dominated by its grammar. Man produces values and discovers that he feels guilt when he contravenes them.'[5] Berger sees no difference between speaking

168

a language within which it makes sense to speak of inventive activities, and speaking of language itself as if it could be the product of invention. Inventiveness presupposes intelligibility, and therefore cannot be postulated in order to explain its origin. Berger confuses internal conceptual relations by treating them as though they were events and consequences. Conformity to grammar, or moral guilt, are not consequences discovered subsequent to the alleged inventions of language and values, since grammar and guilt are internally related to the speaking of a language and to morality, respectively.

Having postulated man as the radical inventor of meanings, Berger is faced with the problem of explaining why the meanings of words are not at our disposal, to do with them what we will. He has to admit, of course, that after the initial inventions, the rest of us are born into a world not of our making. He says, 'the basic co-ordinates within which one must move and decide have still been drawn by others, most of them strangers, many of them long in their graves'.[6] So, in this, the second stage of the story, man is presented as the radical victim of his own inventions.

Berger's analysis of the sense in which a man is a victim is extremely confusing, and obscures from us the reality of the victimisations to which people may be subject. For example, people may be victimised when they are made subject to coercive institutions. But Berger claims that institutions are, by nature, coercive. 'Above all,' he says, 'society manifests itself by its coercive power.'[7] When he gives the law as an example of coercion, we may be tempted to think that he is going to give instances of institutions, or features of institutions, he considers to be coercive. Yet this is not so. Berger claims, 'the same coercive objectivity characterises society *as a whole* and is present in all social institutions, including those institutions that were founded on consensus'.[8] Clearly, for Berger, 'coercive' cannot mean a character possessed by some institutions, but not others. He says, 'It is important to stress that this controlling character is inherent in institutionalization as such.'[9] Berger insists,

This (most emphatically) does *not* mean that all societies are variations of tyranny. It *does* mean that no human construction can be accurately called a social phenomenon unless it has achieved that measure of objectivity that compels the individual to recognise it as real. In other words, the fundamental coerciveness of society lies not in its

169

machineries of social control, but in its power to constitute and impose itself as reality.[10]

Berger's metaphysical abstractions in these remarks obscure from us the realities of personal and social life. We may want to call some institutions coercive, but not others. In calling them all coercive, Berger robs this distinction of its point. Again, within certain institutions, we may be coerced to say or do what we would prefer not to do. At other times, we may initiate policies we want to promote or be glad of policies others have initiated. All this is obscured if we say that, of necessity, every institution is coercive. If we tried to find a context which would give Berger's words some application, it would be that of someone, born out of time, to whom all the institutions are coercive. But it is grotesque to offer an analysis which would fit an extreme case as the analysis of all cases of institutional life.

The same confusion arises when Berger says that all institutions are limited. He also says, 'It is impossible to understand an institution adequately without an understanding of the historical process in which it was produced.'[11] Yet it is ahistorical to call an institution limited, in a pejorative sense, because it is limited to (in the sense of belonging to) a certain time and place. All institutions are subject to the limits of time and place, so that is not what we mean when we distinguish between great institutions, and limited or narrow institutions. Once again, a metaphysical abstraction obscures the ordinary distinctions we make.

Yet Berger's story needs to emphasise that man the radical inventor has become the victim of coercion, for this enables its third stage to develop by asking why man has allowed this to happen. Berger replies, 'What lies at the bottom of this apparently inevitable pressure towards consensus is probably a profound human desire to be accepted, presumably by whatever group is around to do the accepting.'[12] Once again, this description would be familiar enough in a specific context. An individual may want to belong to some group or other and he does not care which. He simply wants to be accepted by 'whatever group is around to do the accepting'. We recognise the phenomenon. But it is absurd to offer that as an analysis of all our engagements in social affairs. People do not have common interests in order to have common bonds. Their interests are their bonds. Since he cannot recognise this, Berger has to search for a motive for man's desire to belong.

The fourth stage of the story provides this motive. Man desires to belong because he is protected by an ordered and meaningful life. Berger says, 'every nomos is an area of meaning carved out of a vast mass of meaninglessness, a small clearing of lucidity in a formless, dark, always ominous jungle'.[13] Berger concludes, 'to live in the social world is to live an ordered and meaningful life'.[14] Again, the abstract identification 'living in the social world' with 'living an ordered and meaningful life', obscures more than it illuminates.

The meaningful and the social cannot be identified. Family relationships have their character within the social institution of the family, but those relationships may be destructive as well as constructive; they may tear apart as well as bind together. Again, if the social entailed the ordered and the meaningful, one would have to say that the bankrupt businessman who commits suicide, whose distress is unintelligible apart from social factors, has lived an ordered and meaningful life.

Similar difficulties arise when Berger tries to identify 'being social' with 'being sane' and to say that to live a social life is to live a sane life. Sometimes, when he speaks of the contrast between sanity and insanity, Berger means to contrast man as a language-user and the state he might have been in had he had no language at all. But this contrast does not have a bearing on the other contexts in which Berger wants to talk about the threat of life appearing meaningless. Living a social life is no protection, as such, against these threats. On the contrary, the threats only have their meaning in that very context. My disorders, troubles, etc., are unintelligible apart from the social activities and personal relationships I am involved in. So it will not do to say, 'Seen in the perspective of the individual, every nomos represents the bright "dayside" of life, tenuously held onto against the sinister shadows of the "night".'[15] So far from the social world of men having the function of staving off nightmares, it gives to such nightmares the only sense they could have. It will not do to say that 'the individual is provided by society with various methods to stave off the nightmare world of anomy and to stay within the safe boundaries of the established nomos',[16] since, but for society and the established nomos, there would not be anything to stave off.

So far, we have encountered four metaphysical abstractions in Berger's sociological story: man the *inventor* of meanings becomes *coerced* by his own meanings due to his desire to be *accepted by a group*, an acceptance which provides him with *protection against anomy*. As we have seen, it is possible, for the most part, to find

171

situations where the abstractions can be grounded and transformed into specific descriptions, descriptions which apply to these situations, but not to others. But, of course, that is not what Berger takes himself to be doing in telling us his story. He is claiming, as we have seen, to be giving us a language 'which reflects what people "know" as "reality" in their everyday non- or pre-theoretical lives'.[17] The story is supposed to be grounded in the commonsense which philosophy distorts. What in fact is happening is that Berger's story itself obscures our ordinary world from us and becomes an obstacle to any understanding of it.

This fact can be illustrated by asking what place can be given to values in terms of the story we have heard so far. It is clear that, for Berger, values have become organisational concepts. Whether something is of value is discussed in terms of its leading to personal integration or social solidarity. Ultimately, such discussion cannot accommodate the concept of value at all. Whether organisation at an individual or social level is worth while depends on its *character*, not simply on its efficacy. To say that something is moral simply because it belongs to some form of organisation can never be a mode of vindication, let alone a final vindication. In these matters, the values are primary, a primacy in terms of which any form of organisation would be subject to an additional moral, political or religious mode of discrimination.

From a certain psychological perspective, beliefs and values are seen as the means by which an individual achieves the integration of his personality. According to such a popular psychological ethic, an ethic to be found in Berger's story, personal integration, feeling comfortable with oneself, is what is of primary importance. Of course, the requirements of this ethic are satisfied by the well-integrated rogue and mediocrity of many kinds. There is no room in such an ethic for the notion of a goodness which is out of reach, or of a grace one might stand in need of. Flannery O'Connor reacted robustly to such an ethic:

> There is a question whether faith can or is supposed to be emotionally satisfying. I must say that the thought of everyone lolling about in an emotionally satisfying faith is repugnant to me. I believe that we are ultimately directed Godward but that the journey is often impeded by emotion.[18]

Religion is not a function of integrated emotions. On the contrary, emotions are subject to the demands of faith.

Similar difficulties arise if, from a sociological perspective, we say that beliefs and values are the means by which social solidarity is achieved. No concern with good and evil can give primacy to rules of association as such. To allow such primacy is to stay at the level of manners, where no space can be found for good or evil, grace or mystery. This is a level at which we are content with relativistic judgements about the customs, practices and values we see around us. We are content with saying that according to one group, such-and-such is of value, but that according to another group, something else is of value. Within such relativities there is little room for mystery. There is no room for the question, 'What *is* of value?' Once again, Flannery O'Connor will not allow such questions to be put aside. She says, in her typically forthright manner: 'My standard is: when in Rome, do as you done in Milledgeville.'[19] Writing to John Hawkes, she says,

> You say one becomes 'evil' when one leaves the herd. I say that depends on what the herd is doing. The herd has been known to be right, in which case the one who leaves it is doing evil. When the herd is wrong, the one who leaves it is not doing evil but the right thing. If I remember rightly, you put that word, evil, in quotation marks which means the standards you judge it by are relative: in fact you would be looking at it there with the eyes of the herd.[20]

It is interesting to note Berger's use of quotation marks too. So far, in his story, and it is a matter I shall not pursue further, he has spoken of 'real', 'know', 'reality', 'knowledge', 'ideas', 'dayside', 'night'. Are these words being used in a special sense? Hardly. They are supposed to shed light on our ordinary senses of these terms. Yet Berger's use of quotation marks indicates that he is half-aware that he is deviating from our normal usage and meanings. Unfortunately half-awareness proves to be insufficient to deter him from continuing his story in such a way that the difficulties we have already met are compounded. When I chose the title of this chapter I deliberately included a barbarism in the word 'sociologising'. This is because the fate of values in Berger's analysis is akin to the fate of conversation in Rorty's hermeneutics: they are vulgarised.

Berger's sociological story is one in which, as we have seen, man, after his invention of language, is quickly imprisoned by it and its meanings. This imprisonment is not irksome to him because he has a deep desire to be accepted by some group or other. This sense of belonging protects him from anomy. We have seen what happens to any concept of value on this analysis. Yet, surely, it may be said, Berger is aware of the myriad ways in which criticism goes on in a society. How does social change occur if his all too static story is accepted? The answer is that Berger is indeed aware of criticism and change, but he analyses them in such a way that the misunderstandings we have already encountered are compounded.

For Berger, as we have seen, giving oneself to certain movements and institutions is analysed in terms of an expression of a desire for security and protection. It is not surprising, therefore, to find him characterising criticisms of movements and institutions as threats to the *status quo*, and answers to such criticisms as legitimations of the *status quo*. We are told that legitimations are what pass for knowledge in a social collectivity, and that they have the function of defending and obscuring the inherent fragility of the nomos being questioned. 'Let the institutional order be so interpreted as to hide as much as possible, its *constructed* character. Let that which has been stamped out of the ground *ex nihilo* appear as the manifestation of something that has been existent from the beginning of time, or at least from the beginning of this group.'[21] Once again, Berger's metaphysical abstraction leaves no room for familiar distinctions which we draw. For example, we distinguish, in various ways, between reasons and rationalisations, but, on Berger's analysis, reasons *are* rationalisations. Again, we are acquainted with the specific circumstances which give Berger's analysis its surface plausibility. Genuine criticisms of institutions may and have run into a blank wall of protectiveness. The phenomenon is a well-known one, and Kafka and Solzhenitsyn have shown us how sinister and soul-destroying that lack of response can be. As usual, however, Berger robs this real phenomenon of its force by transforming it into a metaphysical theory about social movements and institutions as such. What does he make of traditions which are themselves critical by nature — science or philosophy, for example? Questions cannot threaten such traditions, since they are a condition of their continuance. Even where criticism is forbidden, we cannot leap to the conclusion that this is a device to protect the fragility of what cannot be criticised. Criticism of a saga may be forbidden because of the status of the saga. It may be thought to express eternal truths.

One is asked either to come to terms with these truths, or to be estranged from them. They are not there to be bargained with, not because they are fragile and this needs to be covered up somehow or other, but because bargaining is ruled out by their grammar as eternal truths.

What of the man who does not criticise his place in an institution, but finds himself in it? Berger does not allow this possibility. He thinks that a man who identifies himself with such a role, is necessarily in bad faith: 'The professor putting on an act that pretends to wisdom comes to feel wise. The preacher finds himself believing what he preaches. The soldier discovers martial stirrings in his breast as he puts on his uniform.'[22] We have no difficulty in recognising these examples, but we are able to recognise them only because we are also aware of what they are trying to distort. They cannot be the whole story. This is not to deny that some forms of bad faith, such as the desire for social esteem or flattery, need not be distortions of anything. The desire for flattery may be a primitive one. Berger, however, is committed to the view that to be absorbed in an activity is necessarily a form of bad faith.

Berger is not saying that absorption in a role is the result of deliberate play-acting:

> Deliberate deception requires a degree of psychological self-control that few people are capable of. That is why insincerity is rather a rare phenomenon. Most people are sincere, because this is the easiest course to take psychologically ... Sincerity is the consciousness of the man who is taken in by his own act. Or as it has been put by David Riesman, the sincere man is the one who believes in his own propaganda.[23]

The analogy throughout *Invitation to Sociology* is with the theatre: a man is more than his roles, just as an actor is more than his parts. The analogy does not hold. An actor has a life apart from all the parts he plays. Even here, of course, an actor may say that acting *is* his life, but, then, he is not acting when he says that. Again, we can often distinguish between a man who conforms to, or plays at, being this or that, and a man who gives himself to it and in so doing becomes as much part of it as it is part of him. Berger seems to think that individuality is preserved when *all* such activities and relations are stripped away, whereas, in fact, this would destroy the conditions of its possibility.

Similar conclusions are arrived at if we look at two further concepts which play an important rôle in Berger's sociological story: the concept of alienation and the the concept of human liberation. What is Berger's definition of alienation? He says, 'The essence of all alienation is the imposition of a fictitious inexorability upon the humanly constructed world' by which 'choices become destiny'.[24] In criticism of my earlier remarks about the bankrupt who commits suicide, it might be said that I am insensitive to the fact that the poor devil who goes out of the window is coerced by the institutions within which he has his being, and which give to his life the only order he thinks is available to him. Is he not precisely Berger's alienated man who thinks, mistakenly, that a social construct is an inescapable fact? He kills himself because within the parameters of the institutions which define his reality, he has only one option open to him: total rejection and the loss of meaning and order. This total rejection he sees as a necessary consequence of his social destruction — his bankruptcy.[25] But, of course, it is no part of my case to deny that a man may be wrong in denying that he has no alternatives open to him. In fact, it is the very *generality* of Berger's analysis which robs such specific instances of their point. For him, a man is *always* in bad faith if he thinks that no choices are open to him. By embracing such a thesis, Berger divorces the concept of responsibility from that of necessity. On his view, responsibilities may be put aside when disaster threatens. Such a generalised policy would surely not be called responsible at all. Berger tells us that

> the faithful husband may tell himself that he has 'no choice' but to 'programme' his sexual activity in accordance with his marital role, suppressing any lustful alternatives as 'impossibilities' ... Or again, the faithful executioner may tell himself that he has 'no choice' but to follow the 'programme' of head-chopping, suppressing both the emotional and moral inhibitions (compassion and scruples, say) to this course of action, which he posits as inexorable necessity for himself *qua* executioner.[26]

The indiscriminate nature of Berger's analysis can be seen in the way he runs together the example of the executioner who wants to evade his responsibility, and the husband for whom infidelity is not an option. On Berger's analysis, *both* have to be seen as the products of alienation. This is deeply confused. The refusal to regard infidelity as an option is itself an expression of the moral perspective the husband embraces. His adherence need have nothing to do with the threat of anomy or with the fear of conscience which Berger often discusses as though it were no more than a fear of emotional disturbance. It is Berger, not the husband, who is blind to possibilities, namely, the possibility of a moral perspective having an absolute claim on an individual. Berger thinks such absolute claims are confused because 'the plurality of social worlds in modern society' implies that 'the structures of each particular world are experienced as relatively unstable and unreliable'.[27] We have already seen, in our discussions of epistemology, that the possibility, or even actuality, of different ways of doing things, different ways of thinking, need not lead us to doubt our ways of thought and behaviour. What *is* shown is that our ways of proceeding are not underpinned by any kind of metaphysical necessity. No doubt Berger would agree with this latter point but in his thinking it leads to the equally metaphysical view that 'Sociology uncovers the infinite precariousness of all socially assigned identities.'[28] No more than in the epistemological case must it follow that, noting the mere existence of values other than his own, a man must experience his own as relatively unstable or unreliable. On the contrary, his allegiance to his own values may be strengthened, and he may combat the others in a fight which, for him, will be informed and instructed by the perspective he embraces.

We have already seen, in Berger's sociological story, that the absorption in pervasive social perspectives is explained in terms of the desire to be protected against anomy. Such protection is said to be the function of the perspective. Among perspectives, religion is one of the prime agents of alienation, since it makes a man think that the religious order is fixed and unchanging. Since that order is meant to speak to the whole world, religion becomes for Berger, 'the audacious attempt to conceive of the entire universe as being humanly significant'.[29] How is this audacious attempt to succeed? Berger replies, 'The fundamental "recipe" of religious legitimation is the transformation of human products into supra- or non-human facticities. The humanly made world is explained in terms that deny its human production.'[30]

Once again, as in the other examples we have considered, this analysis impoverishes and distorts the values which are present in religious perspectives. For example, instead of asking what might be meant by saying that God remembers when men have forgotten, an enquiry which would involve looking at the roles this remark plays in people's lives, Berger simply says that the reference to God is a protective device against the precariousness of human memories.[31] In his analysis, the religious fear of sinning against God, becomes the extreme form of sanction against any form of enquiry, and the loss of the strongest form of protection against anomy: 'To go against the order of society is always to risk plunging into anomy. To go against the order of society as religiously legitimated, however, is to make a compact with the primeval forces of darkness.'[32] No one would deny that the examples Berger gives have application: they are deviations and distortions of religious ideas. But Berger does not offer them as examples. On the contrary, the language of the deviant cases is offered as the analysis of standard religious concepts.

This becomes patently obvious once Berger begins to offer more detailed instances of what he takes religious belief to be. He joins that chorus of voices who see in religious belief little more than a craving for comfort and shelter. Berger could make nothing of the insistence of someone like Simone Weil who points out that dying to the desire for compensation is a necessary precondition of coming to see how events in one's life can be seen as the will of God who sends rain on the just and the unjust. It is not that Berger is unacquainted with such ideas, but, to make them fit his sociological story, he gives them grotesque analyses. For example, the acceptance of suffering is seen as a masochistic surrender of the self in the other, due to fear of loneliness. Just imagine offering that as the explanation of the life of someone like St John of the Cross. In Berger's hands it would become a life of sublimated self-interest. Here is what he makes of surrender to God:

The 'I am nothing — He is everything' now becomes enhanced by the empirical unavailability of the other to whom the masochistic surrender is made. After all, one of the inherent difficulties of masochism in human relations is that the other may not play the sadistic role to satisfaction. — The sadistic fellowman may refuse or forget to be properly all-powerful, or may simply be incapable of pulling off the act. Even if he succeeds in being something of a credible master for a while, he remains vulnerable, limited, mortal — in fact remains human. The sadistic god is not handicapped by these empirical imperfections. He remains invulnerable, infinite, immortal by definition. The surrender to him is *ipso facto* protected from the contingencies and uncertainties of merely social masochism — for ever.[33]

Yet, having concentrated on religion as the prime agent of alienation, Berger also insists, in passing, that religion can also legitimise de-alienation.

In the Biblical tradition the confrontation of the social order with the majesty of the transcendent God may also relativize this order to such an extent that one may validly speak of de-alienation — in the sense that, before the face of God, the institutions are revealed as nothing but *human* works, devoid of inherent sanctity or immortality.[34]

True enough, but to see what this comes to, religious language must be explored. The difficulty is that the main emphases of that language have been analysed by Berger in terms of the effects of an alienating agency. For this reason, Berger's disclaimer when he says, 'We would also emphasize very strongly that religion need not necessarily entail bad faith',[35] does not carry a great deal of conviction.

Having seen what Berger means by alienation, what account does he give of human liberation? He gives at least two accounts. The first is psychological in character. We simply find ourselves making absolute judgements in face of evil monstrosities. Berger finds this fact curious since, he claims, within a scientific frame of reference, we have to say of these judgements, 'Well, we may not like this at all, we may be outraged or appalled, but that is only because we come from a certain background and have been socialized into certain values.'[36] But do we have to say this? Obviously we must come into contact with values before we can come to have a regard for them, but, as we have already seen, there is an important difference between making these values one's own and simply conforming to them; a difference which will show in the rôle the values play in a person's life. Because Berger does not see the importance of this distinction, he is somewhat puzzled as to why we do not want to speak of our reactions to evil monstrosities in relativistic terms. All he can say is, 'The imperative to save a child from murder, even at the cost of killing the putative murderer, appears to be curiously immune to relativizing analysis.'[37] But there is nothing to be curious about if we reject Berger's analysis.

Berger's second, and main, account of the nature of human liberation is sociological in character, and far more in keeping with the general tenor of his analysis. Man frees himself from alienation by seeing that there are no absolute claims on us; he breaks through to a Machiavellian understanding. 'It is as relief from social determinism that we would explain the sympathy that we frequently feel for the swindler, the impostor or the charlatan ... These figures symbolize a social Machiavellianism that understands society thoroughly and then, untrammelled by illusions, finds a way of manipulating society for its own ends.'[38] But now the liberated man seems to be no more than an unprincipled opportunist: 'Only he who understands the rules of the game is in a position to cheat.'[39]

Berger is aware that his analysis might be thought to lead to cynicism, and he tries to draw back from this consequence: 'Let no one quickly jump to the conclusion that such an ambition is always ethically reprehensible. That depends, after all, on how one evaluates the ethical status of the system in question.'[40] This escape route is not open to Berger, since he cannot reintroduce morality into his analysis to get him out of his difficulties, having already said at an earlier stage of his analysis that 'Another system of social control that exerts its pressures towards the solitary figure in the centre is that of morality, custom and manners.'[41] The figure at the centre is solitary indeed, and Berger has to admit on his analysis that 'The concept of the naked self, beyond institutions and roles as the *ens realissimum* of human being, is at the very heart of modernity.'[42] But is this 'self' the liberated man or the alienated rootless man?

Berger wants to claim that there is 'a humanity behind or beneath the roles and norms imposed by society, and that this humanity has profound dignity'.[43] But where is this to be found? Berger's answer is in terms of the individual's *choice*. 'For instance, it is possible to be fully aware of the relativity and the precariousness of the ways by which men organize their sexuality, and yet commit oneself absolutely to one's own marriage. Such commitment, however, does not require any ontological underpinnings. It dares to choose and to act.'[44] Choice will not play the role Berger assigns to it. Choice must be informed. The act of choice cannot in itself create what is worth while, since unless one had some conception of what is worth while the occasion for

180

choice would not arise. By placing the self beyond everything which could inform its choices, Berger cannot reintroduce choice as the act which bestows humanity and dignity on a person's convictions.

There are times when Berger seems to realise this. In fact, his sociological story turns full circle and ends in contradiction. At the beginning of the story we were told that to be alienated was to find one's identity within institutions and relationships and to see it as some kind of necessity in one's life. To be free from such alienation is to see that there are no such necessities. Liberation from alienation consists in sheer choice. Consequently, at the end of the story, the self, which is now supposed to be free, is placed beyond all institutions and relationships. But, Berger says, when this is done, ' "alienation" is the price of individuation'.[45]

Notes

1. Peter Berger and Thomas Luckmann, *The Social Construction of Reality* (Penguin Books, Harmondsworth, Middx, 1966), p. 27.
2. Ibid., p. 14.
3. Ibid., pp. 210–11.
4. Peter Berger, *The Social Reality of Religion* (Penguin Books, Harmondsworth, Middx, 1973), p. 19.
5. Ibid.
6. Peter Berger, *Invitation to Sociology* (Penguin Books, Harmondsworth, Middx, 1975), p. 53.
7. Berger, *The Social Reality of Religion*, p. 21.
8. Ibid.
9. Berger, *The Social Construction of Reality*, p. 72.
10. Berger, *The Social Reality of Religion*, p. 21.
11. Berger, *The Social Construction of Reality*, p. 72.
12. Berger, *Invitation to Sociology*, p. 87.
13. Berger, *The Social Reality of Religion*, p. 33.
14. Ibid., p. 30.
15. Ibid., p. 33.
16. Ibid.
17. Berger, *The Social Construction of Reality*, p. 27.
18. Flannery O'Connor, *Letters of Flannery O'Connor: The Habit of Being*, sel. and ed. Sally Fitzgerald (Vintage Books, Random House, New York, 1980), p. 100.
19. Ibid., p. 220.
20. Ibid., p. 456.
21. Berger, *The Social Reality of Religion*, p. 42.
22. Berger, *Invitation to Sociology*, p. 113.
23. Ibid., p. 127.
24. Berger, *The Social Reality of Religion*, pp. 101–2.

25. These criticisms were expressed by C.G. Prado, who commented on an earlier unpublished paper which concentrated entirely on Berger's *The Social Reality of Religion*, when it was read to the philosophical section of the annual meeting of the Canadian Learned Societies at the University of Laval in 1976.

26. Berger, *The Social Reality of Religion*, p. 99.

27. Peter Berger, Brigitte Berger and Hansfried Kellner, *The Homeless Mind* (Pelican Books, Harmondsworth, Middx, 1974), pp. 73–4.

28. Berger, *Invitation to Sociology*, p. 178.

29. Berger, *The Social Reality of Religion*, p. 37.

30. Ibid., p. 96.

31. Ibid., p. 49.

32. Ibid., p. 48.

33. Ibid., p. 65.

34. Ibid., p. 105.

35. Ibid., p. 101.

36. Peter Berger, *A Rumour of Angels* (Doubleday, New York, 1970), p. 66.

37. Ibid.

38. Berger, *Invitation to Sociology*, p. 155.

39. Ibid., p. 173.

40. Ibid.

41. Ibid., p. 90.

42. Berger *et al.*, *The Homeless Mind*, p. 190.

43. Ibid., p. 83.

44. Berger, *Invitation to Sociology*, p. 180.

45. Berger *et al.*, *The Homeless Mind*, p. 175.

14
Religion in the Marketplace

The sociological story Berger has told determines the account he gives of the problems facing religion in an increasingly secular culture. He says that as a result of secularisation the man in the street, confronted by a range of options, does not know what to believe. But, as we have seen, the individual who is the product of Berger's story *cannot* know what to believe, since he has been reduced to sheer uninformed choice. As for the various movements, including religion, which compete for the allegiance of individuals, the situation facing them is said to be obvious: 'The pluralistic situation is, above all, a *market situation*.'[1] 'In such a situation, all social movements may be faced with the problem of how to keep going in a milieu that no longer takes for granted their definitions of reality.'[2] In so far as Berger is simply describing what in fact may happen, and, indeed, what has happened, no one could object to his analysis. But, then, from religious perspectives, criticisms will be made of attempts to accommodate secularisation in various ways. Berger does not offer any language within which such criticism could be made. On the contrary, the language of strategic accommodation is offered as though it were the only language available to religion. His claim therefore is an ambitious one: 'the crucial sociological and social-psychological characteristic of the pluralistic situation is that religion can no longer be imposed but must be marketed'.[3]

Two confusions must be noted in these arguments. First, a movement is not sustained by making 'how to keep going' its aim. There is only talk of how to keep going when things have already begun to fall apart. A movement is strong when its adherents are absorbed in its characteristic concerns. Believers say that they are sustained by their faith. The sociological story gives the believers the task of sustaining their faith. It is a kind of joke, after all, when priests and ministers thank people for attending church! Second, if a movement tries to meet pressures from other movements in terms of pragmatic accommodation, what is distinctively its own will be destroyed. A pervasive consumer-orientated mentality will be prepared to sacrifice what is distinctive in any movement. Yet Berger advocates policies which reflect precisely this mentality:

> The practical difficulties must be met by means of 'social engineering' — in the accommodating posture, reorganising the institution in order to make it 'more relevant' to the modern world; in the resisting posture, maintaining or revamping the institution so as to serve as a viable plausibility structure for reality-definitions that are not confirmed by the larger society.[4]

Of course, there are real problems which face religion when, of necessity, it comes into contact with other social movements. But everything depends on the religious significance of such contact. Berger reviews the various pacts he takes religion to have made with secular thought, but, once again, the trouble is that the language at his disposal only allows him to give an external, pragmatic account of them. Berger sees the pacts as having been made by the liberal theology which came in Schleiermacher's wake and which Barth repudiated in his reassertion of God's objectivity. He says, 'Put a little crudely, the objectivity of the tradition having being defined as independent of all these contingencies, "nothing can really happen" to the theologian.'[5] This is more than a little crude, since no effort is made to see what is at stake religiously. There is a danger, no doubt, in early Barthianism, of cutting religion off, too severely, from all that surrounds it. But this is not a danger of failure to accommodate secular rival movements. Rather, it is the danger of religion becoming a private, esoteric game, the concepts of which are unmediated in the world around it. The mediation of religious concepts is not an optional strategy, but the context in which religion informs the daily lives of believers. On the other hand, Barth's repudiation of liberalism had to do with his conviction that religion had been far too accommodating to secular features of the surrounding culture. Instead of judging religion by its secular success, Barth insisted on the secular being brought under the judgement of the sacred. If Barth says that, by the grace of God, all will be well, he does not mean that wordly misfortunes could not befall believers. He knew, all too well, that they could. What he meant was that, by the grace of God, such misfortunes would be met in terms of the Faith.

Berger thinks that the absolutism of neo-orthodoxy is very hard to maintain, but his reason for thinking so is extremely odd. He says, 'the "outside" world is attractive'.[6] Berger might have been making the unobjectionable point that religion cannot exist by cutting itself off from the world and pretending that its attractions do not exist. Unfortunately, this is not what he means. He is saying that worldliness is attractive. That would hardly be news to believers. What would be news to them is the suggestion that the attractiveness of worldliness should be the very reason for accommodating it!

The impoverished language of his analysis does not allow him either to take account of the serious doubts which may exist about co-operative developments within religion, such as the ecumenical movement. Berger's account is purely pragmatic. For him, the ecumenical movement is simply the 'increasingly friendly collaboration between the different groups engaged in the religious market' as 'demanded by the pluralistic situation'.[7] But does the ecumenical movement flow from religious convictions or pragmatic convenience? Without a discussion of such issues, no proper account can be taken of the religious support or opposition to such a development. In terms of his own analysis religious beliefs can be no more than Berger, himself, calls them, namely, 'subjects of "fashion"'.[8]

As to co-operation between religion and other disciplines, for example, psychiatry or psychoanalysis, this, again, for Berger, seems to be a purely pragmatic matter. When he gives an account of what he takes to be the purpose and result of such accommodating co-operation, the example is not encouraging:

Psychologism, be it of a Freudian, neo-Freudian, or Jungian variety, allows the interpretation of religion as a 'symbol system' that 'really' refers to psychological phenomena. This particular lesson has the great advantage, realized particularly in America, of legitimating religious activities as some sort of psychotherapy.[9]

This is an excellent example of what I mean by an external

185

account which pays little critical attention to the concepts involved in religion, psychoanalysis or psychiatry, and to what it is that happens if one tries to run them into each other. Contrast with Berger's wildly general remarks the critical discussions of Freud by Wittgenstein,[10] or the discussions by M. O'C. Drury in which psychiatry and religion bear on each other.[11] In these discussions attention is paid to the grammar of the different concepts involved; something which Berger does not even embark on.

It is not surprising to find such external accounts of concepts in Berger, since there are times when he seems to take the passing away of standards and concepts as itself an indication of their lack of value: 'At best, honour and chastity are seen as ideological leftovers in the consciousness of obsolete classes, such as military officers or ethnic grandmothers.'[12] J.L. Austin once claimed that 'our common stock of words embodies all the distinctions men have found worth drawing and the connections they have found worth making, in the lifetime of many generations'.[13] But it has been rightly pointed out that 'Austin gives no reason for ignoring the possibility that some distinctions and connections which might be worth preserving have disappeared. How does their disappearance show they were not "worth preserving"?'[14] Berger's analysis of value in terms of what survives is close in spirit to the idea of value being equated with whoever happens to win the hermeneutic conversation. Berger says, bluntly, 'He who has the bigger stick has the better chance of imposing his definitions of reality.'[15] At other times, Berger himself recognises that 'A lot will depend, naturally, on one's basic assumptions about man whether one will bemoan or welcome these transformations. What to one will appear as a profound loss will be seen by another as the prelude to liberation.'[16] Quite so. Yet, such judgements of gain and loss cannot be appreciated in terms of the externalities of Berger's sociological story. The point is not to determine what is to constitute gain or loss, philosophy cannot determine that any more than sociology, but to see to it that the philosophical or sociological analysis does not result in a language which makes it hard to see what discussions of gain or loss could amount to. In Berger's story, for the most part, standards become strategies. To see the kind of sense talk of gain and loss have in these contexts, philosophy and sociology must wait on the moral and religious perspectives in which such judgements are made, without imposing an alien analysis on them. Thus when Berger says, 'The argument in this book has moved strictly within the frame of reference of sociological theory. No theological, or for that matter, anti-theological implications are to be sought anywhere in the argument — if anyone should believe such implications to be present, I can only assure him that he is mistaken,'[17] the assurance is not enough. He may have stayed within the confines of sociological theory, but it is the very language of that theory which needs to be examined.

It is the language of his sociological theory which leads Berger into further trouble when, having surveyed all his options, he suddenly asks what might be meant by asking which of them is true. Theorising as he is, after foundationalism, and having failed to do justice to the grammars of moral and religious discourse, Berger cannot find 'truth' or 'absolute judgements' either in any common rational basis underlying the practices he has spoken of, or in any specific concepts of truth or absolute judgement within any of the practices themselves. As a result, we find him thinking that some form of absolute truth must depend on finding some unchanging states of affairs among all the relativities. Thus we find him wondering whether these are 'prototypical human gestures that appear timeless and that may be considered as constants in history',[18] or whether there is an 'intrinsic linkage between certain institutional processes and certain structures of consciousness'.[19] Had Berger waited on the grammar of moral and religious beliefs and explored what talk of absolute commitments mean in those contexts, he would have seen the needlessness of asking these questions.

He would have seen, as Flannery O'Connor has said, that

> when we are invited to represent the country according to survey, what we are asked to do is to separate mystery from manners and judgements from vision, in order to produce something a little more palatable to the modern temper. We are asked to form our consciences in the light of statistics, which is to establish the relative as absolute.[20]

In the same way, he would not have to go searching for hints of religious realities. He says,

> Only after the theologian has confronted the historical relativity of religion can he genuinely ask where in this history, it may, perhaps, be possible to speak of *discoveries* — discoveries, that is, that transcend the relative character

187

of their infrastructures. And only after he has really grasped what it means to say that religion is a human product or projection can he begin to search, *within* this array of projections, for what may turn out to be signals of transcendence.[21]

Given the analysis of 'transcendence' in the sociological story, it is difficult to see how a religious notion of it can be reintroduced in this way, at the end of the day. That criticism apart, the notion reintroduced is not in fact a religious one. Berger searches for hints when all he needs is already provided in the concepts of a transcendent God in religious discourse. These concepts are not hints of transcendence, but expressions of the grammar of talk of transcendence, where God is concerned. No doubt some may be torn between what different traditions within a religion, or different religions, say about God. Even so, that is to be torn about what *is* said, and the problem will be resolved or not resolved in terms of what a person comes to think of the relations between traditions or religions. It is in *that* context that an answer will or will not be found. If we say each context hints at a reality it does not exhaust, that is itself a religious reaction to these contexts. A person may say that they all have something to teach each other. If the different religious contexts, on the other hand, are regarded as hints of a reality which *none* of them possess, the notion of this reality becomes an idle one, having no application or grammar which can be explored or discussed. For Berger, the different practices have no discernible foundations which guarantee their truth. Neither does he wait on them to explore what they mean by a transcendent God. He must therefore rely on what he calls 'hints of transcendence' to give application to concepts which, if he but realised it, are already given to him. The trouble is that he does not wait on the concepts in moral and religious practices. Berger himself provides the reason why: 'The sociologist will be driven time and again, by the very logic of his discipline, to debunk the social systems he is studying.'[22] Instead of debunking them, he should have waited on them.

We can recall that at the beginning of Berger's sociological story, he asserted that the sociologist, somewhat surprisingly, inherited from the philosopher the question of the nature of reality. After foundationalism, the sociologist sees that the intelligibility of social practices cannot be shown to depend on rational foundations or a logic which are supposed to be given, in some sense or other, prior to the practices themselves. Reacting to foundationalism, Berger promised that the sociologist of knowledge would concern himself 'with what people "know" as "reality" in their everyday, non-or pre-theoretical lives. In other words, common-sense "knowledge" rather than "ideas" must be the central focus for the sociology of knowledge.'[23] Berger assures us, 'The sociologist tries to see what is there. He may have hopes or fears concerning what he may find. But he will try to see regardless of his hopes or fears.'[24]

But is this what has happened? We have seen that this is the last thing Berger has achieved. His analyses have a surface plausibility because they refer to situations in which moral concepts, religious concepts, or absorption in the values of certain movements, are distorted or deviated from. In Berger's analysis, the language of deviation and distortion becomes the only language available to give an account of the original concepts which are distorted or deviated from. Berger gives the following descriptions of his sociologist at work:

> the sociologist, but for the grace of his academic title, is the man who must listen to gossip despite himself, who is tempted to look through keyholes, to read other people's mail, to open closed cabinets... What interests us is the curiosity that grips any sociologist in front of a closed door behind which there are human voices. If he is a good sociologist, he will want to open that door, to understand these voices.[25]

And again:

> Sociological perspective can then be understood in terms of such phrases as 'seeing through', 'looking behind', very much as such phrases would be employed in common speech — 'seeing through his game', 'looking behind the scenes' — in other words, 'being up on all the tricks'.[26]

The difficulty with Berger's sociological story can be expressed as follows: it is indeed true that we have the expressions, to which Berger refers, in common speech. Their use there, however, depends on well-known contrasts. When I look behind the scene, I find what is the case, as distinct from what appeared to be the case. When I see through someone's game or am up to all his

189

tricks, I see what he is doing as distinct from what he wanted me to think he was doing. In short, these deceptions are logically parasitic on truth. Berger's sociological story, however, cannot accommodate truth or what is the case, for it is precisely these concepts which are analysed in terms of deception. Berger cannot tell us what is behind the scene or what trick is to be seen through, since the only language his story offers us is a language of scenes and tricks. His story is necessarily incomplete, being logically parasitic on those very conceptions of values and truths which he cannot give an account of.

What would Berger make of these conceptual objections? It is hard to say, since, for one so given to accommodations between different movements in the culture, he is strangely reluctant to enter into any kind of dialogue with other disciplines. He says that if a theologian were to find his remarks relevant, they would be relevant in his universe of discourse. On the other hand, he says that this does not mean that theology is immune from observations in other disciplines, since, 'if the theologian asserts something that can be shown to have never taken place historically or to have taken place in quite a different way from what he asserts, and if this assertion is essential to his position, then he can no longer be reassured that he has nothing to fear from the historian's work.'[27] But this cuts both ways. If having, by his own admission, taken over traditional philosophical questions, a sociologist's analysis is full of conceptual confusions, the sociologist can no longer reassure himself that he has nothing to fear from a philosopher's work.

Finally, it may be asked how a story which is conceptually confused can, nevertheless, be a dangerous story, having a damaging effect on the way we think philosophically and practically about the matters it concerns itself with. In answering, I adapt words used by Hanna Pitkin in replying to the same question asked of Rationalism in politics:

> [The sociological story] as an interpretation of what we do is always wrong, because it is logically impossible to do what [the sociological story] says we do. Yet people may — and many do — believe in the truth of this false, impossible doctrine and act on it. The result is not that they act [out the story] for that is impossible, but that they act differently from people who believe otherwise... There is thus an identifiable and pernicious style... that results from

believing in the false doctrine of [the sociological story]. That is why [the believer in the story] misunderstands what he is doing, 'fails to recognise' the 'true spring' of his activity. Acting *in accord with* [the sociological story] is impossible, acting *on* it, unfortunately is not.[28]

As Berger says, 'non-existent sticks can draw real blood.'[29]

Notes

1. Berger, *The Social Reality of Religion*, p. 142.
2. Ibid., p. 158.
3. Ibid., p. 148.
4. Ibid., p. 158.
5. Ibid., p. 162.
6. Ibid., p. 163.
7. Ibid., p. 140.
8. Ibid., p. 145.
9. Ibid., p. 167.
10. Wittgenstein, *Lectures and Conversations*.
11. M. O'C. Drury, *The Danger of Words* (Routledge and Kegan Paul, London, 1973).
12. Berger *et al.*, *The Homeless Mind*, p. 78.
13. J.L. Austin, 'A Plea for Excuses' in J.O. Urmson and G.J. Warnock (eds) *Philosophical Papers* (Clarendon Press, Oxford, 1961), p. 130.
14. Henry Le Roy Finch, *Wittgenstein — the Later Philosophy* (Humanities Press, Atlantic Highlands, New Jersey, 1977), p. 22 fn.
15. Berger, *The Social Construction of Reality*, p. 127.
16. Berger *et al.*, *The Homeless Mind*, p. 87.
17. Berger, *The Social Reality of Religion*, p. 181.
18. Berger, *A Rumour of Angels*, p. 73.
19. Berger *et al.*, *The Homeless Mind*, p. 159.
20. O'Connor, *The Habit of Being*, p. 100.
21. Berger, *The Social Reality of Religion*, p. 189.
22. Berger, *Invitation to Sociology*, p. 51.
23. Berger, *The Social Construction of Reality*, p. 27.
24. Berger, *Invitation to Sociology*, p. 16.
25. Ibid., p. 30.
26. Ibid., p. 42.
27. Berger, *The Social Reality of Religion*, p. 184.
28. Hanna Fenichel Pitkin, 'The Roots of Conservatism', *Dissent*, Fall 1973, p. 503.
29. Berger, *Invitation to Sociology*, p. 185.

Part Three
Grammar and Theology

How do I know that two people mean the same when each says he believes in God? And just the same goes for belief in the Trinity. A theology which insists on the use of *certain particular* words and phrases, and outlaws others, does not make anything clearer (Karl Barth). It gesticulates with words, as one might say, because it wants to say something and does not know how to express it. *Practice* gives the words their sense.

Wittgenstein, *Culture and Value*

15
Grammar and the Nature of Doctrine

So far, we have discussed three claimants to the succession to epistemological foundationalism: Reformed epistemology, philosophical hermeneutics, and Berger's conception of a sociology of knowledge. Running through all our discussions has been the treatment of a recurring misunderstanding: the assumption that the language in which we make judgements regarding what is true or false, is *itself* a description of the nature of reality. The persistence of this misunderstanding determines the form which reactions to foundationalism have taken. In the absence of an adequate criterion of basicality by means of which it can be shown that our practices and beliefs are well founded, it has been said, either that we simply rely on faith that they are well founded, or that the beliefs and practices are reduced to the level of relativities where the status of notions such as 'knowledge' and 'truth' become problematic. In these reactions, one philosophical theory is succeeded by another. What is not realised is that what we need is not another, better, theory to succeed foundationalism, but no theory at all. Instead of calling my remarks *Faith After Foundationalism*, they could equally well have been called *Against Theory*.

Yet, it must not be thought that when such theories are put aside our difficulties are over. It may be the case that theologians and philosophers may use the very notion of grammar which has featured large in our criticisms of theories, and construct another kind of theory around it. They may think that the notion of grammar in Wittgenstein can *itself* be used to determine the direction in which theological doctrines should develop. In this way, Wittgenstein's observation regarding theology as grammar, can itself become the handmaid of a *particular* theological development. To see how this has come about in one influential theologian, it is necessary, first of all, to see how the notion of grammar does throw light on the nature of theological doctrine.

In his book *The Nature of Doctrine*,[1] we learn that George Lindbeck has been engaged in ecumenical discussions for 25 years. Like others, he is disappointed, even ashamed, of the slow progress which has been made. When we think of the complex relations between theological speculation and the wider church communities, such slow progress may not surprise us, depressing though it may be for ecumenical enthusiasts. Peter Winch has emphasised that the traffic between theology and these wider constituents is by no means one way:

> Theological doctrines are not developed independently of their possibilities of application in the worship and religious lives of believers; and these latter have a certain, though not complete, autonomy. I mean that if a doctrine were felt by believers to be hostile to their practices of prayer and worship, that would create a difficulty for the theological doctrine itself. I emphasise that the traffic goes in both directions and there is give and take. Believers' attitudes towards worship may be modified under the pressure of priests, for example, who in their turn are influenced by the theological doctrines in which they are trained in their church. But the attitude of priests towards theological doctrines may also be affected by the resistances they encounter in the attitudes toward worship among their flocks. Of course, not all believers (or priests) will react in the same way, and thus arise possibilities of schism and heresy.[2]

Winch's purpose in emphasising these complexities is to disabuse us of a simplistic picture in which religious practices are founded on the truth of theological doctrines, the latter being given in isolation, unmediated in the life of worship. When we think of these complexities, we must also remember that they are repeated in different religious traditions and denominations. We have to remember too, that, for many, the tradition in which they find themselves is, to a large extent, an accident, their sense of the original religious reasons for separation having eroded long ago or never having been a reality for them. This has serious implications, obviously, for the possibility of informed discussion. Progress may be dictated more by convenience than conviction.

Administrative and economic pressures may weigh more than religious and theological considerations. Other intrusions may also complicate matters. Philosophical and other theories may influence ecumenical discussion. These theories may have ambitions to refine, revise, or even replace the primary languages of faith. As if all this were not enough, it cannot be forgotten that these factors occur in a pervasively secular culture.

In what I have said so far, I have described an audience which is familiar. Someone with sufficient skill could give a fascinating account of attempts to conduct an ecumenical discussion in such a context. He would need to be the William James of the varieties of ecumenical discussion. His would be no static summary of the different traditions or endless parade of committee resolutions. Rather, he would present us with an array of promising and unpromising conversations. Some would go far, others would barely begin. Some would have much to say to each other, while others would hardly be on speaking terms. The presenter of such a spectrum would not be looking for one big explanation of these differences, the kind so much in vogue at the moment, but we might learn from the very variety he displays. He might teach us differences. Should such a writer emerge, then, once again, I'd recognise the audience he is talking about and addressing.

My difficulty with Lindbeck's book can be put by saying that I cannot locate his audience. When I now go on to discuss possible audiences he may be addressing, I do not say they *are* his audience. I mean what I say: I can't find his audience. No sooner do I think I have, than some feature or other of his analysis forces me to the conclusion that this is not the case. So I keep looking without finding. Is there an audience there to find?

Lindbeck says that the ecumenical audience is a confused audience. He says that they lack the concepts which are central to their situation. Central in ecumenical discussion is talk of faithfulness or unfaithfulness to doctrine. But according to Lindbeck, the audience does not know what it means to be faithful or unfaithful to a doctrine. At times, he goes as far as to say that they do not know what it means to speak of a doctrine. They lack the concepts which would enable them to do so. But this talk of 'lacking concepts' needs to be examined.

Lacking concepts is not like lacking resources. Without resources, you do the best you can. Without concepts, you do not cope as best you can with a situation, because concepts are constitutive of the situation. Without the concepts, the situation does not even exist for you. But, now, think of the complex relations between theology and religious practices Winch reminded us of. Within them, all sorts of judgements are made about faithfulness and unfaithfulness to doctrines. Doctrines will be referred to in many different ways. How, then can it be said that these people lack the concepts of faithfulness or unfaithfulness to doctrine, or the concept of doctrine itself? Their grasp of these concepts shows itself *in* the judgements and references they make. If Lindbeck's audience is *this* audience, and he wants to say that they lack the concepts referred to, then I can make little sense of what is being said. I cannot give this notion of a confused audience any substance.

But perhaps Lindbeck's audience is a different audience. This is not an audience which is confused *in* the judgements it makes, but an audience which gives confused answers when asked what it *means* to make these judgements. While actually *employing* doctrines and *making* judgements concerning faithfulness or unfaithfulness to them, they know what they are doing. But when asked to give an account of their employment and judgements they get conceptually confused. Lindbeck tempts us to think that this is the kind of audience he has in mind when he says, 'Doctrines... do not behave in the way they should given our customary suppositions about the kinds of things they are.'[3] So, on the one hand, we have the life of the doctrines, and, on the other hand, our confused suppositions about them. The religious–theological audience seems to be in the condition Augustine was in when he said that he knew what time was if no one asked him, but that if someone asked him he did not know. If this were Lindbeck's audience, it would be the familiar audience of the philosophically confused. Attempts might be made to rescue them from their confusion by getting them to see where they were led astray in reflecting on the life of the doctrines.

But this audience does not seem to be Lindbeck's audience either. If it were, its ecumenical discussions would proceed unhampered by the philosophical confusions. But the ecumenical discussions do not proceed unhampered. On the contrary, the participants are said to be muddled *in* their discussions. After 25 years, the author's experience seems to be that ecumenical discussion is muddling along. But what sort of muddle is this? Is it a religious muddle? A theological muddle? A philosophical muddle? No doubt sharp boundaries cannot be drawn in all cases, but we do not seem even to make a beginning. But, it may be said, this is to ignore the most obvious answer Lindbeck provides, an answer which identifies his audience immediately. After all, Lindbeck states clearly that his audience is confused because it is in the grip of inadequate theories. What they stand in need of is a correct theory. That theory, according to Lindbeck, is provided by the social sciences and philosophy. The difficulty, however, is this: all this assumes the intelligibility of the way in which Lindbeck speaks of theories. If his notion of a theory is confused, whether he is referring to adequate or inadequate theories, then the audience characterised in terms of his conception of theory will not be a real audience. The situation will be one in which Lindbeck *is* confronted by an audience which is muddling along, but which he himself gives a confused account of. If Lindbeck's talk of theories is an instance of language idling, then an audience thought of in terms of such theories will itself be a conceptual fantasy. That is going to be my contention.

Before looking at his actual concept of a theory, let us look first at the expectations he has of theories, expectations which no theory from the social studies or philosophy could satisfy. First, Lindbeck wants to avoid any suggestion that the theory is simply the best which can be devised to meet the interests of the ecumenical movement. He says, 'A theory of religion and doctrine cannot be ecumenically useful unless it is nonecumenically plausible.'[4] On the other hand, in seeking a theory, Lindbeck says he is 'seeking concepts which will remove anomalies'.[5] There are times when Lindbeck seems to equate 'anomalies' with religious differences. Why should the differences be so regarded? Of course, they may be so regarded from an ecumenical perspective, but, then, this is a religious or theological view of the difficulties. But Lindbeck says that the theories he is looking for are 'meant to be ecumenically and religiously neutral. They do not in themselves imply decisions either for or against the communally authoritative teachings of particular religious bodies'.[6] In fact, the theory sought for is meant to be neutral with respect to the claims of Christianity on the one hand, and Judaism and Islam on the other. The neutrality does not extend as far as Hinduism or Buddhism. Does not this give the game away? Surely, for better or for worse, all we have here is a search for religious reconciliation within a religion, or between religions, where there is enough in common doctrinally to make the search realistic.[7] But if that is the case, we have a religious and theological enterprise already firmly rooted in an ecumenical tradition. Take that tradition away and deep-going differences will re-emerge, making the quest for a unifying neutral theory seem bizarre. For example, let us say an ecumenical service of worship is arranged. As we all know, responses will vary. The service is held. Down the road, in another service, people are praying for the people in the ecumenical service. At the ecumenical service, they are praying for the estranged fellow-Christians. No doubt some headway can be made with anomalies which are due to inconsistencies and factual errors, but they do not take us far. Where the major differences are concerned, to talk of these as anomalies is already to invoke a religious and theological perspective. Anti-ecumenicals may agree that all should be one in Christ, but that unity is taken to be defined by the doctrinal unity of their perspective. They will invite the ecumenical enthusiasts to become one in Christ too. It is difficult to see, therefore, how Lindbeck's expectations of theories are real expectations. Are they not an instance of language idling?

But what of the theories of which Lindbeck speaks? He speaks of theories of the natural sciences, the social sciences and philosophy all in the same breath. There are important differences, however, which need to be noted, differences which have far-reaching consequences for Lindbeck's whole enterprise. The first thing to note is that in examining the behaviour of human beings, we are examining behaviour *in which concepts are already at work.* This is not true of the natural sciences. 'Gravity' is a concept which belongs to the modes of representation in physics, not to the existence of, let us say, the apple. But when we speak of concepts such as 'war', 'discussion', 'family', etc., etc., we are not talking of concepts we employ to explain people's behaviour. On the contrary, these concepts are constitutive of the appropriate forms of human behaviour.[8] Of course, social scientists may be interested in explanations and correlations which do not interest the participants they are investigating. But if they want to understand the behaviour of human beings, they cannot ignore the concepts which are constitutive of that behaviour. This is as true of religious concepts as of any other. The social sciences may help ecumenical investigations in all sorts of ways, but, unless the religious and theological character of these investigations are abandoned, attention must be paid to the meaning of the religious concepts involved. This is not a matter of testing a theory, as Lindbeck seems to think, but a matter of endeavouring to grasp the role of the religious and theological concepts in ecumenical thought. Of course, the creative theologian goes further. He is able to discuss these concepts in such a way that they inform the wider religious communities, in the complex ways Winch outlined, of a vision of what it is to seek unity in Christ. That no such creative theologian seems to be forthcoming does not affect the conceptual points at issue.

But Lindbeck also speaks of philosophical theories. There is one difficulty with doing so: there are no theories in philosophy and, hence, nothing to be tested. Of course, theories are devised, but they turn out, on examination, to be generalisations from limited cases, or products of conceptual confusion. What we do with such 'theories' in philosophy is not to confirm or disconfirm them, but to show the knots in the understanding which led to their formulation. When these theories are given up, they are not replaced by better theories. Rather, the enquirer is free of the confusion which led him to devise the theories in the first place. The unravelling of the route to the confused theory may be a long and complex business. Each person must come to clarity for himself. So in philosophy, we are not testing theories, but struggling with confusions to which we are all prone. Despite what he says about theories, when we turn to look at what Lindbeck means by inadequate theories, we find that they, too, are examples of conceptual confusion. In his discussions of this confusion, however, we can see how deep its hold can be on us. Despite some important insights, Lindbeck does not always free himself from the very conceptual confusion he thinks he has identified. In so far as that is true, the audience he thinks he is talking from and to will remain an elusive one to identify.

Lindbeck's ecumenical audience is said to be confused in a way which obscures from it the reconciliation it is seeking. The audience thinks that it is self-contradictory to speak of doctrinal reconciliation without this entailing doctrinal capitulation. Lindbeck wants to show that this is not so. Inadequate theories stand in the audience's way in appreciating this fact. Two rival theories have dominated the discussion and it is on these, following Lindbeck, that we shall concentrate. Is Lindbeck in the audience which is free from the confusion of these theories, or is he one of the confused audience, the very audience he claims to be identifying? As we shall see, there is no unequivocal answer to this question.

The first theory of religion and doctrine Lindbeck considers is what might be called the cognitivist theory. He says that this theory 'emphasizes the cognitive aspects of religion and stresses the ways in which church doctrines function as informative propositions or truth claims about objective realities'.[9] As we shall see, there are problems about the generality of that description, but what Lindbeck wants to oppose is fairly clear. He rightly wants to oppose that strong tradition in which propositions about the existence of God are treated as the *presuppositions* of religion. On this view, those propositions stand in isolation, their sense being entirely unmediated. Given such a view, the nature of doctrinal disagreements is understood accordingly. Two theologians advancing conflicting doctrines are understood to be like two men trying to describe an object in less than ideal circumstances. If the two theological descriptions conflict, then, given one is correct, the other cannot be reconciled to it without capitulation. As Lindbeck says, 'on this view, doctrinal reconciliation without capitulation is impossible because there is no significant sense in which the meaning of a doctrine can change while remaining the same'.[10]

Here, Lindbeck is accusing the cognitivist theory of conceptual confusion. He is saying that we misunderstand the logic of theological doctrines if we think of them as descriptions of an object, a phenomenon, given independently of them. I think he is absolutely right. What we do not find in Lindbeck, however, is any actual philosophical elucidation of the ways in which we are tempted by these confused views of theology. Some of these ways have been illuminatingly explored by Rush Rhees. He says,

If one lays emphasis ... on the fact that 'God' is a substantive, and especially if one goes on, ... to say that it is a proper name, then the natural thing will be to assume that meaning the same by 'God' is something like meaning the same by 'the sun' or meaning the same by 'Churchill'. You might even want to use some such phrase as 'stands for' the same. But nothing of that sort will do here. Questions about 'meaning the same' in connection with the names of physical objects are connected with the kind of criteria to which we may appeal in saying that this is the same object — 'that is the same planet as I saw in the south west last night', 'that is the same car that was standing here this morning'. Supposing someone said 'The word "God" stands for a different object now.' What could that mean? I know what it means to say that 'the Queen' stands for a different person now, and I know what it means to say that St. Mary's

Church now is not the St. Mary's Church that was here in So-and-So's day. I know the sort of thing that might be said if I were to question either of these statements. But *nothing* of that sort could be said in connection with any question about the meaning of 'God'. Consider the way in which we learn the meaning of 'God'. It is not having someone point and say '*That's* God'. Now this is not a trivial or inessential matter. It hangs together in very important ways with what I call the grammar of the word 'God'. And it is one reason why I do not think it is helpful just to say that the word is a substantive.[11]

I have quoted Rhees at length, and shall do so again, because his discussion is an example of philosophy at work, a revealing of the ways in which we may be misled when we say we are talking *about* God. Now, at times, Lindbeck seems to be endorsing the kind of analysis Rhees has provided. At other times, he seems to be still in the grip of the very confusion he is hoping to eradicate. This shows in the very generality by which he expresses the theory he thinks is confused. He wants to avoid the confusion Rhees shows we can fall into, but does so by attacking the notion that theological statements have to do with an objective reality or with truth claims. But, of course, all Rhees shows is the confusion of construing talk of 'objective reality' and 'truth' in religion in a certain way, namely, in the way we construe them where talk of physical objects is concerned. To be prepared to jettison talk of an independent reality, as Lindbeck seems to be, is to fall back into the grammatical trap which led one astray in the first place. It is to assume that the notion of an independent reality *only* has application where talk of physical objects is concerned. Yet, when a believer strays from the ways of God, he clearly thinks of himself as departing from a reality which is independent of himself. God's independence, however, is not like the independence of a physical object. Philosophy of religion is faced with the task of bringing out the grammatical differences between them should they become confused in someone's mind. This can be brought out by showing that in the case of God, there is no question of anything like a material investigation to find out *whether* there is a God. That would be complete nonsense. Again, Rhees brings out why:

We use 'it exists' chiefly in connection with physical objects, and anyway we use it where we can ask whether it exists

or not. This goes with the sense of *finding out* whether it
exists. Now the 'it', whatever it is, is something we could
identify in such an investigation — by, for example, the
methods by which we commonly identify a particular
physical object. We might also confuse it with something
else, or mistake something else for it. But in any case, the
question *whether* it was the same object would involve those
sorts of criteria. But the question whether we mean the same
by 'God', I have said, is not a question whether we are
referring to the same object. The question whether we are
still talking about God now, or whether we are really
worshipping God now, cannot be settled by referring to any
object. And I do not think it would mean anything to ask
'whether any such object exists'. Nor does it change anything
if you say 'being' instead of 'object'.[12]

If this analysis has revealed a confusion, then the so-called
cognitivist theory, which depends on such confusion, must be
seen as itself the product of confusion. The purpose of Rhees's
analysis is not to prohibit talk of the existence of God or of truth
in religion, but to become clear about what such talk amounts
to. The cognitivist theory is a confused account of such talk. Such
talk misrepresented religious realities. There are times, however,
when Lindbeck speaks as if the cognitivist theory is an optional
way of talking about religion which one might choose to adopt.
For example, he says:

> Fewer and fewer contemporary people are deeply embedded
> in particular religious traditions or thoroughly involved in
> particular religious communities. This makes it hard for
> them to perceive or experience religion in cognitivist fashion
> as the acceptance of sets of objectively and immutably true
> propositions. Perhaps only those among whom the sects
> chiefly recruit who combine unusual insecurity with naivete
> can easily manage to do this.[13]

This seems to miss entirely the role which conceptual clarity plays
in Rhees's analysis. Even if people *were* deeply embedded in
religious practices, the cognitivist theory, if it has the implications
Rhees makes explicit, would still be the result of a confused
understanding of their religious practices. Lindbeck seems almost
to be saying that this understanding would be a viable one if the

people were deeply embedded in religious practices. Again, we can see that Lindbeck is not entirely free from the grammatical confusions of the cognitivist theory when he says: 'Christians ... go on and assert that it is propositionally true that Christ is Lord: i.e. the particular individual of which the stories are told is, was, and will be definitively and unsurpassably the Lord. The great strength of a cognitivist–propositional theory of religion is that, it admits the possibility of such truth claims.'[14] Here is an excellent example of Lindbeck relying on unmediated religious concepts. If the cognitivist theory were applicable to these religious claims, in the ways Rhees outlined, then it would make sense to speak of conducting an investigation to *find out* whether Christ is Lord, much in the same way as one might conduct an investigation to find out whether a title to the Lordship of a manor is a valid title or not. Here, one has a conception of what a valid title is, the criterion to be satisfied, before the investigation starts. But nothing like this applies in acknowledging Christ as Lord. Notoriously, the concepts involved in Messianic expectations prior to Christ's coming cannot be regarded as having the logical status of tests of entitlement which could be applied impersonally to whichever pretender to the title came along. The discussion over whether Christ is Lord is itself a theological and religious discussion. Lindbeck's use of language betrays the fact when he speaks of Christ as 'definitively and unsurpassably Lord'. He offers this as evidence of the strength of the appropriateness of the cognitivist theory in this context, whereas his use of this very language should have shown him the confusion of grammar involved in thinking so.

What we have seen is that Lindbeck, while half-realising that theological doctrines are not descriptions of an object given independently of them, cannot free himself from the tempting and prestigious grammar of that relation, a grammar drawn, in the main, from our talk of physical objects. Here is a good example of Lindbeck oscillating between clarity and confusion. He says:

> The ontological truth of religious utterances, like their intrasystematic truth, is different as well as similar to what holds in other realms of discourse. Their correspondence to reality in the view we are expounding is not an attribute that they have when considered in and for themselves, but is only a function of their role in constituting a form of life, a way of being in the world, which itself corresponds to the Most Important, the Ultimately Real.[15]

Put in a more recognisable contemporary philosophical idiom, the tensions and contradictions in Lindbeck's remarks can be expressed as follows: if we want to understand the force of the 'independently real' in religion, what that comes to, we must not consider that notion in isolation, since it has no sense there. Further, in the attempt to so consider it, what we are likely to do is to give it a sense from a restricted area of discourse, and confusedly make that sense paradigmatic for religion. To avoid this confusion, we must look to the forms of life in which talk of God has a role to see what application the notion of the independently real has there. So far, so good. But, of course, Lindbeck had coined the term 'intrasystematic truth' only because, impressed by the way in which we talk of truths where physical objects are concerned, he had jettisoned talk of 'ontological truth' where religion is concerned. Instead of doing so, he should have explored the grammar of 'the independently real' in a religious context. Finally, having said that it is essential to look at the use of concepts in their natural homes, in this case, in their religious contexts, we find Lindbeck speaking of these natural homes, these grammatical parameters, as *themselves* corresponding to something he calls the 'Most Important' and the 'Ultimately Real'. Here this notion of 'correspondence' is entirely unmediated. No context has been given for it. It is another instance of language idling. No analysis is being referred to since the talk is itself a product of conceptual confusion. No use of capitals in talking of the 'Most Important' and the 'Ultimately Real' can hide the fact that he is trying to place these concepts, whatever they are, in a logical space which transcends the language-games and forms of life in which concepts have their life. The notion of such a logical space is an illusion. So much for Lindbeck's treatment of the first inadequate theory by which he thinks his ecumenical audience is confused. As we can see from it, Lindbeck's own position is an equivocal one. At times, he seems to identify grammatical confusions. At other times, he seems to be still in the grip of the very confusions he identifies.

Lindbeck has a much surer grasp of his criticism of the second inadequate theory which, according to him, confuses the ecumenical audience. This theory is called the 'experiential–expressive approach', by which doctrines are interpreted as 'noninformative and nondiscursive symbols of inner feelings, attitudes, or existential orientations'.[16] On this view, doctrines, in the end, can be dispensed with, since religious agreement or disagreement 'are constituted by harmony or conflict in under-lying feelings, attitudes, existential orientations, or practices, rather than by what happens on the level of symbolic (including doctrinal) objectifications. There is thus at least the logical possibility that a Buddhist and a Christian might have basically the same faith, although expressed very differently.'[17] As Lindbeck says, 'The rationale suggested, though not necessitated, by an experiential–expressive approach is that the various religions are diverse symbolizations of one and the same core experience of the Ultimate, and that therefore they must respect each other, learn from each other, and reciprocally enrich each other.'[18]

There are times when Lindbeck's objections to the so-called 'experiential–expressive' approach amount to saying that other theories are to be preferred because of their greater economy, or because they correspond more closely to the facts. On these views, there is nothing conceptually confused about the theory as such. When Lindbeck is at his best, however, he recognises that the main difficulty with the theory is that it is incoherent. No intelligible account can be given of the notion of an experience which is not only supposed to be contingently related to the language in which it is expressed, but which is supposed to remain constant in character while the linguistic expressions of it vary enormously. No content can be given to this notion of experience because it is confused in its conception. As Lindbeck says, 'it is difficult or impossible to specify its distinctive features, and yet unless this is done, the assertion of commonality becomes logically and empirically vacuous'.[19] Lindbeck sees that the possibility of religious experience is logically parasitic on a language and behaviour which is already religious. Religious experience does not stand to language as a melody stands to a song. We can take away the words of the song, and we are still left with the melody. But we cannot subtract the language and behaviour, in the case of religion, and say that we are left with the experience. *What* experience? The notion is entirely vacuous.[20]

It may well seem that these philosophical observations are borne out by the temporal sequence in which people's religious experiences are formed. After all, it might be said, when a child is first taken to church he has no religious experiences. They come later. What happens is that he is introduced to a context of ritual and worship in which the possibility of religious experience has its sense. In criticism of those theories of religion which explain ritual as emanating from experience, it might be said that so far from experience creating rites and rituals, the rites and rituals create the possibility of religious experience. Lindbeck may be taken to be saying something similar when he says,

> just as a language (or 'language game', to use Wittgenstein's phrase) is correlated with a form of life, and just as a culture has both cognitive and behavioral dimensions, so it is also in the case of religious tradition. Its doctrines, cosmic stories or myths, and ethical directives are integrally related to the rituals it practices, the sentiments or experiences it evokes, the actions it recommends, and the institutional forms it develops.[21]

Yet, as Lindbeck recognises, remarks such as these can easily be misunderstood. If the temporal sequence is emphasised in such a way that the religious experience is thought of as a subsequent development from the practices, the existence of the practices becomes utterly mysterious. Practices divorced from religious experience are just as unintelligible as religious experiences divorced from religious practices. We need to get away from this whole 'chicken-or-the-egg' way of thinking about the relation of experience to practice.[22] Instead, what is needed is to emphasise, from the outset, the character of religious practices where, as Lindbeck says 'The primary knowledge is not *about* the religion, nor *that* the religion teaches such and such, but rather *how* to be religious in such and such ways.'[23]

Having voiced his objections to the two theories he regards as confused, Lindbeck moves on to a consideration of the theory he favours, namely, one in which he adopts what he calls a 'cultural–linguistic' approach to religion in which religions are said to resemble languages. Before going on to consider this third alternative, a brief word is necessary about a tension which runs through Lindbeck's treatment of the two theories he rejects. I have already argued that what he rejects are not theories, but well-known and deep-rooted confusions we can fall into when we reflect on the character of religious belief. There are times when Lindbeck seems to recognise the confusion involved in these ways of thinking. At other times, however, he speaks as though these ways of thinking, that is, thinking of doctrinal statements as descriptively related to a phenomenon which is given independently of these doctrines, or thinking that radically different religious ways of talking could all be expressions of the same underlying experience, could be *options* which we can take up for certain purposes. There are two fundamental objections to this suggestion. First, those in the grip of these ways of thinking do not regard them as options. On the contrary, although they are confused, they, not seeing this, think they are giving a faithful conceptual account of the religious practices they are talking about. Second, those no longer in the grip of these ways of talking, who have seen the confusion involved in them, certainly cannot view them as options which they can take up again. The difficulty I have with Lindbeck's strategies is that he claims to see the confusions and yet continues to talk of these ways of talking as options.

Lindbeck's own suggestion is that theological doctrines should be compared to grammatical rules. He echoes Wittgenstein's remark that theology is a kind of grammar. Theological doctrines become regulative rules for the use of the word 'God', not descriptions of an object given independently of themselves. Once again, Rhees's analysis in this connection is extremely illuminating. We have already seen that in asking whether we mean the same by God, we can get confused if we think that this has anything in common with referring to the same object. Theological speculation is at the centre of any discussion about God's identity. I want to quote Rhees at some length to show just how central it is.[24]

First, Rhees points out how children acquire a primitive theology in the stories they are taught and how their ideas may change as they grow older:

> We may say that children acquire a sort of primitive theology in the stories of the Creation and the Garden of Eden and other stories about God in the book of Genesis, for example. They learn to think about God in these terms and in this way. They generally learn this in connection with elementary notions of worship and prayer too; and it is important to remember that. The stories of God walking in the garden are not taught them in the same way that stories of King Arthur or the battle of Hastings are. I know you may say that children do not draw much distinction; but there is one all the same, and this is important for the role which these stories come to play in later developments or for the way in which they are connected with later developments. The children are not being given primitive ideas of history. Through these stories ideas are being formed, but they are

the ideas that enter into worship.

This theology may be altered as the children grow older.
It may take on a new form when they become familiar with
the Hebrew prophets, for instance. In all this — from the
beginning and on through the later changes — they have
learned a certain way of using the expression 'God', a way
of using the expression 'Creator', a way of using the
expressions 'God's will', 'sin against God', 'serving God',
'love of God' and others.[25]

Rhees emphasises, however, that theology must not be thought
of as a set of propositions which are given, in some sense, prior
to religious practices, and from which the religious practices could
be derived:

I say that without this theology religious devotion, reverence
and religious exaltation would have no sense at all. And yet
— once more — I do not mean that this theology, the
learning of these ways of speaking, is what has produced
religion. If children learn to speak of God through having
the Bible read to them, the Bible itself was the outcome of
religion before it was the source of it. In general, one might
say that theology grows out of religious devotion just as
much as the other way about. And no theology is conceivable
except in connection with a religious tradition.[26]

Someone may still think that all this makes theology
unimportant. But, on the contrary, it is concerned with *the* most
important question for a believer: What *is* worshipping God?
Rhees says:

Someone might ask 'Well why have all this theology at all,
then? Is it not just so much trellis-work or ornamentation
that could as well be left out?' Well, consider 'To know God
is to worship *him*'. What is worshipping *God*, precisely? Could
you speak of worshipping God — would that mean anything
— without some sort of theology?[27]

So Rhees is bringing out that theological speculation at its most
important is speculation about what it is to worship God.
Doctrinal disagreement is disagreement, in the end, about that,
a disagreement which has implications for the role of worship in

a man's life. Doctrines are seen as laying down the grammatical parameters of the faith: they are concerned with what should and should not be said about God. But such considerations are important only in so far as they are related to the realities of the spiritual life. Here, we are far away from the misleading picture of doctrinal disagreement as competing descriptions of an object seen in less than ideal circumstances, or as divergent expressions of an underlying experience which never changes. We see that theology is far more serious than that.

There is reason to believe that Lindbeck would agree with a great deal of Rhees's discussion concerning the character of theology. As we have already seen, he wrongly concludes that seeing theology as a kind of grammar entails not talking of God as an independent reality and ceasing to make truth claims concerning him. All that follows from the analysis, in fact, is that such talk should be understood within the grammar of the religious discourse in which it is made. All we are rescued from is the confusion of thinking that the notions of 'independent reality' and 'truth' in this context have the same grammar as they do in others.

Notes

1. The Westminster Press, Philadelphia, 1984.
2. Peter Winch, 'Meaning and Religious Language' in Brown (ed.), *Reason and religion*, p. 202.
3. Lindbeck, *The Nature of Doctrine*, p. 7.
4. Ibid., p. 8.
5. Ibid.
6. Ibid., p. 9.
7. In a discussion with Lindbeck at Yale Divinity School, he gave an illuminating example of a reconciling theological discussion. Before Vatican II, there was an impasse in discussion between Catholics and Protestants over the status of the Mass. The Protestants insisted that, on Calvary, Christ's sacrifice was sufficient once and for all. They took the Catholic view of the Mass as implying that Christ is sacrificed anew in each celebration. This was denied by the Catholics, but without any effect. After Vatican II the deadlock was broken by the Catholic declaration that two masses are no better than one. Here, reconciliation comes about through the further elucidation of a doctrine. At his best, Lindbeck settles for a straightforward account of what happened. At other times, he is tempted to resort to 'theory', suggesting that what happened entails a principle of sacramental realism.
   Of course, there are still deep differences between the above cases and those who would deny that the mass is a sacrifice, insisting that it does no more than remember a sacrifice.
8. See Peter Winch, *The Idea of a Social Science* (Routledge and Kegan Paul, London, 1958), pp. 127–8.
9. Lindbeck, *The Nature of Doctrine*, p. 16.
10. Ibid., p. 17.
11. Rush Rhees, 'Religion and Language' in *Without Answers* (Routledge and Kegan Paul, London, 1969), pp. 127–8.
12. Ibid., p. 131.
13. Lindbeck, *The Nature of Doctrine*, p. 21.
14. Ibid., pp. 63–4.
15. Ibid., p. 65.
16. Ibid., p. 16.
17. Ibid., p. 17.
18. Ibid., p. 23.
19. Ibid., p. 32.
20. The question of whether there could be a religion without a religious language is a separate issue.
21. Lindbeck, *The Nature of Doctrine*, p. 33.
22. See Part Four.
23. Lindbeck, *The Nature of Doctrine*, p. 35.
24. See too D.Z. Phillips, 'Philosophy, Theology and the Reality of God', *Philosophical Quarterly*, Oct. 1963, reprinted in D.Z. Phillips, *Faith and Philosophical Enquiry* (Routledge and Kegan Paul, London, 1970).
25. Rhees, 'Religion and Language', pp. 125–6.
26. Ibid., p. 126.
27. Ibid., p. 127.

16
Grammar and Doctrinal Disagreement

At the outset of the last chapter, I said that it is tempting to think that Wittgenstein's notion of grammar can *in itself* determine the direction which theological development shall take. It is now time to see how one can succumb to this temptation. Lindbeck does so in thinking that, once one recognises that doctrinal statements are grammatical statements, it is easier to see, of necessity, in ecumenical discussion, how there can be doctrinal reconciliation without capitulation. It is difficult to see how he is able to come to any such conclusion. If doctrinal statements are seen as grammatical remarks, it is extremely important to note that, within doctrinal contexts, there may still be deep doctrinal differences. In other words, there will be grammatical tensions as well as grammatical agreements. In many cases, if the tensions are to be resolved, there will have to be doctrinal capitulation. Of course, the logic of this capitulation is no longer the logic of capitulation where one man sees that a description of an object he has provided is incorrect. But just because the grammar of capitulation is different, it is no less capitulation. Capitulation now would take the form of the admission that one had not been speaking properly about God. Given the essential relations we have noted between theology and the life of worship, it would be an admission made in the light of a new awareness of spiritual truths. There are times when Lindbeck seems to appreciate this momentous fact. It is momentous because in saying 'God is ——' one is providing a rule for the use of the word 'God'; a provision which should be made in fear and trembling. At other times, however, Lindbeck reverts to the tempting charm of the cognitivist theory and speaks as though a truth concerning God has to do with the relation between the grammatical rule and a reality independent of itself. But this is to misunderstand the sense of the very notion of grammar Lindbeck wants to employ in referring to doctrines. Here is a good example of Lindbeck oscillating between, and thereby confusing, the two different grammars:

> if the form of life and understanding of the world shaped by an authentic use of the Christian stories does in fact correspond to God's being and will, then the proper use of *Christus est Dominus* is not only intrasystematically but ontologically true. Utterances within any not totally incoherent religion can on this account be intrasystematically true, but this in no sense assures their ontological truth or meaningfulness.[1]

If Lindbeck had properly understood the notion of a form of life, he would have seen that it is only within such contexts that the question of what it means to ask whether a statement is true or false can arise. So if we want to ask whether a doctrine is true or false, we have first to ask what it means to speak of truth or falsity in this religious context. As we have seen, to speak of truth here is already to make a religious judgement. To ask whether the way you make religious judgements is true is to contemplate a religious change or to contemplate giving up one's religious allegiances. But in the above quotation, Lindbeck is speaking as though he had introduced us to a conception of truth (what he calls ontological truth) which has an application independently of religion and independent of any form of life we could specify. Of course, it is no accident that he can give no substance to this conception. Lindbeck says 'This is not the place to pursue in detail the logical issues raised by truth claims in religion.'[2] Perhaps it is because he does not do so, or has not done so, that Lindbeck is still in the grip of the very grammatical confusion from which he thinks he has freed himself. Having apparently seen through the grammatical confusions of the cognitivist theory, he nevertheless thinks that these grammatical confusions can be incorporated in his new grammatical insights: 'There is nothing in the cultural-linguistic approach that requires the rejection (or the acceptance) of the epistemological realism and correspondence theory of truth, which, according to most of the theological tradition, is implicit in the conviction of believers that when they rightly use a sentence such as 'Christ is Lord' they are uttering a true first-order proposition.'[3] Nothing that requires the rejection?

214

Surely, a grammatical gain logically entails abandoning one's grammatical confusion. If Lindbeck is claiming to offer any gains in grammatical insight in his discussion of the status of doctrines, he cannot combine this with an accommodation of the confusions such a gain logically requires us to put aside. It is because Lindbeck attempts to do so that his own location, the audience from which he speaks, is so difficult to determine.

We shall find the same difficulty in turning to our final topic, namely, the nature of doctrinal disagreement. There are times when Lindbeck states, quite clearly, the grammatical status of religious doctrines, and how those doctrines set the parameters for the discourse and identity of a religious community: 'Church doctrines are communally authoritative teachings regarding beliefs and practices that are considered essential to the identity or welfare of the group in question. They may be formally stated or informally operative, but in any case they indicate what constitutes faithful adherence to a community.'[4] Lindbeck points out that this view of doctrines itself contains complexities which need not be apparent at first. For example, the reality of doctrine need not correspond always to what is explicitly stated in formal terms in the religious community. This is because in terms of its actual use, its actual interpenetration within the life of worship, an explicitly stated doctrine may have little more than a nominal reality, while one not stated formally may be at work in the life of worship. Further, formal agreement on the doctrine may hide the extent of theological disagreement, for how that doctrine is explained and mediated in the life of the religious community may reveal theological differences. When these differences become acute some people react, as many did in the 1960s, by saying that the differences do not matter, and that underlying religious experiences survive them. As we have seen, however, no serious religion is possible without some kind of theology, without some concern being expressed about what ought and ought not to be said about God. In this context, there are two extremes which Lindbeck, rightly, wants to avoid. On the one hand, he wants to avoid the radical relativism of those who say that Christianity has no central core. Everything is in flux and what is called Christianity today is no more than the traditions which have evolved to meet our present historical situation. On the other hand, he wants to oppose Catholic and Protestant attempts to hold onto old forms which, once historically valid, cannot speak to the present situation.

How, then, is doctrinal faithfulness to be combined with the need for relevant proclamation? This is a question which theology cannot ignore. The philosophical issue I am exploring, however, is whether a certain philosophical clarity concerning doctrine and doctrinal disagreement of itself gives one kind of theological answer to this question. This seems to be Lindbeck's hope, but it is a hope which cannot be realised.

It is hard to follow Lindbeck's analysis because he claims that doctrines are not first-order propositions. He says this because, for him, first-order propositions make claims about extra-linguistic realities. Once again this involves the confusion of grammars which we have already had occasion to note. It is necessary at this stage to make some further comparisons to re-emphasise these. Consider two uses of 'This is red'. In the first, we are offering a description of a particular object. Someone has asked us what colour it is and we reply 'This is red'. But in the second use of 'This is red', nothing is being described. Rather, we are being given the rule for the use of the word 'red'. We are being taught the meaning of the word 'red'. It seems to me that theological or doctrinal statements are often of the second form. They are giving us rules for the use of the word 'God'. Within this use we may disagree about a particular application of the concept. We may argue over whether it is proper to speak of an incident as an expression of God's love. But in saying 'God is love' we are being taught one of the meanings of the word 'God'. The description of a particular object is not given in the sample 'This is red'. To find out whether the particular object is red you have to look. But in the doctrinal statements we are given the parameters of what can be said of God. *If, then, the doctrine is opposed and another proposed, the conflict in question is itself a grammatical conflict, not a factual conflict within an already agreed grammar.* Rhees draws the contrast as follows:

Winston Churchill may be a Prime Minister and also a company director, but I might come to know him without knowing this. But I could not know God without knowing that he was the Creator and Father of all things. That would be like saying that I might come to know Churchill without knowing that he had face, hands, body, voice or any of the attributes of a human being.[5]

Now this has an important bearing on the issue of doctrinal

216

and religious disagreement. We see that the differences show in the different roles which religious ideas play in people's lives. Rhees asks, 'How would the peoples of different races know whether they meant the same or whether they meant something different in speaking of God? Or the members of different sects?'[6] He replies,

> I suppose it would be the role which the word played in connexion with the different manifestations of religion and religious belief — in the one race and in the other say. Within a single tradition, like that of the Hebrew religion, it can be said that the author of the second half of Isaiah meant the same by 'God' as the author (or authors) of Genesis did, and that St. Paul meant the same by 'God' as both of them because of the continuity of Hebrew worship and of the kind of worship that was, the importance of such conceptions as 'the God of our fathers', 'the God of Abraham and the God of Jacob', and so on. But for Paul the same God could be worshipped by gentiles who were not the seed of Abraham and Jacob. And if the gentiles worship the same God, then this must appear in what they say about God, in the way they worship and in what it means to them to be creatures and children of God. To ask '*Do* they worship the same God or not?' is to ask about that.[7]

And when we examine the role these ideas play we'll discover differences. Again, as Rhees says,

> Obviously there is no clear line which divides those who worship the same God from those who do not (or even those who worship God at all from those who do not), and we find that some sects are tolerant of one another and some are not. (I think there are still Scottish Presbyterians who refer to the Roman Catholic church as 'the Whore of Babylon'.) But the fact that there is no sharp line does not mean that there is no distinction. And the question whether we mean the same by 'God' may be an important one. It is a question of the role which our statements about God play in our worship and in our lives. Or, if we are outside religion and discussing it, the reference is still to the use the language has among those who practise it.[8]

As far as the philosopher is concerned, his work is over when he notes this situation, ragged as it is, with as much clarity as he can achieve. An ecumenically minded theologian, on the other hand, is working within the situation, hoping to change it in certain respects. The difficulty in locating the audience to which Lindbeck belongs is due to the fact that while, on the one hand, he is undoubtedly an ecumenically minded theologian, he seems to think, on the other hand, that the theological enterprise can be furthered by philosophical means. But he is not consistent in these matters, hence the difficulty of locating his audience.

Having noted that doctrinal statements are grammatical statements, Lindbeck says that the grammar is 'inevitably imperfect' because it has exceptions, and may only express surface grammar and miss the depth grammar. These remarks, borrowed it seems from Wittgenstein's use of 'grammar', are confused. If a doctrinal statement is understood to be a grammatical statement, it cannot have exceptions, since it is in terms of the grammar that we determine what is to count as the rule and what is to count as an exception to it. In Wittgenstein, the contrast between surface grammar and depth grammar refers to one source of philosophical confusion. We may be confused by the surface grammar of a proposition into thinking its logic is quite different from what would be revealed if we examined the actual contexts of its application (its depth grammar). Thus 'God is love' may mislead us into thinking that it is a descriptive statement rather than a rule for the use of the word 'God'. Once we grasp Wittgenstein's use of the distinction between surface and depth grammar, we can see that we cannot speak of the real grammar of a doctrine as confused, or as only expressing surface grammar. That way of speaking is unintelligible if 'grammar' is being used in anything like the way in which Wittgenstein used the term.

As we have seen, the mediation of a doctrinal statement may vary enormously, as widely, Lindbeck tells us, as the difference between a medieval scholastic and a contemporary liberationist. He thinks, however, that despite the different mediations they are still mediations of the same doctrine. I think this may be contested. We have to remember that grammar is explicated, not in the formal identification of a form of words, but in the way it shows itself in the roles religious ideas have in the lives of the believers. That being so, when some of these roles are spelled out, others may react to them by saying that they are not instances of faithfulness to that doctrine at all. The only identity the 'unfaithful' mediation has with the 'faithful' doctrine is that in judging it, it is an additional sin on its part to have desecrated so hallowed a form of words. So there are no grounds for Lindbeck's optimistic assertion, 'To the degree that religions are like languages they can obviously remain the same amid vast transformations of affirmation and experience.'[9] To so argue would be like saying that when someone comments on a contemporary barbarism by saying 'Look what the English language has become', the identity of the English language remains the same despite the barbaric transformation! Lindbeck's distinction between conditional and unconditional rules does not circumvent this difficulty. To love God and to love one's neighbour may be said to be unconditional rules, but, given certain mediations of them, there is still an issue whether we can be said to be talking of the *same* commandment in all cases. This is not to deny Lindbeck's point that some doctrines and theological formulations are more central than others. The point is that even in the central cases, not to mention the others, no judgement of sameness and continuity can be guaranteed in the way Lindbeck thinks it can. All he says about the flexibility and sensitivity which is necessary in changing circumstances can be accepted. It still remains the case that theological judgements about the character of what is happening may vary. Looked at externally, this situation is unlikely to change. That being so, the philosopher looking at it, leaves ragged what is ragged. Lindbeck, as a theologian, works for different ends. What we have seen is that the appreciation of theology as a form of grammar is not, in itself, a servant of his theological perspective.

Lindbeck does not deny the vast variety of perspectives both within the mainstream Christian traditions and within the sects. Of course, to speak of mainstream traditions and of sects is already to invoke a theological distinction. In the midst of this variety he asks 'Who are the competent practitioners? Who have the pious ears?'[10] But whose question is this? From what audience does it come? A non-theological investigator simply takes the question as one referring to a sample of what most people believe. All that answers, however, is the question of what most people believe at a certain time. It does not tell one whether those people are pious or not. Lindbeck's own attempts at locating this pious audience are extremely puzzling. On the same page we find him saying first this:

Membership in a mainstream community does not

guarantee competence ... most Christians through most of Christian history have spoken their own official tongue very poorly. It has not become a native language, the primary medium in which they can think, feel, act, dream. Thus lacking competence, they *cannot,* from the cultural-linguistic perspective, be part of that *consensus fidelium* against which doctrinal proposals are tested.[11]

And, then, this:

The linguistically competent, to recapitulate, are to be sought in the mainstream, rather than in isolated backwaters or ingrown sects uninterested in communicating widely. They must, in other words, be what in the past centuries was meant by 'catholic' or 'orthodox' and what we now generally call 'ecumenical'. Further, the competence that they have must to some extent be empirically recognizable. As in the case of native speakers of natural languages, they are not tied to fixed formulas, but rather can understand, speak and discriminate between the endless varieties of necessarily innovative ways of using both old and new vocabularies to address unprecedented situations. While they have no formal theological training they are likely to be saturated with the language of Scripture and/or liturgy. One might, perhaps, call them flexibly devout: they have so interiorized the grammar of their religion that they are reliable judges, not directly of doctrinal formulations (for these may be too technical for them to understand), but of the acceptability or unacceptability of the consequences of these formulations in ordinary religious life and language.[12]

The two quotations contradict each other in their non-reliance and reliance on mainstream traditions. Whatever of that, the analogy between religion and language will not do. We can have regrets about what is happening in the language; regrets about ways of talking and thinking that come to dominate people's minds. There is no logical contradiction, therefore, in calling the state of religion, at any time, mainstream and decadent. As we saw earlier, the survival of a set of formulae does not in itself constitute the continuity of the one Faith, if the mediation of the formulae varies enormously from what one takes the Faith to be. It is staggering, therefore, to hear Lindbeck conclude: 'The

220

reliability of their agreement in doctrinal matters may not be improperly called infallible.'[13] But before we proceed with the obvious criticism that agreement in procedures cannot be identified with religious truth, we find Lindbeck changing his ground. Recall that his original question was 'Who have the pious ears?' Suddenly, we find that the only question he can answer is the question of what is to count as dominant Christian practice at any given time, where this is to be understood in a purely formal sense. There, of course, the majority have it. But questions of religious truth and piety cannot be settled in this way. Think of applying this method to the beginnings of Christianity. On these criteria, the Christians could only be called a sect. Lindbeck has to admit that questions of religious truth are themselves matters of religious judgement. More should be heard on this issue, for there are times when Lindbeck seems dangerously close to conflating the truth with what in fact proves acceptable. In so far as he does so, his conception of religious truth comes dangerously close to Rorty's conception of the dominant voice in the hermeneutic conversation, or to Berger's claim that what we mean by reality is determined by who wields the bigger stick. In fact he *is* influenced by the vulgarisation of social movements in the analysis of them provided by Berger. When movements find themselves in a competitive marketplace Berger says, as we saw, that their policies should be determined by the dynamics of consumer preference. In this way, the genuine interests of the movements themselves are treated with a complete lack of seriousness.

Despite the twists and turns of his argument, the audience Lindbeck has to face is the familiar ragged one of different religious traditions and emphases present to us within Christianity, not to mention different religions. Lindbeck is quite right when he says that within this variety the disagreements are often disagreements over an appropriate grammar for the word 'God': 'they would involve disagreements on where proper grammar is to be found, on who are the competent speakers of a religious language. The progressives would appeal to rebels, the conservatives to establishments, and Catholics and Protestants would continue to differ in their understandings of the relation of Scripture and tradition.'[14] Despite this variety, Lindbeck wants to conclude, 'Nevertheless, the common framework would make possible, though not guarantee, genuine arguments over the relative adequacy of specifically different positions.'[15] Of course, discussion may occur, but my argument has been that there is nothing in Lindbeck's grammatical insights, at their best, which prescribes that this should be so. The variety to which he should direct his attention shows as many grammatical contrasts as grammatical similarities in theology. He has to admit 'such arguments are difficult, however, when theologies have formally different views of religion. The problem ... is that each theology is embedded in a conceptual framework so comprehensive that it shapes its own criteria of adequacy.'[16] Lindbeck hopes to get over this difficulty by his distinction between revisible and irrevisible theological explications of doctrine. As we have already seen, however, this distinction does not remove such difficulties.

Lindbeck's chief concern, at the end of the book, must be a concern for any serious theologian: the question of how religion is to be proclaimed in the world in which we find ourselves. He says rightly, 'The grammar of religion, like that of language, cannot be explicated or learned by analysis of experience, but only by practice.'[17] But what has that practice become? For many, religion has lost its distinctiveness by becoming subsumed in some wider non-religious enterprise. As Lindbeck puts it, it has been transposed into alien speech. Modern problems have to be identified, but a distinctively Christian perspective must be brought to bear on them. The theologian must renew 'the ancient practice of absorbing the universe into the biblical world. May their tribe increase.'[18] This is a prayer most theologians will echo, but finding an answer to the prayer cannot be made a matter of policy. Lindbeck says that Reinhold Niebuhr was the last theologian who made great efforts in this direction. But, then, he was able to do so, not because he made doing so a policy. The question of why he was able to do so can usually only be answered, with any profit, retrospectively. One can point to many factors in the situation in which he wrote and so on. But, at the end of the day, we are faced with the brute fact that this man was able to write in the way he did. What we have to understand is not a general theory, but him and what he had to say. Put religiously, we would say that the Holy Spirit used *these* people in a distinctive way (or deny that they were so used). But these are retrospective judgements. Lindbeck indulges in predictive judgements: 'God will not withold his guidance from theologians who pray for it, and perhaps not even from some who do not pray.'[19] On both scores, I do not think we can indulge in *a priori* pessimism or optimism.

I have had difficulty in locating the audience Lindbeck is addressing or speaking from. Now and again I seem to have identified it only for its character to elude me. I do not think Lindbeck himself could identify it for me, since I think he is the victim of more than one audience and their voices have become confused in his. There are times when the voice with which he speaks is clear and important. There are other times when the voice is muddled and confused. I think he has inflated hopes of the help philosophy can give to theologians faced with the phenomenon of doctrinal disagreement. He says that he has been influenced by Wittgenstein but that Wittgenstein's influence in general 'does not appear to have yet inspired consideration of problems of doctrinal constancy and change and of agreement and disagreement with which this book is concerned.'[20] Perhaps not, but I hope my comments have indicated the limits of what one's expectations should be. Someone learned in doctrine and its disputes, in a way I am not, could give illuminating examples to illustrate what agreement and disagreement come to in this area. The philosopher could bring out, as I hope to have done to some extent, the *kind* of dispute a theological dispute is; how it is often a matter of a conflict of grammar. As far as philosophy is concerned, that ragged scene must be left ragged. Of course, the scene may change. A theologian may arise with such a vision that long-standing differences dissolve in some wider all-embracing perspective. Some may think the coming of such a vision likely, others may think it unlikely. If it came, many would greet it as the work of the Holy Spirit. I should be surprised if there were not others who would see it as the work of the Devil. That these disagreements are likely is no trivial matter. It shows that religious and theological questions are matters over which people *do* disagree in this way. It is part of their grammar, one might say.

Notes

1. Lindbeck, *The Nature of Doctrine*, p. 65.
2. Ibid., p. 66.
3. Ibid., p. 69.
4. Ibid., p. 74.
5. Rhees, 'Religion and Language', p. 131.
6. Ibid., p. 129.
7. Ibid.
8. Ibid., pp. 129–30.
9. Lindbeck, *The Nature of Doctrine*, p. 84.
10. Ibid., p. 99.
11. Ibid., p. 100.
12. Ibid.
13. Ibid.
14. Ibid., p. 113.
15. Ibid.
16. Ibid.
17. Ibid., p. 129.
18. Ibid., p. 135.
19. Ibid., p. 102.
20. Ibid., p. 24.

17
Grammar Without Foundations

Epistemological foundationalism claimed to have the means to assess epistemic practices, showing which were rational and which were irrational. Theologians often accept, uncritically, that philosophers will tell them what it is for statements to be meaningful. Armed with the answer, the theologians claim to establish the meaningfulness of religious statements. Or so the story goes. What usually happens is that the theologian is already convinced that religion has meaning and then searches around, in a somewhat unedifying fashion, for the philosophical theory best suited to what he wants to say about religion. Many philosophers are all too ready to assess religion by arriving at some generic concept of meaning by which to judge it. As a result, 'it has been solemnly declared that there are kinds of meaning and that some language is cognitively meaningful, some is emotively meaningful, and some is altogether meaningless.'[1] We saw such distinctions at work in George Lindbeck's discussion of the logical status of doctrinal statements. Instead of discussing the actual meanings they are puzzled or confused by, philosophers proceed to discuss the *kinds* of meaning they believe these meanings are. The philosophical terms take on a life of their own, their characters being thought of as commendatory or pejorative. Thus, it is sufficient to say, in certain philosophical circles, that an analysis is non-cognitive and emotive, to condemn it. When discussion is carried on at this level, the primary language which occasioned the original puzzlement is soon forgotten.

In opposing these tendencies, Paul Holmer has learned from Wittgenstein in coming to see for himself

that there can be no generic theory of meaning by which

225

we can say that scientific language is more meaningful than religious language ... In fact, the whole notion of meaning is itself confused and it might be better simply to say that we can learn the differences between ways of speaking and ways of understanding ... One way to express this fully is to declare that the logic of the discourse of science is not the same as the logic of religion. Another way is to note all the different ways that we explain things to ourselves. For again there are many kinds of explanation. Each kind has its context, its occasion, its own province, and its own function, relative to a specific need. We are gradually learning that kinds of explanations are not necessarily incompatible. They are in fact incommensurable with one another, and hence there is no logical incompatibility of the radical sort.[2]

If this incommensurability is ignored, then, as we have seen, one kind of explanation can easily be taken as a paradigm for all others. Religious uses of language are not logically odd, as Ian Ramsey used to claim. If ordinary uses are primary uses, then, in the appropriate context, religious uses are primary uses, ordinary uses. We can never understand these uses if we ignore their natural contexts. It was this conviction, Holmer argues, which was at the heart of Kierkegaard's and Barth's protests against the alien paradigms of rationality to which religious belief was subjected or which it was all too ready to appropriate. Both thinkers expressed themselves over-lavishly at times, but, even so, there is little excuse for calling them irrationalists and subjectivists. The same fate has befallen Wittgenstein and those influenced by him in the philosophy of religion. Holmer brings out why:

The fact that Wittgenstein and other analytic logicians have made strong remarks about forms of life having an ultimacy has also created the notion that theology is like metaphysics in not being any longer the final court of justification. If forms of life are foundational, then it looks as though fideism is more crucial than theology.[3] So it is that followers of Wittgenstein and Wittgenstein himself are assumed to be of the mind that denies that there is a recognizable kind of knowledge of God and that therefore theology is not truly cognitive, objective and rational. Oddly enough, Barthians,

Kierkegaardians, and Wittgensteinians together look like the opponents of cognitivity and rationality in religion, but only if a certain pattern of rationality is taken to be normative.[4]

Holmer's main point here is that, once again, the categorising of the philosophers he mentions is characterised by a woefully impoverished and one-sided conception of rationality. I am just a little concerned, however, at the extent to which Holmer is anxious to have a philosophical term like 'cognitive' applied to religion, almost as if it were the very kind of stamp of approval he criticises so well. Holmer says

> it is an academic and hence a confoundedly difficult prejudice to eradicate, namely, that *objective, real, true, logical, rational,* and other words of this extensive criteriological sort are manifest in meaning, unvariegated in use, simple to understand, and plainly rudimentary and underived in import. Though we use them in every context, and though we are all endowed with sufficient capacity to use some of them in telling ways, they are still not transcendentals and context-free. The fact is that they are used in several contexts, and they become context-dependent. So we have to be clear about the specifics in each case. *Rational, objective, true, real,* etc., are always 'in respect to so and so'; and then the expressions make sense and engage a subject matter and a thinker.[5]

What Holmer does not consider, however, is the possibility that the status of some of these criteriological words is bound up with their confused philosophical use. In that case, insisting that they be applied to religion and other forms of discourse may do more harm than good. It may perpetuate the very philosophical malaise Holmer says is so difficult to eradicate. After all, does a term like 'cognitive' belong to the primary language of either religion or theology? Would using it help us to understand something we would not arrive at by considering ordinary language in this context? To repeat Holmer's own earlier suggestion, 'it might be better simply to say that we can learn the differences between ways of speaking and ways of understanding'.[6]

Once these grammatical differences are appreciated, we see that the respective grammars do not stand in need of justifications or foundations. Yet many theologians insist on providing such foundations in one form or another, and much of Holmer's work is concerned with exposing their confusions. There are four categories of theologians whom he sees as would-be providers of foundations for religious belief.

First, Holmer mentions those who think that implicit in the living Faith is the philosophical foundation of it. They call it theism. Indeed, there are those for whom a rejection of philosophical theism is tantamount to a rejection of religion.[7] As Holmer says, 'There is something absurd about this. Crucifying Jesus, living faithlessly, and loving the world with all one's heart, soul, mind and strength tend then to become trivialities compared with denying theism. It is almost as if the academics have made crucial what was not so initially.'[8] Further, theism is thought to be a conceptual scheme common to Christianity, Judaism and Islam, on which their rationality depends. But, in countless philosophy classes, the traditional arguments associated with theism are subjected to devastating criticisms. The traditional proofs for the existence of God which, arguably, began as attempts to understand the Faith from within it, are now made to stand alone as external attempts at proof which, of course, invariably fail. But if a severe displacement of the so-called proofs has occurred, we can see that concepts at work in a living Faith do not derive their meaning and vitality from the abstract concepts of theism. On the contrary, whatever life theism ever had in it was derived from the special, but ordinary concepts of a working Faith. I am not overlooking the fact that abstract concepts have found their way, by various routes, into creeds and declarations of Faith. Even so, to the extent that they have any life there, it will not be by forming the abstract foundations of Faith, but by having a lively application within it.

Second, Holmer mentions those theologians who think that Faith needs to be made secure through historical investigation. Here, the notion of a paradigm of what it is to be real plays a prominent part. History offers a seductive paradigm: to be real is to answer to the facts. It is no part of Holmer's intention to denigrate historical scholarship. On the contrary, he praises its achievements in relation to the history of religions as much as he does elsewhere. His concern is different. It is a concern with someone who comes to equate knowledge of religions with religious knowledge. The fact that the latter phrase is often used in schools to refer to the former does not help. The term 'religious instruction' fares no better. Holmer is worried at signs of many settling for historical knowledge as if it were an adequate substitute for theology. There is a desperate confusion in the assumption that such a substitution makes sense. Holmer says:

> Theology does not at every juncture demand an historical understanding before it can be reasserted in our day. To make that case supposes far too standardized a view ... there may be instances of literature, New Testament and Old, Shakespeare, Molière, or Plato, where one needs to know the time and occasion before one gets the drift of what was said. But these are particular instances where historical understanding is a necessary priority. Most instances of the New Testament, for example, are not like that. One suspects that it is far more important than most historical material to learn to hunger and thirst for righteousness, to learn to love a neighbour, and to achieve a high degree of self-concern, in order to understand the religious themes of the New Testament. There are, in short, personality qualifications that are also required. Perhaps it is even essential to have learned guilt because one has not done as he ought to have done. In any case, these forms of human consciousness are closer to the prerequisites for a Christian's understanding than is most knowledge supplied by other scholars.[9]

But the metaphysical notion of 'factuality' dies hard. When someone becomes convinced that the truths of religion cannot be ascertained by historical investigation, he may be tempted to create a conception of a different kind of history, religious history, which has to do with special facts — religious facts. Alternatively, he will stick to the notion of historical factuality and simply claim the authority of the Bible for saying that the facts are such-and-such. In this way, historical fruits can be enjoyed without historical labours. The Bible, in its turn, is said to be based on the facts, facts to do with God himself. So the elevation of actuality in the third group of theologians in Holmer's audience, characterises a whole theological spectrum, from liberalism to conservatism. I do not want to enter into a discussion over whether there is more loss than profit involved in talking of factuality where the existence of God is concerned. I suppose that when Kierkegaard said, 'God does not exist, he is eternal'[10] he was noting the limits of usefulness in talking of facts and of finding out the facts. Still, the important point, and one with which Holmer concurs, is that if we are going to speak of religious facts, all the grammatical work has still to be done. We have to show how talk of facts in this context differs from talk of facts in other contexts. We would need to be clear about what finding out the facts, discovering the facts, or being mistaken about the facts, would amount to where religious matters are concerned. There would be similarities enough with other contexts, but there would be huge differences. I suspect what is important would lie in these differences.

Holmer's complaint against the liberal is that he either thinks that what is fundamental can be discovered by historical investigation or else extends the notions of history and factuality in a technical usage of his own devising. If historical investigation is put aside as a means of arriving at the fundamental facts, their discovery is said to be dependent on these new conceptual categories of the theologian's making. Neither alternative yields what is fundamental. What is needed is an understanding of the fact that God has reconciled the world to himself in Christ and other fundamental facts of the Gospel. Of course, to reach this understanding we must come to terms with the Gospel. But this Gospel, Holmer insists, is waiting for us to come to terms with it. It is not itself waiting on the latest theories of theologians.

Holmer's complaint against the conservative is that in his eagerness to be faithful to what he thinks are the plain facts of the Gospel, he in fact displaces them from their natural context. The conservative wishes to say that the whole of the revelation he embraces is based on something called 'the facts'. He wants to begin with the facts and found his religion on them. But, Holmer insists, it is only in the context of revelation that we can come to see what talk of facts amounts to here. The conservative, in invoking a conception of factuality outside this context, is himself in the grip of the very metaphysical conceptions he claims to have no room for. More importantly, for Holmer, the conservative's desire to be given the facts before he begins, as it were, is an instance of what Kierkegaard called 'foreshortening eternity' or 'taking eternity by storm'.[11] The appropriation of religious facts cannot be achieved all at once in the way the conservative seems to think. What does it mean to appropriate the fact that God has reconciled the world to himself in Christ? That appropriation, Holmer would say, is a personal matter. It cannot be done on behalf of anyone by another. To take that truth into one's life is what accepting it, appropriating it, amounts to. It is an appropriation which is never over and done with in this life. It involves Christian patience to the end. When we remember contexts such as these, we see how misplaced it is to speak of an appropriation of facts effected, somehow, before one even begins to consider matters of religious import. O.K. Bouwsma spoke humorously of the lost first book of the Bible, 'Pre-Genesis', in which all the facts were given on which the rest of the Bible depends. Many theologians of different schools are engaged on enterprises which assume that, although we may never find it, 'Pre-Genesis' exists or existed.[12]

The fourth group of theologians which make up Holmer's audience react against the endeavours of those theologians we have already mentioned. Despairing at those attempts to make religious assent intellectual assent, and dismayed at the array of theologies from which they are asked to choose, these theologians emphasise the importance of religious experience, a religious experience free from theology. Holmer sympathises with the initial reactions of these theologians, but not with the implications they draw from them. Despair at confused theologies should not lead one to jettison theology altogether. Experience without the governance of theology is wild and undisciplined. Furthermore, turning away from the concepts of the Christian Faith towards experience is to misunderstand the role of these concepts. When they are not intellectualised beyond all recognition by theologians, we can see that to grasp a concept is to develop a capacity.

> The Christian concept of *agape*, or love, is a typically familiar one. But there are more — God, hope, grace, repentance, sin, guilt, sanctification, holiness, faith, creation, Saviour, Lord, crucifixion, gospel, forgiveness, and many others. Many of these words are otherwise familiar; but it does seem that in specifically Jewish and Christian contexts, one does something distinctive with them. This distinctive power is tied up very concretely with the expectations and qualities of being a Jew and/or a Christian with attendant forms of life, of concern, and of emotion.[13]

So to appropriate theological concepts is to learn the authorisation for

> all kinds of dispositions, feelings, passions, virtues, and deeds that make one's daily living something distinctive. They

even produce another view of the world and human life ...
So we have to remember that theological teachings have
also the power to commission their hearers. To be
commissioned is to be given something to do. Religious
teaching challenges people out of their complacency into a
radical kind of behaviour. It makes disciples of the hearers.
Therefore, to understand theology and to evince a command
of its concepts is to be spurned, to be humiliated, to be
stirred to contrition, to be prepared for joy. There is even
a way to understand all human beings as if they were pro-
foundly sick. This is also a Christian way. The Christian
mode of talking is supposed to completely alter the way of
sick lives, and the task is to cure one person at a time.[14]

When theology is appreciated in the light of these remarks, we
see that the desire to have religious experience free from theology
is a deeply confused one. It is often characteristic of religious
forms of romanticism.

We have now noted four kinds of theologians who feature large
in the confused audience Holmer takes himself to be addressing.
I have simply commented on and illustrated the ideas Holmer
attacks without mentioning any theologians by name. Suffice it
to say that in the course of his criticisms Holmer provides plenty
of examples of theologians from all periods of theology, including
our own, who have been guilty of the confusions to which he
addresses himself. One feature dominates these confused
theologies: instead of being *of* the Faith, they are *about* the Faith.
They stand in external relations to a living faith. As a result, is
it any wonder to see the discredit in which theology stands today?
From the point of view of the religious laity 'theology is painfully
abstract ... a specialist's domain ... impractical ... of no use to the
laity ... about matters that do not and cannot concern those who
are nonacademic'.[15] Within theological circles the study of
theology tends to become an end in itself. So within universities
and centres for the study of religion theology can itself become
an academic game. In this context, Holmer's words are likely to
cut deep.

In such places, the sheer opulence of points of view and the
thick harvest of historical antecedents give a revivification
by scholarship and cause dim overviews to develop about
the development of doctrine and the necessity that one

succeed another. After a while, it becomes a lot easier to believe this vague metaview that makes one sceptical about any particular theology of an individual or of a church than it is to be a lively believer and hearty participant in any one theology and its related practices. The point that seems so disturbing here is that these chaotic developmental views are so easy to teach and that they are no longer linked to anything save the most obvious accommodation to the 'Zeitgeist'. They serve also to divorce most people from the practice of religion itself, and instead create a sophisticated clientele that is interested in theology as one more artifact cast up in the course of time.[16]

But this so-called sophisticated clientele is doomed within the circles it desperately wants to belong to, the cherished circle of academia. Since theology has been uprooted from its proper role and turned into an intellectual system it cannot be, the fate of such systems in the light of any worthwhile intellectual judgement is inevitable: 'And then theology is (just as unfortunately) lumped with speculative concerns, with metaphysics, with subjectivity and special interests, and, by its detractors, finally, with astrology, prescientific thought, mythology, and make-believe.'[17]

When we turn aside from these confusions to theology's proper task we find it is the grammar of the Faith. It teaches us the parameters within which, as believers, we can come to know God. It may appear in a codified form, but it cannot be learned by rote. Appropriation in this context, as we have seen, is always personal appropriation.

Theology answers the question — what is Christianity? But it tells us the answer by giving us the order and priorities, the structure and morphology of the Christian faith. It does this by placing the big words, like *man, God, Jesus, world*, in such a sequence and context that their use becomes ruled for us. And if we begin to use words like that, with the appropriate zest and pathos, then we, too, become Godly as those earlier believers were.[18]

Appreciating the grammatical role of theology has two important consequences. First we see that 'the theologian gets no new revelation and has no special organ for knowledge. He is debtor to what we, in one sense, have already — the Scriptures and the lives and the thoughts of the faithful.'[19] Second, 'this puts theology within the grasp of conscientious tentmakers, tinkers like Bunyan, lay people like Brother Lawrence, and maybe someone you know down the street who shames you with his or her grasp'.[20] It may seem that compared with everything that has been rejected, the task that remains for theology is a relatively modest one. Nothing could be further from the truth. Many theologies think that to be comprehensive they have to be systematic. Starting from the true apprehension that religious faith informs the whole of life, they conclude, wrongly, that one thing can bear on another only as parts of a system bear on one another. Conversations bear on one another too, but not in a systematic way. The language of sermons and worship bears on the language of everyday speech and its multitude of concerns. As Holmer says,

> The point is that the language of faith is not an artificial or contrived tongue. People speak in this way and in conjunction with Apostles, saints and the proposers of law and gospel. *Faith, hope, grace*, and other words become internal to one's life and its vicissitudes. Fairly soon, that language of faith is extended to all of one's planning, judging, wishing, and even remembrance of things past. Judgements are formed and ideas are formulated as to what life is all about.[21]

All this could never take the form of a system. Holmer says that 'Orthodoxy in theology is never capable of much more refined definition than that supposed by the somewhat loose consensus of the faithful.'[22] But, in the middle of this richly variegated context, the theologian dares to become the guardian of the central remarks of the Faith.[23] We have seen that throughout all he has said, Holmer has wanted to emphasise over and over again that religious belief is a matter of striving to be near to God; the practice of the presence of God, to use Brother Lawrence's apt phrase. The practice of God's presence involves humbling ourselves. We become aware of our pride, weakness and sin. Holmer concludes: 'Surely the one who is then humbled is also the one to whom the Lord God gives his grace and his spirit (1 Peter 5:5). But this is also how one becomes a true theologian, one who actually knows God.'[24]

In expounding the four categories of foundationalist theologians, Holmer, presumably, has two aims in mind. First, he wants them to stop doing what they are doing, since it is confused and confusing. This is why what Holmer has to say appears so negative to his critics. But this is to miss the fact that he wants to recall theologians to a momentous task: that of being guardians of the Faith. Second, he wants to protect the laity against these theological trends; to impress on ordinary believers that everything needful already surrounds them, and that they are not dependent on whatever intellectual systems theologians are able to devise.

How is Holmer's theological audience likely to react to his criticisms? There is, of course, the well-known academic strategy of ignoring anything that will upset the game being played. That apart, what is their reaction likely to be? If theologians are confronted by wholesale attacks on the metaphysical views on which they think religious belief depends, they will search desperately for alternative metaphysical views. As we have already suggested, there is something comic in the way theologians have hopped from one metaphysical view to another. What they will not admit, any more than their philosophical counterparts, is that when a metaphysical view falls, it need not be replaced by another one. We can settle for the gain in clarity achieved by seeing the confusions which led us to devise the theory in the first place. So what is to be done about Holmer's book? After all, almost the whole of *The Grammar of Faith* is an attempt to rescue theology from its metaphysical view of itself, to bring the practice of theology back from its metaphysical to its ordinary use. How can that attack be blunted, if not ignored? Holmer predicted the method to be employed: blunt the attack by treating it as if it were an *additional* metaphysical perspective. An excellent example of this is found in Cornel West's review of *The Grammar of Faith*. West outlines four major paradigms in North American theology today. The first, which he calls the *historicized Kantian paradigm*, derives from the influence of H. Richard Niebuhr. The second, the *process paradigm*, stems from the work of Alfred North Whitehead and Charles Hartshorne. The writings of Husserl and Heidegger inform the third paradigm, *the hermeneutical paradigm*, while James Cone initiated the fourth paradigm, the *liberation paradigm*. In each case, West notes not only the inspirers of the paradigms, but also the promising theologians working today under the influence of each. He also notes drawbacks he sees in each. Against such a background he has Holmer make an entry as someone who is offering us a fifth paradigm, a *Wittgensteinian–Kierkegaardian paradigm*. Despite the fact that West shows what

Holmer is opposed to, nevertheless, characterising him as offering a paradigm, a fifth to better the four which have proved unsatisfactory, suggests a continuity of enterprise where none exists, any more than there is a continuity between the desire to devise metaphysical systems and Kierkegaard's and Wittgenstein's attacks on them. Holmer would not say he had brought a new viewpoint to bear on theology, but tried to recall it to what, in one sense, it already is. But, for West, 'Holmer has performed an invaluable service by presenting and promoting a new and exciting viewpoint—the Wittgensteinian-Kierkegaardian paradigm — on the North American theological scene.'[25] The academic practitioners can breathe a sigh of relief: a label has been provided and now *it* can be discussed. I am reminded of Kierkegaard's satirical story in this connection. One day a man went to get his suit pressed. He saw a shop with a sign in the window, 'Suits Pressed Here'. He went inside, but found that only the sign was for sale. So Holmer's paradigm will become the topic of discussion instead of the primary language of religion and theology. I write this with some sympathy having suffered a similar fate. Having tried, in ways not dissimilar to Holmer's, to criticise perceived relations between philosophy and religious belief, my attempts were met, at first, with some puzzlement. Before many of Wittgenstein's remarks relating to religion were available, my views were accounted for as a philosophical expression of Welsh evangelical theology — a view which amused some and outraged others among my Welsh evangelical acquaintances. Then, briefly, the analyses were said to be Barthian. Finally, the very thing: Kai Nielsen's ingenious label, *Wittgensteinian fideism*.[26] I am not in the original list of so-called fideists. Those named make a very odd collection, since they differ widely in their views.[27] Still, it worked, and instead of discussing the primary language of religion, discussions of Wittgensteinian fideism flourished. Whenever I read papers, someone was sure to ask about fideism. At one American university, having been asked for the hundredth time, 'When did you decide to become a Wittgensteinian fideist?' I gave my best reply, 'Shortly after the operation, as a matter of fact'.[28] Holmer was spared discussions of the *Wittgensteinian-Kierkegaardian paradigm* because, fortunately for him, it lacks the consumer appeal of Wittgensteinian fideism. Nevertheless, in other respects, his fate is similar. We have seen that Holmer endeavours to get theology back from its metaphysical to its proper, ordinary use. But in West's exposition, this very attempt

236

becomes a meta-physical thesis: 'Holmer's metaphysical thesis is that theology ought to be a *part of* the language of the faithful, not *about* this language.'[29] Thus the metaphysical game perpetuates itself.

Notes

1. Paul Holmer, *The Grammar of Faith* (Harper and Row, New York, 1978), p. 56.
2. Ibid., pp. 68–9.
3. I do not think it ought to be said that forms of life are foundational, since, as we have seen, the notion of a form of life is used, in part, precisely to combat philosophical foundationalism. 'To imagine a language is to imagine it in a form of life', but a form of life is not the foundation of the language.

As well as the previous discussion in this book see D.Z. Phillips, *Belief, Change and Forms of Life* (Macmillan, London and Humanities Press, Atlantic Heights, New Jersey, 1986).
4. Holmer, *The Grammar of Faith*, p. 184.
5. Ibid., pp. 189–90.
6. Ibid., p. 68.
7. See Part Four, ch. 19.
8. Holmer, *The Grammar of Faith*, p. 162.
9. Ibid., p. 9.
10. Søren Kierkegaard, *Concluding Unscientific Postscript*, trans. David Swenson (Princeton University Press, Princeton, New Jersey, 1944), p. 296.
11. Kierkegaard, *Purity of Heart*.
12. See O.K. Bouwsma, *Without Proof or Evidence*, ed. J. L. Craft and R. E. Hustwit (University of Nebraska Press, Lincoln, 1984).
13. Holmer, *The Grammar of Faith*, p. 142.
14. Ibid., pp. 145–6.
15. Ibid., p. 1.
16. Ibid., p. 3.
17. Ibid., p. 1.
18. Ibid., p. 20.
19. Ibid., p. 21.
20. Ibid.
21. Ibid., pp. 198–9.
22. Ibid., p. 198.
23. Ibid., p. 192.
24. Ibid., p. 212.
25. Cornel West, review of Paul Holmer, *The Grammar of Faith*, Union Seminary Quarterly Review, vol. 35, Nos 3 and 4 (Spring/Summer 1980), p. 284.
26. Kai Nielsen, 'Wittgensteinian Fideism', *Philosophy* vol. 42, 1967.
27. The original names of the so-called fideists are: Peter Winch, G.E. Hughes, Norman Malcolm, Peter Geach, Stanley Cavell, J.M. Cameron, Robert Coburn.
28. For a more philosophical response see Phillips, *Belief, Change and Forms of Life*.
29. West, review of Holmer's *The Grammar of Faith*, p. 281.

18
Grammarians and Guardians

The philosopher, it might be said, is the guardian of grammar. The theologian is the guardian of the Faith. Yet, as we have seen, Paul Holmer in his book *The Grammar of Faith* spends most of his time discussing the sense in which a theologian is the guardian of the grammar of the Faith. Naturally, therefore, there will be considerable overlaps between philosophical and theological concerns. Nevertheless, the two concerns are different and they occasion some questions about Holmer's analysis.

The tensions to which I refer appear on the book's jacket. First, reference is made to the misunderstandings of theology's tasks which, as we saw in the last chapter, Holmer wants to rectify:

One of the steady voices in today's cacophonous theological world here proposes that there is a logic and a grammar of faith, the rules of which theologians must adhere to or risk being unworthy of the name. *The Grammar of Faith* discloses that theology is not a succession of rival intellectual positions or new knowledge unavailable to the ordinary believer, but a way to organize and understand faith itself ... What then is theology's central task? According to Dr. Holmer, theology must stand in vigilance against faddism. It must never allow the needs of the day to take primacy over the needs of the eternal ... in the New Testament, Christian liturgy, and the ways of obeying God and being faithful to him are the very means by which the language of faith regains its essence and vitality. This is — or should be — theology's natural home. Far from dubiously examining the central tenets which Christians through the centuries have held dear, theologians must give dignity to the ordinary believer's doubts and beliefs. Theology has no privileged access to either doubt or faith.[1]

Here, it is clear that Holmer is setting himself against, and grappling with, conceptual misunderstandings of the nature of theology.

Second, we are told, 'To speculate on the "meaning" of faith is to vitiate its language.' Holmer is referring here to those who see it as their function to provide more refined 'meanings' to replace the primary language of faith. Holmer is insisting that what has to be understood is the ragged primary language of faith.

But, third, we are told that this primary meaning 'has to be earned and achieved in its original forms'. Who is being addressed in these words? What kind of understanding is being referred to? To earn the understanding *he* seeks, the philosopher must pay attention to the role of religious concepts in their natural contexts. But if the philosopher *earned* and *achieved* these meanings *in their original form,* the philosopher would be a *hearer* of the word in its primitive form too, namely, a believer. Is to understand the Word to hear the Word? We seem to be close to saying so in the following: 'The state of us all is to wrestle with the same mighty matters; and the grammar that is theology is the grammar of our lives.' There is an oscillation in Holmer's work between theological and philosophical concerns. There is nothing amiss with this oscillation, if one is aware of it, but it is not clear that this is always the case. For example, we are told, *'The Grammar of Faith* calls for a grasp that does not substitute for piety or belief, does not foreshorten understanding or grace, but gives one access to them.' But what sort of access is being referred to here? Is it access to the natural contexts of concepts which may prevent conceptual misunderstandings, or access to a living faith without foreshortening the path to it? Is it an access which leads to conceptual clarity or one which leads to spiritual growth? Is clarity enough for Holmer, or is he hoping for something more?

What this something more might be can be brought out by considering two questions which arise from the analysis we expounded in the last chapter. The first arises from aspects of religion which get little attention in Holmer's essays, namely, the heterogeneity within Christianity itself and its relations to the other religious and secular movements which surround it.

As we have seen, Holmer takes as his main task a constant recalling of what he takes to be the primary language of faith.

But is that language as homogeneous as he thinks? Does not Holmer's phrase 'the somewhat loose consensus of the faithful'[2] cover a multitude of differences? In this respect, Cornel West has a point when he says that Holmer's analysis reflects 'those situations in which there has been close personal contact, or when a group is culturally homogeneous or held together by bonds of trust — in short ... those situations in which an organic, cohesive tradition exists'.[3] Even, then, in such contexts there are a variety of religious traditions and deep-going theological disputes: predestination, double predestination, grace and works, the place of the sacraments, mediated or immediate authority, limited or universal salvation, etc., etc. These theological differences cannot be treated as though they were misunderstandings of the one primary language of faith, misunderstandings which would disappear if only theology could be recalled to its proper task. No, these theological differences reflect deep religious differences. What is more, at the primary language of faith, we have a language in which these differences address one another. It is a language in which there is talk of truth and falsity, of departing from the truth and embracing falsehood. These ways of speaking enter into accusation and counter-accusation. If Holmer wants to give a faithful presentation of the primary language of faith, surely this is one prominent feature of it which should be taken into account. We need to become clear about what using conceptions of truth and falsehood come to in this context. For example, it is hard to see how these warring conceptions can be judged by some common measure to determine their rationality or their value. Here, as Wittgenstein says, when people disagree, they are apt to call each other fools and heretics. No doubt confusions and superstitions will come to light, but there is no reason to think that after such revelations and exposures we shall be left with common agreement in religion and theology. All we can say in this realm is that one conception is deep and another shabby. But, of course, there is no guarantee of agreement in such judgements.[4] If there were such agreement within religion there would not be any need to make them. Holmer is so interested in reminding theologians of what they are tempted to forget that he makes the ragged character of the primary language of faith a secondary consideration. Yet, is not remembering this raggedness an essential part of the task he says he has set himself, namely, not to settle all theological issues or internecine controversies, but 'to give them a better setting'.[5]

When we turn to consider the relation of religious faith to secular movements in the surrounding culture, the difficulties deepen. Here, too, there is talk of truth and falsity, of the true way and of false ways. The ways which may be called false from within the perspective of the faith cannot be shown to be misunderstandings. Misunderstandings of the Faith? Not even that much can always be said. For example Holmer admits,

> Nietzsche's aversion to Christianity was so profound and so detailed that his pages outline a faith in Jesus that is worthy of offence. For this reason, his work helps us to see how blessed someone is who is not offended by Jesus. Nietzsche understood but was antipathetic. Voltaire's conception that Pascal's account of Christianity is misanthropic suggests that both Voltaire and Pascal had seen the logic of faith correctly. In one sense, both had the grammar straight — one so that he could accept it, the other so that he could at least reject the right thing.[6]

Here is a genuine clash. Each side may call what the other has to say false and what he proclaims the truth. What is the logic of these undoubted uses of truth and falsity? In an age in which theology cannot take its audience for granted, surely this is something to which we ought to pay more attention than Holmer does.

There are times, however, when Holmer speaks as though, underlying the different perspectives, there is a measure in terms of which the perspectives turn out to be commensurable after all. Holmer suggests that the way one's life develops as a believer will be different from the way it will develop if one is not a believer, and that this difference in development can serve as an external check on the faithfulness of Faith's promises and their superiority over the alternatives. Holmer says that theology 'is more like the teaching that leads to a truly successful, deeply satisfactory, even blessed and happy life ... We get a notion of what the world is, of what we are, and who God is.'[7] Is this a case of 'Taste and see that the Lord is good' becoming 'Test and see that the Lord is good'? Are the notions of success, satisfaction, blessedness, happiness, the world, identity, which Holmer invokes, given *independently* of religious belief, in such a way that the belief can be shown to be superior to the alternatives *according to a common measure*? Any such suggestion would lead to difficulties comparable

241

to those which have accompanied attempts to revive ethical naturalism. No one has succeeded in showing that it is in a rogue's interests to be moral, where those interests have to be understood in the rogue's terms. In the question, 'What profiteth it a man if he gain the whole world and lose his own soul?', the 'gain' and 'loss' cannot be understood as referring to a common coinage.[8] Similarly, where different moral viewpoints are concerned, one cannot point to a conception of human flourishing to act as a judge between them. No doubt there are overlaps between such viewpoints, but they will also differ in what they take human flourishing to be. These differences are not different hypotheses about an agreed something or other, called human flourishing, but *different conceptions of flourishing.*

Yet, in so far as Holmer is tempted, sometimes, to speak as if experience confirms the Christian way to be the *right* way, this way of talking conflicts with his more general emphasis on the *incommensurability* of religious perspectives and other perspectives with which it can so easily be confused. He insists on the dangers of thinking that religious concepts can always be cashed, without loss, into whatever happens to be the conceptual coin of the realm. It seems, then, that we have a tension between conceptual analysis in Homer's work and the theological desire to guard a gospel; a desire which leads him sometimes to use language which is at home within the Faith as if it were an external experiential confirmation of that Faith. What is at issue can be brought out in the following comparison. When Socrates says that the just man is happier than the unjust man, it may seem that he is advocating a naturalism by means of which the superiority of justice over injustice can be demonstrated. The use of the comparative 'happier' may mislead us. Similarly, if Socrates says that the just man is *more* happy than the unjust man, we may be misled in the same way. But Socrates is to be read as saying, 'Let justice be your conception of happiness', or 'Happy is the man who is just.' A neutral conception of happiness is not being used to judge between justice and injustice. Rather, moral conceptions determine what is meant by happiness. When the Faith promises to the believer a satisfactory, blessed and happy life, is it not the case that, despite overlaps, here, too, it is the Faith which determines what these conceptions of satisfaction, blessedness and happiness amount to. Holmer the philosopher never forgets this, but Holmer the theologian is tempted to.

Theological temptations to deviate from conceptual analysis

are more in evidence in the second question which needs to be asked of the analysis expounded in the last chapter. This has to do with what I take to be an over-confidence in Holmer in the way he appeals to the abiding character of the primary language of faith. Holmer speaks of this language as an abiding truth:

> There is a deep and abiding truth that theology proposes, which, like a 'de profundis' is a criterion and standard for all human life. Amid the mad whirl of our common life, this theological stuff, this news about God and man, helps to redefine the human boundaries, to tame its vagrants, stimulate the indifferent, energize the slothful, and give scope and promise to all those who feel hedged in and even utterly defeated. Amid the highs and lows, where ethico-political aims engulf us, where empires organize and disorganize human passions so that we stumble to confusion, there is still a great and level *via*, a narrow way, across these frightening chasms.[9]

In any given situation, it is the task of theology to express this truth in the vernacular, but not by appropriating the intellectual or political language of the day. It is mediated, rather, in 'that residual language, that common diction, within which we all understand and describe the bitterness of grief, the anguish of hopelessness, the fate of the defeated, the cries of the weary, the hurt feelings of the neglected, and the elation of the victor'.[10] Here, Holmer is describing the ordinary but important contexts in which he firmly believes that theology must do its work.

Given this conviction, he is deeply alarmed at those theologians and other thinkers who say that this traditional task cannot be continued because it is outmoded.

> The diagnoses are rather vague and several; and the prognoses are equally disquieting. The themes that are struck are rather familiar in the long historical scene. Popular religion is vague, more chauvinistic than Christian, not well-conceived, and not quite responsible socially and intellectually. The churches with their avid members are pictured as grand but ill-founded. In fact, there are cracks everywhere ... Who are the specialists for God's creaking house? Are there any at all? Quite a few hands are up.[11]

We have already noted the various theological enterprises he goes on to criticise. These enterprises distort and thereby seek to displace the primary language of faith. This being so 'it only sustains a confusion to ask for a revision of language, as if this were the seat of the difficulties'.[12] In resisting such revisions, West thinks that Holmer is not being Wittgensteinian enough. He accuses him of making religious concepts non-historical and, to that extent, context-free. Holmer, as we have seen, is not denying that theology has to be mediated in a concrete historical situation, but its ethico-religious values are brought to bear on that situation and cannot be understood simply as a product of it. West is right in suggesting that Holmer has not given the notion of religious disagreement as much attention as he might have done, but wrong to deny that there are cores to the religious traditions which may disagree with each other in unimportant respects. Once these core concepts are denied, it seems as if everything becomes a matter of interpretation, and that Wittgenstein's insights allow us to say no more than that whatever is called religion, at any time, *is* religion. West says that it is precisely the ideal situations Holmer has in mind 'which are being called into question by the realities facing our churches, our seminaries, our communities, our society, our world'.[13] West does not say what he takes these challenging realities to be, or how they are to be responded to. But since he is questioning Holmer's notion of an adequate response, let us assume that his suggested responses would be ones which, for Holmer, distort the primary language of the faith. What bearing has Wittgenstein's emphasis on the natural context of concepts on this disagreement? On the one hand, it is true that if the responses to challenges West speaks of become pervasive, then, this is now what religion has become. It does not follow at all, of course, that Holmer has to accept this conception of religion. West has forgotten that Wittgenstein said that language-games can pass away and be forgotten. If the changes West envisages come to pass, Holmer, remembering how it used to be, could say that in so far as these new practices seek to travel in the name of the old, they are confused, for they have eroded and distorted the old language-games.

Yet, although Holmer *should* have no difficulty in answering West's misplaced criticism, he may seem to have a difficulty in answering it, because there are times when he seems to suggest that the primary language of faith cannot be in jeopardy, that it cannot lose its meaning. I am not referring now to confused suggestions that it *has* to lose its meaning once its pre-scientific character is realised and its demythologisation is realised. I am talking of the primary language of faith losing its meaning because it gradually ceases to be available to people: the well becomes poisoned at the source. It does not seem to me that Holmer gives serious enough attention to that possibility. He asks, 'Do beliefs crack, sag and sink?'[14] Well, T.S. Eliot certainly thought it made sense to speak in this way of words. In *Burnt Norton*, he says:

> ... Words strain,
> Crack and sometimes break, under the burden,
> Under the tension, slip, slide, perish,
> Decay with imprecision, will not stay in place,
> Will not stay still ...

Does Holmer allow these possibilities? He is so preoccupied with the dead metaphysical language that hangs about the neck of the language of faith, that that is the dead language he tends to concentrate on.

> For it is a question of which part of religious language is really so dead today. Is it the discourse of the metaphysical theologians? Is it the language of the hymn writer? Is it the language of the psalmist and other Biblical authors? If we are talking about certain kinds of elaborate metaphysical theology, I believe it is quite clear that much of this is very dead indeed.[15]

But what of the primary language of faith? Can it be placed in jeopardy? Holmer is quite aware that religious words, like any other words, have their meanings in the life that surrounds them.

> For the way that concepts are finally achieved, even concepts like 'God', 'sin', 'grace', 'salvation' and many more, is also by a kind of interaction between human responses and language. And this supposes a religious context of worship, faith, and concern. Indeed, there are concepts by which people refer to God and a host of other things in profoundly religious ways, but these concepts are achievements constituted in the long pull of educating the human spirit as to what religion is. If the concepts no longer have any life in them, if they mean nothing, then it must be that all

the rest that goes into giving people confidence and faith that there is a God has also disappeared.[16]

But does Holmer believe this could happen or that it, at least, makes sense to hold that, on a large scale, it has already happened in many contexts? It is difficult to give an unequivocal answer. Sometimes, he seems to want to separate the meaning of the words from the common usage, a separation which would run counter to his main emphasis on the internal relations between the meanings and the uses of words. For example, he says,

It is not the words that are at fault, as much as the persons speaking them. Therefore, the religious words are vain when nothing follows their usage, when the individual does not seem to know anything about the matters to which they refer and the way of life in which they were born. Then we can say sadly that people do not know what they are saying. To teach them is one of the theologian's tasks.[17]

But what if the sad commentators grow few and the shabby speech becomes pervasive? It will then become not a matter of people not knowing what they are saying, but of their coming to say different things. It will be impossible to say that the trouble is not in their words, for given their usage, this is what their words have become, despite the fact that they may have the same form as the old words. In such circumstances, it cannot be said that the theologian will teach them anew, for he will be as much a part of the predicament as anyone else. In such a situation there will be those who, remembering what it was possible to say, find attempts to speak like that now, forced, strained. Holmer would admit that we would be hard pressed now to find a concern and discussion of religious questions such as those which surrounded the work of the sixteenth- and seventeenth-century Reformers. One may be surrounded by ways of talking about and discussing religion which one considers shabby and vulgar, and which place serious limitations on what it is possible for one to say. When one tries to say what one believes, in such a context, one finds it, almost of necessity, having a polemical character one might have not wanted it to exhibit. But the choice of one's voice being heard in any other way may be taken from one. The prevailing circumstances have seen to that. There are others, who, perceiving the shabbiness of what prevails, find in it echoes of what used to be, but cannot make these echoes more explicit.[18]

At this point, a possible misunderstanding needs to be avoided. The argument may give the impression that it is being said that, in order to flourish, Christianity needs the presence of a high culture. In reply it might be said that Christianity was *not* part of the high culture of its day, but, at best, a sub-culture which protested against it; a sub-culture which spoke directly to simple people. The point of this reply is well taken. But simple people may have their style too, as may their protest against the prevailing culture. My question would include the possibility of *that* style declining too. Defences and attacks concerning religion become shabby. That is part of what Kafka shows us in *The Castle*, and which led him to say in the fourth of his Prometheus legends: 'Everyone grew weary of the meaningless affair. The gods grew weary, the eagles grew weary, the wound closed wearily.'[19] If it is said that this *cannot* happen, I am puzzled by the character of this 'cannot'. If reference were made to the *power of the Word*, a power which sustains itself come what may, a power which accompanies the words no matter what the surroundings, these views seem to entail saying that meaning is something which 'accompanies' the words. Holmer would be among the first to see what is wrong with that suggestion, and to emphasise that words depend on what we do with them. In that case, is there anything that guarantees the impossibility of a decline in our religious concepts? If not, does not that allow the possibility of religion losing its hold on a people?

Holmer and I could have a discussion about the extent to which we think this has happened already. Perhaps I would cite Ian Robinson's essay 'Religious English' in which he shows what cannot be said in the language of the New English Bible.[20] But, again, that would not be the *philosophical* point at issue. But Holmer seems reluctant to raise the specifically philosophical question. His reluctance may well have a theological source. There are times when teachers feel that they put doubts into the minds of their students; doubts which would never have existed if the philosopher had not spoken. Perhaps Holmer reacts in the same way to my question about the possibility of religious decline. He may think that the question is of a 'What if ...?' character. Posing such questions *in vacuo* may create unnecessary obstacles for the faithful. Abstract speculation about such matters, he may think, is a bad thing. Instead of speculating in asking, 'What if ..?' difficulties should be met piecemeal, as they occur.

This theological reaction is not without its point, but it does not address the philosophical issue at hand. That issue is not about possible eventualities, but about what is involved in believing *now*. In asking 'What if ...?' light is thrown on the logic of religious belief. The citing of possibilities, as in Wittgenstein's *On Certainty*, is not meant to pose threats to the faithful, but to get us away from thinking that religious language depends on some kind of necessity provided by a metaphysical underpinning. In seeming, at times, to deny the possibility of a loss of religious meaning, Holmer seems to hanker after a notion of necessity he spends most of his time attacking. If the language Robinson decries becomes the standard language children inherit, will not their inheritance be one in which certain things can no longer be said? As we have seen, it cannot be said that Holmer denies this of the primary language of faith, but it is not clear either how much room he leaves for it. He says 'And if we are weary of it, it must be that our understanding has waned. When that waxes, the words take wing again and theology becomes once more the Gospel according to God.'[21] But *must* the understanding wax; *must* the words take wing again? The ideal commerce of discourse is characterised by Eliot in *Little Gidding* as follows:

> And every phrase
> And sentence that is right (where every word is at home,
> Taking its place to support the others,
> The word neither diffident nor ostentatious,
> An easy commerce of the old and the new,
> The common word exact without vulgarity,
> The formal word precise but not pedantic,
> The complete consort dancing together)
> Every phrase and every sentence is an end and a beginning,
> Every poem an epitaph ...

Eliot, looking at our prospects, goes on to say:

> And all shall be well and
> All manner of thing shall be well

This is not an optimistic prediction, as some have thought. Rather, it is a kind of prayer for us which the poet has earned the right to make.[22] What I want to insist on is that whether that prayer has been or will be answered is an open question: it can go either way.

As we have seen, Holmer has been concerned to disentangle conceptual confusions about theology and religion which may lead philosophers and others astray. If a philosopher endeavours to free himself from these confusions, he will achieve a certain conceptual and grammatical clarity about the primary texts of faith and theology. But, for theology, clarity is not enough, nor should it be. When theology plays its part in clearing away confusions about the primary language of faith, its task is 'to get persons familiar and intimate with what these texts require'.[23]

Is clarity enough for Holmer? Certainly, he does not disparage the analytic philosopher's search for it.

> On the contrary, it can be asserted that the most detailed and seemingly disinterested analysis is very frequently also the most useful. Great detail and great skill are essential to becoming clear. Furthermore, religions, not least Christianity, do live in part by concepts, and these, in turn become muddied by dubious associations and are frequently mis-construed by virtue of their resemblances to concepts found in the sciences, in aesthetics, and surely in morals.[24]

This struggle for conceptual clarity is itself obscured if we think that the philosophical analysis is a provider of meanings. The analysis is simply trying to clarify meanings already given, about which, for some reason or another, we have become confused or puzzled. Therefore, for those who want the meanings of religion to be provided from without,

> the recent shift in philosophical emphasis is not the better way, analytic instead of speculative, to do the same thing. In fact, Wittgenstein's reflections on these matters are more in the direction of liquidating philosophy as the science of meanings than of inventing one more permutation of methods to provide them.[25]

Philosophy leaves everything where it is and simply endeavours for clarity concerning it; the primary language of faith and theology included.

It seems to me that Holmer's *The Grammar of Faith* does not settle for such clarity. For such clarity is still knowledge *about* religion, a clarity the philosopher seeks with respect to a host of other subjects too. The search for such clarity must be exercised with a cherished freedom from what, Holmer rightly says, 'are considered alien and extraneous demands, be they political, religious, ethical, or even institutional'. But, then, Holmer goes on to say this:

> All of these things remembered, is there not still another way of speaking that is theology proper? Is there not a way of speaking that is a more intimate expression *of* the religious life, a greater clue to its province, a greater help to learning to be religious, than all the learning *about* religion?[26]

The philosopher leaves the theologian of the proper kind where he is. It is right that he should do so. But the theologian of the kind Holmer wants to show us does not leave the philosopher where he is, because it is not right that he should do so. This is because, Holmer tells us, 'the true judgements that theology proffers, like the judgements of the morally enflamed man, are made to incite, not merely to inform'.[27] Of course, the philosopher can, in turn, inform himself of *this* feature of theology's task; he can become clear about that without being incited or without inciting anyone else.

But when we read *The Grammar of Faith*, it is clear that Holmer is doing far more than informing himself and his audience of theology's proper task. He is also engaged in the task himself. Holmer not only informs; he also incites. As we have seen, Holmer says that when he does his work properly, the Christian teacher, the theologian, dares to become the guardian of the language of the Faith. So does Paul Holmer.

Notes

1. Holmer, *The Grammar of Faith*, bookjacket.
2. Ibid., p. 198.
3. West, review of Holmer's *The Grammar of Faith*, p. 284.
4. For a striking example of disagreement involving myself see the symposium I participated in with Richard Swinburne on 'The Problem of Evil' in Brown (ed.), *Reason and Religion*. Swinburne gives a portrayal of a good God to which he thinks morally sensitive people will respond, whereas I see the *same* portrayal as the product of moral insensitivity. I have expanded my comments to take account of Swinburne's response, John Hick's comments as chairman, and the general discussion on that occasion, in *Belief, Change and Forms of Life*.
5. Holmer, *The Grammar of Faith*, p. xi.
6. Ibid., p. 194.
7. Ibid., p. 22.
8. For further discussion see D.Z. Phillips, 'Does it pay to be good?', *Proceedings of the Aristotelian Society*, vol. 65 (1964/5) and D.Z. Phillips and H.O. Mounce, 'On morality's having a point', *Philosophy* (1965). Both papers are developed further in D.Z. Phillips and H.O. Mounce, *Moral Practices* (Routledge and Kegan Paul, London, 1970).
9. Holmer, *The Grammar of Faith*, p. 12.
10. Ibid., pp. 15–16.
11. Ibid., p. 85.
12. Ibid., p. 117.
13. West, review of Holmer's *The Grammar of Faith*, p. 284.
14. Holmer, *The Grammar of Faith*, p. 83.
15. Ibid., p. 128.
16. Ibid., p. 131.
17. Ibid., pp. 134–5.
18. I explore these issues at greater length in 'Meaning, Memory and Longing' in my *Through a Darkening Glass* (University of Notre Dame Press and Basil Blackwell, Oxford, 1982). See too 'Only Words' in my book *No Main Road: Religion in Twentieth Century Literature*, forthcoming (Routledge).
19. See 'A Place without Qualities' in Phillips, *No Main Road*.
20. Ian Robinson, 'Religious English' in *The Survival of English*, Cambridge University Press, 1973.
21. Holmer, *The Grammar of Faith*, p. 36.
22. I owe this observation to my former colleague, David Sims.
23. Holmer, *The Grammar of Faith*, p. 49.
24. Ibid., p. 167.
25. Ibid., p. 132.
26. Ibid., p. 62.
27. Ibid., p. 67.

Part Four

Religion and Concept-Formation

Christianity is not a doctrine, not, I mean, a theory about what has happened and will happen to the human soul, but a description of something that actually takes place in human life. For 'consciousness of sin' is a real event and so are despair and salvation through faith. Those who speak of such things (Bunyan for instance) are simply describing what has happened to them, whatever gloss anyone may want to put on it.

Wittgenstein, *Culture and Value*

19
Epistemological Mysteries

Looking back at the epistemological difficulties which we have discussed in the first three parts of the book, we can sum them up in the form of a sceptical epistemological question: by what right *can* we speak of God? The question is one concerning what *can* be known. It is as if we find ourselves talking about something which we do not have any obvious right to talk about, and so our talk stands in need of rational foundations, justifications. But when we have looked at the form these foundations and justifications have taken, they have not proved to be satisfactory. The situation has been well described by O.K. Bouwsma:

It's as though man lived in an enclosure with thick walls and dummy doors. Men pull and push against the dummy doors ... trying to push open or pull open, but apart from their illusions that the dummy door has given way just a chink, the dummy door does not open. Men cannot find their way to look out. All the same they cannot get rid of the idea that there is something outside the wall. So they talk about it and talk about it — some say that there is nothing but darkness there, nothing at all. It frightens them. Others say that there is indeed something there, that the door opened just a chink. 'I had a glimpse of it. I saw it and it vanished. The door closed.' But when they talk about this they discover no agreement. 'I saw a dragon.' 'He saw a beautiful woman with a veil.' 'I saw a high mountain; and splendid giants lived on that mountain.' When they asked other questions, such as 'And what has that to do with life in the city, with us, and with our prospects, and what about death?' again there is no agreement. People begin to mistrust the chinks and to say, 'They are all dummy doors.' They may even have some account of how the dummy doors got there. And they say, 'If you keep on pushing and pulling on a dummy door, the exhaustion and the desperation — as though your push and your pull were your only hope — may soon produce the illusion of chinks and of light coming through.' And the people pity one another. But they do not respect one another. To every man his chink, his illusion.[1]

That seems to me to be an accurate description of the state of contemporary philosophy of religion. We have encountered many dummy doors in our discussions, doors which claim to give, but cannot provide, the required knowledge of God. For all pushers and pullers at these doors, God is indeed a mystery, a reality beyond the reach of our epistemic practices. Religious mysteries are turned into epistemological mysteries. Once this transition has taken place the problem is characterised as one of showing how we in the world, inside the enclosure, can talk of God, who is outside the enclosure.

At its starkest, the epistemological problem seems to be one which threatens the very *possibility* of talking about God. When religious mysteries are turned into epistemological mysteries, religious language itself can be used to fuel scepticism. After all, it will be said, does not religion itself proclaim that God is beyond human understanding? That being so, how can we, situated as we are, be expected to speak meaningfully about God? John Whittaker has expressed the difficulty as follows:

One of the most peculiar features of the belief in God is the accompanying claim that God is an indescribable mystery, an object of faith but never an object of knowledge. In certain contexts — in worship, for example — this claim undoubtedly serves a useful purpose; and so I do not want to dismiss the idea altogether. But when pious remarks about the ineffable nature of God are taken out of context and turned into philosophy, the result is usually an epistemological muddle. The trouble, of course, is that those who insist on God's mysteriousness still manage to say all sorts of things about him; he is an incorporeal spirit, he created the world, he loves his creatures, and so on. To assert these things is to presume *some* understanding of God, but no understanding is possible if God is completely incomprehensible. So if that is how it is, if the object of religious belief is *utterly* incomprehensible, then it makes no sense to say — or believe — anything about God.[2]

Notice the slide in Whittaker's remarks from talk of the mystery of God to talk of God as incomprehensible, as though being bidden to feed on mysteries was like being asked to swallow the incomprehensible. That is an instance of sliding from the religious to the epistemological. Once we start on the slide, problems abound. How can we ever *say* anything about God so conceived? On this view, 'God' is an abstract postulate needed to explain the world as we know it. But how do we move from the alleged necessity of such a postulate to the nature of God? As Whittaker says, although, on this view, 'we must postulate something to satisfy a bill of explanation ... that something, as long as it does that, could be *anything*.'[3] As Hume showed, we could believe that the world is the work of an infant deity, a world which, since his act of creation, has been allowed to run on uncontrolled. On the other hand, the world may have been created by a superannuated senile deity, the product of his dotage. We could devise all sorts of fancies. They are not genuine hypotheses, since we have no idea what would count for or against them; no idea how to assess them. As Hume might say, with his customary irony, the nature of the creator is indeed a mystery!

We push at the dummy door of constructing belief in God as a hypothesis and nothing comes of it. It neither fails nor succeeds — the whole enterprise cannot even get off the ground. But what if it did? We saw at the outset that, at best, all it could deliver is a belief in a God whose existence is highly probable — certainly not the God in whose inescapable reality our exemplars of faith believed.

Again, if we try to speak of a God, thought of as a mysterious being in the metaphysical sense we are now considering, ascribing to him any definite attributes, dire consequences follow for the notion of his mysteriousness. Once we postulate these attributes, how do we know that they are not his only attributes? If this were thought to be the case, 'the mysteriousness of his nature would disappear as soon as the properties were deduced.'[4] On the other hand, what if we say that these properties do not exhaust God's properties? How can we know that if we say that God is utterly mysterious? To make the judgement seems to presuppose knowledge of the very God we say cannot be known. On either view, God's mysteriousness seems to be destroyed.

Similar difficulties arise if we say, on this view, that we have encountered the mystery of God in religious experience. Our language is supposed to be inadequate to describe the experience. This inadequacy is not conceived of as a temporary or initial difficulty. Otherwise, as Whittaker says, 'As long as the experience of God — or any other experience — occurs often enough and widely enough to permit a common usage to develop, words can be instituted to refer to it.'[5] On the other hand, if the experience is said to be of a God it cannot capture, an unbridgeable logical gap opens up between the experience and its object. How is the experience to serve as a reason for saying that its alleged object has any reality? Whittaker points out that the very insistence that all our experiences *must* refer to objects may be due to no more than 'an unexamined mental habit'. After all,

> Some non-perceptual experiences have no objects. Feelings, moods, premonitions, forebodings, and other emotional experiences often arise without any identifiable objects serving as their source. These states of mind may have causes, of course; but they need not be tied to objects which one can experience in various other ways, as one can experience objects of perception. Religious experience may be no different, despite the fact that we speak of such experience as if did have an object, namely, God. And therefore the appeal to experience as an explanation of the limitations of religious understanding ultimately begs the question. For we don't know that experience partially reveals an unexhausted mystery unless we already know that the experience in question comes from an objective ground in a hidden reality. The experiential view of religious understanding trades on this assumption, but it does not justify it. Apparently faith supplies the knowledge that there is more to God than we know by experience. But how? That is the original problem.[6]

As we saw, Reformed epistemology rejects the original problem by refusing to accept it on its own terms. Those terms would commit us to epistemological foundationalism; to search for reasons which justify us in saying that we believe in God. Reformed epistemology spurns any appeal to such evidentialist reasons. It insists that religious epistemic practices are justified by faith, not by reason. This is not anything peculiar to religion. Other epistemic practices are based on faith, too, since their adherents commit themselves to their epistemic endowments without reason. Yet, as we saw, Reformed epistemology turned out to be a dummy door too, despite its exposure of the pretensions of foundationalism. For although Reformed epistemologists denied that belief in God is based on foundations, they insisted that it was not groundless. The belief is grounded in experiences such as hearing God's voice, fearing his wrath, wanting to praise him, and so on. These experiences, however, are said to be the prima-facie grounds or the prima-facie justifications of the belief, always open to possible defeaters. As we saw, this left belief in God in a strangely isolated position as a foundational belief in the believer's noetic structure. The belief did not seem to be mediated in the detail of the believer's life. The restriction of apologetics to negative apologetics, meant that the elucidation of religious concepts, giving a perspicuous representation of them in their natural contexts, is neglected in favour of the stark assertion of a believer's right to place belief in God among his foundational beliefs.

But, as we turn from these dummy doors, others confront us. It may be said that we should not be alarmed at Bouwsma's depiction of us as confined within an enclosure, necessarily limited in our situation as we try to talk about God. On the contrary, it is an accurate description of the state of philosophy of religion, simply because it is an accurate description of how things are with us religiously. The epistemological difficulties we have encountered, it might be said, are simply due to our wanting to say we have knowledge or experience of an essentially mysterious God. Why not say that we have no knowledge or experience of such a God? If the reality we are referring to is a 'higher' one, it is not surprising that it cannot be captured in a finite language. Why not recognise that human language is inherently inadequate to express the nature of a mysterious God? Some philosophers have argued that failure to recognise this involves the denial of most, if not all, of philosophical theology. Such a startling conclusion can be embraced if we understand philosophical theology as David Conway does when he says:

A large part of the history of that discipline can be constructed as reactions to, attempts to cope with, the nearly universally accepted premiss that we, as finite, limited beings, cannot fully understand the nature of an infinite, unlimited being, as a result of which our language, as such, is inherently inadequate for expressing and so for understanding the nature of the deity.[7]

Conway's comments were occasioned by a claim I had made in passing in *Death and Immortality* to the effect that I found the notion of the inherent inadequacy of human language a problematic one. I said:

> Our language is not a poor alternative to other means of communication. To say 'We only have our language' in this context, is not like saying, 'I only have English'. In the latter case one might say, 'If you could speak Welsh you'd see why *hwyl* is untranslatable.' But one cannot say, 'Because we only have language we cannot say what the world beyond the grave is like.' There can be an inadequate use of language, but it makes no sense to say that language itself is inadequate.[8]

For Conway, the possibility of philosophical theology depends on the admission of the inherent inadequacy of human language. His reaction to my comments is, therefore, to be expected: 'Thus Phillips would dispose of much of philosophical theology.'[9]

For Conway, the two notions, the mysteriousness of God and the inherent inadequacy of human language, stand or fall together. Anyone denying this, according to him, disposes, not only of philosophical theology, but of any form of theistic religion. According to Conway, if we say that human language is inherently adequate, the only God such a view can accommodate is a finite God who is fully within our comprehension. It follows, for Conway, that Judaism and Christianity necessarily involve acceptance of the inherent inadequacy of human language. Only in this way, Conway thinks, can the notion of God's mysteriousness be accommodated.

Anyone contemplating strategies to be adopted by Conway faces the initial task of showing that it makes sense to speak of the inherent inadequacy of human language. Conway's first attempt to fulfil this task depends on the possibility of making retrospective judgements on the state of a language prior to the occurrence of certain developments in the language. Apparently, all we have to do is to imagine that an actual feature of the language, *hwyl*, for example, had never existed. Since we now know what *hwyl* is, we can say that language, prior to its existence, was inadequate to express it. Since the existence of any pheno-menon such as *hwyl* is contingent, the possibility of such phenomena occurring always counts against a claim, at any time, that language is necessarily adequate.

How are we to respond to these arguments? Where the example of *hwyl* is concerned, we could simply say that the phenomenon did not exist prior to the existence of the Welsh language. *Hwyl* has no meaning, in a religious context, apart from certain traditions of preaching and worship. So when Conway says that languages other than Welsh could not have expressed *hwyl* had the Welsh language never existed, the fact is that there would be no *hwyl* which these languages were failing to express. Conway's case would have been stronger had he chosen different examples. Consider situations in science where particular problems remain unsolved for a considerable time. It may be said that until the breakthrough occurs, the science in question is conceptually inadequate to deal with the problem. Here, however, the difficulty is located in the problem and not in the alleged inherent inadequacy of language. Conway's own way of talking testifies to this fact, since he refers to later stages where the successful conceptual development has taken place. One can think of many different examples where attention is drawn to inadequacies of a temporary or contingent kind. For example, it may be said, rightly or wrongly, that the New English Bible cannot express divine authority as we find it in the King James version. Here, the argument depends on an appeal to how in fact things have gone. What would it mean to say that things had to go this way? Where such necessity is at home, as in the assertion that there *cannot* be another Elizabethan age, it has little to do with inadequacy of any kind. The necessity is understood by anyone who understands the notion of historical development.

In all cases where it makes sense to speak of temporary inadequacies, all we can say is, 'We are stuck at the moment. We cannot see our way ahead.' But this is hardly enough for those who want to argue for the necessary mysteriousness of God. In their case, the inadequacy of language to express the nature of God, cannot be thought of as a temporary inadequacy. Otherwise, as Whittaker has already said, in time a language will develop in which the experience may be adequately expressed.

Those who want to say that language is inherently inadequate to express the nature of the metaphysical object of faith, or who want to speak of religious experience as the manifestation of an inexpressible higher reality, need a stronger thesis than the one we have been considering. For them, the inability of language to express the divine is no temporary setback. According to the stronger thesis, we are not stuck for the moment, but necessarily stuck. At times, Conway slides from the weaker thesis to the stronger thesis without realising that he is doing so. He is anxious to warn against the danger of actually saying that which, it is said, language cannot express. Someone may want to say, 'Perhaps the English language is not yet equipped to indicate the more-than-drizzling but less-than-sprinkling condition of the atmosphere.' Conway says that this difficulty could be avoided by saying, 'Perhaps the English language is not yet equipped to describe some conditions of the atmosphere.' Where religion is concerned, similar difficulties could be avoided, Conway suggests, by saying, 'Human language is not able to describe the nature of a being that is worthy of a worshipful attitude.'[10] Note the difference between the two statements: 'Perhaps the English language is not yet equipped ...' and 'Human language is not able ...' Clearly, the spirit of the second statement is not captured if we substitute, 'Perhaps human language is not yet able ...' The spirit is not captured because the claim being made is that human language, by its very own nature, can give no adequate expression of the reality of God.

Conway admits, later in his article, that all his arguments hitherto depend on interpreting me as saying 'that at any time the language that we have cannot be inadequate'. On the other hand, he recognises that I may have been arguing against a rather different claim, namely, that there can be things which cannot be expressed in any *possible* language. This is why Conway turns to his second attempt to show that the notion of the inherent inadequacy of human language is a coherent one. Conway says that the denial that God's nature could be adequately expressed in any possible language, would be compatible with saying that higher realities will be revealed to us only beyond the grave and 'that our language, i.e. the language of mere earthly beings, will always be too limited to allow us to understand the future condition, that the condition is expressible in a language which we can learn and understand only when we are in that condition.'[11] These remarks, of course, occasion other difficulties about the grammar of the notion of a higher reality and the notion of a world beyond. These difficulties, as we shall see, have a vital bearing on the intelligibility of Conway's idea of a 'higher reality'.[12] Yet, irrespective of these issues, it is now clear, on his own admission, that the possibility Conway envisages in no way depends on his thesis concerning the inherent inadequacy of language. All that is being said is that a breakthrough of the kind described is needed before we can come to understand certain things. This places the argument in the contexts we have already discussed.

The main objection to Conway's thesis, however, does not depend on answering his two attempts to give sense to the notion of the inherent inadequacy of human language. Such an assumption would give the impression that the question as to whether human language is or is not inherently inadequate is a genuine question. In fact, this is not the case. By this I do not mean that the question has been resolved. On the contrary, it is unclear what sense the question has. Conway has assumed, throughout, that I want to counter the thesis that human language is inherently inadequate, with the thesis that human language is inherently adequate. But the claim that human language is inherently adequate is as senseless as the claim that human language is inherently inadequate. To say that human language as such is either inherently adequate or inadequate requires finding sense in the notion of a complete language, such that looking at its completeness (all that can ever be said), we can say that it, this complete language, is either adequate or inadequate. Since this notion of completeness is unintelligible, talk of the adequacy or inadequacy of a complete language is also unintelligible. An attempt has been made to say something which cannot be said.

As far as Conway is concerned, God's mysteriousness refers either to something which our language cannot express now or to something which will be expressed in an adequate language after death. But the language in which we talk of God's mysteriousness is language we *do* have. It is not a report on language we do not have. Similarly, it is not language which we may speak some day, but a language which the believer speaks every day. After all, it must be remembered that religious mysteries are supposed to constitute food for the faithful in their daily lives.

Running through our discussions has been a critique of the basic assumptions involved in foundationalism and Reformed epistemology, a critique dependent on insights derived from

Wittgenstein. In terms of this critique, we rejected the starting point of epistemological scepticism. Instead of asking how we *can* speak of God, we must begin by noting that we *do* speak of God. Surely, what we need to do is to enquire into the grammar of that talk. Bouwsma says,

> In such an enclosure as I have described ... there are not only dummy doors which tempt people, but there are also doors, or at least one door, which opens only from the outside of that enclosure. And when that door is opened — it is obviously opened by what is outside the wall and does not even show from inside the enclosure — and one sees what is to be seen, naturally he has no interest in those other doors others try so hard to open ... 'The door was opened.' And he might have said, 'The door walked among us.' 'Verily, Verily, I say unto you. I am the door of the sheep.'[13]

So although we want to say that the door is opened by something outside the wall, it is how that notion walks among us, how it illuminates human lives, which determines the sense which saying that has. We are *not* faced with the epistemological problem of inferring, or justifying by faith, from within the enclosure, that there is something outside the wall. The *sense* in which something is said to be outside the enclosure is given in how we speak within the enclosure. Kierkegaard makes the same point as follows: '... let us understand one another; the journey of which we speak is not long ... it is only a single step, a decisive step, and you, too, have emigrated, for the Eternal lies much nearer to you than any foreign country to the emigrant, and yet when you are there the change is infinitely greater.'[14] The same emphasis is found in Wittgenstein's insistence that what we need to deal with our philosophical problems is already given to us, already lies before us, if only we can give it a right arrangement. When we can arrive at a perspicuous representation our puzzlement is eased. So if we can arrange matters properly within the enclosure, we will see the sense of saying that a door has opened from outside the wall.

Yet, as we have seen, concentrating on what is within the enclosure may simply lead to a further confrontation with dummy doors. As Bouwsma says, the possibility of an open door, from outside the wall, may not even be seen from within the enclosure. As a result of the hermeneutical conversation, for example, it became impossible to retain a proper context for religious belief.

In fact, hermeneutics seemed to harbour ambitions to replace religion in its promise to make 'new beings' of participants in its conversation. But even when we turned to efforts to convey the sense of *religious* beliefs we found ourselves running into dummy doors. Religious concepts were seen to be vulgarised in certain analyses propounded in the sociology of knowledge, while in the treatment of the *imago Dei*, said to be in all men, Reformed epistemologists were seen to force and falsify too much of our familiar acquaintance with unbelief among our neighbours.

John Whittaker is free of these confusions, but when he attempts to show what talk of God's mysteriousness amounts to by turning to the practical contexts of a living faith, we find the notion of divine mystery eluding him too. In seeing how this comes about, we will see at the same time why religious mysteries are not epistemological mysteries.

The practical context Whittaker speaks of is the working relationship a believer has with God's teachings; a relationship which in no way depends on metaphysical knowledge. We are able, however, from the standpoint of this 'working knowledge of truths to live by',[15] to muster criticisms of various misunderstandings of these truths, misunderstandings which Whittaker accuses of 'literalness'. Such misunderstandings ignore the normative and regulative character of religious beliefs. What needs to be recognised, Whittaker argues, is that 'The claim that God watches over us, that he hears our prayers, that he knows our hearts, that he forgives our sins — even the claim that he created the world — all these teachings serve as truths to live by, and all promise a kind of practical proverbial wisdom.'[16] The knowledge which one possesses in knowing these truths is a capacity, the capacity to live according to God's will.

Whittaker is quite aware that this so-called practical account will seem reductive to many philosophers because it ignores what they would call the ontological foundations of faith. But, Whittaker asks, what if this appeal to ontology is itself the product of confusion? Underlying the appeal is the assumption that 'God' is a name which refers to some kind of object. But this assumption is itself philosophically dubious. The ontological foundation is thought to be necessary in order 'to assure the possible *truth* of religious assertions by giving them something to be *true about*'.[17] Whittaker says that there is a tendency to think that 'the practical truths of religious belief must rest on prior truths about what there is in the universe'.[18] In criticising this tendency, a tendency which goes deep in the philosophy of religion, Whittaker shares insights which have been shown by others influenced by Wittgenstein in this context and who have voiced similar criticisms. For example, Peter Winch has argued:

> It is true that there would be something wrong with a man who claimed to be praying to God while saying he did not believe in God's existence. But would the same kind of thing be amiss as with a man who claimed to be writing to the Yugoslav ambassador while saying that he did not believe in the existence of such a person? I feel inclined to say that, in the latter case, ceasing to see any point in writing is a *consequence* of ceasing to believe in the ambassador's existence, whereas ceasing to see any point in praying is an *aspect* of ceasing to believe in God. In other words there are internal connections between ceasing to believe in God's existence and ceasing to see any point in prayer of a sort which do not hold between ceasing to believe in the ambassador's existence and ceasing to see any point in addressing letters to him.'[19]

In *The Concept of Prayer*, I argued against the assumption that there could be an investigation of whether there is a God which is quite independent of the context of prayer and worship.[20] Rush Rhees has argued:

> All that theology can do is to indicate, perhaps even with some sort of formal proof, what it is correct to say, what is the correct way of speaking about God. The question of 'what God is' could only be answered through 'coming to know God is' in worship and religious life. 'To know God is to worship him'.[21]

These observations are the opposite of the view expressed by Roger Trigg: 'The belief is distinct from the commitment which may follow it and is the justification for it.'[22] To this Norman Malcolm has replied,

> According to Trigg ... a man who was entirely devoid of any inclination to religious action or consequence might believe in *the existence* of God. What would be the marks of this? Would it be that the man knows some theology, can

recite the Creeds, is well-read in Scripture? Or is his belief in the existence of God something different from this? If so, what? What would be the difference between a man who knows some articles of faith, heresies, Scriptural writings, and in addition believes in the existence of God, and one who knows these things but does not believe in the existence of God? I assume both of them are indifferent to the acts and commitments of religious life. I do not comprehend this notion of belief in the *existence* of God which is thought to be distinct from belief *in* God. It seems to be an artificial construction of philosophy.[23]

Malcolm calls this craving for justification, the desire to ground religious belief in some kind of ontology, 'one of the primary pathologies of philosophy'.[24]

Whittaker's own contribution is to insist that if metaphysical speculation has a role to play, it is one of reflection on prior religious understanding. So far from religious beliefs being founded on prior truths about the world, in religion, Whittaker argues, 'we postulate certain items of the world's furniture because we already feel certain of some practical truths'.[25] Whittaker finds a parallel in Socrates' discussion of the immortality of the soul. Socrates would warn us against literalism, that is, the temptation to turn what he shows us into abstract, theoretical truths, rather than see them as truths to live by. Here, the metaphysical arguments actually promote misunderstanding. They take us away from the contexts in which the Socratic truths have their sense. If we appreciate this sense, 'we need not and should not expect to know any truths more profound than the truth by which Socrates lived and died — that a good man cannot be harmed'.[26] Whittaker intends similar points to be made of religious beliefs, since, although 'they may not have quite the same point ... if they have any truth in them at all, their truth need not belong to any other domain of understanding'.[27]

It is important to recognise the grammatical character of Whittaker's remarks. He is not referring to contingent facts. In the Socratic context, the point is not that the truths found there *happen* to be found there, but could be found elsewhere. The very possibility of such truths is internally related to such contexts. So when Whittaker says that we need not and should not seek elsewhere for such truths, he is not making a moral or religious recommendation. Rather, it is a recognition of the appropriate grammatical parameters of the mode of discourse he is discussing. Similarly, when Whittaker says that truths found in religious beliefs 'need not belong to any other domain of understanding', he is locating the appropriate grammatical context for such truths and not referring to a contingent fact.

I have no doubt that the above conclusions are those which Whittaker wants to emphasise in the main. His presentation of them, however, sometimes suffers from ambiguity. For example, he ends his paper with the following comment: 'With wisdom of that kind faith can afford to be modest about its ontological claims.'[28] Unless we read the reference to modesty ironically, the comment is far too weak given what has preceded it. On Whittaker's analysis, ontological claims are not claims which call for modesty; they should be abandoned as part of a misleading philosophical picture. Yet, the ambiguity in Whittaker's presentation is no mere slip.[29] It is connected with the analysis he wishes to give of religious mystery. It is this analysis which marks my disagreement with Whittaker, despite my agreement with much of what he has said hitherto.

How is the practical context of a living religious faith to give an adequate account of religious mystery? Attempts to arrive at such an account via metaphysics or the experiential content of religious belief simply revealed that the mystery they grappled with was nothing more than a pseudo-concept. If the understanding of religious mystery claims by a living faith is not to meet a similar fate, certain conditions must be met: 'Unless the possibility of this understanding can be explained, and unless it can be reconciled with traditional claims about the unknowable nature of God, the philosophical suspicions which surround theology are likely to increase.'[30] Whittaker thinks that the reconciliation between a living faith and traditional claims regarding God's mysteriousness can be secured if we remember one thing: 'The language of faith never directly captures its object, so to speak; and so the mystery remains.'[31] As we shall see, the reminder Whittaker thinks we need is, in fact, a far-reaching confusion. As a result of it, the same unbridgeable gap will open up between faith and its object as we saw open up between metaphysics and its object and between religious experience and its object. Let us see how this comes about.

The place of mystery is made secure by a living faith, according to Whittaker, if we pay attention to the knowledge which faith *presumes* and to the knowledge which faith *disclaims*. What kind of understanding does faith presume to possess? Whittaker replies,

> Such understanding is largely a practical matter. Instead
> of a theoretical knowledge of a metaphysical being, gained
> through an intellectual inquiry, it represents a working
> knowledge of truths to live by. And instead of an extra-
> ordinary experience of a transcendent reality, it reflects an
> ability to deal meaningfully with the garden varieties of
> human experience.[32]

Given an understanding of what such a working faith involves,
one will be in a position to point out misunderstandings of it.
Having seen what understanding faith presumes to possess, what
knowledge does it disclaim? Whittaker replies, 'The wisdom
gained from language of God does not advance the frontiers of
any science, empirical or philosophical. It does not reveal any
new objects in the universe and does not provide any independent
information about a metaphysical postulate.'[33] So faith disclaims
possession of metaphysical knowledge or experiences of a transcendent object. So far, so good. But then we hear Whittaker saying
of that which faith possesses, 'This lower form of understanding
needs no apology, though. A working understanding of God —
i.e., of teachings about God — is just what faith requires to retain
its epistemological modesty.'[34] But why should faith be called a
lower form of understanding, especially when the higher form
with which it is to be contrasted is a form of metaphysical
speculation which, earlier, Whittaker has characterised as a
product of confusion?

On this analysis, the place preserved for mystery is marked by
what is said to be beyond faith. Whittaker calls religious understanding modest 'because there is no direct way to convert it into
theoretical knowledge of metaphysical realities. In that sense God
remains a mystery for religious believers, despite their practical
understanding.'[35] But is *this* to be the analysis of what faith means
by God's mysteriousness; this 'kind of extra knowledge which
faith in its modesty need not pretend to possess'?[36] Surely not.
On such a view, religious mysteries would refer to an alleged
knowledge which is absent from faith; a 'knowledge' which,
elsewhere, Whittaker characterises as the pitfalls of confusion we
should endeavour to avoid. We recall his earlier remark: 'when
pious remarks about the ineffable nature of God are taken out of
context and turned into philosophy, the result is usually an

epistemological muddle'.[37] Is there any way out of this inconsistency?

One way forward would be to suggest that faith's ignorance of metaphysical truths about religion is akin to an ironic conception of Socrates' ignorance of essences. A great deal depends, however, on what we take Socratic ignorance to be. On one reading, when Socrates asks, 'What is justice?' he is searching for essences. He rejects any definition offered by producing a counter-example. Not realising that justice does not have an essence, Socrates says it is a mystery to him. On this view, a view devoid of irony, when Socrates says that the only difference between himself and others is that he knows that he does not know, Socrates, along with the others, is searching for the essence of justice. They think they have found the essence, whereas he knows that they and he have not — that is the only difference. If, on the other hand, we do see irony in Socratic ignorance, as Kierkegaard did, the picture is very different. On this view, Socrates asks, 'What is justice?' not because he seeks an answer to the question, but because the others do. He reminds them of a question that haunts them. He offers his counter-example, not in order to help answer their question, but in an effort to get them to stop asking it. When Socrates says that he does not know what they say they know, he is referring to the knowledge of essences which they think they possess. Such 'knowledge' is indeed a mystery to Socrates, but 'mystery' is being used here in a pejorative sense; the sense in which Hume was to affirm that theism is indeed a miracle. Socratic ignorance, on this view, is an ironic expression of freedom from metaphysical confusion.

Similar choices face us in reading Whittaker. On one reading, faith finds metaphysical knowledge of God a mystery because it cannot attain it. Faith is a lesser form of knowledge. On the alternative reading, faith finds this metaphysical knowledge a mystery in a pejorative sense of 'mystery'. Understanding faith enables us to see that the so-called metaphysical knowledge of God is a confusion.

Yet, no matter how we read Whittaker, a major problem concerning the notion of religious mystery still confronts us. On either reading, mystery simply refers to what faith *excludes*. My argument is that mystery is essentially what faith *includes*. At no time does Whittaker consider whether mystery is internally related to religious belief. He is wedded disastrously to the claim that 'The language of faith never directly captures its objects, so to speak;

and so the mystery remains.'[38] It is not surprising, therefore, to find Whittaker, as we have seen, claiming that there are tensions between making positive religious claims and believing in the mysteriousness of God: 'The trouble, of course, is that those who insist on God's mysteriousness still manage to say all sorts of things about him; he is an incorporeal spirit, he created the world, he loves his creatures, and so on.'[39] But what if the notion of mystery, so far from creating a difficulty for these religious beliefs, is internally related to them? Indeed, what if such internal relations are central to an understanding of concept formation where the notion of God is concerned? If that is the case, we can see, once again, that religious mysteries will only be prevented from becoming epistemological mysteries if we take full cognisance of concept-formation in religious belief.

Notes

1. O.K. Bouwsma, 'Faith, Evidence and Proof' in *Without Proof or Evidence*, p. 2.
2. John H. Whittaker, 'Literal and Figurative Language of God', *Religious Studies*, vol. 17, no. 1 (March 1981), p. 39.
3. Ibid., p. 43.
4. Ibid., p. 44.
5. Ibid., p. 47.
6. Ibid., p. 48.
7. David A. Conway, 'D.Z. Phillips and "The inadequacy of language" ', *Analysis*, vol. 35 (1974/75), p. 93.
8. Phillips, *Death and Immortality*, p. 14.
9. Conway, 'Phillips and "The inadequacy of language" '.
10. Ibid., p. 94, fn.
11. Ibid., pp. 95–6.
12. Such difficulties were my main concern in *Death and Immortality*. See also *Religion Without Explanation*, ch. 8: 'Perspectives on the Dead'.
13. Bouwsma, *Without Proof or Evidence*, pp. 4–5.
14. Kierkegaard, *Purity of Heart*, p. 154.
15. Whittaker, 'Literal and Figurative Language', p. 49.
16. Ibid., p. 51.
17. Ibid., p. 52.
18. Ibid.
19. Winch, 'Meaning and Religious Language', pp. 207–8.
20. Phillips, *Concept of Prayer*.
21. Rhees, 'Religion and Language', p. 127.
22. Roger Trigg, *Reason and Commitment* (Cambridge University Press, 1973), p. 75.

23. Malcolm, 'The Groundlessness of Belief', pp. 211–12. The articles by Winch, Rhees and Malcolm I cite are central to any discussion of reference in religious belief.
24. Ibid., p. 208.
25. Whittaker, 'Literal and Figurative Language', p. 52.
26. Ibid., p. 54.
27. Ibid.
28. Ibid.
29. As we shall see, however, the rejection of a philosophical ontology is not, as Whittaker seems to think, the rejection of the literal.
30. Whittaker, 'Literal and Figurative Language', p. 49.
31. Ibid., p. 39.
32. Ibid., p. 49.
33. Ibid., p. 52.
34. Ibid., p. 49.
35. Ibid., p. 52.
36. Ibid.
37. Ibid., p. 39.
38. Ibid.
39. Ibid.

20
A Place for Mystery

If religious mysteries are not epistemological mysteries, what kind of mysteries are they? What place do they have in our discourse? When we listen to Kierkegaard's description of this place it may strike one as singularly unpromising:

> Suppose Christianity to be a mystery ... Suppose a revelation must be a mystery ... Suppose that it were after all a blessed thing, critically situated in the extreme press of existence, to sustain a relation to this mystery without understanding it, merely as a believer. Suppose Christianity never intended to be understood ... Suppose it refuses to be understood and that the maximum of understanding which could come in question is to understand that it cannot be understood.[1]

Why does this sound so unpromising to us? Is it not because, if asked, we would paraphrase Kierkegaard as follows? — 'Suppose Christianity to be a mystery ... Suppose a revelation must be incomprehensible ... Suppose it were a blessing, in the press of existence, to admit that there is something to be understood which you cannot understand and that the most you can achieve on earth is to admit this.' And why *should* we paraphrase it in this way? Largely because, as O.K. Bouwsma has pointed out, we are so accustomed to being masters in our own house:

> There is our language, the language we do understand. We use it. We write the books. We coin the words as we need them. We are almost virtuosos in this language. We pun. We play on words. We make jokes. It is ours. And what do we do with it? We tell stories. We write novels. We write

273

biographies. We write history. We publish books on what we found in Mexico and South America. We tell the world what we found out about the stars. You and I know the names of many authors. They are people like us. If we read books or read a magazine or a newspaper and do not understand it, ordinarily we are aware of this and can find out what we need to find out; if we do not understand and think we do, it is not a matter of importance. It may be that our misunderstanding will be discovered and we will come to understand. And what now does this depend on? There is the one community of agreement within which we understand and misunderstand one another. It is our language. Within it we move and speak and write and understand and have our being. I do not mean by this only that we agree in our vocabulary. There is something more subtle. We undo what it is we do speaking and writing. When you tell a joke I get the point. When you explain it I get the explanation, though I may lose the point, not of the explanation but of the joke. When you give a demonstration, I see. And so on. We have a common background and common interests of which our language is the medium in which we get on together. I must emphasize that it is we whose language this is. We are at home in it. It is our native land, our city, our ultimate surroundings. We live here. We are the masters.[2]

These remarks certainly need a corrective. They give too great an emphasis to common backgrounds and common interests, almost as if speaking a language entailed this commonality. It isn't only jokes and magazines we may fail to get the point of. We find each other puzzling too. Often, we can make little of each other. We are far from being masters in our own houses, let alone masters of our language in some unqualified sense. This is not the place to explore these qualifications, but, even if we make them, kinds of understanding prevail. Even if others are often enigmas to us, we do not say that there is nothing there to understand. Sometimes, with a little effort, or a greater effort, we could come to understand. At other times, we would have to change as persons to understand and, if we did, we might then say that we cannot understand what we saw in our previous point of view. Even then, what we have is one kind of understanding succeeding and even eroding another.

But Kierkegaard's remarks seem far more radical. He seems to be saying that we have been given a language of revelation, which, naturally, we take to be a history or a report of transcendental things, and told simply to accept it even though we do not understand it. We are told to swallow the incomprehensible because so-and-so says it is true. No wonder many balk at giving the language of religion any serious attention. As Bouwsma says, the reaction of many is predictable: 'What shall we do with it? We can ignore it. That is no doubt what most people do ... Of course, one might still want to read a little now and then to remind ourselves of how men who could read spent their time before civilization and the higher mind came along.'[3]

But these reactions miss the point of Kierkegaard's remarks. He does not talk of a blind acceptance of what we can see is incomprehensible. He speaks rather of coming to an understanding, even though it is an understanding that something cannot be understood. Kierkegaard does not say we come to see that something which *could* be understood cannot be understood by us. He says that we come to something, something in relation to which 'understanding' is not the appropriate response. And *that* is something we can come to understand. We are told that Moses forsook Egypt, not fearing the wrath of the king, for he endured as *seeing him who is invisible*. Now, how is this to be understood? Did Moses see the one who is invisible because, for a while, he became invisible? There is a series of films about the invisible man. Now and again, however, the invisible man becomes visible to his friends. Of course, he's there all the time, you understand — only invisible. Is that how it was with Moses? Was he one of the favoured few to whom the invisible one became visible? No, that's not how it was. He is said to have seen the unseen. When you see the invisible man he ceases to be invisible. You can't see him unless he's visible. But when the invisible one of whom Kierkegaard speaks is seen — he is seen as invisible. So the question now becomes this: what is it like among the many things we see to see the invisible one? In other words, what is it like among the many things we see, to see God?

Simone Weil answers this question in a way which startles us with its boldness:

There is a reality outside the world, that is to say, outside space and time, outside man's mental universe, outside any sphere whatsoever that is accessible to human faculties.

Corresponding to this reality at the centre of the human heart, is the longing for an absolute good, a longing which is always there and is never appeased by any object in this world.[4]

Reflecting the difficulties such words have come to have for us, M. O'C. Drury says: 'but suppose someone was to say to me, "what in the world do you mean, outside of space and time? The word 'outside' only has a meaning *within* the categories of space and time'." Drury concedes,

This is a perfectly logical objection, the words 'outside space and time' have no more meaning than Plato's beautiful expression 'the other side of the sky'. Again if someone were to object, 'I don't feel any longing for an absolute good which is never appeased by any object in this world', how could you arouse such a desire? What right have you to make the psychological assertion that such a desire lies at the centre of the human heart?

Despite these difficulties, some of which we have discussed already, Drury says,

Yet I believe Simone Weil is right when she goes on to say that we must never *assume* that any man, whatsoever he may be, has been deprived of the power of having the longing come to birth. But how can this desire for the absolute good be aroused? Only, I believe, by means of an indirect communication. By so limiting the sphere 'of what can be said' that we create a feeling of spiritual claustrophobia. The dialectic must work from the inside as it were.[5]

There are difficulties about these remarks which need not detain us at this stage of our argument. We may wonder how a beautiful expression can lack meaning or how the notion of an absolute good, if it is something we long for, can be outside 'what can be said'. What is important in Drury's remarks is the insistence that talk of a God who is beyond us must be communicated by means of indirect communication; that is, the sense of such talk is found in the way it is mediated in the context of human life. Again, we find in Simone Weil a striking expression of what is at stake here: 'Earthly things are the criterion of spiritual things ... Only spiritual things are of value, but only physical things have a verifiable existence. Therefore the value of the former can only be verified as an illumination projected on to the latter.'[6] Commenting on these remarks, Peter Winch says, 'This is not to say that the expression "God" really *refers* to such facts; it is to say that the reality which it expresses is to be found in the conditions of its application.'[7] These conceptual requirements are, of course, essential if we are to have any grasp of the notion of religious mystery. Here, too, there are constant temptations to sever the notion from the contexts in which it has its sense. Speaking of writers who want to show this sense in their stories, Flannery O'Connery said, 'if the writer believes that our life is and will remain essentially mysterious, if he looks upon us as human beings existing in a created order to whose laws we freely respond, then what he sees on the surface will be of interest to him only as he can go through it into an experience of mystery itself.'[8] But this working through the surface phenomena to the experience of mystery, what Drury called indirect communication, is no optional strategy for the writer or for the philosopher. The mediation of mystery in the detail of people's lives is a precondition of seeing the sense it has; a precondition of mystery being able to come in at the right place.

If we think of passages in the Old and New Testaments where God is said to be beyond human understanding, it is likely that some of the following would come to mind. Job seeks a God who 'doeth great things and unsearchable' (5:9); the Psalmist testifies, 'Great is the Lord; and greatly to be praised: and his greatness is unsearchable' (145:3); St Paul exclaims as he wonders at the knowledge and wisdom of God, 'how unsearchable are his judgements, and his ways past finding out' (Rom. 11:33). All are agreed on the Psalmist's view of God's knowledge: 'Such knowledge is too wonderful for me; it is high, I cannot attain unto it.' (139:6).

Here we have expressions of God's mysteriousness in their natural settings. The reference to mystery in these contexts is certainly not pejorative. Looking back at Whittaker's suggestion that mystery refers to metaphysical knowledge of God, which is a mystery to faith, since faith in fact cannot attain it, it does not even begin to be plausible in this context. It is equally implausible to say that the mystery refers to metaphysical knowledge which it makes no sense to say we can attain. The reference is not to metaphysics, but to the ways of God, his greatness, knowledge and wisdom. These considerations rule out the two readings of mystery offered in Whittaker's analysis. At the outset of his paper, he said of the notion of God as an indescribable mystery: 'In certain contexts — in worship, for example — this claim undoubtedly serves a useful purpose, and so I do not want to dismiss the idea altogether.'[9] As we have also seen, Whittaker is right in saying that the natural context of worship is often distorted by philosophy. On the other hand, as we have seen, his own analysis makes mystery no more than a means of indicating what is excluded from the context of faith and worship. But, as we shall see, the notion of mystery does far more than play a 'useful purpose' in the context of faith and worship. Mystery is an integral part of concept-formation in faith and worship.

In so far as Whittaker emphasises mystery as that which faith excludes, as that which lies beyond it, his reading of the natural religious setting would come close to that of Conway. Conway, no doubt, sees the religious expressions of mystery as examples of the 'nearly universally accepted premiss that we, as finite limited beings, cannot fully understand the nature of an infinite, unlimited being, as a result of which our language, as such, is inherently inadequate for expressing, and so for understanding the nature of the deity.'[10] But is this what the religious expressions of mystery tell us? Are they confessions of the inherent inadequacy of human language?

The first thing it is essential to note is that Job, the Psalmist and St Paul are not making statements *about* human language. Their expressions of religious mystery are expressions *in* language. They are not telling us that, because of the inadequacy of language, they cannot praise God. Praising God is precisely what they are doing! Consider the following example, which may throw some light on the matter. I happen to meet a married friend in a fairground. She is accompanied by her young child. I buy the child an ice-cream, to which the mother responds by saying, 'Words can't tell you how grateful I am.' Naturally, I am embarrassed, maybe amused, by this response. Depending on the circumstances, what I take them to be, I shall react to these words in one of many possible ways. But I certainly do not regard them as a normal response — it was, after all, only an ice-cream cone. But, now, consider the words in a situation where I know that my friend, who is a tense, rather nervous person, is having a lot of trouble coping with her difficult child. She has promised the child an ice-cream, but has forgotten her purse which has all her money in it. The child is having a tantrum, screaming the place down, and the mother is panicking. I buy the ice-cream cone, to which she responds by saying, 'Words can't tell you how grateful I am.' Does the mother fail to express her gratitude in those words? No, she succeeds. Similarly, Job, the Psalmist and St Paul are not telling us that God is hidden from them because of the inadequacy of their language. Rather, they are showing us that the notion of God, *in* their language, *is* that of a hidden God: 'Verily thou are a God that hidest thyself, O God of Israel, the Saviour' (Isaiah 45:15). Weil says, 'the very reason why God has decided to hide himself is that we might have an idea of what he is like'.[11] In that penetrating remark Weil is emphasising that mystery is bound up with the very grammar of our notion of God. Turn that into an epistemological muddle and one has the following misleading gloss on Weil's remark: 'It might seem more reasonable to say that God hides himself so that we might have no idea of what he is like.'[12] If this remark were taken ironically it would have a point: Job, the Psalmist and St Paul have no metaphysical idea of God. Without the irony, we would be saying that Job, the Psalmist and St Paul are glorifying a God with no idea of what he is like!

The picture changes when mystery is seen as part of the grammar of our notion of God. When we see the way in which mysteries enter human life, and how the notion of God's will is related to them, we see concept-formation at work in the emergence of a sense of the mysterious will of God. God's will does not *happen* to be inscrutable to us, due to our limitations. Rather, the notion of God's will is born of what is necessarily inscrutable in human life. Sometimes, this inscrutability is related to a specific incident, as when it is called 'an act of God'. No one did it, if our notion of someone doing something is an action done for such-and-such a reason, on impulse or by accident. In *that* sense no one performed an act of God. That is why it is called an act of God — 'It just happened. It was an act of God.' How ironic it is therefore, to lose sight of this contrast in passing from our ordinary understanding of 'an act of God', to our philosophical analyses of 'God acts' into which we import reasons, impulses or accidents which, we say, God must have acted from.

The notion of the will of God, of course, has more general application to events in the natural world and to the course of our own lives. When all explanations have been given, in specific instances — the death of a child, the failure of a marriage, the way events in themselves unrelated have formed a problematic pattern — people still ask, 'What is the meaning of all this?' They are not looking for further explanations, but for ways of coming to terms with explanations which they have been given. Sometimes, it is true, they may be confused. Because they have been acquainted with the purpose of some things, they may think it makes sense to search for the purpose of everything, as though 'everything' were one big thing or process. On the other hand, they may not harbour these confusions, and asking what sense can be made of things need not be an instance of harbouring them. After all, it is not as if religion has a monopoly of the answers which have been given to the question of what sense life has. Faced with the events which befall them men have said, 'It's Fate', 'It's absurd', 'It's meaningless', 'That's how things are', 'That's life', 'That's the way the cookie crumbles' as well as 'It's the will of God'. To bring out the force of these responses would be to show the life or lack of life which surrounds them, what role they play in the lives of those who make them. What is clear, however, is that certain forms of reflection on human life occasion these responses, responses which could not be replaced by piecemeal explanations. People make these responses while knowing all about the piecemeal explanations.

Let us explore some of the surroundings of acceptance of God's will which illustrate the internal relations between such acceptance and the notion of mystery. First, let us look at the notion of the mysterious will of God in relation to events in the natural world. A striking illustration of what I mean by concept-formation in this context is to be found in the work of Jakob Fries.

> when I find myself in the power of nature, with neither advice nor assistance, the fortifying and elevating thought of eternal Destiny presents itself to my soul and my fear vanishes. Never shall I forget the sublime impression made upon me on the evening when I made my first acquaintance with the raging power of the sea. I was sitting in the stern of a little open boat and we were quietly exchanging jests about our unaccustomed pastime. Suddenly the storm fell upon us, ploughing up the floods of the sea and hurling foaming waves against the sheer and rocky cliffs nearby. The imperilled boatmen hauled in the sail. The pallid oarsmen exchanged terrified glances with each other and silently struck into the wild flood. On that havenless coast there was no other salvation than that of Fate. A single

wave breaking over us from the cliff would have been sufficient to drag us down into the flood. Our little bark pitched to and fro, one moment riding the crest of a wave and the next plummeting the depths of a trough. I turned my gaze upon the roaring tumult and then at the black and threatening heavens above. But of my anxious trembling there was no more trace. I was seized by a sublime thrill at the thought of the holy omnipotence of God. So vivid was that impression that I would today fain issue forth once more to renew my acquaintance with that tumult. And thus am I wont happily to stand, free and proud, confronting the thunder. Thus, in the thick of battle, does the sublime thought steady my nerve and elevate my mind. For, in battle, although it is true that the boldness and composure of the commanders and the valour of the troops secures the army victory, whether or not the individual is to fall a sacrifice to victory, a victim of the enemy sword, or whether, mourning his brother who has given his life upon the field of battle, he is destined to join the celebrations of the victory gained — that is decided by the hand of Destiny alone.[13]

These are primitive reactions which play a central role in the formation of the concept of God's inscrutable will. I do not know how any further justification could be given of these reactions, or how any alternative account could explain them away. In moments of extreme peril, such as being in a storm at sea, a person may say that his life is in God's hands. God's will will be made manifest in his survival or destruction, as it is in the raging storm. Above the waves, above the thunder and the lightning, is the omnipotence of God — an omnipotence the writer finds both terrible and wonderful. The notion of God's will gets its sense *in* such reactions. Contrast this with the view that primitive man responds in this way because of a *prior* conclusion he has reached, namely, that because he is not responsible for the storm, someone else, greater than himself, must be responsible. On this view, the reactions in the storm are a *consequence* of previously held beliefs. Such a view ignores concept-formation in religious belief. The sense of belief in God is itself rooted in reactions such as reactions to the storm.

The notion of God's will is not related to what has happened as a higher *explanation*. On the contrary, although the divine will is higher in so far as it holds together, with a certain sense, the events I have described, that sense does not explain away the sheer contingency of human life in face of the storm. 'It is the will of God' is not an answer to the question 'Why is this happening?' but one way in which someone may die to the desire to ask the question. The notion of God's will is formed, not in a search for explanations, but in the abandonment of explanations. It is not as if there was something, an explanation, which *could* be understood, but which, as a matter of fact, we cannot understand. There is nothing to understand; no explanation. It is precisely in the absence of anything to show why he should perish or survive the storm, that the person comes to see that his own fate is not the primary consideration. Being at the mercy of God's will leads to a sense of wonder, wonder at the contingency of life, the miracle of existence. In face of it, a man dies to the understanding, but not in the sense of failing in, or waiving, an understanding of what could be understood. On the contrary, he dies to the understanding in the sense of seeing that what confronts him is not a matter for the understanding. This is what Job recognises in his reaction to the contingencies which came to him: 'The Lord gave, the Lord hath taken away, blessed be the name of the Lord.'[14] Theodicies distort this mode of religious acceptance. They want to make our ways God's ways, and our thoughts his thoughts. They do not recognise that what needs to come in at the right place in this context is not explanation, but awe, wonder and mystery. We could say, in this context, what Weil said of suffering, that religion has a use, but no remedy for it.

I am not saying, of course, that a sense of the contingencies of life must lead to the notion of the mystery of God's will. On the contrary, reactions to the storm need amount to no more than a cry in the dark, a desperate need for comfort. The surroundings will show that that is what these reactions amount to. On the other hand, we could imagine rites developing around these reactions of terror which, so far from seeking comfortable reassurances, seek to celebrate the contingency of human life through its expression of what is terrible. Imagine a rite in which children dance around a pit of fire. The wizard points at one of the children, and immediately the child is thrown into the pit. One minute dancing, the next consumed in the flames: life is in the hands of a terrible God.

It is tempting to argue that since man may be depicted as bowing in subjection before the inscrutableness of an omnipotent will in most of the examples I have given, the only rational reaction is resigned acceptance of whatever happens. 'All things come from God' seems to mean no more than 'Whatever happens happens'. Surely, it might be thought, the only justifiable response is an undifferentiating resignation.[15] We have seen why these conclusions do not follow. First, resignation is as much a reaction to contingencies as any other. It *is* a reaction, not an inference or argument. It does not represent something called a *rational* reaction as opposed to the others we have considered. Instead of denying that the others are rational, attention must be paid, in the ways we have suggested, to concept-formation in these contexts. When we do this we can, as philosophers, allow senses of mystery to come in at the right place. Further, when this is done, when we see what recognition of the will of God comes to, we can also see how this would have a bearing on specific events in people's lives. For example, if a sense of being in the hands of God leads a person to see that nothing is his by right, then this will have consequences for the satisfaction and disappointment of his desires. After all his efforts are done, he sees the outcome is in God's hands. In this way he mediates the sense of the will of God in his attitude to both success and failure.

To illustrate this point further, we can consider the notion of the mysterious will of God in relation to our judgements concerning ourselves and others. Here, too, we can see how dying to the understanding, in a certain sense, is called for.

Consider the following words: 'The first shall be last, and the last first.'[16] How are these words to be understood? We may think that these words report a mistake, a rather serious miscalculation. After all, we seem to be talking about more than a mere slip — the first actually last, and the last first! Think of the chaos which would ensue if this mistake were repeated in other walks of life. Think of horse-races: those horses tipped to be first coming in last and those horses tipped to be last coming in first. Only odds-makers would be happy! But it is difficult to see how the world of life insurance could survive: all-American boys dying like flies and the chronically ill getting congratulatory telegrams on their hundredth birthdays. The first last and the last first. And what of those graduates of first-class universities hoping to take the world by storm? Those hoping for honours failing and failures getting high honours. What would be our reactions to these catastrophes which have swept through our institutions and practices? Well, after the initial shock, surely, we would try to find out what had gone wrong. We would want to rectify matters so that our judgements could be on a firm footing again; rectify matters so that the first and the last could be in their proper places again.

Yet, the words of the text have to do with something far more important than horse-racing, insurance or academic grades. They have to do with the soul's destiny in the sight of God. And our reaction to hearing that a mistake has been made in this area, might be the same as our reaction to the other mistakes: we strive to rectify matters, to see that those who deserve to be first are first, and those who deserve to be last, really are last. With such a thing as how we stand in God's final judgement, surely we want to be sure that those who are in are really in and those who are out are really out. The attitude has some similarities to those who, from time to time, attempt to find out what has been written about them in the obituary columns of the London *Times*. They want to know, before they die, what is going to be said about them after they die.

But, now, do not these comparisons badly mislead us where the scriptural words are concerned, those words which speak of the first being last and the last being first? We have assumed that these words refer to a mistake, a mistake of miscalculation. But that was not the sin involved. The sin was not to miscalculate where they stood in the sight of God, *but to want to calculate at all*. They thought they were dealing with something which could be seen and that their mistake was to see it incorrectly. It looks as if they were ignorant of an eschatological state of affairs, which, for reasons of self-interest, they would like to know about. Perhaps it appears to be something that you could merely be curious about. But to let mystery come in at the right place where the destiny of the human soul before God is concerned, is, once again, to see what is unseen. To accept the mystery is not a matter of being content with ignorance where knowledge could be had, but, rather, a matter of coming to accept a spiritual truth. This can be illustrated by reference to Flannery O'Connor's wonderful short story, 'Revelation'.

To the large Mrs Turpin in the doctor's waiting-room, there is no mystery about how people are to be understood.

Sometimes Mrs Turpin occupied herself at night naming the classes of people. On the bottom of the heap were most coloured people, not the kind she would have been if she had been one, but most of them; then next to them — not above, just away from — were the white-trash; then above them were the home-owners, and above them the home-and-land owners to which she and Claud (her husband) belonged. Above she and Claud were people with a lot of money and much more land.[17]

There were times when she wondered what she would do if Jesus were to confront her with the following dilemma: 'There's only two places available for you. You can either be a nigger or white-trash.'[18] Because of the changing circumstances in the community about her, operating her categories posed difficulties for her:

> But here the complexity of it would begin to bear in on her, for some of the people with a lot of money were common and ought to be below she and Claud and some of the people who had good blood had lost their money and had to rent and then there were coloured people who owned their homes and land as well. There was a coloured dentist in town who had two red Lincolns and a swimming pool and a farm with registered white-face cattle on it. Usually by the time she had fallen asleep all the classes of people were moiling and roiling around in her head, and she would dream they were all crammed in together in a boxcar being ridden off to be put in a gas oven.[19]

In the waiting-room there is another respectable white lady in whom Mrs Turpin senses a kindred soul. Unfortunately, she is accompanied by her sullen ugly daughter. The question occurs to Mrs Turpin, 'What if Jesus had said, "All right, you can be white-trash or a nigger or ugly!" '[20] Her own destiny is certainly no mystery to her. A gospel song is being played, 'When I looked up and He looked down' and she supplies the response in her mind, 'And wona these days I know I'll we-eara crown.'[21]

During the wait in the surgery, various conversations take place, all of which annoy the sullen daughter more and more. Her mother begins to discuss her daughter's lack of manners with Mrs Turpin, complaining that studying at Wellesley College has not improved her.

> 'If it's one thing I am,' Mrs Turpin said with feeling, 'it's grateful. When I think who all I could have been besides myself and all I got, a little of everything, and a good

disposition besides. I just feel like shouting, "Thank you, Jesus, for making everything the way it is!" It could have been different!' For one thing, somebody else could have got Claud. At the thought of this, she was flooded with gratitude and a terrible pang of joy ran through her. 'Oh thank you, Jesus, Jesus, thank you!' she cried aloud.[22]

At that moment the girl's book hits her in the eye and her nails are in the flesh of her neck. The girl kicks Claud's ulcerated leg. The girl has some kind of fit, and has to be sedated, but her eyes are fixed on Mrs Turpin. Mrs Turpin leans over her:

'What you got to say to me?' she asked hoarsely and held her breath, waiting, as for a revelation. The girl raised her head. Her gaze locked with Mrs Turpin's. 'Go back to hell where you came from, you old wart hog,' she whispered. Her voice was low but clear. Her eyes burned for a moment as if she saw with pleasure that her message had struck its target.[23]

They all agree that the girl has had a fit. Some say she is destined to be a lunatic. ' "I thank Gawd," the white-trash woman said fervently, "I ain't a lunatic".'[24]

Back on the farm Mrs Turpin cannot get the image out of her mind — a wart hog from hell. She tries to greet her black workhands in the usual way. She had always said that black people should be shown love, for in that way they worked better for you. She has to tell them of the incident in the doctor's waiting-room, but, seeing through their flattery and reassurance, she finds no consolation.

In the final scene in the story, Mrs Turpin is hosing down her hogs. Suddenly, she speaks, ' "What do you send me a message like that for?" she said in a low fierce voice, barely above a whisper but with the force of a shout in the concentrated fury. "How am I a hog and me both? How am I saved and from hell too?" '[25] Her fury against God grows and in it is revealed once again the way in which she thinks of other people:

'Why me?' she mumbled. 'It's no trash around here, black or white, that I haven't given to. And break my back to the bone every day working. And do for the church.' ... 'How am I a hog?' she demanded. 'Exactly how am I like them

... There was plenty of trash there. It didn't have to be me.
If you like trash better, go get yourself some trash then,'
she railed. 'You could have made me trash. Or a nigger. If
trash is what you wanted why didn't you make me trash?'
... 'I could quit working and take it easy and be filthy,' she
growled. 'Lounge about the sidewalks all day drinking root
beer. Dip snuff and spit in every puddle and have it all over
my face. I could be nasty. Or you could have made me a
nigger. It's too late for me to be a nigger,' she said with
deep sarcasm, 'but I could act like one. Lay down in the
middle of the road and stop traffic. Roll on the ground.'[26]

Her railings against God come to their climax:

'Go on,' she yelled, 'call me a hog! Call me a hog again.
From hell. Call me a wart hog from hell! Put that bottom
rail on top. There'll still be a top and bottom!' ... A final
surge of fury shook her and she roared, 'Who do you think
you are?' The colour of everything, field and crimson sky,
burned for a moment with a transparent intensity. The
question carried over the pasture and across the highway
and the cotton field and returned to her clearly like an
answer from beyond the wood.[27]

Who do you think you are? — in the echo is the beginning of
her new realisation. Alone, with the hogs, the final revelation
arrives:

There was only a purple streak in the sky, cutting through
a field of crimson and leading, like an extension of the
highway, into the descending dusk. She raised her hands
from the side of the pen in a gesture hieratic and profound.
A visionary light settled in her eyes. She saw the streak as
a vast swinging bridge extending upward from the earth
through a field of living fire. Upon it a vast horde of souls
were rumbling toward heaven. There were whole companies
of white-trash clean for the first time in their lives, and
bands of black niggers in white robes, and battalions of
freaks and lunatics shouting and clapping and leaping like
frogs. And bringing up the end of the procession were a
tribe of people whom she recognised at once as those who,
like herself and Claud, had always had a little of everything

287

and the God-given wit to use it right. She leaned forward to observe them closer. They were marching behind the others with great dignity, accountable as they had always been for good order and common sense and respectable behaviour. They alone were on key. Yet she could see by their shocked and altered faces that even their virtues were being burned away. She lowered her hands and gripped the rail of the hog pen, her eyes small but fixed unblinkingly on what lay ahead. In a moment the vision faded but she remained where she was, immobile.

At length she got down and turned off the faucet and made her slow way on the darkening path to the house. In the woods around her the invisible cricket choruses had struck up, but what she heard were the voices of the souls climbing upward into the starry field and shouting hallelujah.[28]

The necessary mystery of the soul's destiny remains. A mystery revealed is not like a practical problem solved or a philosophical puzzle dissolved. One feeds on the mystery. What the story shows is one possibility of the way in which the acceptance of a mystery is mediated through the way it is possible to think of other people. The possibility does not mean, and neither did Flannery O'Connor mean, that all judgements of others should cease, but a great deal depends on the spirit in which the judgements are made. We are not to claim a final knowledge of ourselves and others such that we, but not they, are to have access to God. Here we are to die to the understanding, it is something no human can claim to have. To claim such knowledge, to attribute a spiritual superiority to oneself, is itself an offence against the spirit. Frantic desires and attempts to determine who is in and who is out in the sight of God, receive the reply — who do you think you are? The eternal destiny of the individual soul must be left to God. In one of her letters, Flannery O'Connor says, 'I read recently somewhere about a priest up for canonization. It was reported in the findings about him that he had said of a man on the scaffold who had been blasphemous up to the last that this man would surely go to hell; on the basis of this remark he was denied canonization.'[29]

By waiting on Flannery O'Connor's story we can see how it shows one way in which mystery comes in at the right place. It shows how leaving things to God is not a theoretical matter or an inevitability. On the contrary, it is something men find difficult to do. It is something which has to be worked at; something which may be revealed as it was to Mrs Turpin.

As a result of letting mystery come in at the right place, what has happened to the epistemological context in which our problem was thought to be one of showing how we *can* speak of God, given that our language hides from him from us? What we have seen is that language is not a screen which hides God from us. On the contrary, the idea of God *in* the language we have been explaining, is the idea of a hidden God — *Vere tu es Deus absconditus.*[30]

Notes

1. Kierkegaard, *Concluding Unscientific Postscript*, pp. 191 f. Quoted by Bouwsma in 'The Invisible' in *Without Proof or Evidence*, p. 31.

2. Bouwsma, *Without Proof or Evidence*, p. 28.

3. Ibid., p. 34.

4. Simone Weil, 'Draft for a Statement of Human Obligations' (1943) in *Selected Essays 1934–1943*, trans. Richard Rees (Clarendon Press, Oxford, 1962).

5. M.O'C Drury, 'Some Notes on Conversations with Wittgenstein' in Rush Rhees (ed.), *Ludwig Wittgenstein — Personal Recollections* (Basil Blackwell, Oxford, 1981), p. 99.

6. Simone Weil, *First and Last Notebooks*, trans. Richard Rees (Clarendon Press, Oxford, 1970), p. 147.

7. Winch, 'Meaning and Religious Language,' p. 210.

8. Flannery O'Connor, *Mystery and Manners*, sel. and ed. Sally and Robert Fitzgerald (Farrar, Straus and Giroux, New York, 1969), p. 41.

9. Whittaker, 'Literal and Figurative Language', p. 48.

10. Conway, 'Phillips and "The inadequacy of language" ', p. 93.

11. Simone Weil, *Lectures on Philosophy*, trans. H.S. Price, intro. Peter Winch (Cambridge University Press, 1978), pp. 171–2.

12. Translator's note by H.S. Price, ibid., p. 172.

13. Jakob Fries, *Dialogues on Morality and Religion*, trans. David Walford, intro. Rush Rhees, ed. D.Z. Phillips (Basil Blackwell, Oxford, 1982), pp. 10–11. I am indebted to Rush Rhees for discussions of Fries.

14. See Phillips, *Concept of Prayer*, pp. 61–2; 98–100; 155–6.

15. These pertinent questions were put to me by Eric Mack at Tulane University when I read a version of 'Grace and works'. The questions resemble those of C.W.K. Mundle who asked why, if all prayers end with 'Thy will be done' one should make any *specific* requests at all. See *Concept of Prayer*, p. 121 f.

16. *Matt.* 19:30.

17. Flannery O'Connor, 'Revelation' in *Everything That Rises Must Converge* (Faber and Faber, London, 1965), p. 195.

18. Ibid., p. 195.

19. Ibid., pp. 195–6.

20. Ibid., p. 196.
21. Ibid., p. 194.
22. Ibid., pp. 205–6.
23. Ibid., pp. 207–8.
24. Ibid., p. 209.
25. Ibid., p. 215.
26. Ibid., pp. 215–16.
27. Ibid., pp. 216–17.
28. Ibid., pp. 217–18.
29. O'Connor, *Habit of Being*, p. 102.
30. For a philosophical and literary discussion of a poet's hard-won celebration of belief in such a God, see D.Z. Phillips, *R.S. Thomas: Poet of the Hidden God* (Macmillan, London, 1986).

21
Morality, Grace and Concept-Formation

We began the final part of this book by showing, in Chapter 18, how easily religious mysteries can become epistemological mysteries. It is so easy to see our task as that of leaping over the wall of the enclosure we are in, to a metaphysical reality which lies without. And all the time, as we have seen, what was needed was all about us if only we would wait on it. For various reasons, the enclosure we find ourselves in is not one, for the most part, in which the majority speak of the inescapable reality of God. As we have said, for us the problem seems to be one of finding God rather than of escaping from him. Nevertheless, as we saw in the last chapter, it is still possible to grasp the sense of talking of an inescapable God if only we let mystery come in at the right place. We saw this in relation to the notion of the mysterious will of God in connection with natural events and our judgements of other people. When we can wait on these conceptual reminders, we see that while religious belief talks of a sense which lies outside the enclosure, the grasping of that sense depends on seeing how it illuminates what is within the enclosure.

It is difficult in philosophy of religion to give a perspicuous representation of the mode of application which religious concepts have. As we have seen, it is difficult to recognise the place of mystery in religious belief. Indeed, there are plenty of voices within the enclosure which say that these difficulties are insurmountable, since they come from a desire to say what cannot be said. According to these voices, talk of mystery distorts too much of what we know within the enclosure. Talk of a mystery of grace in nature or in our dealings with others seems to be no more than indulgence in magical concepts. We are better off, it is said, with the honest endeavours we are aquainted with. These endeavours, very often, do not amount to much, but at least they are ours and we do not falsify them. The help which is said to come from God's grace is no help at all. It threatens our understanding of moral endeavour with magical promises of divine deliverance.[1] In face of objections such as these, our task, as before, is to pay attention to concept-formation in religious belief, in this case, the conceptual relations between grace and works.

Here is a familiar religious setting in which talk of grace and works has a natural home: man, it is said, wishes to be accepted by a holy and just God. In order to be accepted, he endeavours to keep God's commandments. His justification before God will then depend on the merits of his works. Yet, if he is honest with himself, he has to admit that he fails in his endeavours again and again. He has to admit that he is a sinner. But how can a sinner be justified before a holy and just God? If his salvation depends on the merits of his works, he is without hope. Yet, he is saved from despair by good news of God's grace. God has elected to save the sinner without regard to the believer's good works. Man's salvation does not depend on what man has done for God, but on what God has done for man. Salvation is the free gift of God's grace. Man need not despair at his lack of good works. All he has to do is to believe what God has done for him and be grateful for it.

Yet, it is this familiar religious context which has led to so much theological controversy within religion and to so many philosophical objections to religion. The most extreme interpretation of the religious setting to cause these diverse reactions has been, undoubtedly, the doctrine of predestination. My purpose here, even if I could fulfil it, is not to provide a full discussion of this doctrine, but simply to illustrate, by reference to it, how the difficulties concerning recognising concept-formation in religious belief arise. John Whittaker has shown what happens when the doctrine of predestination is taken out of its religious setting and made the subject of abstract metaphysical speculation.

> On the face of it, the doctrine seems ... frightening ... since it is terrifying to think that one might be arbitrarily excluded from salvation by divine fiat ... Such a God makes all of us the victims of an arbitrary destiny, a destiny which seems unspeakably cruel to those who through no fault of their own are left to misery and damnation. Unless, of course,

God somehow foreknows the virtues of his elect; but in that case God's foreknowledge seems to close our futures in the stifling grip of determinism. How can God know what people are going to do in order to reward or punish them in advance of their deeds, if it lies within their power to do as they please? Or if it does not lie within their power, how can they be said to be worthy or unworthy of his grace? And how can God be said to be just in dispensing this grace?[2]

According to Whittaker, this is a metaphysical caricature of the doctrine, one which it is fatal to entertain on its own terms. What is needed is a change of direction which shows the irrelevance of the metaphysical arguments. This is what Luther tried to achieve. Whittaker tells us that Luther tried to bring out the religious point of the doctrine in terms of the fears the doctrine was meant to allay. These fears had to do with the question of how a man's soul can be saved if he has to rely on his good works. Only by taking this into account can we come to see what reliance on God's grace can mean in a believer's life.

In elucidating the development of belief in God's grace in Luther, Whittaker reminds us that Luther had been taught

> that God's grace was freely available, but only to those who were properly repentant. Only those who sincerely and completely confessed their failings, and who sincerely willed to live according to the law of God, would be forgiven and strengthened. For them the sacraments would be the ever-available means of grace, but for those who lacked or lost a properly receptive heart, the sacraments would become ineffectual.[3]

When he reflected on his own life, this became a doctrine of despair for Luther, because he had to recognise that he failed repeatedly in good works and even in wanting to have a pure heart, and the more he tried to have a pure intention, the more artificial the very trying made his endeavour seem. On the view with which he was presented, what 'grace' came to was a belief that 'God makes up the difference between what we intend and what we actually accomplish in the way of doing his will, so that we can actually *achieve* the righteousness needed for salvation.'[4]

The doctrine of predestination came as a liberating force to Luther, one which rescued him from his despair. What he came to realise is that salvation comes from *election*, that God offers his grace prior to anything a man does, 'so that it remains only for one to believe in it and be grateful for it.'[5] In this way, Whittaker argues, a harsh doctrine was transformed, 'for as long as God offers His grace *in consequence* of the believer's merit, the acutely conscious sinner is left without hope. If God grants his grace *prior* to the sinner's hopeless attempts to rectify his impure will, however, then the happiness which he could not possess through his own effort becomes possible through God.'[6] Whittaker would claim, I think, that, in this way, the doctrine of grace ceases to be a doctrine of fairness and becomes a doctrine of love.

Yet, despite this hoped-for transformation in the doctrine, it is precisely to the details of how this transformation is effected that objecting voices have been raised. We can see how the objections occur if we look at Whittaker's own attempt to provide details of the nature of the transformation from reliance on works to reliance on grace. He characterises the change in two ways: first, he suggests that reliance on works has a self-defeating character, and, second, that reliance on works relies on ineffective attempts to further one's self-interest. As we shall see, both characterisations lead to insuperable difficulties.

First, what of the suggestion that attempts to save one's soul by reliance on good works are self-defeating? Whittaker says that Luther's attempts to possess a pure heart were self-defeating. The more he tried, the more he despaired. Whittaker claims that Luther is in a confused state: 'Luther was like one who on some grievous occasion tries to feel appropriately saddened, but in *trying* to feel sad feels only unnatural and insincere.'[7] The confusion consists in thinking that one can be sad by trying to be sad. Whittaker seems to equate Luther's despair with the confusion involved in the self-defeating attempt to attain righteousness by making righteousness an end to which one's actions are supposed to be the means. A transition from a state of reliance on good works, to a state of reliance on divine grace, involves, for Whittaker, freeing oneself from a state of conceptual confusion.

The obvious difficulty with this analysis of reliance on good works is that a man who *is* in despair about his moral endeavours need not be conceptually confused in the way Whittaker describes at all. On the contrary, he may be clear-sightedly free of such confusion. Consider one of Simone Weil's examples of a pure action, that of a father absorbed in play with his children. Another father may recognise that he is not like this. But he may also see quite clearly that he can never become like this by making spontaneous absorption in play with his children an end which he can aim for. He cannot plan to be spontaneous! He appreciates the confusion involved in that. But he is dejected nevertheless, and so his dejection does not depend on the confusion. A man may be dejected simply because of what he is. This being so, there are difficulties for the way in which Whittaker wants to describe the distinctive liberation which comes to a man who comes to rely on divine grace. That *distinctive* liberation cannot be said to consist essentially in seeing that moral purity cannot be made the goal of moral endeavour. *That* recognition would mark a transition from a confusion about a regard for decency to a clearer view of it. The attainment of such clarity, however, need not lead to any sense of reliance on divine grace and so certainly cannot be equated with a transition to such reliance. Neither, as we have seen, is it a necessary condition of such a transition, since neither the man who endeavours to be decent nor the man who comes to rely on divine grace need ever have been confused in the way Whittaker describes.

What of Whittaker's second attempt to account for the transition from reliance on works to reliance on grace? It has the unfortunate consequence of reducing morality to the pursuit of self-interest. Whittaker says that prior to his recognition of what God has done, a person performed good deeds 'for his own self-acceptance', whereas after he has recognised what God has done, the believer performs these deeds 'out of gratitude' for what God has done for him.[8] This depiction of moral endeavour has far-reaching difficulties. Does a man do good works *in order* to save his soul? What if a man says that he jumped into a river to save a child from drowning in order to save his soul? Wouldn't it make sense to reply: 'We thought you jumped in for the sake of the child?' Purity of soul is not achieved by making purity of heart an aim. Purity or otherwise is shown *in* the character of one's actions. Decency does not depend on one's actions leading to some further end called salvation, which is thought of as contingently related to them. Any goal postulated as the goal of our actions is as answerable to the demands of decency as the means which lead to it.

Whittaker should have come to these conclusions, too, for when he accounts for the transition from a concern with purely prudential considerations to a concern with moral considerations, he is fully aware of a conception of moral endeavour which is not self-defeating in character and which is obviously inexplicable in terms of enlightened self-interest. Whittaker shows how futile it would be to attempt to demonstrate, according to some common measure of interest, that moral considerations serve men's interests more than prudential considerations. Whittaker argues, rightly, that

> as long as the point of moral principles is to override ... prudential considerations by instituting prescriptive judgements of *obligation*, the moralist cannot afford to defend his principles on his opponent's ground. The moral believer would defeat his own purposes if he set aside the point of his principles merely to win their acceptance on prudential grounds, for the acceptance of these principles as prudent policies would not require the believer to exercise any higher ideals. Such a believer would not enter into any *new*, peculiarly *moral* domain of judgement. Without adhering to moral beliefs as the foundation of a different kind of reflection, beyond prudential reasoning, he simply would not become a dutiful person. And for all those who believe that we have moral duties, that makes no sense at all.[9]

Here, moral duties, as depicted by Whittaker, neither exhibit a self-defeating character, nor serve as mere means to a further end.

On the other hand, given this depiction of moral duties, Whittaker's account of the transition from reliance on moral endeavour to reliance on grace becomes problematic: '*Rather than thinking that his ultimate happiness and fulfilment might be secured as the end product of moral achievement, the believer forgoes the whole range of means/ends judgements in connection with his happiness.*'[10] But in his account of the transition from a concern with prudence to a moral concern, Whittaker's whole point was that morality, unlike prudence, should *not* be construed in terms of conduct determined by the relation of means to ends. In that case, Whittaker is construing the reliance on divine grace as involving the giving up of a conception of moral endeavour which, on his own admission, is confused.

This being so, those who want to resist any suggestion of a *necessary* transition to reliance on grace from reliance on moral endeavour will point out, quite correctly, that there is nothing self-defeating or prudentially instrumental in a concern for moral considerations. If someone expounding how a reliance on grace may come about relies on imputing such characteristics to moral endeavour, objectors will justifiably point out the groundlessness of the imputation. Of course, it may still be the case, as we shall see, that reliance on divine grace is internally related to moral endeavour, but that connection has yet to be elucidated satisfactorily.

Before exploring the internal relations between the notions of grace and moral endeavour, there is a second way in which objecting voices may be raised against reliance on divine grace. So far from stressing internal relations with moral endeavour, it might be said, talk of reliance on grace fails to treat such endeavour seriously by advocating, instead, a magical conception of salvation and deliverance. But, as Flannery O'Connor has said, 'you cannot show the operation of grace when grace is cut off from nature.'[11]

Whittaker is aware of the dangers involved and he points out that Luther was aware of them too. Luther called the doctrine of predestination 'strong meat', not to be given to those not ready for it. One way of not being ready to understand the doctrine is to divorce it from everything in Luther's life which led him to embrace it. If we take away the consciousness of sin, if we take away the heavy conscience and the threat of despair, then we won't understand what we are being told when it is said that God has already prescribed for man's salvation 'so that it remains only for one to believe it and to be grateful for it.'[12] We may find ourselves saying that, according to such a view, we can do what we like since God has made salvation secure whatever we do. Here, the sense of the notion of grace is unmediated. It becomes a magical operation. It is this magical conception of grace which becomes the deserving object of philosophical criticism.

The emphasis on grace as God's free gift is meant to take us away from a self-calculating religion of desert. To put such matters as emphatically as possible, the doctrine of predestination says that God's election to salvation was made 'before the foundations of the world were laid'. Yet, dangers of misreading similar to those we have considered threaten these words too. So far from ridding men from prudential considerations, this emphasis can actually reinforce them. If prudential considerations are coupled with the thought that divine rewards and punishments have already been determined, people may grow anxious about whether they are included among the beneficiaries. Believers begin to search frantically for signs of their election; they want to know who is in and who is out in the sight of God. What began as a mystery degenerates into a probing of secrets, and, as we saw in the last chapter, mystery and grace come in at the wrong place as a result.

If we say that the gift of God's grace has nothing to do with human endeavour, and that all men have to do is to recognise what God has done for them, how do we avoid a magical conception of grace? This is one of the issues which bothered Pelagius. If there is only a contingent connection between recognising what God has done and the gratitude which is supposed to ensue, the door is opened to some highly embarrassing conclusions. If a man is in prison, then, normally, he will be glad to hear that someone has secured his release. But this need not lead to any change in his behaviour or any sense of gratitude to the person who releases him. On the contrary, the released person may take up the life which led to his imprisonment and regard the one who set him free as a soft-hearted fool.

Pelagius did not think that talk of God's grace is intelligible without reference to good works. He did not think such works should be despised. As Flannery O'Connor observes, Manichean-type theologies see 'the natural world as unworthy of penetration'.[13] But this is tantamount to refusing to mediate the sense which the notion of grace may have. In saying, mistakenly, that a man's soul could be saved by his good works, Pelagius was wanting to avoid confusions not dissimilar to those to which Whittaker calls our attention. He wanted to avoid a magical conception of grace or religious experience which is quite cut off from moral conduct. It is for the same reason that Flannery O'Connor says, 'Today's reader, if he believes in grace at all, sees it as something which can be separated from nature and served to him raw as Instant Uplift.'[14] So although their doctrines are diametrically opposed to each other, Luther and Pelagius want to avoid magical conceptions of grace unmediated in the detail of the believer's life. In its most extreme form a believer could be said to recognise what God has done for him, but be completely indifferent to it, or even to live a life contrary to God's commands. Perhaps he could even say with impunity, 'If God has done all that is necessary already, why should I bother?'

Clearly, Whittaker wants to avoid these unhappy conclusions. He sees the dangers involved in trying to speak of reliance on works or reliance on grace while ignoring the internal relations between them. He tries to move in this direction when he says that the doctrine of grace is expressed less misleadingly if we say 'that the grace by which we are able to live at peace with ourselves is given *logically*, not *chronologically*, prior to our efforts to attain it.'[15] In other words, we should try to see how a concept of grace may inform moral endeavour from the outset. But Whittaker's analysis, as we have seen, does not allow him to bring out the internal relations which may exist between the notions of grace and works. Instead, he lays himself open to the familiar objections that talk of grace often suggests that moral endeavour has a self-defeating character or is based on enlightened self-interest. There can be no doubt that many advocates of doctrines of grace do talk in this way. There can be no doubt either that the doctrine of grace advocated is often what we have called a magical conception of grace.

On the other hand, there are other conceptions of grace which do not fall foul of these objections. Let us consider some examples which bring out the internal relations between grace and works. The vulnerability of human beings is an important element in the formation of the notion of divine grace. We saw, in the last chapter, how a sense of being at the mercy of God's will can give rise to a certain wonder, wonder at the miracle of existence. In such a reaction, the very contingency of events takes on the aspect of a gift — a gift of grace, one might say. These reactions are not *arguments* from contingency to God. That is why Whittaker's depiction of the reaction will not do; it is too much like an argument:

> Sheer existence, with all its mysterious givens and disturbing contingencies, must have some higher rationale, some end that renders individual existence worthwhile and capable of fulfilment. This is the theme on which the world's religions play their different variations. The point of postulating a higher order in the cosmos is to legitimate the individual's search for a worthwhile end in his own existence.[16]

Here we are back with the view that religious reactions are legitimated by beliefs which precede them. The man in awe before the majesty of God's will in the storm can hardly be characterised as someone who postulates a higher order in the cosmos in order to legitimate his own worthwhileness. His reactions are not based on prior beliefs; rather, his beliefs get their sense in the context of these reactions. Furthermore, his awe at the majesty of God, so far from establishing his own worthwhileness, shows him that he is nothing before God. He may well remember the man who planned a vast expansion in barn building, not knowing that God required his soul that very night.

If human beings, like the storm, are seen as in the hands of God, then human beings too are seen as dependent on grace. To see men as God's creatures is to deny at the same time that others should play at being God with respect to them. In this way, coming to see people as God's creatures is inextricably bound up with one's own conduct. It is no accident that wondering at God's creation, seeing human beings as God's creatures, are closely linked to dying to the self, since making the self central would be a denial of the religious sense I am trying to elucidate. The picture of an acknowledgement of God's grace, completely divorced from any moral endeavour is, therefore, a confused picture. It is not confused, however, because the possession of divine grace *causally* brings about good works. Neither is it confused because good works are a *natural consequence* of the acknowledgement of divine grace. Rather, it is because there are *internal conceptual relations* between the acknowledgement of grace and moral endeavour.

When these internal relations are stressed, we see what is wrong in an analysis of a transition from reliance on works to reliance on grace, where works cease to be a means of attaining salvation ('Look at what I have done') and become the means by which gratitude to God is shown ('Look at what he has done'). On such a view, there is no change in the instrumental conception of good works and grace remains something magical, quite independent of them. In the religious possibility I have elucidated, grace transforms the very conception of a person's endeavours, not by making them the means of achieving something different from what was achieved before, *but by seeing the possibility of the works themselves as the gift of grace.* This is what I take Paul to be emphasising to the Ephesians in those words which are so often the victim of incomplete quotation: 'For by grace are ye saved through faith; and that not of yourselves: it is the gift of God. Not of works, lest any man should boast.' (Here, those who want to separate grace from works usually end their quotation, but Paul continues.) 'For we are his workmanship, created in Christ Jesus unto good works, which God hath before ordained that we should walk in them.'[17] Here, there is no issue of bridging a gap *between* grace and works, since grace informs one's very conception of human endeavour. Such a perspective indeed changes one's whole attitude to works, attainment, failure, praise, blame, judgement, pity, compassion and forgiveness. Weil shows us part of what is involved when she illuminatingly locates Peter's denial of Jesus, not in the breaking of his promise, but in the making of it. 'Denial of Saint Peter. To say to Christ: "I will never deny Thee" was to deny him already, for it was supposing the source of faithfulness to be in himself and not in grace.'[18] Peter thought that his loyalty, his allegiance, his faith, were entirely within his control, the product of his purposeful endeavours. What Jesus reveals to him is that even his ability to make the promise is in the hands of God, dependent on grace, on factors over which he has little control. Hence, when someone is guilty of denial, as Peter was, the believer's response is, 'But for the grace of God, there go I.' The opposite response is the sin of pride: 'God, I thank thee that I am not as other men are', which is what Peter was saying in effect in his confident prediction that no matter who deserted Jesus, he never would. In this way, his promise to be faithful was already an act of unfaithfulness, a denial of grace.

All I have said about an internal relation between grace and works can be spoken of in the way in which Whittaker speaks of Luther's faith. He says that it 'ultimately rested on the new vista of understanding which opened up when he grasped the point of this belief and took it to his heart. Any other way of "grounding" this belief by detaching its credibility from the role it plays as a principle would have been completely illogical.'[19] This insight is not regarded as an achievement or another form of salvation by desert. The insight itself is regarded by the believer as a work of grace, the work of God in him. That is why such a believer would say, with Paul, 'Not I, but Christ liveth in me.'[20]

I agree entirely with Whittaker when he says, 'A doctrine like that of predestination acquires its point by virtue of the role it plays in reorienting the judgements a believer makes.'[21] I am less happy with what Whittaker takes to be the central concern of these judgements, namely, the believer and his prospects for happiness. Theologically, I may be taken as making a plea to emphasise God's *electing to save*, rather than God *saving the elect*. If this is done, the place of the self is determined as a consequence. Thus, a higher order is not postulated in order to legitimise an individual's search for what is worthwhile (Whittaker), but, rather, faced with the mediated reality of God's grace, what is worthwhile for the individual is determined thereby. Why such grace is revealed at all remains, as it must, a necessary mystery. This priority takes more seriously Whittaker's own recognition that the doctrine of predestination plays a supporting role to 'the more fundamental doctrine of divine grace'.[22]

Despite my plea to emphasise God's electing to save, rather than God saving the elect, I do not want to be taken as issuing theological prescriptions. My main concern has been with the conceptual confusions which result from a failure to mediate the sense of the notions of grace and works; a failure which leads, as we have seen, to a distortion of moral endeavour and to a magical conception of grace and religious experience. It is in this context that a final point has to be made. Whittaker has emphasised, rightly, that we cannot see the point of a religious belief if we divorce it from the role it plays in the religious life. He goes on to claim, however, that 'one can see how a faithful adherence to such a belief depends entirely on a grasp of its point'.[23] Here we part company.

Let us assume that I, philosophically, have succeeded in showing the point of stressing an internal relation between grace and works. If this is all a faithful adherence to belief depends on, my exposition, if faithful, amounts to faithful adherence to the belief. But, surely, Whittaker would not be happy with this. By 'adherence to belief' he clearly means adherence to it in one's life. The equation of such faithful adherence to philosophical or even theological analysis will not do. Something is missing. Furthermore, we have reason to suppose that Whittaker, on reflection, would know what is missing, for he gives us the answer elsewhere in his essay. In describing Luther's faith, Whittaker tells us that it depended, not simply on Luther grasping its point, but also on his *taking it to his heart*.[24] The philosopher who strives for some measure of clarity concerning the transition from reliance on works to reliance on grace may or may not make such a transition his own; may or may not take it to his heart. To say that reliance on divine grace has a certain conceptual character is not to rely on divine grace. To receive such grace the philosopher would have to confess 'I have arrived at my analysis by the grace of God.' That confession is not made simply in writing his book.

Notes

1. For a philosophical and literary discussion of these protesting voices from within the enclosure together with religious counter-voices see Phillips, *No Main Road: Religion in Twentieth Century Literature*.

2. John H. Whittaker, *Matters of Faith and Matters of Principle*, Trinity University Monograph Series in Religion, vol. 6 (Trinity University Press, San Antonio, 1981), pp. 70–1.

3. Ibid., pp. 71–2.

4. Ibid., p. 73.

5. Ibid.

6. Ibid.

7. Ibid., p. 72.

8. See ibid., p. 80.

9. Ibid., p. 88.

10. Ibid., p. 82.

11. O'Connor, 'Novelist and Believer' in *Mystery and Manners*, p. 166.

12. Whittaker, *Matters of Faith and Matters of Principle*, p. 73.

13. O'Connor, 'Novelist and Believer' in *Mystery and Manners*, p. 163.

14. Ibid., p. 165.

15. Whittaker, *Matters of Faith and Matters of Principle*, p. 85.

16. Ibid., p. 60.

17. *Eph.* 2:8–10.

18. Simone Weil, *Gravity and Grace*, trans. Emma Craufurd, introd. Gustave Thibon (Routledge and Kegan Paul, London, 1947), p. 22.

19. Whittaker, *Matters of Faith and Matters of Principle*, p. 82.

20. *Gal.* 2:20.

21. Whittaker, *Matters of Faith and Matters of Principle*, pp. 85–6.

22. Ibid., p. 84.

23. Ibid., p. 70.

24. See ibid., p. 82.

22
Religious Concepts: Misunderstanding and Lack of Understanding

We began the book by referring to a scandal in contemporary philosophy of religion, namely, the assumption that an acceptable account of religious belief can only be given within the perspective of epistemological foundationalism. We saw that such a perspective distorted the grammar of religious belief. On the other hand, Reformed epistemology made the basic propositions of religion seem isolated from the contexts in which they have their life. We saw, in other ways, how hermeneutics, the sociology of knowledge, and even attempts at giving theology its proper status, may all create difficulties for giving perspicuous representations of religious belief. In my criticisms, I have tried to provide conceptual reminders of the kind of life religious beliefs may have. But I have been writing philosophy of religion long enough to know that the provision of these conceptual reminders is not unproblematic. A philosopher must not be over-confident and take his audience for granted. Why is it important to recognise this?

The first thing to recognise is that in contemporary philosophy there *is* an enormous confidence about the analysis of religious belief, a confidence that the analysis shows such beliefs to be meaningless. We have already noted Norman Malcolm's observation that religious belief is regarded in Western academic philosophy with condescension or even contempt.[1] Responding to these remarks, Kai Nielsen says,

> Surely the response of intellectuals to religion is more complex and varied than that, but there is enough truth in this exaggeration and in Malcolm's further remark 'that by and large religion is to university people an alien form of

304

life' to make it an important sociological datum to keep
before our minds when we consider religion. A religious
human being, a person who prays and goes to church and
all that, is something of an anomaly among present day
Western intellectuals and particularly among philosophers.
That form of life does seem very alien to many of us.[2]

In attempting to provide conceptual reminders of the grammar
of religious belief, we have to realise that we are faced by Nielsen's
'important sociological datum'.

The situation we have arrived at, in which religious belief has
come to be alien to many, is a situation with a history. Religious
beliefs, as we noted at the outset of the book, are said to have
failed the tests of rationality. Religious belief is seen as an
aberration of the human mind from which enlightenment should
rescue us. Hume, having shown how an argument from world to
God is logically flawed, bequeathed to the nineteenth and
twentieth centuries the task of explaining how people, despite the
enlightenment at hand, can continue to believe what is irrational.
Philosophy, aided by anthropology and psychoanalysis, was to
be the angel of light which was to bring enlightenment to the
dark recesses of the human mind. The confident tone of the
intellectual partnership is found in the following remarks by E.B.
Tylor:

> To the promoters of what is sound and reformers of what
> is faulty in modern culture, ethnography has double help
> to give. To impress men's minds with a doctrine of
> development will lead them in all honour to their ancestors
> to continue the progressive work of past ages, to continue
> it the more vigorously because light has increased in the
> world, and where barbaric hordes groped blindly, cultured
> men can often move onward with clear view.[3]

The cultured, modern man Tylor refers to is described by
Flannery O'Connor as one who

> recognises spirit in himself but who fails to recognise a being
> outside himself whom he can adore as Creator and Lord;
> consequently he has become his own ultimate concern. He
> says with Swinburne, 'Glory to man in the highest, for he
> is the master of things,' or with Steinbeck, 'In the end was

the word and the word was with man.' For him, man has his own natural spirit of courage and dignity and pride and must consider it a point of honour to be satisfied with this.[4]

Freud too was anxious to show that courage, dignity and pride are not incompatible with seeing through the other-worldly promises of religion:

> And, as for the great necessities of Fate, against which there is no help, they will learn to endure with resignation. Of what use to them is the mirage of wide acres in the moon, whose harvest no one has ever yet seen? As honest smallholders on this earth they will know how to cultivate their plot in such a way that it supports them.[5]

They learn to endure with resignation because they have come to realise, as primitive man did not, that the forces of nature to which they are subject, winds and rains, come when they do, and that no amount of magic will make any difference. When man dispenses with such magical rites as rain dances, he is coming of age, seeing that there is no causal connection between the dances and the coming of the rain.

Despite the fact that many writers, Tylor and Freud included, insisted that primitive people could not be blamed for thinking as they did, inevitably it was hard to keep out a congratulatory element from the claim that they were speaking from an intellectually superior vantage point in human development. This intellectual superiority, however, has been challenged from many directions. It never was very plausible, since the primitives were skilled hunters, farmers, metal-workers. Had they been as ignorant of causal connections as some said they were, they could never have survived. On the other hand, alongside their ordinary purposive activities they perform rituals. How are the rituals related to the other activities? Wittgenstein made the telling observation that rain dances were performed when the rains were due anyway.[6] The dance did not cause the rains to come; it celebrated their coming. When we see the dances as part of a celebratory activity, we no longer speak of confusion. Wittgenstein also gives the following examples: 'Towards morning, when the sun is about to rise, people celebrate rites of the coming of day, but not at night, for then they simply burn lamps.'[7] Again: 'The same savage who, apparently in order to kill his enemy, sticks his knife through a picture of him, really does build his hut of wood and cuts his arrow with skill and not in effigy.'[8] By waiting on the rituals, conceptual clarity rescues us from a condescending misunderstanding.

Yet, contemporary philosophers may well see these conclusions as premature. Because it is quite right to say, as Wittgenstein does, that the primitives are not guilty of ignorance of causal connections, it does not follow that their ritualistic practices cannot be criticised. They can be criticised, it is said, because what the rituals exhibit are not causal mistakes, but conceptual confusions. This view has been argued by John Cook:

> Wittgenstein was going beyond the mere rejection of Frazer's theory. He was offering a theory of his own, a theory to the effect that the primitive magician in the performance of his rites no more intends to help his crops flourish or to harm his enemy than we intend to bring about some effect by kissing the picture of a loved one. But merely finding good reason for rejecting Frazer's theory does not give us a reason for embracing this new theory of Wittgenstein's — unless, of course, we assume that these are the only possibilities from which to choose. Wittgenstein, perhaps, thought that they were the only alternatives and that his own positive theory could therefore be adequately supported by simply finding good reason to dismiss Frazer's.[9]

But does Wittgenstein embrace such a theory? On the contrary he is opposed to *a priori* theorising and in fact recognises the very possibility Cook claims he has missed, namely, that the primitives may be guilty, not of mistakes about causality, but of deep conceptual confusions.[10] For example, Wittgenstein thought the ritual of scapegoat in *Leviticus* a jarring symbolism. The scapegoat is said to carry the sins of the people with it into the wilderness. Here, as Rush Rhees says, ' "carry" seems to mean what it does in "The goat carries on his back the basket in which we put our firewood"; and yet it *cannot* mean that.'[11] But we would not say a mistake is made in the ritual. We would say it is confused. Wittgenstein concludes, 'The scapegoat on which sins are laid and which goes out into the wilderness with them, is a false picture, like all the false pictures of philosophy. Philosophy might be said to purify thought from a misleading mythology.'[12]

The difference between mistakes and confusions in this context may be brought out by the following example. A person who wants to poison another mistakenly buys a harmless potion. His belief that the potion is harmful is false, but it might have been true. But can we say the same when I stick pins in a picture of someone, believing it will harm him? Can we say that sticking pins in the picture might have been effective, but in fact is not? Of course not. We have not the slightest idea of what it could mean to say that sticking pins in the picture could harm someone else. What we have is not a false, but a meaningless belief, and yet people believe it. None of this should surprise us, since we are by no means immune from these confusions ourselves. Although we are not ignorant of causal connections, nevertheless, our superstitions flourish alongside them.

Once we identify the confusion, the next step is to see how it came about. Here are some suggestions from John Beattie's influential book on social anthropology:

> I am not saying that ritual and magical activities are not commonly thought to be causally efficacious; they certainly are. But they are expressive *as well* as being instrumental, and it is this that distinguishes them from strictly empirical, instrumental activity. Indeed often they are believed to be instrumental just because they are expressive; many people think that the word, the *logos*, has its own special power. Often it is believed that to say or even to think something solemnly and emphatically enough is somehow to make it more likely to happen. Even members of modern societies may be frightened or ashamed when they become conscious of hidden wishes for the death or injury of someone they dislike, and may feel guilty when the object of their antipathy is run over by a bus. Belief in the power of words, thoughts and symbols is by no means the monopoly of simpler peoples.[13]

The confusion involved here is not like a mistake *about* anything; about causal connections, for example. What we have is a confusion which springs from a misunderstanding of the logic of our language, a misunderstanding which has a deep hold on us. These misunderstandings give rise to metaphysics. Wittgenstein began an earlier version of his remarks on Frazer by saying, 'I think now that the right thing would be to start my book with remarks on metaphysics as a kind of magic.'[14]

308

The formality of rituals marks them off from the ordinary discourse of daily affairs. On the other hand, there is an affinity between the words and gestures used in ritual and those words and gestures used elsewhere. For example, I may express the wish that someone should come to me by beckoning or calling out to him. When he comes, I may feel this is due to some inherent power in the beckoning or calling; almost as if a power accompanies the gesture or words. When the beckoning by gesture or word expresses a wish in the ritual, we may then feel that since the power is in the beckoning, the condition of fulfilling the wish is given in the inherent power of the beckoning, although the persons or spirits beckoned are absent. In this context, the misunderstandings involved could be called a kind of magical treatment of words — belief in the power of words.[15]

So far from wanting to defend magical or religious rituals against all charges of confusion, as Cook thinks, Wittgenstein is recognising possibilities — and, I emphasise, *possibilities* — of confusion in the rituals, confusion which may still go deep with us.[16] The spirit in which these possibilities are noted by Wittgenstein is very different, however, from the attitude to religion we find among most contemporary philosophers. The *a priorism* is not his, but theirs, since they want to say that *all* forms of magic and religion are confused. Not content with saying that conceptual confusion *may* be present, they say that they are *necessarily* present. How does this come about? E.E. Evans-Pritchard said of the anthropologist:

> As I understand the matter, there is no possibility of his *knowing* whether the spiritual beings of primitive religions or of any others have any existence or not, and since this is the case he cannot take the question into consideration. The beliefs are for him sociological facts, not theological facts, and his sole concern is with their relation to each other and to other social facts ... The validity of the belief lies in the domain of what may be broadly designated the philosophy of religion.[17]

For most contemporary philosophers, however, the reference to philosophy simply postpones the issue. Philosophy shows that religion necessarily involves metaphysics. But metaphysics, it is argued, is not a theory *about* anything. On the contrary it is itself the product of deep confusions about the logic of our language.

Cook points out that Evans-Pritchard argues that because gods, ancestral spirits, etc., 'if they exist, have a mode of being that is not open to empirical investigation ... anthropologists must leave their existence an open question'. Cook replies:

> This seems like an eminently sensible view to take — so long as it assumed that religious beliefs are either true or false, i.e. that either there are or there are not ancestral spirits who deserve human consideration, that either reincarnation occurs or it does not occur, etc. Yet this is not how philosophers generally see the matter. Take the matter of disembodied existence after death. Philosophers nowadays do not regard this as an obviously possible state of affairs which may or may not occur. On the contrary, viewed philosophically the issue is whether this idea makes any sense at all, and at least most philosophers think it has been shown that the idea does not make sense. Extrapolating from this example, then, what I am suggesting is that if we think carefully about gods and spirits and so on, we may find that these ideas are in some way confused, unintelligible. If they are, then of course there is no possibility that gods and spirits exist.[18]

Notice that Cook is able to speak confidently of 'how philosophers generally see the matter', 'philosophers nowadays', and of what 'at least most philosophers think'. I said that *within* the practice of the philosophy of religion, animistic modes of argument prevail; religious beliefs are true or false, reasonable or unreasonable hypotheses. What has to be said, however, is that the majority of philosophers pay little, if any, attention to religious beliefs, believing that the conceptual confusions they necessarily exhibit have been exposed long ago.

The first reason, then, why a philosopher who seeks to give perspicuous representations cannot take his audience for granted is the enormous confidence of many philosophers in thinking that the meaninglessness of religious belief has been amply demonstrated. Second, however, the difficulty of finding a receptive audience has to do with the price many philosophers would have to pay to have their confidence shaken. I believe this price has much to do with the anger and resentment which has greeted the conceptual reminders which Wittgenstein and others have presented; an anger and resentment rare, even in philosophy.

In order to trace some of the sources of this anger, and the kind of change which would have to take place in the philosophers I have in mind were the conceptual reminders to be accepted, I shall compare the philosophical task of providing these reminders with the task of providing religious reminders in literature.

Like the philosopher of religion, Flannery O'Connor, as a Catholic writer, faced the problem of how to convey a religious perspective in literature in a pervasively secular American culture. Just as many philosophers regard religious belief as a cultural divergence needing rational enlightenment, so many in the North in the 1960s regarded the South with its racial problems and evangelical religion as being in the grip of irrationality. Robert Coles observed of Flannery O'Connor and her South:

> Surely neither she, nor other Georgia writers, nor the black rural field hands of the state, have ever had much say in the matter of what in this nation is and is not considered 'appropriate,' 'seemly,' 'desirable,' let alone 'grotesque.' The standards come from elsewhere.[19]

Yet, there were voices raised in Georgia which refused to accept the North's version of what was happening. Here is one such voice, which accuses the Northern critics of lacking the very virtues in terms of which they claimed to be making their criticisms. The speaker insists that the distinction between North and South was not a distinction between purity and impurity:

> You think the coloured people don't know who's here to stay, and who's just passing through — looking for a *cause* ... to find people to look down on, and people who will look up to them as if each and every one of them was Jesus Christ Himself. So they say to each other: let's go South and have us a damn good time down there, with all those dumb crackers. There will come a day when the shoe will be on the other foot, and all the trouble we have down here won't look so bad, when you see what's going on up there. And when that day comes, I'll promise you something: no one from Georgia is going to go up there, pointing his finger at people, and telling them they're no good, and they're ignorant, and they have to change by federal law, or else. It's not our way, down here, to go poking into the business of others, so we can have our fun. If these people would

take themselves to church, other than to organize integration rallies, while they're down here staying among us, they might learn something — about pride, the worst sin of all. But they'd laugh if I went and told them that — because I didn't go to college.[20]

We can see why the reminder about pride from the South would be hard to accept. To accept it would be to admit to the very sin one was accusing others of so confidently. Flannery O'Connor's reminders in her stories had a similar effect. They outraged her critics because they took the form of using the secularist's perspective as a testimony to the reality of the religion it attacked. She realised that in a pervasively secular culture she could not give her reminders in a straightforward way. Flannery O'Connor said that she, 'instead of reflecting the image at the heart of things ... has only reflected our broken condition and, through it, the face of the devil we are possessed by. This is a modest achievement, but perhaps a necessary one.'[21] In the Georgian censure of Northern attitudes, the sting came, as we saw, in the location of pride and condescension in the very attitudes which prided themselves on being those of concern and fellow-feeling. So in Flannery O'Connor's short stories, the very age which prides itself on freedom from superstitions such as belief in the devil, is accused of demon possession. Flannery O'Connor observes, 'Probably the devil plays the greatest role in the production of that fiction from which he himself is absent as an actor.'[22] These considerations are embodied in Flannery O'Connor's short story, 'The Lame Shall Enter First'.

In the story, Sheppard, a part-time social worker, befriends a lame delinquent called Johnson. He compares his own son, Norton, unfavourably with him. Norton's mother has died, but Sheppard believes his son's grief is excessive, and that instead of moping he should build for the future. Sheppard sees more spirit in the delinquent, despite all his disadvantages. Johnson is brought into the house. Sheppard is appalled to find that the delinquent attributes his deviance to the fact that he is in the Devil's power. He promises to explain his devil to him. Johnson is bought a telescope to encourage his interest in astronomy. Yet, when Johnson is alone with Norton he reveals his contempt for the attention of the social worker, ' "God, kid," Johnson said in a cracked voice, "how do you stand it?" His face was stiff with outrage. "He thinks he's Jesus Christ." '[23] He feeds the young son with crude pictures of heaven and hell. He tells him that if his mother was a good woman she is in heaven, but that he would have to die to reach her. Norton is convinced that through the telescope he can see his mother waving at him. Sheppard tells him that all he can see are star clusters, but to no avail. The story ends with Sheppard's discovery that the delinquent has misled him all along; has used his trust as a cover for committing further crimes. Johnson is led away compounding lies and it is at this point that revelation comes to Sheppard:

> 'I have nothing to reproach myself with,' he began again. 'I did more for him that I did for my own child.' He heard his voice as if it were the voice of his accuser. He repeated the sentence silently.
> Slowly his face drained of colour. It became almost grey beneath the white halo of his hair. The sentence echoed in his mind, each syllable like a dull blow ... He had stuffed his own emptiness with good works like a glutton. He had ignored his own child to feed his vision of himself. He saw the clear-eyed Devil, the sounder of hearts, leering at him from the eyes of Johnson...[24]

He rushes back to his son, to ask for his forgiveness, to tell him he loved him. He finds him in the attic: 'The tripod had fallen and the telescope lay on the floor. A few feet over it, the child hung in the jungle of shadows, just below the beam from which he had launched his flight into space.'[25]

The social worker had promised to explain away Johnson's devil. Flannery O'Connor's reminder shows how, from a religious perspective, the social worker's confidence in his explanatory categories is an aspect of the Devil's victory. Johnson wanted to be caught by the police. When asked why he replies, referring to the social worker, 'To show up that big tin Jesus... He thinks he's God. I'd rather be in the reformatory than in his house. I'd rather be in the pen! The Devil has him in his power.'[26] The irony is that the social worker is seen as possessed by the very Devil he set out to explain away.

Philosophers may call attention to the kind of criticism from Georgia I quoted or to a story from Flannery O'Connor, as I have done, in order to show that there are perspectives from which matters can be seen in ways which the secular rationalist cannot account for. While the secularist may not embrace these

313

perspectives, he cannot explain them away, as he thinks, in terms of their irrationality. Yet, that is not my main reason for using these examples. I have used them to show how the moral criticism and Flannery O'Connor's story, in their different ways, accuse certain attitudes of possessing a character they prided themselves on being free of. This is why both caused so much anger and controversy. It is in this respect that they throw light on the earlier question we posed: why should the reminders of the philosopher of religion cause so much agitation among those who deny that religious beliefs can mean anything? Is it not because they too, if accepted, would involve the philosophical sceptic in recognising that he was possessed by that very thing he prided himself on being free of ? While we do not object to saying that we are blind to science, we do object to saying that we are blind to religion. Why? We must remember that for many philosophy is supposed to be an angel of light ministering to the darkness of superstition. But in being reminded of the character of certain religious beliefs, philosophers are being asked to accept that they may be in the grip of the very superstition they take themselves to be attacking. Consider the following gloss given by Tylor on the ritual among the Seminoles of Florida of holding a newborn infant over a mother's face to receive her parting breath if she was dying after childbirth. Speaking of the notion of the soul involved in the ritual he says,

> It is a thin unsubstantial human image, in its nature a sort of vapour, film or shadow; the cause of life and thought in the individual it animates; independently possessing the personal consciousness and volition of its corporeal owner, past or present; capable of leaving the body far behind to flash swiftly from place to place; mostly impalpable and invisible, yet also manifesting physical power, and especially appearing to man waking or asleep as a phantasm separate from the body of which it bears the likeness; able to enter into, possess, and act in the bodies of other men, of animals, and even of things.[27]

Commenting on Tylor's conception of the soul I said:

> Tylor thinks that the meaning of his examples are unequivocal and that it is accounted for in his analysis. As a matter of fact, his analysis is more influenced by a

314

philosophical dualism concerning soul and body than by the examples under consideration ... What Tylor fails to take account of is the significance these gestures have in the relationship between a dying mother and the child she is giving birth to ... A mother has given her life for her child and this is expressed in the ritual by the child receiving her parting breath. What more needs to be said? ... these acts are not based on hypotheses or opinions concerning strange invisible substances which, by mysterious means, are transferred from one person to another. On the contrary, the gestures are expressions of something. What they express can be indicated in the ways we have just noted. Ironically, it is Tylor, the rational critic, who is in the grip of the very conception of the soul he sets out to criticise. It is precisely because for him there would have to be a strange substance called the soul in order for the notion to have any meaning that he finds the examples he discusses unintelligible. It is his own positivistic conception of the soul which prevents him from appreciating what the notion may mean in its natural setting.[28]

We can appreciate why a philosopher would find it hard to accept these criticisms. He is accused of being in the grip of the very superstition he prides himself on exposing. In the same way it is a shock to hear Wittgenstein saying, 'Frazer is much more savage than most of his savages, for these savages will not be so far from any understanding of spiritual matters as an Englishman of the twentieth century. His explanation of the primitive observances are much cruder than the sense of the observances themselves.'[29] The words are a shock because, once again, the rational enquirer is said to be possessed by the very savagery and crudity he claims to be exposing. Little wonder, then, that certain philosophical reminders have aroused controversy among philosophical critics, for in accepting the reminders it is as though they were accepting a philosophical version of Matthew's admonition, 'If therefore the light that is in thee be darkness, how great is that darkness!',[30] which might be rendered, 'If therefore your very conception of rationality is confused, how great is the confusion!'

Yet, having noted two reasons why a philosopher of religion cannot take his audience for granted, namely, the pervasive confidence among philosophers that they have demonstrated the meaninglessness of religious belief, and the price they would have to pay if that confidence is shaken, our story is not quite over. There are other features of *any* audience which a philosopher of religion addresses which must be taken into account. In attempting to give perspicuous representations of religious belief I am asking philosophers to reopen a road on which they have put a 'no through road' sign. I have said that their irritation at this will be compounded by the fact that they are not being told that they have not investigated the road on which they have chosen to travel thoroughly enough. Rather, they are told that they should not have turned down that road in the first place. Yet the irritation may go deeper. Philosophers may not appreciate the force of conceptual reminders presented to them. This would, then, be not a matter of misunderstanding, but of *failure to understand*. This is a feature which will be present in any audience which is unsympathetic to religious belief. For philosophers to accept *this* possibility, would be to recognise not simply that they have turned down a wrong road, but that there is a road, a flourishing neighbourhood even, which they know little about. We cannot take for granted that that ignorance can be rectified in all cases, although it is not for us to say that it is impossible in any given case. This possibility leads to the third and fourth reasons why a philosopher of religion cannot take his audience for granted.

The third reason has to do with the character of the actual audience being addressed today. Flannery O'Connor describes an audience with which the philosopher is also faced: 'My audience are the people who think God is dead. At least these are the people I am conscious of writing for.'[31] She describes the difficulties with which she is faced as follows:

> I don't believe that our present society is one whose basic beliefs are religious, except in the South.[32] In any case, you can't have effective allegory in times when people are swept this way and that by momentary convictions, because everyone will read it differently. You can't indicate moral values when morality changes with what is being done, because there is no accepted basis of judgement.[33]

What did she think she had to do as a result?

The novelist with Christian concerns will find in modern

life distortions which are repugnant to him, and his problem will be to make these appear as distortions to an audience which is used to seeing them as natural; and he may well be forced to take ever more violent means to get his vision across to his hostile audience. When you can assume that your audience holds the same beliefs as you do, you can relax a little and use more normal means of talking to it; when you have to assume that it does not then you have to make your vision apparent by shock — to the hard of hearing you shout, and for the almost-blind you draw large and startling figures.[34]

But she was under no illusions about the failure rate among her audience even when she employed such distortions. Critics accused her of wallowing in the grotesque. Yet her use of distortion is like Kafka's. She says of his *Metamorphosis*, 'a story about a man who wakes up one morning to find that he has turned into a cockroach overnight, while not discarding his human nature ... The truth is not distorted here, but rather, a certain distortion is used to get at the truth.'[35] But many critics failed to see what kind of truths she was talking about. Looking at what they had said about one of her stories concerning the action of grace in human life she responded, 'The story has been called grotesque, but I prefer to call it literal.'[36]

At this point, a comparison can be made with similar critical responses to what I have endeavoured to say in the philosophy of religion. My critics want to face me with the following choice: either the word 'God' refers to a fact or it is a metaphorical use of language. Two of my critics, J.L. Mackie and T.A. Roberts, recognise that, on the one hand, I deny that the word 'God' refers to an object, and that, on the other hand, I deny that 'God' is a metaphorical use of language. Given the exclusive choice with which they think I am faced, it is little wonder that neither Mackie nor Roberts can make much of my positive remarks concerning the word 'God'. Of course, what we need to do is to reject the simple choice which Mackie and Roberts wish to impose on us.

In *The Concept of Prayer, Faith and Philosophical Enquiry*, and *Death and Immortality* I gave many examples of the use of the word 'God'. Mackie and Roberts do not consider these, but confine themselves to *Religion Without Explanation*. More particularly, they concentrate on the belief that God watches over us all the time and that there is a Last Judgement at the end of time. Mackie and Roberts want to confront us with the same exclusive choice once again: either the language has literal meaning, one which refers to objects, facts, or the language is metaphorical. I had said of belief in the Last Judgement:

> One is taught about a day of judgement, not as just one more matter of fact which is to occur in the future. One is told that it is necessary, unavoidable, something that confronts us all ... This is not a version of the belief that you will be caught out in the end. On the contrary, it gets its force from the conviction that one is known for what one is all the time ... The word 'God' has its sense in this context from this conviction of a necessary scrutiny of love and goodness, a scrutiny unlike that of any human agency since any idea of its being mistaken or misinformed is ruled out.[37]

Mackie responds to these remarks as follows:

> This sounds impressive, but what exactly is Phillips saying? Perhaps the talk about an ultimate judgement should be taken as a metaphor which represents rather a continuous scrutiny. But if one is known continuously for what one is, one must be so known by someone or something. If it is not known by any (other) human agency, it must be either oneself or some supernatural being. If Phillips means that the content of the conviction is literally true, then he must after all defend the literal, objective, existence of a god or something like a god. If instead he means that what one is known by is oneself, or a part of oneself, then his view is substantially identical with (those who hold) that religious statements represent and support moral sentiments and resolves, but they are only metaphorically true.[38]

Roberts has great admiration for Mackie's response and echoes it in his own remarks:

> If a theologian says that his belief is literally true, then Phillips responds by saying that he has fallen into superstition in believing that an assertion like 'God exists' is a factual assertion. If a philosopher (for example, Braithwaite) says that religious assertions are not literally true and that their function is to express a moral conviction

along with a resolution to live a certain kind of life, then Phillips says 'he has reduced religion to something which lacks some of the fundamental characteristics of religious beliefs'. To quote Mackie's words, 'Phillips's talk about a different grammar of "truth" is a vain attempt to evade this simple but inescapable dilemma.' The dilemma Phillips tries to avoid is this: Either religious assertions are factually true or they are not; if they are not factually true, then they are not true except in some metaphorical sense.[39]

In reading Mackie and Roberts, the reader may be forgiven for gaining the impression that I have failed to recognise or sought to avoid the dilemma with which they say I am confronted. As a matter of fact I discuss the issue quite explicitly in relation to Braithwaite's views:

> The fundamental confusion in Braithwaite's argument can be found in the choice with which he takes himself to be confronted. If we take the religious belief in a last judgement as our example, Braithwaite thinks that it must either be construed as an empirical proposition, such that believing in it is to predict that an event of a certain kind is going to take place some time in the future, or the story of a last judgement must be seen as a psychological aid to moral endeavour, the question of whether one believes in the truth of the story being unimportant.[40]

Is not this, word for word, more or less, the 'dilemma' which Mackie and Roberts wish to bring to my attention? They share Braithwaite's confusion in thinking that the dilemma must be accepted on its own terms. All three see the choice as simple because they simplify epistemological possibilities. In discussing the 'dilemma' I rejected the exclusive alternatives it seeks to impose on us. 'In reacting to these exclusive alternatives most contemporary philosophers of religion call Braithwaite a reductionist because he does not stress the first alternative.'[41] But, in my opinion, Braithwaite did not take the language of religion seriously enough in his second alternative. In saying that religious stories give psychological aid to moral endeavour, Braithwaite characterises the relation between moral endeavour and the religious stories as an external one. As far as his analysis is concerned, the same psychological help could be given to the same moral endeavour by a different story. As I said, 'For Braithwaite, the content of one's moral intentions is quite independent of the religious stories. The stories simply provide psychological aid for these intentions.'[42] But there is another possibility I mentioned which never suggested itself to Braithwaite or Roberts:

> He never considers the possibility that the religious belief is itself the expression of a moral vision ... The language is not contingently related to the believer's conduct as a psychological aid to it. On the contrary, it is internally related to it in that it is in terms of this language that the believer's conduct is to be understood. It is a language which in itself gives the believer certain possibilities in which to live and judge this life. Hence the kind of necessity connected with religious beliefs. They are certainly not hypotheses. It is even misleading to call them propositions. Though the term has dangers of its own, to avoid the associations of the above terms it would be better to call the religious beliefs dogmas: the absolutes of faith.[43]

I have already mentioned the possibilities connected with the Christian conception of the Last Judgement, but in *Religion Without Explanation* I also referred to the notion of an eternal pact between lovers in death and to the very different conception of eternity we find in the notion of Valhalla. In all these examples we have neither the language of facts nor reference to external help to some prescriptive policy for action. From my treatment of them it can be seen that I do not ignore or evade the 'dilemma' with which Mackie and Roberts seek to confront me. On the contrary, the remarkable feature of Roberts's paper is that he ignores the answer I give to it. Mackie does not ignore the answer. He completely misunderstands it in equating what I mean by internal relations with psychological aid or superstition.[44] In order to understand the ignoring or misunderstanding of my response to the 'dilemma' in which they think I am caught, we need a closer look at some of their philosophical assumptions.

Let us remind ourselves of Roberts's words: 'The dilemma Phillips tries to avoid is this: Either religious assertions are factually true or they are not; if they are not factually true, then they are not true except in some metaphorical sense.' Consider the existence of God in this context. Mackie and Roberts tend to speak of his existence as something literal, factual and objective. Mackie says 'Phillips has given us no grounds for denying that "the God of religion" is a possible subject of simple truth or falsehood: in consequence what he offers is either disguised atheism or unsupported theism — since he declines to support its factual claims — or else an unresolved tension between the two.'[45] Is this true? I had referred to Wittgenstein's remarks on the logical status of the word 'God': 'The word "God" is amongst the earliest learnt — pictures and catechisms, etc. But not the same consequences as with pictures of aunts. I wasn't shown [that which the picture pictured].'[46] Wittgenstein says that he can show Moore the pictures of plants: 'There is a technique of comparison between picture and plant.'[47] If someone were only to see the picture of plants he would be justified in saying, 'I will not believe that the plants exist unless I see them.' But what if someone, on hearing worshippers praise the Creator of heaven and earth, asks to see the object referred to in their worship? Would not this reveal a massive misunderstanding on his part? But note Mackie's equally revealing question, 'To talk of "God", Phillips claims, is not to refer to an individual, an object. But then what is it?'[48] The irony is, of course, that if, *per impossibile,* any object *were* said to correspond to the word 'God', one thing would be certain, that object would not be God. For similar reasons, no actual dining hall could be Valhalla. Mackie and Roberts ask for factual verification, but no such verification could be verification of the reality of God. As John Wisdom has said,

> Now what would it be like to see God? Suppose some seer were to see, imagine we all saw, move upwards from the sea to the sky some prodigious figure which declared in dreadful tones the moral law or prophesied most truly — our fate. Would this be to see God? Wouldn't it just be a phenomenon which later we were able to explain or not able to explain, but in neither case the proof of a living God.[49]

Neither Mackie nor Roberts understand what Norman Malcolm was trying to do in relation to Anselm's proof, namely, to show that Anselm had realised that God is not an object among objects, not something that can come to be and pass away. Mackie and Roberts, in speaking of the factual character of God's existence, mislocate the logic of the word 'God'.

But what of Mackie's and Roberts's conception of the distinction between the literal and the metaphorical? It is evident that the literal and the factual are synonymous for them. Such an equivalence is a gross over-simplification, nowhere more so than in relation to religious belief. Consider the following examples from the Psalms to which O.K. Bouwsma draws our attention:

Great is Jehovah and *greatly* to be praised... (*Ps.* 48)

Jehovah reigneth; let the people tremble;
He sitteth above the cherubim;
Let the earth be moved.
Jehovah is great in Zion. (*Ps* .99)

Bless Jehovah, O my soul,
O Jehovah, My God, thou art very great. (*Ps.* 104)

Great is Jehovah and *greatly* to be praised.
And his *greatness* is unsearchable. (*Ps.* 145)[50]

What is the primary use of these sentences? According to Mackie and Roberts I have to choose between the factual and the metaphorical. For Mackie and Roberts, if we say that God's greatness is literal or that his height is literal, then they are factual matters. It would be appropriate to ask how great or high God is. What exactly are the measurements? I assume that neither Mackie nor Roberts would want to answer such questions. Therefore, it seems that we do not have factual language here. But what of the suggestion that what we have here is an instance of metaphorical language? Neither Mackie nor Roberts are relying on a narrow, technical use of the term 'metaphorical'. Notice how Roberts puts the matter with respect to religious beliefs: 'if they are not factually true, then they are not true except *in some metaphorical sense.*'[51] It is likely, therefore, that they would say that if 'Great is our God above all gods' is not factually true, it can only be true in some idiomatic sense. But the sense cannot be that found in idioms. Stanley Cavell has shown that idioms, if taken factually, *could* be true or false.[52] Referring to the idioms, 'He fell flat on his face' and 'I sent him away with a flea in his ear', Cavell says, 'it is fair to say that their words literally say something that is quite false; something, that is, which could easily, though maybe comically, be imagined to be true.'[53] But in the case of 'Great is our God above all gods', the so-called factual component yields nonsense. Therefore we do not have an instance of an idiomatic use of language here.

But what if we take Mackie and Roberts to be referring to 'metaphor' in a narrow, technical sense? Metaphors do not behave like idioms. As Cavell says, 'to say that Juliet is the sun is not to say something false; it is, at best, wildly false, and that is not being just false. This is part of the fact that if we are to suggest that what the metaphor says is true, we shall have to say it is wildly true — mythically or magically or primitively true.'[54] So since there is this difference, with respect to factual truth, between idioms and metaphors, showing that 'truth' is not used idiomatically in religious beliefs is not to show that it is not used metaphorically.

But even if religious language *were* characteristically metaphorical (as distinct from including metaphors on specific occasions), neither Mackie nor Roberts could have done justice to metaphors. Take 'Juliet is the sun'. Here you can offer a paraphrase if someone does not get the point, but you normally add 'and so on'. The 'and so on', as Cavell says, registers what William Empson calls the 'pregnancy' of metaphors. We wouldn't want to replace the metaphor with the paraphrase. But if we say that the metaphor expresses a truth we do not mean that the truth it expresses is a kind of substandard 'truth'. What is expressed is the truth *in* the metaphor. To think otherwise would be like thinking that the only truth which a distortion can contain, is a distorted truth. If Mackie and Roberts think that only empirical, factual statements can be true, or convey truths, that is their problem.

But the primary form of religious language is not metaphorical language. As Cavell says, 'To give the paraphrase, to understand the metaphor, I must understand the ordinary or dictionary meaning of the words it contains, *and* understand that they are not being used there in their ordinary way.'[55] With religious expressions it is different. Cavell considers the expressions, 'a man stands before God' and 'This night shall thy soul be required of thee'. He says that Kierkegaard is right in not calling such uses metaphorical. Cavell argues

'Speaking metaphorically' is a matter of speaking in certain ways using a definite form of language for some purpose; 'speaking religiously' is not accomplished by using a given form, or set of forms, of words, and is not done for any further purpose: it is to speak from a particular perspective, as it were to mean anything you say in a special way. To understand a metaphor you must be able to interpret it; to understand an utterance religiously you have to be able to share its perspective.[56]

A philosopher can understand that without himself sharing the perspective. But he cannot understand that without understanding, as Cavell says, that

> The religious is a Kierkegaardian Stage of life; and I suggest that it should be thought of as a Wittgensteinian form of life.[57] There seems no reason not to believe that, as a given person may never occupy this stage, so a given age, and all future ages, may as a whole not occupy it — that the form will be lost from men's lives altogether.[58]

But religious expressions have not been lost yet. In the Psalms we have examples of a primary use of religious language. *Now, if we want to call primary use a literal use, then the believers are saying something they want to say is literally true, without its being either factual or metaphorical.* Referring to my analysis Mackie says, 'But now the firm ground beneath our feet has disappeared and we are struggling helplessly in a bog ... To speak of a different grammar of "truth" is to demand a licence for evasion and double-talk.'[59] Roberts approves of this reaction. What we have seen, however, is that what needs questioning is their philosophical confidence that they were standing on firm ground in the first place. Instead of determining, without looking at human practices, what that firm ground has to consist in, they ought to look at the concepts at work in those practices. No more licence is demanded than that required for a clear elucidation of the primary uses of language in these diverse practices.

When we bring examples of the primary use of language in religion to Mackie's attention, he fails to appreciate them. For him, to say that God exists is to say that an object exists. If you think like Mackie, you will not understand why, if you spit in God's face, you can't miss. Wittgenstein says, 'The way you use the word "God" does not show *whom* you mean — but rather, what you mean.'[60] Think how different it would be if Wittgenstein had written 'but rather, *what* you mean.'[61]

Mackie reacts in similar ways when he considers religious art. Mackie says, 'a somewhat old-fashioned Christian may believe, literally, that there will be a last judgement. He need not, indeed, suppose that there will be such a scene as that depicted by Michelangelo on the wall of the Sistine Chapel ... I am saying only that talk about a last judgement *can* be understood literally.'[62] The main deficiency in these remarks is not lack of analysis, but lack of imagination. To say that God is in a picture is not to say that it is a picture of God. But for Mackie and Roberts there is one simple standard conception of truth and everything else is a deviation from it, an idiomatic or metaphorical use of truth. Because it may well share this simple conception, a modern audience too may feel helpless in trying to come to grips with religious beliefs. They too have *a priori* conceptions of what 'truth' must amount to; conceptions arrived at without waiting on religious beliefs. Thus a modern audience is unlikely to be a sympathetic audience.

There is a fourth reason why we may think all our elucidations of human practices should be clear to everyone given that we have sufficient analytic ability. We are, after all, in philosophy, striving for clarity concerning the concepts we employ. If we pay attention to concept-formation, to the various primitive reactions in which such concepts are grounded, what stands in the way of our appreciation of them? This confident expectation overlooks a very important fact: although all concepts are public, this does not mean that they are universal; common reactions are not universal reactions. A language which we share is not a language we share with everyone. This fact has important consequences for the practice of philosophy. Let us see how this comes about.

Wittgenstein said, 'Language does not emerge from reasoning.'[63] We do not reason our way to our primitive reactions concerning pain, colours, sounds. At later, more refined stages, reasons and discriminations become appropriate. Such refinements, however, are dependent on the brute fact that we react as we do — jump with fright, call colours light or dark, call sounds loud or quiet, cry out in pain or express concern or shock at the pain of others. We do not agree to react in these ways. Rather, the fact that we agree shows itself *in* these reactions. The possibility of the development of the concepts concerned is rooted in such reactions. Primitive reactions play a central role too in enquiries where, we are inclined to think, the interest must emerge from intellectual reflection and experimentation. We think this must apply to our interest in causal connections. But Malcolm asks us to consider the following example: 'Suppose that a child runs into another child, knocking him down ... The child would not be doubting or wondering what made him fall. He would not want to observe what happens in other cases. Nor would he be said to *assume* that in similar cases the same thing occurs.'[64] Wittgenstein remarks,

> There is a reaction which can be called 'reacting to the cause' — We also speak of 'tracing the cause', a simple case would be, say, following a string to see who is pulling it. If I then find him — how did I know that he, his pulling, is the cause of the string's moving? Do I establish this by a series of experiments?[65]

In calling our attention to primitive reactions, Wittgenstein is opposing the rationalistic view of language which suggests that language is the result of intellectual reflection. There is a striking similarity between what he has to say and remarks by Weil on concept-formation. She says

> The very nature of the relationship between ourselves and what is external to us, a relationship which consists in a reaction, a reflex, is our perception of the external world. Perception of nature, pure and simple, is a sort of dance;[66] it is this dance that makes perception possible for us.

Peter Winch comments:

> Simone Weil's account, like Wittgenstein's, achieves this by making the notion of *action* central. Action is conceived, in the first instance, as a series of bodily movements having a certain determinate temporal order. In its primitive form action is quite unreflective. Human beings, and other animate creatures, naturally react in characteristic ways to objects in their environments. They salivate in the presence of food and eat it; this already effects a rudimentary classification which doesn't have to be based on any reflection between 'food' and 'not food'. Our eyes scan objects and connect with other characteristic movements of our bodies, we sniff things (or sometimes hold our noses), we exhibit subtly different reactions to things we put into

our mouths — corresponding to such tastes as 'sour', 'sweet', 'salty', etc. — and so on. The reactions are developed and refined as we mature; and some of these refinements and developments are responses to training by other human beings around us. A staircase is something to be climbed, a chair is something to be sat in: compare Wittgenstein's remark: 'It is part of the grammar of the word "chair" that this is what we call "to sit in a chair".'[67] As Simone Weil expresses it: 'everything that we see suggests some kind of movement'[68].[69]

Speaking of these primitive reactions, Wittgenstein says,

> The origin and the primitive form of the language-game is a reaction; only from this can the more complicated forms grow.
> Language — I want to say — is a refinement; 'in the beginning was the deed'.[70]

Wittgenstein and Weil are saying: in the beginning was the dance. Language concerning fear, pain, surprise, causation and perception develops from primitive reactions, the dance of the body; it is hardly surprising, then, that such reactions should be of central importance in magical and religious practices.

These practices may not be appreciated because people are alive to the possibilities of confusion in them. But what we have here are possible confusions, not necessary confusions. The same is true of the other confusions about the logic of our language which may mislead us. Although the language of wishing or expectation may mislead us, so that we think that what is wished for is somehow in the wish and can make it come true, Wittgenstein did *not* conclude that the language in which wishes are expressed needs revising. Rush Rhees emphasises,

> Wittgenstein would not have said there need be anything mistaken in our using the different forms of expression: 'I am expecting him', 'I am expecting him to come', and 'I expect that he will come'. He would not have said that only the second of these expresses correctly what the fulfilment of my expectation would be. If you asked 'What are you waiting for?' and I answered 'I'm waiting for my brother', there would be nothing inaccurate or inadequate in this;

and Wittgenstein would not have said, 'what you *really* mean
is you are waiting for your brother to come'.[71]

We cannot say, simply by looking at a form of words, whether
these words are going to be confused or not. What we need is not
to look at the sentence, but at what we do with it. The same
lesson must be applied to the language of magic and religion. We
cannot say *a priori* simply by looking at the language of curses,
prayers and sacrifices, that it leads to confusion. Where rituals
express a wish, then, to know in what sense the ritual acts out
the wish, we would have to take account of the role played by
the ritual in the details of the lives of the people who celebrate
it. As elsewhere, to see whether the 'acting out' is confused or
not, we must not think — impose our *a priori* assumptions — but
look.

When we follow this good philosophical advice in relation to
magic and religion, we see possibilities come to light which we
are tempted to ignore. We may ignore them because we are not
alive to them as possibilities. Let us think again of sticking pins
in a picture as the expression of a wish. We have already seen
the possibilities of confusion the 'acting out' of the wish may
involve, but are these the only possibilities? Let us consider a
version of sticking pins in an effigy put forward by my colleague,
H.O. Mounce. He asks us to imagine someone who has drawn
an excellent likeness of one's mother asking one to stick a pin in
the picture, taking special care to aim at one of the eyes. Mounce
comments, 'There is hardly anyone, I suppose, who would not
find it very difficult to comply with this request. This reaction ...
so far as I can see, is neither rational nor irrational; it is just the
way most people would happen to react.'[72] Mounce does not tell
us what he thinks of this reaction. He does not consider the
possibility of its being a primitive moral reaction. This is
important, since it might be vital in determining how one reads
the acting out of the fulfilment of the wish. This is how Mounce
does in fact continue to unfold the example:

> Suppose, however, that one does comply with the request
> and then discovers, a short time later, that one's mother
> has developed an affliction in the eye and is in danger of
> going blind. I wonder how many people would resist the
> feeling, if only momentarily, that there was some connection

between the two events. But this belief ... is just as absurd as anything held by the Azande.[73]

By 'some connection' Mounce means some causal connection, but we cannot assume that the 'acting out' must take this form. When I discussed Mounce's example with a class of forty students,[74] fifteen of them said that they would have no difficulty in sticking pins in the picture, and that if they did, they would feel no guilt if the mother were visited later with the affliction. 'It's only a picture,' they said, 'how can it have anything to do with it?' When asked to elaborate, they said that there was no causal connection between the two events. The others in the class said they could not stick pins in the picture, and that if they did, they would feel guilty if the affliction developed. For them there would be a connection between the two events. The fifteen were surprised to discover, however, that by some connection, the others did *not* mean some causal connection. In discussion it emerged that what they meant was something like this: they felt that sticking pins in the picture reduces serious possibilities to a game; it plays around with things. When the affliction occurs, an internal relation between the 'playing around' and the event makes the guilt understandable. What this elucidation shows, however, is not that people refused to stick in the pins as a *consequence* of such beliefs, but that primitive moral responses occur and that people, if asked to reflect on them, may reply in this way.

For the fifteen students, no causal connection meant no connection at all. For some of them, the reactions of the others served as reminders of possibilities they had not thought of. But what I want to emphasise is that the others could still make nothing of those responses. Shall we say that they misunderstood? Not if this means misunderstanding the logic of the language. The language does not get off the ground with them. *They fail to understand, but they do not misunderstand.*[75] They cannot take the reactions in the right spirit. This is a constant problem for the philosopher of religion's task of providing reminders to achieve clarity.

Think again of Beattie's examples of contemporary beliefs in the power of words. He says that even we, let alone primitives, feel frightened or ashamed at hidden wishes for someone's injury or death, and feel guilty if the event wished for occurs. But need such reactions lead us into confusions? Only if the injury or death is seen as a *consequence* of the wish. Think again of what the wish is for — the injury or death of someone else. Here, what is longed for is expressed in the portrayal of it, as may be the case with sticking pins in an effigy, and the 'tendency to confuse what belongs to the symbolism with what is expressed in the symbolism', to which Beattie refers, need not be present. The wish shows something about me. In that sense, I have my wish in the expression of it. Think of Wittgenstein's remark, 'The description (Darstellung) of a wish is, eo ipso, the description of its fulfilment.'[76] Rhees comments, 'If I translate *'Darstellung'* roughly in the phrases: "portrayal of my wish ... portrayal of that which would satisfy my wish", then this second phrase is not the same as, "portraying the *satisfaction* of my wish" or "portraying the arrival of what I wish for".'[77] When, however, what I have wished for is satisfied, does arrive, my guilt, if guilt there be, can be understood in terms of the internal relation between my wish, the wish which frightens me or makes me feel ashamed, and the actual occurrence of what I had wished for. Such reactions, free of the confusions Beattie refers to, are as common among ourselves as they are among primitives. *That* is a reminder we stand in need of. But we *also* need reminding that some will fail to understand such reactions; fail to see any sense in them. So giving religious primitive reactions and subsequent concept-formation their proper place in our reflections depends on more than not being misled by the logic of our language. It depends, more fundamentally, on the spirit in which we are able to respond to the language in question.

We have seen four reasons why a contemporary philosopher of religion, seeking to give a perspicuous representation of religious beliefs, cannot take his audience for granted. First, the confidence of philosophers in thinking that they have shown religious belief to be meaningless. Second, the high price such philosophers would have to pay if this confidence were undermined. They would have to admit to being in the grip of the very superstitions they took themselves to be attacking. Third, the secular character of the modern audience which makes it unsympathetic to religion. Fourth, that we do not share *all* the concepts in our language. Some we do not misunderstand, but fail to understand. Of course, there may well be perspectives which the philosophers of religion I have in mind are as blind to as others are to the perspectives they are trying to elucidate. In any event, the conception of philosophy as a subject which has, by its own inherent resources, all it needs to understand any human practice presented to it, will have to be revised. That conception may well be another illusion, which, after foundationalism, philosophy is called on to surrender.

Notes

1. See p. 8.
2. Kai Nielsen, 'On the Rationality of Groundless Believing', *Idealistic Studies*, vol. 11, no. 3 (Sept. 1981), p. 215.
3. E.B. Tylor, *Primitive Culture* (John Murray, London, 1920), p. 453.
4. O'Connor, *Mystery and Manners*, p. 159.
5. Sigmund Freud, *The Future of an Illusion* (Hogarth Press, London, 1962), p. 46.
6. Ludwig Wittgenstein, 'Remarks on Frazer's *The Golden Bough*', *The Human World*, no. 3 (May 1971).
7. Ibid., p. 37.
8. Ibid., p. 31.
9. John W. Cook, 'Magic, Witchcraft and Science', *Philosophical Investigations*, vol. 6, no. 1 (1983).
10. Rush Rhees had anticipated the kind of reaction we find in Cook: ' "So Wittgenstein was coming forward in defence of the ancient rituals!" That remark could have sense only if Wittgenstein had recognised no other "co-ordinates", no other standards than that of knowledge, of what may be established in science, and error; (and probably it would not have sense even then).' Rush Rhees, 'Wittgenstein on Language and Ritual' in Brian McGuinness (ed.), *Wittgenstein and His Times* (Basil Blackwell, Oxford, 1982), pp. 80–1.
11. Ibid., p. 82.
12. Wittgenstein, MS 109, 210f.
13. John Beattie, *Other Cultures* (Cohen and West, London, 1964), p. 204. Cook quotes this passage in 'Magic, Witchcraft and Science', p. 6.
14. Wittgenstein, 'Frazer's *Golden Bough*', p. 19.
15. Compare the following: 'The gestures made in these rituals had been learned in the daily life and language of those who made them — or many, and probably most of them were. The gestures used *only* in the ceremony had their role as gestures — they were seen as gestures — through some affinity with the gestures made in daily life and practical affairs (in building, planting, hunting, fighting, and so on). And the same goes for words and sentences, which are as important in many ritual or magical practices as gestures are, in incantations, spells, curses, in prayers, vows, and so on. There may be words used only in ritual magic, but these are taken as *words* with the power that words have in speech — conversation, instructions, orders, quarrels, etc., outside ritual — a power which they bring with them into ritual.' Rhees, 'Wittgenstein on Language and Ritual', p. 72.
16. For further discussion of this issue see my paper 'Wittgenstein's

331

Full Stop' in I. Block (ed.), *Perspectives on the Philosophy of Wittgenstein* (Basil Blackwell, Oxford, 1981). This paper is used in a wider context in my *Belief, Change and Forms of Life*.

17. Evans-Pritchard, *Primitive Religion*, p. 17.

18. Cook, 'Magic, Witchcraft and Science', p. 35.

19. Robert Coles, *Flannery O'Connor's South* (Louisiana State University Press, Baton Rouge, 1980), pp. 6–7.

20. Ibid., pp. 10–11.

21. O'Connor, *Mystery and Manners*, p. 168.

22. Ibid., p. 189.

23. Flannery O'Connor, 'The Lame Shall Enter First' in *Everything That Rises Must Converge*, p. 161.

24. Ibid., pp. 189–90.

25. Ibid.

26. Ibid., p. 187.

27. Tylor, *Primitive Culture*, p. 429.

28. Phillips, *Religion Without Explanation*, pp. 40–1.

29. Wittgenstein, 'Frazer's *Golden Bough*', p. 34.

30. *Matt.* 6:23.

31. Quoted in Coles, *Flannery O'Connor's South*, p. 154.

32. Whether this could be said with the same conviction now is another matter.

33. Coles, *Flannery O'Connor's South*, p. 166.

34. Ibid., pp. 33–4.

35. Ibid., pp. 97–8.

36. Ibid., p. 113. The story was 'A Good Man is Hard to Find'. I have discussed it in this connection in 'The Devil's Disguises' in Stuart Brown (ed.), *Objectivity and Cultural Divergence* (Cambridge University Press, 1984).

37. Phillips, *Religion Without Explanation*, p. 143.

38. Mackie, *Miracle of Theism*, p. 225.

39. T.A. Roberts, 'Crefydd a Rheswm' (Religion and Reason), *Y Traethodydd* (April 1984), p. 77.

40. Phillips, *Religion Without Explanation*, p. 142.

41. Ibid.

42. Ibid., p. 143.

43. Ibid., pp. 143–4.

44. See Mackie, *Miracle of Theism*, p. 226.

45. Ibid., p. 228.

46. Wittgenstein, *Lectures and Conversations*, p. 59.

47. Ibid., p. 63.

48. Mackie, *Miracle of Theism*, p. 226.

49. John Wisdom, 'Gods' in *Philosophy and Psychoanalysis* (Basil Blackwell, Oxford, 1964), p. 11.

50. Bouwsma, 'Anselm's Argument' in *Without Proof or Evidence*.

51. Roberts, 'Crefydd a Rheswm', p. 77. My italics.

52. Stanley Cavell, 'Aesthetic Problems in Modern Philosophy' in *Must We Mean What We Say* (Cambridge University Press, 1976); see pp. 80–1.

53. Ibid., p. 80.

54. Ibid.

55. Ibid., p. 79.

56. Stanley Cavell, 'Kierkegaard's *On Authority and Revelation*', in *Must We Mean What We Say*, p. 172.

57. I should prefer to say that to imagine a religion is to imagine it in a form of life. For my reasons for this preference see *Belief, Change and Forms of Life*, ch. 5.

58. Cavell, 'Kierkegaard's *On Authority*'.

59. Mackie, *Miracle of Theism*, p. 225.

60. Ludwig Wittgenstein, *Culture and Value*, trans. Peter Winch (Basil Blackwell, Oxford, 1977), p. 50e.

61. I owe this observation to Peter Winch.

62. Mackie, *Miracle of Theism*, p. 3.

63. Wittgenstein, *On Certainty*, para. 475.

64. Norman Malcolm, 'The Relation of Language to Instinctive Behaviour', *Philosophical Investigations*, vol. 5, no. 1 (Jan. 1982), pp. 5–6.

65. Ludwig Wittgenstein, 'Cause and Effect: Intuitive Awareness', *Philosophia*, vol. 6, nos. 3–4 (Sept.–Dec. 1976), pp. 391–408: selected and edited by Rush Rhees, English translation by Peter Winch, p. 416.

66. Weil, *Lectures on Philosophy*, p. 51.

67. Ludwig Wittgenstein, *The Blue and Brown books* (Basil Blackwell, Oxford, 1978), p. 52.

68. Weil, *Lectures on Philosophy*, p. 31.

69. Ibid., Peter Winch, Introduction, p. 12.

70. Wittgenstein, *Culture and Value*, p. 31.

71. Rhees, 'Wittgenstein on Language and Ritual', p. 88.

72. H.O. Mounce, 'Understanding a Primitive Society', *Philosophy*, vol. 48 (Oct. 1973), pp. 347–62.

73. Ibid., p. 353.

74. At the University of Carleton, Ottawa.

75. For a development of the important distinction between 'misunderstanding' and 'failing to understand' see Rhees, 'Wittgenstein on Language and Ritual'.

76. Wittgenstein, 'Frazer's *Golden Bough*', p. 31.

77. Rhees, 'Wittgenstein on Language and Ritual', p. 90.

Bibliography

Alston, W.P. (1983) 'Christian experience and Christian belief' in Alvin Plantinga and Nicholas Wolterstorff (eds), *Faith and Rationality*, University of Notre Dame Press, Indiana

Austin, J.L. (1961) 'A plea for excuses' in J.O. Urmson and G.J. Warnock (eds), *Philosophical Papers*, Clarendon Press, Oxford

—— (1962) ed. G.J. Warnock, *Sense and Sensibilia*, Clarendon Press, Oxford

Barth, Karl (1946) '*No!*' in John Baillie (ed.), *Natural Theology*, Geoffrey Bles, The Centenary Press, London

Beattie, John (1964) *Other Cultures*, Cohen and West, London

Bennett, Jonathan (1971) *Locke, Berkeley, Hume: Central Themes*, Clarendon Press, Oxford

Berger, Peter (1970) *A Rumour of Angels*, Doubleday Anchor Book, New York

—— (1973) *The Social Reality of Religion*, Penguin Books, Harmondsworth, Middx. (First published in America as *The Sacred Canopy*.)

—— (1975) *Invitation to Sociology*, Penguin Books, Harmondsworth, Middx

—— and Luckmann, Thomas (1966) *The Social Construction of Reality*, Penguin Books, Harmondsworth, Middx

Berger, Brigitte, and Kellner, Hansfried (1974) *The Homeless Mind*, Pelican Books, Harmondsworth, Middx

Boer, Jesse de (1982) 'Reformed Epistemology', *The Reformed Journal*, vol. 32, issue 4, April 1982

Bouwsma, O.K. (1984) *Without Proof or Evidence*, essays of O.K. Bouwsma, ed. J.L. Croft and Ronald E. Hustwit, University of Nebraska Press, Lincoln

Brown, S. (ed.) (1977) *Reason and Religion*, Cornell University Press, Ithaca, New York

Brunner, Emil (1946) 'Nature and Grace' in John Baillie (ed.), *Natural Theology*, Geoffrey Bles, The Centenary Press, London

Calvin, John (1813) *Institutes of the Christian Religion*, vol. I, trans. John Allen, Presbyterian Board of Publication, Philadelphia

Cameron, James (1962) *The Night Battle*, Helicon Press, Baltimore

Cavell, Stanley (1976) 'Aesthetic problems in modern philosophy' and 'Kierkegaard's *On Authority and Revelation*' in *Must We Mean What We Say*, Cambridge University Press

Clifford, W.K. (1879) 'The ethics of belief' in *Lectures and Essays*, Macmillan, London

Coles, Robert (1980) *Flannery O'Connor's South*, Louisiana State University Press, Baton Rouge

Conway, David (1974/5) 'D.Z. Phillips and "The Inadequacy of Language" ', *Analysis*, vol. 35

Cook, John (1983) 'Magic, Witchcraft and Science', *Philosophical Investigations*, vol. 6, no. 1

Davidson, A.B. (1904) *Theology of the Old Testament*, Edinburgh

Dilman, Ilham and D.Z. Phillips (1971) *Sense and Delusion*, Routledge and Kegan Paul, London

Drury, M.O'C. (1973) *The Danger of Words*, Routledge and Kegan Paul, London

—— (1981) 'Some notes on conversations with Wittgenstein' in Rush Rhees (ed.), *Ludwig Wittgenstein—Personal Recollections*, Basil Blackwell, Oxford

Eliot, T.S. (1973) 'Four Quartets' in *The Complete Poems and Plays of T.S. Eliot*, Faber and Faber, London

Evans-Pritchard, E.E. (1965) *Theories of Primitive Religion*, Clarendon Press, Oxford

Ferreira, M. Jamie (1980) *Doubt and Religious Commitment*, Clarendon Press, Oxford

Finch, Henry Le Roy (1977) *Wittgenstein — The Later Philosophy*, Humanities Press, Atlantic Highlands, New Jersey

Frazer, James (1922) *The Golden Bough* (abridged edn), Macmillan, London

Freud, Sigmund (1962) *The Future of an Illusion*, Hogarth Press, London

Fries, Jakob (1982) *Dialogues on Morality and Religion*, ed. D.Z. Phillips; trans. David Walford; Introduction by Rush Rhees, Basil Blackwell, Oxford

Gutting, Gary (1985) 'The Calvinist and the Catholic: a dialogue on faith and reason', *Faith and Philosophy*, vol. 2, no. 3

Holmer, Paul (1978) *The Grammar of Faith*, Harper and Row, New York

Hume, David (1822) *Essays and Treatises on Several Subjects*, a new edition

—— (1896) *A Treatise of Human Nature*, ed. L.A. Selby-Bigge, Clarendon Press, Oxford

Kamenka, Eugene (1970) *The Philosophy of Ludwig Feuerbach*, Routledge and Kegan Paul, London

Kenyon, J.D. (1985) 'Doubts about the concept of reason', *Proceedings of the Aristotelian Society*, supp. vol. LIX

Kierkegaard, Søren (1944) *Concluding Unscientific Postscript*, trans. David Swenson, Princeton University Press, Princeton, New Jersey

—— (1956) *Purity of Heart*, trans. Douglas Steere, Harper Torch Books, New York

Lear, Jonathan (1982) 'Leaving the world alone', *Journal of Philosophy*

Lindbeck, George (1984) *The Nature of Doctrine*, The Westminster Press, Philadelphia

Locke, John (1969) *An Essay Concerning Human Understanding*, ed. and abridged with an introduction by A.D. Woozley, The Fontana Library, London

Losin, Peter (1982) 'Reformed epistemology', *The Reformed Journal*, vol. 32, issue 4

Lyas, Colin (1977) 'The groundlessness of religious belief' in S. Brown (ed.), *Reason and Religion*, Cornell University Press, Ithaca, New York

Mackie, J.L. (1982) *The Miracle of Theism*, Oxford University Press

Malcolm, Norman (1977) 'The groundlessness of belief' in *Thought and Knowledge*, Cornell University Press, Ithaca, New York

—— (1982) 'The relation of language to instinctive behaviour', *Philosophical Investigations*, vol. 5, no. 1

Mavrodes, George I. (1983) 'Jerusalem and Athens revisited' in Alvin

335

Plantinga and Nicholas Wolterstorff (eds), *Faith and Rationality*, University of Notre Dame Press, Indiana

Mitchell, Basil (1973) *The Justification of Religious Belief*, Macmillan, London

Mounce, H.O. (1973) 'Understanding a primitive society', *Philosophy*, vol. 48

—— and Phillips, D.Z. (1970) *Moral Practices*, Routledge and Kegan Paul, London

Newman, John Henry (1840) 'Lectures on the Scripture proof of the doctrines of the Church', *Tracts for the Times*, no. 85, 2nd edn

—— (1843) *Sermons Chiefly on the Theory of Religious Belief preached before the University of Oxford*, Rivingtons, London

Nielsen, Kai (1967) 'Wittgensteinian fideism', *Philosophy*, vol. 42

—— (1981) 'On the rationality of groundless believing', *Idealistic Studies*, vol. 11, no. 3

O'Connor, Flannery (1965) *Everything That Rises Must Converge*, Faber and Faber, London

—— (1968) *A Good Man is Hard to Find*, Faber and Faber, London

—— (1969) *Mystery and Manners*, sel. and ed. by Sally and Robert Fitzgerald, Farrar, Straus and Giroux, New York

—— (1980) *Letters of Flannery O'Connor: The Habit of Being*, sel. and ed. by Sally Fitzgerald, Vintage Books, Random House, New York

Phillips, D.Z. (1965) *The Concept of Prayer*, Routledge and Kegan Paul, London (paperback edn, Basil Blackwell, Oxford, 1981)

—— (1970) *Faith and Philosophical Enquiry*, Routledge and Kegan Paul, London

—— (1970) *Death and Immortality*, Macmillan, London

—— (1970) (with H.O. Mounce) *Moral Practices*, Routledge and Kegan Paul, London

—— (1971) (with Ilham Dilman) *Sense and Delusion*, Routledge and Kegan Paul, London

—— (1976) *Religion Without Explanation*, Basil Blackwell, Oxford

—— (1984) 'The Devil's Disguises' in S. Brown (ed.), *Objectivity and Cultural Divergence*, Cambridge University Press

—— (1986) *Belief, Change and Forms of Life*, Macmillan, London and Humanities Press, Atlantic Highlands, New Jersey

—— (1986) *R.S. Thomas: Poet of the Hidden God*, Macmillan, London

—— (forthcoming) *No Main Road: Religion in Twentieth Century Literature*

Pitkin, Hanna (1973) 'The roots of conservatism', *Dissent*, Fall 1973

Plantinga, Alvin (1979) 'Is belief in God rational?' in C.F. Delaney (ed.), *Rationality and Religious Belief*, University of Notre Dame Press, Indiana

—— (1982) 'Reformed epistemology again', *The Reformed Journal*, vol. 32, issue 7

—— (1983) 'Reason and belief in God' in Alvin Plantinga and Nicholas Wolterstorff (eds), *Faith and Rationality*, University of Notre Dame Press, Indiana

Price, H.S. (1978) Translator and Notes, Simone Weil, *Lectures on Philosophy*, Cambridge University Press

Rhees, Rush (1969) 'Religion and language' in *Without Answers*, Routledge and Kegan Paul, London

—— (1970) 'On continuity: Wittgenstein's ideas 1938' in *Discussions of Wittgenstein*, Routledge and Kegan Paul, London, and Shocken Books, New York

—— (1982) 'Wittgenstein on Language and Ritual' in Brian McGuinness (ed.), *Wittgenstein and His Times*, Basil Blackwell, Oxford

Roberts, T.A. (1984) 'Crefydd a Rheswm' (Religion and reason), *Y Traethodydd*, April

Robinson, Ian (1973) *The Survival of English*, Cambridge University Press

Rorty, Richard (1980) *Philosophy and the Mirror of Nature*, Princeton University Press, Princeton, New Jersey and Basil Blackwell, Oxford

Swinburne, Richard (1977) *The Coherence of Theism*, Oxford University Press

—— (1981) *The Existence of God*, Oxford University Press

—— (1981) *Faith and Reason*, Oxford University Press

Trigg, Roger (1973) *Reason and Commitment*, Cambridge University Press

Tylor, E.B. (1920) *Primitive Culture*, John Murray, London

Van Til, Cornelius (1969) *A Christian Theory of Knowledge*, Presbyterian and Reformed Publishing Co., New Jersey

Warnock, G.J. (1969) *Berkeley*, Peregrine Books, London

Weil, Simone (1952) *Gravity and Grace*, trans. Emma Craufurd, intro. Gustave Thibon, Routledge and Kegan Paul, London

—— (1962) 'Draft for a statement of human obligations' in *Selected Essays*, ed. Richard Rees, Clarendon Press, Oxford

—— (1970) *First and Last Notebooks*, trans. Richard Rees, Clarendon Press, Oxford

—— (1978) *Lectures on Philosophy*, trans. H.S. Price, intro. Peter Winch, Cambridge University Press

West, Cornel (1980) Review of Paul Holmer, *The Grammar of Faith*, *Union Seminary Quarterly Review*, vol. 35, nos 3 and 4

Whittaker, John (1981) 'Literal and figurative language of God', *Religious Studies*, vol. 17, no. 1

—— (1981) *Matters of Faith and Matters of Principle*, Trinity University Press, San Antonio

Winch, Peter (1958) *The Idea of a Social Science*, Routledge and Kegan Paul, London

—— (1972) *Ethics and Action*, Routledge and Kegan Paul, London

—— (1974) 'Language, Belief and Relativism' in H.D. Lewis (ed.), *Contemporary British Philosophy*, 4th series

—— (1977) 'Meaning and religious language' in S. Brown (ed.) *Reason and Religion*, Cornell University Press, Ithaca, New York

—— (1978) Introduction to Weil, Simone, *Lectures on Philosophy*, trans. H.S. Price, Cambridge University Press

Wisdom, John (1968) 'Gods' in *Philosophy and Psychoanalysis*, Basil Blackwell, Oxford

Wittgenstein, Ludwig (1953) *Philosophical Investigations*, trans. G.E.M. Anscombe, Basil Blackwell, Oxford

—— (1966) *Lectures and Conversations on Aesthetics, Psychology and Religious Belief*, ed. Cyril Barrett, Basil Blackwell, Oxford

—— (1971) 'Remarks on Frazer's *The Golden Bough*', trans. A.C. Miles and Rush Rhees, *The Human World*, no. 3, May 1971

—— (1976) 'Cause and effect: intuitive awareness', *Philosophia*, vol. 6, nos 3–4, Sept.–Dec.

—— (1977) *Culture and Value*, trans. Peter Winch, Basil Blackwell, Oxford

—— (1978) *The Blue and Brown Books*, Basil Blackwell, Oxford

—— (1979) *On Certainty*, trans. Denis Paul and G.E.M. Anscombe, Basil Blackwell, Oxford

Wolterstoff, Nicholas (1983) 'Can belief in God be rational?' in Alvin Plantinga and Nicholas Wolterstorff (eds), *Faith and Rationality*, University of Notre Dame Press, Indiana

—— (1981) 'Is reason enough?' *The Reformed Journal*, vol. 34, no. 4

Wykstra, Stephen J. 'Plantinga versus evidentialism: relocating the issue', unpublished paper

Index

About the Book and Author

Contemporary philosophy of religion is dominated by foundationalism—the belief that there exists a set of "foundational" propositions that provide evidence for all other propositions without themselves requiring such evidence. Today, foundationalism is under heavy fire, and the philosophy of religion is being greatly changed by these debates.

In a brilliant series of essays, the distinguished philosopher D. Z. Phillips explores the alternatives for faith after foundationalism. A significant exploration of post-foundationalist thought in its own right, *Faith After Foundationalism* is also an important evaluation and critique of the theological implications of the views of Alvin Plantinga, Richard Rorty, George Lindbeck, and Peter Berger.

Phillips's own position is that one must resist the philosopher's tendency to turn religious mystery into epistemological mystery. To understand how religious concepts are formed is to understand that to speak of God as "beyond mortal telling" is *not* to confess a failure of language. God's hiddenness is part of our concept of him—a reflection of the mystery of human life as it is lived.

Faith After Foundationalism will be essential reading for philosophers of religion and theologians, as well as for students of contemporary epistemology.

D. Z. Phillips is professor of philosophy at the University of Wales, Swansea, and the Danforth Professor of the Philosophy of Religion at the Claremont Graduate School. He is the author of many important books on philosophy of religion and ethics, including *The Concept of Prayer, Death and Immortality, From Fantasy to Faith, Interventions in Ethics,* and *Wittgenstein and Religion.*

Printed in the United States
64613LVS00002B/191